Planning, Time, and Self-Governance

PLANNING, TIME, AND SELF-GOVERNANCE

Essays in Practical Rationality

Michael E. Bratman

OXFORD
UNIVERSITY PRESS

OXFORD
UNIVERSITY PRESS

Oxford University Press is a department of the University of Oxford. It furthers
the University's objective of excellence in research, scholarship, and education
by publishing worldwide. Oxford is a registered trade mark of Oxford University
Press in the UK and certain other countries.

Published in the United States of America by Oxford University Press
198 Madison Avenue, New York, NY 10016, United States of America.

© Oxford University Press 2018

CIP data is on file at the Library of Congress
ISBN 978–0–19–086786–7 (pbk.)
ISBN 978–0–19–086785–0 (hbk.)

9 8 7 6 5 4 3 2 1

Paperback printed by Webcom, Inc., Canada
Hardback printed by Bridgeport National Bindery, Inc., United States of America

In memory of my mother and father, Anne and Harry Bratman

CONTENTS

PREFACE

From 1987 to 2014 I published a quartet of books that develop what I call the planning theory of intention and of our human agency. These books highlight the fundamental roles of our planning capacities in our agency, both individual and social. These capacities are at the heart of basic forms of cross-temporal organization, social organization, and self-governance. These books seek to provide a theoretical framework for understanding more deeply these fundamental features of our agency. And my hope is that these theoretical resources can do important work both in philosophy and in other related areas of research—where these latter potentially include artificial intelligence, cognitive science, decision theory, legal theory, and political theory.

The main aim of the essays in this present book is to provide a more adequate understanding of the normative foundations of this planning theory of our agency. The essays in this volume must of course be assessed on their own. But I also hope that, taken together with the prior works, they put us in a better position to assess the significance and theoretical value of the overall model of our plan-infused human agency.

While at work on these essays I have twice had the privilege of being a Fellow at the Stanford University Humanities Center; and the Center has also generously provided a work-friendly office during other important stages in this work. I am deeply grateful for this support. While I try to indicate my specific intellectual debts within the essays themselves, let me say here, in a more general vein, that I have benefited enormously from interaction with a wonderful and diverse group of philosophers, including a number of remarkable students here at Stanford. Almost all of these essays have been written in the context of a workshop, conference, or public lecture; and I am grateful for these opportunities for philosophical exchange. Philosophy is, when all goes well, a temporally extended shared cooperative activity.

I have updated the references in the previously published essays. When an essay cited is itself one of the other essays in this volume, I have added that information within the references. In some cases I have added to an essay pointers in brackets to other essays. Many thanks to William Jared Parmer for preparing the overall bibliography, and for his help in preparing the manuscript; and many thanks to Meica Danielle Magnani for preparing the Index.

Essay 1, "Introduction: The Planning Framework," and essay 11, "A Planning Agent's Self-Governance Over Time" have not been previously published. All the other essays have previously been published. Their original locations are as follows:

2. "Intention, Belief, Practical, Theoretical" was originally published in *Spheres of Reason*, edited by Simon Robertson, 29–61. Oxford: Oxford University Press, 2009. Reprinted by permission of Oxford University Press.

3. "Intention, Belief, and Instrumental Rationality" was originally published in *Reasons for Action*, edited by David Sobel and Steven Wall, 13–36. Cambridge: Cambridge University Press, 2009. Reprinted by permission of Cambridge University Press.

4. "Intention, Practical Rationality, and Self-Governance" was originally published in *Ethics* 119, no. 3 (2009): 411–443. © 2009 by the University of Chicago.

5. "Agency, Time, and Sociality" was originally published in *Proceedings and Addresses of the American Philosophical Association* 84, no. 2 (2010): 7–26. Reprinted by permission of the American Philosophical Association.

6. "Time, Rationality, and Self-Governance" was originally published in *Philosophical Issues* 22, no. 1 (2012): 73–88. Reprinted by permission of Wiley-Blackwell.

7. "Temptation and the Agent's Standpoint" was originally published in *Inquiry* 57, no. 3 (2014): 293–310. It was originally published online on March 12th, 2014. It is available online: http://www.tandfonline.com/10.1080/0020174X.2014.894271.

8. "The Interplay of Intention and Reason" was originally published in *Ethics* 123, no. 4 (2013): 657–672. © 2013 by the University of Chicago.

9. "Consistency and Coherence in Plan" is derived from portions of "Rational and Social Agency: Reflections and Replies," which was originally published in *Rational and Social Agency: The Philosophy of Michael Bratman*, edited by Manuel Vargas and Gideon Yaffe, 294–343. New York: Oxford University Press. Reprinted by permission of Oxford University Press.

10. "Rational Planning Agency" was originally published in Anthony O'Hear, ed., *Philosophy of Action, Royal Institute of Philosophy Supplement*: 80 (Cambridge: Cambridge University Press, 2017): 25–48. Reprinted by permission of Cambridge University Press.

Finally, and yet again, my deepest debts are to my family—Susan, Gregory, and Scott.

Planning, Time, and Self-Governance

CHAPTER 1

Introduction

The Planning Framework

We—mature human agents in a broadly modern world—are planning agents. Our practical thinking is shaped in characteristic ways by our future-directed plans. This is a key to the striking forms of cross-temporal organization that are central to our human lives. It is also, I think, a key to important forms of our sociality and our self-governance. Somewhat stable prior partial plans normally provide a background framework within which much of our practical thinking—including the weighing of reasons—proceeds. This framework-providing role of these prior partial plans involves distinctive rationality norms—norms of consistency,[1] coherence, and stability over time. And a fruitful way to understand intention is to see intentions as plan-states in this plan-infused, normatively guided psychic economy. In this way, we can develop a naturalistically plausible and modest theory of the will.

Or so I have argued in a series of works, beginning in the mid-1980s.[2] As this work has progressed, however, it has become clear that there are

---

1. I include here both a norm that precludes planning p while believing not-p, and an agglomerativity norm that precludes planning X and planning Y while believing X and Y are not co-possible. Carlos Núñez develops a deep challenge to the former in his "The Independence of Practical Reason," unpublished manuscript.

2. This work took place against a background of field-defining work by Donald Davidson and under the significant influence of work of Gilbert Harman—and, to some extent, Herbert Simon and Héctor-Neri Castañeda. See Donald Davidson, *Essays on Actions and Events*, 2nd ed. (Oxford: Oxford University Press, 2001). Gilbert

unresolved and difficult issues about practical rationality at the foundations, issues that require further reflection. This collection of essays is my effort, so far, to respond further to these foundational issues.

1.

Let me set the stage. I developed some of these ideas about our planning agency in my 1987 book, *Intention, Plans, and Practical Reason*. I then explored two further ideas. The first was that this planning framework provides substantial resources for a rich model of our *shared* acting and thinking, a model in the space between the work of, among others, Margaret Gilbert and John Searle. This led to a series of papers beginning in the early 1990s, four of which were included in my 1999 collection, *Faces of Intention*; and this then led to my 2014 book, *Shared Agency: A Planning Theory of Acting Together*. The second idea was that this planning framework provides substantial resources for a rich model of our self-governance, one in the space between the work of, among others, Harry Frankfurt and Gary Watson. This led to a series of papers—many of which are in my 2007 collection, *Structures of Agency*—in defense of a plan-based model of self-governance. These twin developments added further support for the idea that our capacity for planning agency is a core capacity, one that supports a wide range of important practical capacities and is in that sense fecund. (See essay 5.)

But unrest was brewing. Why are the planning norms to which I was appealing, norms of *rationality* with a distinctive normative significance or force? In my 1987 book I had proposed a two-tier pragmatic justification for these norms, one that appealed to the ways in which guidance by these norms in general supports, both instrumentally and constitutively, much

Harman, "Practical Reasoning," in *Reasoning, Meaning, and Mind* (Oxford: Oxford University Press, 1999). Gilbert Harman, *Change in View: Principles of Reasoning* (Cambridge, MA: MIT Press, 1986). Herbert Simon, *Reason in Human Affairs* (Stanford, CA: Stanford University Press, 1983). Héctor-Neri Castañeda, *Thinking and Doing* (Dordrecht, The Netherlands: Reidel, 1975). For discussion of Castañeda's views, see Michael E. Bratman, "Castañeda's Theory of Thought and Action," in *Faces of Intention* (New York: Cambridge University Press, 1999.) The main work of mine, prior to this present volume, in which I develop this plan-theoretic view of our agency is the following: Michael E. Bratman, *Intention, Plans, and Practical Reason* (Cambridge, MA: Harvard University Press, 1987; Reissued CSLI Publications, 1999); Michael E. Bratman, *Faces of Intention* (New York: Cambridge University Press, 1999); Michael E. Bratman, *Structures of Agency* (New York: Oxford University Press, 2007); Michael E. Bratman, *Shared Agency: A Planning Theory of Acting Together* (New York: Oxford University Press, 2014).

of what we care about, especially given our cognitive and epistemic limits. And I also tried to block the worry, traceable to J. J. C. Smart's forceful concerns about rule-worship, that a direct inference from pragmatically supported general strategies of thought to a judgment about the particular case is fraught.[3] But as I thought more about this Smart-inspired concern, my confidence waned.[4] And in his criticism of my argument against what I had called the "simple view," Hugh McCann challenged the very idea that the relevant norm of plan consistency is a norm of rationality rather than just a rule of thumb for tracking what really mattered.[5] Related challenges later appeared in work of Joseph Raz and Niko Kolodny who both think that the idea that the cited planning norms are norms of rationality is a "myth."[6]

During the same period, others—including J. David Velleman, Kieran Setiya, and to some extent R. Jay Wallace—developed the idea that these norms were the reflection of more basic norms of theoretical rationality in favor of consistency and coherence of belief. And some such—as I called it—cognitivism could already be discerned in Gilbert Harman's groundbreaking essay, "Practical Reasoning."[7]

3. J. J. C. Smart, "Extreme and Restricted Utilitarianism," *Philosophical Quarterly* 6 (1956): 344–54.

4. See my "Planning and the Stability of Intention," *Minds and Machines* 2, no. 1 (1992): 1–16; my "Following Through with One's Plans: Reply to David Gauthier," in Peter A. Danielson, ed. *Modeling Rationality, Morality, and Evolution* (New York: Oxford University Press, 1998), 55–66; and essays 8 and 9 in this volume. And see Kieran Setiya's reflections on the threat of a "baffling fragmentation of practical reason" in his "Intention, Plans, and Ethical Rationalism," in Manuel Vargas and Gideon Yaffe, eds., *Rational and Social Agency: The Philosophy of Michael Bratman* (New York: Oxford University Press, 2014), at 64.

5. Hugh McCann, "Settled Objectives and Rational Constraints," *American Philosophical Quarterly* 28, no. 1 (1991): 25–36. The simple view says that intentionally A-ing always involves an intention to A. My argument against the simple view first appeared in my "Two Faces of Intention," *The Philosophical Review* 93 (1984): 375–405. Large parts of "Two Faces of Intention" were then incorporated into Chapter 8 of my *Intention, Plans, and Practical Reason.*

6. Joseph Raz, "The Myth of Instrumental Rationality," *Journal of Ethics and Social Philosophy* 1, no. 1 (2005): 1–28. Niko Kolodny, "The Myth of Practical Consistency," *European Journal of Philosophy* 16, no. 3 (2008): 366–402.

7. Gilbert Harman, "Practical Reasoning"; J. David Velleman, *Practical Reflection* (Princeton, NJ: Princeton University Press, 1989; Reissued Stanford, CA: CSLI, 2007); R. Jay Wallace, "Normativity, Commitment, and Instrumental Reason," with postscript in his *Normativity and the Will* (Oxford: Oxford University Press, 2006); Kieran Setiya, "Cognitivism about Instrumental Reason," *Ethics* 117, no. 4 (2007): 649–73. And see also Jacob Ross, "How to Be a Cognitivist about Practical Reason," in R. Shafer-Landau, ed., *Oxford Studies in Metaethics*, Vol. 4 (Oxford: Oxford University Press, 2009), 243–82; John Brunero, "Cognitivism about Practical Rationality," in R. Shafer-Landau, ed., *Oxford Studies in Metaethics*, Vol. 9 (Oxford: Oxford University Press, 2014), 18–44.

I myself was persuaded neither by cognitivism (see essays 2 and 3) nor by the myth-theoretic challenge. (See essay 4.) But I realized that I needed to go beyond the (albeit, qualified) two-tier account in my 1987 book. So beginning in 2009 I published a series of papers in which I tried to work toward a more adequate view.

One idea that was not available to me was that these norms are constitutive of agency—that it is a necessary feature of agency (or, anyway, intentional agency) that it involves guidance by these norms.[8] This was in part because I wanted to situate the planning theory within a theoretical strategy that Paul Grice had called "creature construction."[9] The idea is to build up increasingly rich models of agency and to see planning agency as a specific form of agency, one that appears in later stages of this exercise in creature construction. Given this multiplicity of agency, it is not plausible that these distinctive norms of planning agency are constitutive of agency quite generally.

That said, guidance by these norms is, on the theory, partly constitutive of, in particular, planning agency. But given that you can be an agent without being a planning agent, it is not clear exactly how this—as we might call it, planning-agency constitutivism—helps us defend the claim that these are norms of practical rationality for such an agent.[10]

Velleman in a 2007 essay ["What Good Is a Will?" as reprinted in *Rational and Social Agency: The Philosophy of Michael Bratman*, Manuel Vargas and Gideon Yaffe, eds. (New York: Oxford University Press, 2014)], and Setiya in a 2014 essay ["Intention, Plans, and Ethical Rationalism"] also went on to provide insightful critiques of my approach to these matters. My initial response to Velleman's critique is in essay 2. My initial response to Setiya is in my "Rational and Social Agency: Reflections and Replies," in Manuel Vargas and Gideon Yaffe, eds., *Rational and Social Agency: The Philosophy of Michael Bratman*, at 313–5. This present volume of essays constitutes my overall response to both of these philosophers.

8. Ideas in the spirit of such agency-constitutivism are in Christine Korsgaard, *Self-Constitution: Agency, Identity, and Integrity* (Oxford: Oxford University Press, 2009); and J. David Velleman, *The Possibility of Practical Reason* (Oxford: Oxford University Press, 2000). See also Christine Korsgaard, "The Normative Constitution of Agency," in Manuel Vargas and Gideon Yaffe, eds., *Rational and Social Agency: The Philosophy of Michael Bratman*, at 190–214.

9. Paul Grice, "Method in Philosophical Psychology (From the Banal to the Bizarre)," Presidential Address, *Proceedings and Addresses of the American Philosophical Association* 48 (1974–5): 23–53; Michael E. Bratman, "Valuing and the Will," in *Structures of Agency*.

10. Setiya in his "Intention, Plans, and Ethical Rationalism" insightfully poses this issue in terms of what he calls "pluralistic rationalism." My initial response is in my "Rational and Social Agency: Reflections and Replies," at 313–5. In essay 10 and this Introduction I try to deepen this response. Though my appeal to a two-tier pragmatic rationale contrasts with such pluralistic rationalism, the version of the strategy of self-governance developed here is to some extent in the spirit of such pluralistic rationalism.

So I sought a path between a myth theory and cognitivism, but a path that did not depend on agency-constitutivism. I continued to think that it was important that the general guidance by these norms helps shape our lives in profound ways that are central to much of what we care about. But I concluded that we needed to supplement these two-tier pragmatic ideas. Such a supplement should draw on the common view that rationality is at least in part a matter of coherence.[11] But what I learned from McCann, Raz, and Kolodny was that a mere appeal to coherence was open to the challenge that we were grounding rationality simply in a kind of mental "tidiness."[12] We need to explain why the relevant forms of coherence matter in a way that responds to the concerns of the myth theorist, and we need to understand the philosophical underpinnings and implications of that explanation.

While I was trying to figure this out, I was also developing the approach to a planning agent's self-governance articulated in the essays in my 2007 book.[13] This led me to the conjecture that we can forge a path of the right sort between a myth theory and cognitivism in part by studying the ways in which basic norms of plan rationality reflect conditions of a planning agent's self-governance, both at a time and over time. We begin by explaining what is involved in central cases of a planning agent's self-governance. We then see the demands imposed by planning norms as demands to satisfy certain of these conditions of self-governance. The forms of coherence that are required by these planning norms will be forms of coherence that are among these conditions of a planning agent's self-governance.

The idea, then, is to treat central conditions of a planning agent's self-governance as a starting point and then see relevant norms as demands in favor of satisfying those conditions. In this sense these norms track relevant conditions of self-governance. The (perhaps implicit) acceptance of these norms, once in place, will then support conformity with these conditions of self-governance. So these norms track conditions of self-governance, and their acceptance tends to lead to conformity to those conditions.[14]

11. For example, John Broome writes: "Rationality is concerned with coherence among your attitudes such as your beliefs and intentions . . ." See John Broome, *Rationality Through Reasoning* (Hoboken, NJ: Wiley-Blackwell, 2013), at 193.
12. Niko Kolodny, "How Does Coherence Matter?," *Proceedings of the Aristotelian Society* 107, no. 1 (2007): 229–63, at 241.
13. I was also helped by Kenneth Stalzer's work on his 2004 Stanford University PhD thesis, *On the Normativity of the Instrumental Principle*.
14. This paragraph was aided by correspondence with Sarah Paul.

These essays constitute an interim report of progress, so far, with this line of reflection. The essays reveal a progression of ideas, with adjustments along the way. While there remain many unanswered questions,[15] what emerges is, I think, a plausible strategy for steering a path in our understanding of plan rationality between a myth theory, cognitivism, and agency-constitutivism. This path continues to acknowledge the significance of two-tier pragmatic considerations but supplements those considerations in an important way. My primary aim in this introduction is to pull together, in broad strokes, some of the main ideas about this path to which I have been led in writing these essays.[16] In doing this I leave for those essays many of the details, complexities, qualifications, references, and credits—though I will provide pointers to those essays along the way. And toward the end I will go somewhat beyond these essays, though in a way that draws from ideas in these essays.

2.

As I see it, our main concern is with the reflection of a planning agent on her basic forms of practical thinking, forms of practical thinking guided by distinctive norms of (as I claim) plan rationality. How might she make the most sense of these norms, and would they thereby be reflectively stable? (Essays 2, 9, 10) These queries are motivated both by our interest in the normative force of these norms and by our related interest in the explanatory significance of structures of planning agency. If these norms would not be stable under reflection then it would be to some extent less plausible to say—as the planning theory does say—that these forms of practical thinking are central to the explanation and understanding of our human action.

A planning agent's reflection would take due account of the pragmatic virtues, especially given her epistemic and cognitive limits, of these general forms of thinking. But it would also be sensitive to the Smart-inspired thought that a direct inference from the pragmatic benefits of these general forms of thinking to a conclusion about the particular case is fraught. (Essays 8, 9, 10) Our reflective planning agent will want to know how to

---

15. Since each essay was written to stand on its own, there are also redundancies, for which I request the reader's patience.

16. In writing this Introduction I have drawn also on my "Plan Rationality," in Ruth Chang and Kurt Sylvan, eds., *The Routledge Handbook of Practical Reason* (forthcoming), my Pufendorf Lectures at Lund University in June 2016, and my Franz Brentano Lectures on Practical Philosophy at the University of Vienna in April 2017.

supplement such a two-tier pragmatic account (which is not to say that she will explicitly appeal to such a supplement in each case of her actual practical thinking).

It is here that (beginning with essay 4) I try to develop a *strategy of self-governance*. This involves two ideas. The first is the *tracking thesis*: basic planning norms track certain conditions of a planning agent's self-governance, conditions that are articulated within our model of that self-governance. The second idea is the *reflective significance thesis*: the tracking thesis helps provide the supplemental support for these planning norms that is sought by the reflective planning agent in justifying her application of these norms to the particular case.

Concerning the tracking thesis, begin with a planning agent's self-governance at a time (or, anyway, during a small temporal interval). Here my proposal is a merger of Frankfurt-inspired ideas with elements from the planning theory.[17] Central to such self-governance is guidance by the agent's relevant, suitably coherent practical standpoint. Given the roles of planning in a planning agent's temporally extended agency, this standpoint will, for such a planning agent, be substantially plan-infused. So the plan consistency (including plan-belief consistency) and means-end coherence required by basic planning norms will be needed for the agent's standpoint to be sufficiently unified to play this Frankfurtian role in her synchronic self-governance. And this supports the tracking thesis concerning these synchronic norms.

This brings us to the reflective significance thesis with respect to these synchronic norms. Here I envisage a four-part answer.[18] (1) We can now see why the coherence that is tracked by these norms is, plausibly, a coherence worth wanting: it is not merely mental tidiness but is, rather, partly constitutive of a planning agent's self-governance—where I take it that such self-governance is itself worth wanting. (2) We have thereby identified an important commonality across these norms. Indeed, as we will see below, we have laid the foundation for articulating a common element that underlies not only these synchronic norms but also a plausible diachronic norm. (3) The tracking thesis supports the claim that if (a) one has a normative reason in favor of one's synchronic self-governance, and (b) one has in the particular case the capacity for such self-governance,

---

17. See essays 4 and 5; though see also an important challenge in Elijah Millgram, "Segmented Agency," in Manuel Vargas and Gideon Yaffe, eds., *Rational and Social Agency: The Philosophy of Michael Bratman* (New York: Oxford University Press, 2014), 152–89.

18. See essay 10, though I there in effect collapse the third and fourth element to be distinguished below.

then (c) this normative reason transmits to a distinctive reason of synchronic self-governance to conform to these synchronic norms in that particular case. (See essay 4, where I also respond to related concerns about inappropriate bootstrapping of normative reasons.[19]) And (4): our reflective planning agent will indeed have a normative reason in favor of her self-governance.[20]

Given the tracking thesis, and given (1)–(4), the reflective planning agent will be in a position to supplement her appeal to a two-tier pragmatic rationale for her synchronic planning norms in a way that suitably supports her application of these norms to the particular case. But there remain two issues. First, we are so far without a defense of (4), the claim about a normative reason for self-governance. And second, we have so far not explored whether—and if so, how—this approach could be extended to the diachronic case.

I turn now to this second issue, about the diachronic case. What I say will then be of use when we return later to the first issue.

3.

So what should we say about the tracking thesis and diachronic plan rationality? Here we will need to reflect on a planning agent's self-governance not only at a time, but also *over* time. But first let me note a methodological issue. When we were considering the tracking thesis concerning synchronic norms of plan consistency and coherence, we took as given the basic outlines of those norms and tried to see if, so understood, they did indeed track conditions of a planning agent's synchronic self-governance. In contrast, when we turn to diachronic plan rationality it is less clear, at the start, exactly what the relevant diachronic norm(s) is/are. So in exploring the tracking thesis about diachronic plan rationality we will need to assess an overall package that includes both a model of a planning agent's diachronic self-governance and a view of the associated diachronic norm (or norms).

That said, how should we model a planning agent's self-governance over time? (Essays 6, 10, 11) An initial idea is that a planning agent's

---

19. For a challenge to my response to concerns about inappropriate bootstrapping, see John Brunero "Self-Governance, Means-Ends Coherence, and Unalterable Ends," *Ethics* 120 (2010): 579–91.

20. I discuss below the relation between the desirability of self-governance and such a reason for self-governance.

self-governance over time involves her self-governance at (during) relevant times along the way, together with relevant interconnections across those forms of synchronic self-governance. What interconnections? Here I have been led to two complementary ideas. The first is that these are the (perhaps implicit) plan-infused interconnections that are characteristic of planned temporally extended activity. These include characteristic forms of continuity of intention, cross-references between intentions at different times, intended and actual mesh between sub-plans at different times, and interdependence between relevant intentions at times along the way. The second idea is that these plan-theoretic *intra*personal interconnections are analogues of the (perhaps implicit) *inter*personal intention interconnections characteristic of shared intention and shared intentional activity—where these interpersonal interconnections are those articulated in my planning theory of acting and thinking together. (Essays 5, 11) These analogies between planned temporally extended agency and shared intentional agency support the useful metaphor that in diachronic self-governance one is, as it were, acting "together" with oneself over time. (Essays 10, 11)

So the initial proposal is that a planning agent's self-governance over time involves her self-governance at times along the way together with cross-temporal plan-infused intrapersonal interconnections that are analogues of the plan-infused interpersonal interconnections characteristic of shared intention and shared intentional activity.[21] The next step is to explore implications of this proposal for a pair of cases that have received much attention in the literature. This will lead us to a further element of such diachronic self-governance.

First, there are cases highlighted by John Broome in which one makes a decision in the face of non-comparable considerations and then reflects later on whether to stick with that decision.[22] Since, on the model, a planning agent's diachronic self-governance normally involves relevant plan continuities and connections, it will normally involve sticking with one's earlier decision in such cases of non-comparability over time. (Essays 6, 10, 11)

---

21. A complexity in the background concerns the hierarchical structure of plans: there can be relevant intrapersonal interconnections at the level of an overarching plan despite a breakdown in such interconnections at the level of relevant sub-plans. I discuss this complexity in essay 11.

22. John Broome, "Are Intentions Reasons? And How Should We Cope with Incommensurable Values?," in Christopher W. Morris and Arthur Ripstein, eds., *Practical Rationality and Preference: Essays for David Gauthier* (Cambridge: Cambridge University Press, 2001), 98–120.

Second, there are cases highlighted by Richard Holton of potential will-power in the face of temptation.[23] Here the implications are more complex, and this because of a complex interaction between synchronic and diachronic self-governance. (Essays 7, 10, 11)

Suppose that you know you will be tempted to drink a lot at tonight's party. Since you now think that would be a bad idea, you decide now to stick with one drink tonight. You know, however, that at the party your judgment will temporarily shift and you will at least initially judge that it would be better to have many drinks—though you also know that if you did give into this temptation you would later regret that. If at the party you stick with your prior one-drink intention there will be a salient continuity in intention; in contrast, if you give into temptation there will be a break in this continuity. However, such continuity of prior intention helps constitute diachronic self-governance only given synchronic self-governance at times along the way. But if your judgment shifts at the time of the party it seems that sticking with your prior intention would not be a case of synchronic self-governance: given the judgment shift, where you stand at the time of the party seems to favor drinking more. So it is unclear whether such cases of willpower can satisfy our model of a planning agent's diachronic self-governance. It seems to be built into such cases that there is a breakdown in coordination between self-governance at the time of temptation and the kind of cross-temporal continuity characteristic of self-governance over time. Yet it seems a plausible, commonsense thought that willpower can sometimes be a central case of governing one's life over time.

The solution I propose is to supplement our model of a planning agent's self-governance over time by appeal to an end of the agent's that favors relevant intention continuity and thereby can potentially help re-shift her standpoint at the time of the party back in favor of a single drink. What end? We don't want just to appeal to an end of simple diachronic continuity. That would threaten to be an end in favor of mere cross-temporal mental tidiness; and that would expose our associated account of diachronic rationality to a version of the myth-theoretic charge that these norms are simply tracking mental tidiness. I also think that we should not follow J. David Velleman in appealing here to a theoretical end of self-understanding.[24] Given our pursuit of a uniform account of plan rationality,

23. Richard Holton, *Willing, Wanting, Waiting* (Oxford: Clarendon Press, 2009). And see Michael E. Bratman, "Toxin, Temptation, and the Stability of Intention," in *Faces of Intention*.

24. See, e.g., J. David Velleman, "Centered Self," in his *Self to Self* (Cambridge: Cambridge University Press, 2006), 253–83; J. David Velleman, *How We Get Along* (Cambridge: Cambridge University Press, 2009), chap. 1.

both synchronic and diachronic, this would return us to cognitivism about plan rationality—a view I have offered reasons to reject. (Essays 2, 3)

My proposal is instead to appeal to the end of one's diachronic self-governance itself.[25] (Essays 10, 11) This would help us explain how willpower can sometimes be a form of diachronic self-governance; it would avoid the charge that we are appealing to mere mental tidiness; and it would put us in a position to provide an alternative to a cognitivist account of diachronic plan rationality. So—by way of a kind of inference to the best explanation—I infer that the end of one's diachronic self-governance is itself an element in basic cases of a planning agent's exercise of her capacity for diachronic self-governance. Further, given that diachronic self-governance essentially involves relevant synchronic self-governance at times along the way, the presence of this end of one's diachronic self-governance will normally bring with it an end in favor of relevant synchronic self-governance.

This supplemented model of a planning agent's diachronic self-governance in hand, we can return to our effort to support a norm of diachronic plan rationality by way of the strategy of self-governance. The first step is to consider an extended tracking thesis: as synchronic plan rationality tracks conditions of a planning agent's synchronic self-governance, diachronic plan rationality tracks conditions of a planning agent's diachronic self-governance. This extended tracking thesis would have a pair of implications. First, there would be rational pressure in favor of continuity of intention over time, so long as that continuity coheres with self-governance at times along the way. Second, there would be rational pressure in the direction of an end of one's diachronic self-governance. We could then put these ideas together with our earlier, partial account of synchronic plan rationality and synchronic self-governance.

What should we say about such a package of views about plan rationality and self-governance? Well, given this overall package, norms of both synchronic and diachronic plan rationality are tied together and unified, and thereby made more intelligible, by the ways in which they track conditions of a planning agent's self-governance. Further, given this overall package we can conclude that if one has a normative reason in favor of one's self-governance, both synchronic and diachronic, and if one has the capacity for

25. In essay 7 I say: "a planning agent is committed to shaping present thought and action with an eye to how her planned activities will stably look as they develop over time." (This volume p. 163.) Here (and in essays 10 and 11) I replace this appeal to a concern with how things will look over time with an appeal to a concern with one's self-governance over time; and I interpret this concern with one's self-governance over time as an end of the agent's. I then try, toward the end of this Introduction, to articulate a more nuanced account of the relation between planning agency and this concern.

relevant self-governance, then one will have a distinctive normative reason of self-governance to conform to these norms. (Essays 4 and 6 address potential worries about unacceptable bootstrapping of reasons.)

This returns us to the question postponed earlier: Why think that a reflective planning agent has a normative reason in favor of her self-governance? Now, we are asking about the reflections of a planning agent who is considering the norms that are guiding her practical thinking and wondering whether to continue to think in these ways. And I think that in such reflections a planning agent will be primarily concerned with considerations that are anchored in ends of hers that are desirable. So, for our purposes, it will be reasonable to think of normative reasons as anchored in ends of the agent that are desirable.[26]

So: What to say about a normative reason in favor of one's self-governance? We can, I think, suppose that self-governance is desirable pro tanto, though a specific instance can be on-balance bad. (An example from essay 4 of self-governance that may well be on-balance bad is Iago.) So our question turns on the question: What is the status of the end of one's self-governance?

And here we face a dilemma. If our theory were to say only that

(a) the end of one's self-governance is a contingent, rationally optional end

it would not be in a position to account for the general normative force for us of basic planning norms. But an account that said that

(b) the end of one's self-governance is essential for all intentional agency

would, I think, overburden our theory of intentional agency: there are too many cases of intentional agency that is not plausibly motivated by some such end.

Is there a path between (a) and (b), one that would suffice for our defense of the normative force of basic planning norms? We might try here to appeal to our earlier conclusion that the end of one's diachronic self-governance is involved in central cases of the exercise of the capacity for such self-governance. But it is not clear how this is to work. It seems that at most what we can infer is that a planning agent with the capacity for diachronic self-governance must have the *capacity* for the end of her diachronic self-governance. So we do not have an argument that a planning

---

26. As I discuss in essay 10, not all ends are intentions and not all intentions are ends.

agent with the capacity for diachronic self-governance must in fact have that end.

There are, however, two important truths in this neighborhood. (Essay 10) Consider a planning agent who *does* have this end in favor of her diachronic self-governance (and so, in favor of related synchronic self-governance). This end grounds a normative reason for such self-governance; and, as we have seen, this reason helps support the application of norms of plan rationality to the particular case.[27] And here it is important to note that one of these norms is the cited norm of diachronic plan rationality, a norm that itself supports the presence of this very end (given the role of this end in the normal exercise of the capacity for such self-governance). So in this way this end of diachronic self-governance is, if present within the planning framework, *rationally self-sustaining*: it supports a norm of diachronic plan rationality that in turn supports it. Further, given this rationally self-sustaining end, the agent's package of plan-infused practical thinking, planning norms, ends, and reasons would be reflectively stable: this would be a *rationally stable reflective equilibrium*. This package would be reflectively stable even if it were in some sense possible (though pragmatically problematic, and perhaps not even psychologically possible) for the agent to give up being such a planning agent.

So this end of one's diachronic (and so, synchronic) self-governance is, if present within the planning framework, rationally self-sustaining and a keystone of a rationally stable reflective equilibrium. Let's call this observation about a rationally self-sustaining end of self-governance over time, and an associated rationally stable reflective equilibrium involving the norms of plan rationality, the *keystone claim*. And now we need to ask: How should we understand the significance of this keystone claim?[28] In particular, does this claim help us find the path for which we are looking, a path between

27. And see the discussion at the end of essay 8 of how such an end can help block what Kieran Setiya calls a "fragmentation of practical reason."

28. Part of the answer concerns the relation between this keystone claim and ideas about "self-reinforcement" in essays 8 and 9. Essay 8 considers the idea, within the framework of work of David Gauthier, that a deliberative standard can be "self-reinforcing in the sense that its very acceptance provides, by way of considerations of self-governance, reasons that . . . [can] tip the scales in favor of employing that deliberative standard in the particular case." (Essay 8 at p. 180.) Essay 9 claims that if (a) we take it as given that a planning agent has a normative reason in favor of her self-governance, then we can argue that if we are (as there are strong pragmatic reasons to be) planning agents, and if we have the capacity for self-governance in the particular case, then (b) we have a reason of self-governance in support of the application to that particular case of the norms of plan consistency and coherence whose acceptance is partly constitutive of our planning agency. In this sense our planning agency is, given (a), self-reinforcing.

In each case, the cited self-reinforcement—of a deliberative standard; of planning agency itself—works against a background of a reason or end in favor of

the idea that (a) the end of self-governance is just one among many rationally optional ends, and the idea that (b) the end of self-governance is essential for all intentional agency? While essay 10 provides support for this keystone claim, it stops short of a full answer to this further question. And my hope is that we can make progress here by returning to, and further developing, an idea initially introduced in essay 2.

4.

In section IX of essay 2 I began to explore a parallel between the framework of plan-infused practical thinking and the framework of reactive emotions, as understood by Peter Strawson.[29] And my conjecture here is that by further developing this parallel we can find an appropriate path between (a) and (b), a path supported by the keystone claim.[30]

Strawson famously highlighted the role of the reactive emotions in our practices of holding morally responsible, and so in our understanding of moral responsibility. As Strawson saw it, this framework of reactive attitudes is not strictly necessary for agency or mind; but it is a deeply entrenched framework for us, one that is integrated within much that is humanly significant, and one we may well not have the capacity to change at will. This framework has very many good consequences; but it is also important that built into this framework is an entrenched concern with quality of will, one that helps make sense of the normative structure of the reactive emotions including, in particular, the relevance of excuses of ignorance and absence of control.

Analogously, the planning framework is not strictly necessary for agency; but it is a deeply entrenched framework for us, one that is integrated

---

self-governance. The keystone claim goes on to focus in particular on the end of one's self-governance over time. It claims that this end is, within a planning framework, a rationally self-sustaining element of a reflectively stable psychic economy. And our question now is what exactly this tells us about the status of that end, and thereby also about the kinds of self-reinforcement noted in essays 8 and 9.

For a different development of the metaphor of a keystone see Keith Lehrer's discussion of "the keystone loop of reason," and of a related idea of a self-supporting "power preference," in his *Self-Trust: A Study of Reason, Knowledge, and Autonomy* (Oxford: Oxford University Press, 1997), esp. chaps. 1 and 4. (Quotations are from pp. 22 and 100.) Thanks to John Fischer for reminding me of this work of Lehrer's.

29. Peter Strawson, "Freedom and Resentment," in Gary Watson, ed., *Free Will*, 2nd ed. (Oxford: Oxford University Press 2003), 72–93.

30. For a related discussion, see Luca Ferrero, "Inescapability Revisited" (unpublished manuscript, April 2016), section 2.4. In this present section I have benefited greatly from detailed comments from Ferrero on an earlier draft.

within much that is humanly significant, and one we may well not have the capacity to change at will. This general framework has very many good consequences; but it is also important that built into this framework, at least for us, is an entrenched end of one's self-governance over time, an end that helps make sense of the normative structure of our plan-infused practical thinking including, in particular, the application of basic planning norms, both synchronic and diachronic, to the particular case. This end of one's self-governance over time is (within the planning framework) rationally self-sustaining; favors a central, organizing commonality across the planning norms; and is thereby a keystone of a rationally stable reflective equilibrium involving the agent's plan-infused practical thinking. This is all true even if it is in some sense possible (though pragmatically problematic, and perhaps not even psychologically possible) for the agent to give up being such a planning agent.

Basic planning norms are, for us, embedded in such a rationally self-sustaining and stable reflective equilibrium. Whereas the keystone of the Strawsonian framework of reactive attitudes, and associated practices of holding responsible, is a concern with quality of will, the keystone of our framework of plan-infused practical thinking is a rationally self-sustaining end of one's self-governance over time. In each case the keystone helps make reflective sense of the normatively guided functioning of relevant attitudes—in one case, the system of reactive emotions; in another case, the system of plan-states. In each case the keystone—concern with quality of will/end of diachronic self-governance—while not essential to mind or (intentional) agency per se, is also not merely one among many rationally optional, potential ends. After all, these keystones help make reflective sense of what are, for us, fundamental, pervasive, fecund, and entrenched webs of normatively guided thought and action. And, turning in particular to the planning framework, this puts us in a position to say that while basic planning norms are not (given the multiplicity of agency) essential to (intentional) agency per se, characterizing their purported special status as a "myth" fails to appreciate their keystone-supported status.

This allows that we can sometimes put to one side the end of our diachronic self-governance.[31] As Carlos Núñez has emphasized (in conversation), Strawson noted that we each have the power sometimes to bracket our concern with quality of will, perhaps as "a relief from the strains of involvement."[32] But it remains true, according to Strawson, that our

31. Cp. Sarah Paul, "Diachronic Incontinence Is a Problem in Moral Philosophy," *Inquiry* (2014): 337–55, at 345.
32. Strawson, "Freedom and Resentment," at 82.

normatively guided practice of holding morally responsible is to be understood in terms of the expression of reactive emotions that involve this concern with quality of will. Analogously, we each perhaps have the power sometimes to bracket our concern with our own diachronic self-governance. But it remains true that our normatively guided plan-infused practical thinking is to be understood within an overall framework that involves that basic concern.[33]

A disanalogy is that whereas in holding responsible the primary focus will tend to be on quality of will, in our planning our primary focus will not tend to be on our diachronic self-governance but rather on the specific ends at stake. Nevertheless, in each case, when the relevant practical thinking—holding responsible, normatively guided planning—makes full reflective sense to us in the particular case, that will be in part because of the cited concern/end.

This does not rule out the possibility of a thin kind of planning agency in the absence of a concern with self-governance. Perhaps this is how we should think about the planning of young human children, or the great apes, or certain artificial intelligence systems.[34] About such thin forms of planning agency the myth theorist might be right to say that it involves no distinctive form of practical rationality that goes beyond a two-tier pragmatic rationale, with its limits in supporting the application of general modes of thinking to the particular case. But such a thin planning agent would not be in a position to make direct sense to herself, on reflection, of her direct application of her planning norms to the particular case. In contrast, a planning agent who does have the cited concern with her own diachronic self-governance would be in a position to make reflective sense to herself of this basic aspect of her plan-infused practical thinking.

And my conjecture is that we ourselves are such reflectively successful and reflectively stable planning agents. While the myth theory may be right about, say, very young children, it is not right about us—mature human agents for whom structures of planning play a reflectively supportable and stable role in our cross-temporal organization, our sociality, and

33. As Facundo Alonso has noted (in correspondence), a cognitivist about these planning norms might appeal here to its own version of an analogue of Strawson's framework, one within which a concern with, say, one's self-understanding plays an essential role. However, this would not address the substantive problems for such cognitivism that I discuss in essays 2 and 3. That said, there remains the further question of whether the approach to plan rationality I am sketching here can be extended to norms of theoretical rationality of belief.

34. Concerning this last idea, see Michael E. Bratman, David Israel, and Martha Pollack, "Plans and Resource-Bounded Practical Reasoning," *Computational Intelligence* 4, no. 3 (1988): 349–355.

our self-governance. These pervasive and fecund forms of plan-infused practical thinking are not only in general extremely useful, though they are that. They are for us also in part supported by our entrenched, reflectively stable end of our own self-governance over time, and in that way by who we in fact, and on critical reflection, are.[35]

35. Thanks to Facundo Alonso, Olle Blomberg, Jorah Dannenberg, Luca Ferrero, Carlos Núñez, Sarah Paul, and Steven Woodworth.

CHAPTER 2

Intention, Belief, Practical, Theoretical

I

In my 1987 book *Intention, Plans and Practical Reason* I tried to understand intentions as, in the basic case, elements of larger and typically partial plans whose primary roles in our lives are ones of coordination and organization, both cross-temporal and social. I called this the *planning theory* of intention. Central to the planning theory is the idea that intentions—in contrast with ordinary desires—are both embedded in characteristic regularities and are subject to distinctive rational pressures for consistency and coherence.[1] There is, in particular, a rational demand that one's intentions, taken together with one's beliefs, fit together into a consistent model of one's future. There is, further, a rational demand that one's intentions be means–end coherent in the sense, roughly, that it not be true that one intends E, believes that E requires that one intend means M, and yet not intend M.[2] And these norms of consistency and coherence are operative in a planning agent's practical reasoning.[3]

1. I describe this basic approach in Bratman 1987: 9–10. As I say there, my approach tries to articulate "a web of regularities and norms" characteristic of intention and planning; and it appeals to "an account of the norms of rationality that are appropriate for agents for whom such planning plays a central role" (1987: 10).
2. A complexity that I put to one side here is that it can matter whether one thinks one needs now to intend M, or only needs to intend M by some later time. See Bratman 1987: 31. It is also important to note that this demand for means–end coherence goes beyond a demand for consistency. As I say in Bratman 1987: 33, this demand "provides rational pressure for the addition of further intentions. In contrast, considerations of consistency do not by themselves provide pressure for the addition of further intentions." John Brunero also highlights this last point in his 2005: 6.
3. They are, as I say in Bratman 1987: 109, "internal norms."

How should we understand these rational demands for consistency and coherence of intentions (given relevant beliefs)? Here we may be impressed by two ideas. The first is that intention seems in some way to involve belief. Different views are possible here: some suppose that an intention to *A* involves the belief that one will *A*; some say only that it involves a belief that *A* is, in an appropriate sense, possible. But however we spell out this belief-involvement we may also be struck by a second idea, namely, that one's beliefs are themselves subject to demands for consistency and coherence. Indeed, it is in the context of belief that demands for consistency and coherence may seem to have their most fundamental home. And this leads to a conjecture: the rational demands for consistency and coherence of intention are grounded, by way of the involvement of belief in intention, in rational demands for consistency and coherence of belief. To this extent, practical rationality of one's system of intentions is, at bottom, theoretical rationality of one's associated beliefs. Call this *cognitivism* about the demands of consistency and coherence on intention.[4]

Cognitivism, so understood, is not simply the idea that demands of consistency and coherence on intention parallel demands of consistency and coherence on belief. The idea is, rather, that demands of consistency and coherence on intention *derive from* demands of consistency and coherence on involved belief. And versions of such cognitivism can be found in some of the best recent work on this subject, including work of Gilbert Harman, J. David Velleman, R. Jay Wallace, and, perhaps to some extent, John Broome.[5] One of my aims in this essay is to explore a range of problems that arise for various versions of cognitivism about consistency and coherence of intention.[6] One issue here will be the status of a norm of agglomeration of intention.[7] A second issue will concern the implications for cognitivism of our fallibility about our own intentions. And a third issue will concern the distinction between intended means and expected side

4. I coin this use of "cognitivism" in my "Cognitivism About Practical Reason" as reprinted in Bratman 1999: 250–64. Cognitivism in this sense should be distinguished from cognitivism as a standard position in meta-ethics.
5. See Harman, "Practical Reasoning" (originally published 1976; reprinted, with some changes, in Harman 1999: 46–74, which is the version quoted from here) and 1986a; Velleman 1989, 2000; R. Jay Wallace, 2001; John Broome, 2009. Broome's view is difficult to classify, however, and less clearly cognitivist than that of Harman, Velleman, and Wallace.
6. According to the planning theory, intentions are also subject to certain rational pressures for stability; and we can also ask whether these rational pressures for stability of intention are grounded in corresponding pressures for stability of belief. But I do not address these matters here.
7. The terminology of "agglomeration" can be traced back at least to Bernard Williams, "Ethical Consistency," in Williams 1973: 166–86 (see esp. 179–82).

effects. My view, in the end, is that cognitivism about the norms of consistency and coherence of intention is problematic, and that it is more plausible to see these norms as fundamentally practical norms that are part and parcel of a planning system that is so important to our lives.

II

A first step is to reflect on the very idea that intention involves belief. And here we need to distinguish three different versions of this idea: (a) intending to act just *is* a special kind of belief that one will so act; (b) intending to act *involves* a belief that one will so act; (c) intending to act involves a belief that it is *possible* that one will so act. These three ideas are in descending order of strength: it will be easier to defend (c) than (b), or (b) than (a). Indeed, I argued in my 1987 book that (a) and (b) are sufficiently controversial that we do well to develop the basic theory of intention and planning in a way that does not require such an assumption.[8] It seemed to me plausible that I might, for example, intend to stop at the bookstore on the way home even though I know that once I get on my bike I tend to go into automatic pilot, and so I do not, strictly speaking, believe I will stop (though I do not believe I will not stop). So I thought it best not to tie the theory of intention and planning to such a strong belief-condition. However, it is also true that the stronger our claim about belief-involvement the stronger our resources in defending the idea that certain rational demands on intention are grounded in theoretical demands on involved beliefs.

I should also note a fourth idea here, one that has recently been pursued by John Broome. This is the idea that if you believe you intend *X* then you believe *X*. As Broome notes, this might be true even if you can intend *X* without believing *X*, for you might intend *X* but not believe you intend *X*. And Broome (2009) is interested in this fourth idea because he is interested in practical reasoning in which one brings to bear what one believes one intends.

Now, it does seem that examples like the one just mooted about the absent-minded cyclist raise a problem also for Broome's idea.[9] But in any case this fourth idea is not quite apt for my purposes here, since even if we accept it we could not use it to explain why intentions *quite generally* are

8. Bratman 1987: 37–8. See also my "Practical Reasoning and Acceptance in a Context," as reprinted in Bratman 1999: 15–34, at 31–2.
9. I pursue this concern in Bratman 2009 [this volume, essay 3].

subject to the cited demands. This is because it is granted that intending does not always bring with it a belief that one so intends. So I will put this idea to one side here, and focus on the first three ideas of a belief-condition on intention quite generally.

To explore cognitivism about the demands on intention, then, we will need to consider various combinations of purported belief-involvement together with associated appeals to theoretical reason. And, indeed, recent work on these matters has included efforts to build on each of these three different accounts of belief-involvement. Gilbert Harman, in his groundbreaking 1976 essay "Practical Reasoning," and David Velleman in his 1989 book *Practical Reflection*, both identify intention with a kind of belief, and they both see this as a key to grounding basic rational demands on intention. In his 1986 book, *Change in View*, however, Harman appeals only to the idea that intention involves belief.[10] And in a recent effort to defend a broadly cognitivist account of, as he calls it, the "instrumental principle," R. Jay Wallace (2001) has appealed rather to the even weaker idea that intention involves a belief in the possibility of success. So the issues here are complex. But to get an initial idea of the (as I will argue, misleading) attractions of the cognitivist approach let us briefly consider how, in particular, (b)—the idea that intending to A involves believing one will A—might help ground demands on intention.

Consider consistency of intention and of intention taken together with belief. Given that intending to A involves believing one will A, and given a demand of consistency on one's beliefs, it follows directly that there is a demand of consistency on one's intentions. After all, if one's intentions are inconsistent, or inconsistent with one's beliefs, then, on the assumption, one's beliefs are inconsistent.

Consider now means–end coherence. How might this be seen as grounded in demands of theoretical reason on one's beliefs? We can begin by supposing that there is a demand of theoretical reason that one's beliefs be coherent, where this includes what Gilbert Harman has called explanatory coherence.

One's beliefs fail to conform to this demand when they involve believing things for which there is, within one's beliefs, no explanation. Such beliefs would be explanatory "danglers."[11] Such incoherence in one's system of beliefs may involve inconsistency, but it may not: there can be a significant

---

10. See, for example, Harman's summary of the dialectic concerning the relation between practical and theoretical reasoning in Harman 1986a: 113.
11. Such talk of "danglers" derives from H. Feigl's talk of "nomological danglers" (Feigl 1958).

explanatory gap in one's beliefs even if there is, strictly speaking, no inconsistency.

Suppose now that one intends end E (and so, on our present assumption, believes E), and believes M is a necessary means to E. Suppose also that one believes that M will obtain only if one intends M.[12] And suppose, finally, that one still does not intend M. One's intentions are, taken together with one's beliefs, means–end incoherent: one intends the end but does not intend known, necessary means even though one believes such an intention is needed for those means (and so for the end). Is this a form of theoretical incoherence? It may seem that, given the assumed belief-involvement, it is indeed a form of theoretical incoherence; for it may seem that there will be an explanatory gap in one's beliefs. Given the absence of an intention to M, it seems that one will have no explanation of M even though one needs to believe that M will obtain if one is to have an explanation of E. So it may seem that one's beliefs will be explanatorily incoherent. So it may seem that this kind of means–end incoherence is, indeed, a form of explanatory incoherence.

This is, of course, only a sketch; and we will need to re-visit the details below. But I think it does give one a feel for efforts to ground distinctive rational demands on intention directly in demands of theoretical reason, given certain forms of belief-involvement in intention. I have my doubts, however.

III

The first question is whether a weak belief-condition, along the lines of (c), would suffice for cognitivism. This is important since such a belief-condition is more easily defended than stronger and more controversial conditions along the lines of (a) or (b). And, indeed, R. Jay Wallace has recently sought to defend something like cognitivism concerning the demand for (what I am calling) means–end coherence by appeal to such a weak belief-requirement. As he says:

> Some philosophers have gone so far as to suggest that intentions presuppose (or may in part be identified with) the belief that what one intends will in fact come to pass; but this thesis is controversial, and anyway unnecessary to account for the principle of instrumental rationality. It will suffice to maintain what is at any

12. See Binkley 1965: 443.

rate more plausible, namely that the intention to do X requires at least the belief that it is *possible* that one do X.[13]

Wallace's "principle of instrumental rationality" corresponds to what I am calling the demand for means–end coherence; and I will return to his account of that principle below.[14] But I'd like first to reflect on the demand for consistency of intention. This demand for consistency is not the focus of Wallace's discussion. Nevertheless, a plausible cognitivism needs an account of that demand. So it is worth noting that belief-requirement (c), taken by itself, is too weak to do this.[15]

Suppose I believe it is possible that I A, and I believe it is possible that I B. I am thereby in a position to believe the conjunction: it is possible that I A and it is possible that I B. Nevertheless, I might well not believe—and reasonably so—that it is possible that I do both. A conjunction of beliefs about the possibility of different actions need not ensure a belief that the conjunction is possible. So even if an intention to A involves a belief that A is possible, and similarly concerning an intention to B, we would not yet have explained what is rationally criticizable about intending to A and intending to B when I believe that though each is individually possible it is not possible to do both. To explain that, within a cognitivist framework and given only Wallace's weak belief-condition, we need to suppose that by virtue of this pair of intentions the agent arrives at a single belief that it is possible that he do both A and B. But there is, so far, nothing in Wallace's account that explains why the agent must arrive at this belief, and so no explanation of the relevant demand of consistency on intention.[16]

13. Wallace 2001: 20. My discussion of Wallace's views, as well as a range of related issues about the "instrumental principle," has benefited from discussions with Kenneth Stalzer and from his PhD thesis, "On the Normativity of the Instrumental Principle" (Stanford University, 2004). For further critical discussions of Wallace's view—discussions of Wallace that are (independently) broadly in the spirit of my discussion in this essay—see also Brunero 2005 and Raz 2005.

14. To avoid confusion let me make a terminological remark: Wallace distinguishes between "the instrumental principle," on the one hand; and, on the other hand, normative pressures for coherence "with the agent's larger system of projects and ends" (2001: 24). And Wallace calls coherence with the "larger system of projects and ends" "means–end coherence." However, it is Wallace's "instrumental principle" that corresponds to the demand for means–end coherence, as I am understanding that demand here.

15. Actually, there is an ambiguity in this talk about belief in the possibility that one so acts. Wallace sometimes seems to understand this as a belief that one can, or is able so to, act; but he sometimes seems to understand it only as a belief that one's so acting is consistent with one's beliefs. However, my discussion of Wallace's views does not depend on resolving this ambiguity.

16. So, for example, in the video games case I have discussed elsewhere, Wallace's weak belief condition does not by itself explain what is problematic about intending

Of course, if an intention to act involved a belief that one would so act, matters would be different; for a conjunction of beliefs in the success of each intention does support a belief in conjunctive success. But at this point we would have left Wallace's effort to make do with a weak belief-requirement, and we would have returned to something like (b), or even (a).

Alternatively, we might seek to explain the pressure for agglomerating intentions in a way that does not draw solely on the beliefs purportedly involved in intention. With such an explanation in hand we could explain why, given an intention to A and an intention to B, I am under rational pressure to intend both to A and to B. And given that single intention in favor of the pair of actions, we could then appeal to Wallace's weak belief-condition—that intention brings with it a belief in possibility—to explain why that intention is challenged by a belief that it is not possible to perform both actions.

This would be to supplement cognitivism with a further principle of intention agglomeration, a principle that says, roughly, that if one intends A and intends B then one is to intend A and B.[17] On the present proposal the rationale for this principle does not derive directly from theoretical demands on purportedly involved beliefs (where those involved beliefs are understood along the lines of (c)). And this raises the possibility that it is this nontheoretical rationale that is primarily at work in providing a ground for the consistency demand.[18] Nevertheless, Wallace might say that the full story of consistency demands on intentions would still depend in part on the corresponding consistency demand on involved (c)-type beliefs. So let us call a theory of this sort *supplemented* cognitivism, and contrast such theories with versions of *pure* cognitivism that seek to derive demands of consistency and coherence of intention solely from purported belief-involvement together with theoretical demands on beliefs. And what we have seen is that if we follow Wallace in seeing the belief-involvement along the lines of (c), then there is pressure on our cognitivism about intention consistency to move to a supplemented cognitivism, one that appeals to an independent principle of intention agglomeration.

to hit target 1 and also intending to hit target 2, while knowing these are each, taken individually, possible but are not co-possible. See Bratman 1987: ch. 8.

17. For a very useful discussion of complexities in the formulation of this condition, see Yaffe 2004: 512–13.

18. My own approach to agglomeration—discussed below—has this character.

What about means–end coherence? We might wonder whether Wallace's belief-condition (c) is too weak to support a version of the cognitivist story rehearsed earlier about means–end coherence, since that story drew on the stronger belief-condition (b).[19] For present purposes, however, I want to focus on what seems to me a more basic problem, a problem posed by the possibility of false beliefs about one's own intentions. Indeed, as I see it, this is a problem that Wallace's account shares with cognitivist accounts of means–end coherence that draw on even stronger assumptions about the relation between intention and belief. So I will explore this problem primarily in the context of accounts that appeal to a stronger belief-condition, though I will also return below to a distinctive aspect of Wallace's treatment.

Consider in particular Gilbert Harman's approach in "Practical Reasoning." In that paper Harman identifies intention with a kind of reflexive belief: an intention to A is a belief that this very belief guarantees that A, where this belief is a conclusion of practical reasoning,[20] and where practical reasoning is concerned, in a characteristic way that distinguishes

19. Wallace (2001: 20–1) thinks (c) is strong enough. Stalzer usefully discusses this issue in his "On the Normativity of the Instrumental Principle": ch.2.

20. What Harman says is as follows: "This suggests, then, that an intention is a conclusion of practical reasoning that says that that very conclusion guarantees that something will happen" (1999: 65). This remark comes immediately after referring to an example, due to Derek Parfit, of an insomniac who believes his very belief that he will stay awake guarantees he will stay awake. About this insomniac Harman says that "his belief is not an intention, because it is not a conclusion of practical reasoning." So it is natural to interpret Harman as saying that this belief would be an intention if it were a conclusion of practical reasoning, and so that intention is a *belief* that is "a conclusion of practical reasoning that says that that very conclusion guarantees that something will happen." This reading is also supported by Harman's comments at the 1980 Eastern Division Meetings of the American Philosophical Association, quoted below in note 30.

But how can a belief guarantee that something will happen? I think Harman's answer is not clear in this 1976 essay; but his strategy in a later essay is just to stipulate that intentions are beliefs that also have the further feature of motivating action. See Harman 1986b: 376. (For a related idea, see Setiya 2003: 359.) An alternative strategy here would be to find a desire that is—in some sense, as a matter of necessity—in the background, a desire with which the belief that is the intention would systematically connect to motivate action. This is David Velleman's (1989) strategy, in citing background desires for self-knowledge and self-understanding. In a later version of this idea, Velleman appeals to the "aim" of self-knowledge (2000: ch. 1). I turn to Velleman's views below.

it from theoretical reasoning, with coherence with intrinsic desires.[21] Further:

[s]ince intention involves belief, theoretical and practical reasoning overlap.

In theoretical reasoning, one seeks to increase the coherence of one's overall view of the world . . . Since intention involves belief, and theoretical and practical reasoning overlap, coherence must be relevant to any sort of reasoning about the future, theoretical or practical . . .

The thesis that intention involves belief associates practical reasoning about means and ends with theoretical reasoning. It brings these two sorts of reasoning under a single principle.[22]

What single principle? A principle of coherence. To what does this principle of coherence directly apply? Given the emphasis on "[t]he thesis that intention involves belief" it seems that the idea is that the principle of coherence directly applies to one's beliefs, which constitute the "view" that is the concern of theoretical reasoning. It is because "intention involves belief" that this principle of coherence on belief extends to one's intentions. And, given that intention involves belief, it seems that a failure to intend known necessary means will induce a failure to satisfy this principle of coherence. After all, if I intend E, believe that M is necessary for E and that intending M is necessary for M, and if I do not intend M, and if an intention that E involves a belief that E, then my beliefs are explanatorily incoherent, since E, which I believe, is an explanatory dangler within my system of beliefs. Or so it seems. So the practical demand for coherence of one's intentions that is associated with means–end reasoning within one's intentions is, at bottom, the theoretical demand for coherence of the beliefs that are involved in intentions.

This account of "practical reasoning about means and ends" so far only draws on the idea that intending to act requires a belief that one will; it

21. Harman describes this connection between practical reasoning and intrinsic desires at 1999: 62–3. The idea is that this includes a range of cases: what is intended as a conclusion is intrinsically desired or is thought to contribute to something that is intrinsically desired; the formation of the intention is thought to contribute to the satisfaction of intrinsic desires; or the intention is a conclusion of means–end reasoning from other intentions that persist, by way of inertia, from an earlier view of a connection to the satisfaction of intrinsic desire. Other features of Harman's account of practical reasoning emerge in his discussion of the distinction between intending and predicting. I turn to this discussion below in section VI.

22. Harman 1999: 49–50. In the original 1976 essay, Harman had said that "[I]n theoretical reasoning, one seeks to increase the explanatory coherence of one's overall view of the world." In this more recent version of his essay, he appeals broadly to coherence, where explanatory coherence is one kind of coherence (though the appeal specifically to explanatory coherence remains at 1999: 56, 63).

does not yet draw on the identification of intention and belief. So, even though (as I have interpreted him) Harman does in this 1976 essay endorse such an identification, he is being accurate when he says that what is at work here is the "thesis that intention involves belief." (Indeed, as I have noted, in his 1986a book Harman pulls back from the identification, but still endorses the "thesis that intention involves belief." I turn below to relevant details of his 1986 account.)

Nevertheless, I think that, in the end, the purported identification of intention and belief may well matter to the argument for cognitivism. The first step to seeing why is to turn, as anticipated, to the concern that Harman's cognitivist account of means–end coherence does not work because it is possible for an agent to believe he intends M but, in fact, not intend M.[23]

Suppose I intend E and know that E requires M and that I intend M. If I still do not intend M my intentions suffer from means–end incoherence. But suppose that, while I in fact do not intend M, I nevertheless falsely believe that I intend M. So my beliefs are that E, that E requires M and that I intend M, that I intend M, and that M. There is no incoherence (though there is falsity) in this structure of beliefs. So means–end coherence is not belief coherence.

How might a cognitivist respond to this challenge? I will discuss below an effort to retain, in response, a pure cognitivism by appealing specifically to the identification of intention with belief. But first let us consider a response that explicitly involves a supplemented cognitivism. The idea here is to appeal to some further rational demand that is violated when one believes one intends M but does not so intend. And, indeed, this is Wallace's strategy. Wallace does not say that an intention to A requires a belief that one so intend. But he does aver that if "intentions are readily accessible to consciousness" then it is "independently irrational for you to have false beliefs about the content of your intentions" (2001: 22). As for "intentions that are not readily accessible to consciousness," Wallace says that it is "doubtful that intentions that are cut off in this way from conscious belief really do introduce rational constraints on our further attitudes, of the kind represented by the instrumental principle" (2001: 23).[24]

I will focus on the case in which one's intentions are "accessible." Wallace is clear that, given his appeal to such a rational requirement on beliefs about intentions, his account of "the instrumental principle" is not "merely . . . an application of the considerations that determine coherence

23. I proposed this objection in Bratman 1981: 255–6, note 4.
24. This last remark is in the spirit of Broome's focus on those cases of intention in which one does believe one has the intention.

and consistency relations among beliefs" (2001: 23). His is a supplemented, not a pure cognitivism. But Wallace does think this further requirement is "independently plausible."

Suppose that it is Sunday and I now believe that I now intend to go shopping this coming Thursday. However, if I thought more about it I'd realize that actually what I intend to do is to go on Friday. My intention to shop on Friday is "accessible to consciousness," but I have not right now bothered carefully to access it, since there is no special reason to do that now and other matters are more pressing at the moment. I have a false belief about the content of my "accessible" intention. But not all cases of false belief are cases of irrationality. So we need to ask why we should say that, in the present case, the false belief does involve irrationality.

One idea might be that false beliefs about the contents of one's own attitudes always involve irrationality. But this seems wrong. We are psychologically complex, and it is sometimes difficult for us to discern, for example, what we do in fact want, or fear, or love. If we at times make mistakes about ourselves in these domains that will at least sometimes be a matter of our fallibility, not our irrationality. Granted, there may be a special case to be made concerning false beliefs about what one believes: it might be argued that a false belief about one's own beliefs is an irrational incoherence within one's beliefs.[25] But our present concern, within Wallace's theory, is, rather, with false beliefs about one's own intentions. So we are still without an explanation of why a false belief about one's "accessible" intentions is irrational.[26]

Can we appeal at this point to irrationality in failing to reflect more carefully on what one intends, on failing to bother to access intentions that are accessible? Well, it seems that it is not always irrational not to reflect carefully on all that one intends. Such reflection is an activity that takes time and uses other resources, and one may well have better things to do. We are, after all, agents with limited psychological resources.

In any case, such an appeal to a purported irrationality in failing to reflect more carefully on what one intends seems to involve an appeal to instrumental reason, broadly construed: it will normally be irrational to fail to reflect in this way when (but perhaps not only when) such reflection is, broadly speaking, called for as a means to things one values. If we were

25. An idea I turn to below, in the context of my discussion of Harman's views.
26. Recall that John Broome focuses on cases in which one believes one intends X. So the target of his focus would not include my intention to shop on Friday. Broome's reason for this limitation is that he thinks that it is only when one believes one intends X that one's intention enters into practical reasoning. Wallace's claim here is, in contrast, that a false belief about what one intends, when one's intention is accessible, is irrational. It is this claim of Wallace, a claim about irrationality, which is at issue here.

to proceed in this way, then, the further principle of rationality to which Wallace appeals would itself be grounded, at least in part, in instrumental rationality, broadly construed.[27]

This would be a supplemented cognitivism, but the supplement in this case would bring to bear instrumental reason, broadly construed. In the earlier case of appeal to a principle of intention agglomeration, the supplement to cognitivism, while not derived solely from theoretical demands on belief together with a thesis of belief-involvement in intention, was not itself a principle of instrumental rationality. But now we are considering a supplement that itself depends on considerations of instrumental rationality. To mark this difference let us call this latter kind of supplemented cognitivism *compromised* cognitivism.

It may seem that compromised cognitivism travels in a circle. It seeks an account of means–end coherence; but it appeals to instrumental reason in that account.

I think, though, that there need not be a circle here, strictly speaking. In particular—and this is a point to which I will return below—we can distinguish two forms of instrumental rationality. Our main focus so far has been with means–end coherence specifically of intentions and plans. This is a constraint specifically on planning structures. And this constraint is limited in two important ways. First, it is not a general concern with means to all the various things one values and cares about. It concerns only intended means to ends that are, strictly speaking, intended. Second, there is a substantive question whether means–end coherent plans are more effective than means–end incoherent plans, or indeed than an absence of planning, in promoting the various things one values and cares about—the various concerns that constitute what we can call the *agent's practical standpoint*. There is a substantive question whether means–end coherence in fact supports effective agency—where effectiveness is assessed, broadly, with respect to the agent's practical standpoint.[28] We can ask about this mode of functioning—or, indeed, about any mode of psychological functioning—whether as a matter of fact it tends to support, causally and/or constitutively, the agent's broadly effective agency.

Now, compromised cognitivism would be circular if its support of the demand for means–end coherence simply appealed to the demand for

27. I owe to Nadeem Hussain the idea that at this point in his theory, Wallace's account of the "instrumental principle" might itself need to appeal to instrumental reason.

28. See Railton 1997: 77–8. See also John Broome 2007, at section 4. Concerning the idea that effectiveness of agency is assessed with respect to the agent's practical standpoint, see my "Temptation Revisited," in Bratman 2007: 257–82, at 264–6.

means–end coherence. But it need not proceed in this way. It can instead say, in particular, that certain norms on intentions are supported by an instrumental concern with broadly effective agency. Such a compromised cognitivism need not be circular.

Nevertheless, while such a compromised cognitivism need not be circular, it does not seem to establish that false beliefs about one's own (accessible) intentions *always* involve irrationality, and in any case it departs significantly from the initial intuition behind the cognitivist approach that the basic rational pressure at work in these contexts is one of theoretical reason. Someone who is impressed with the cognitivist program will want to ask whether there is a way of defending, instead, a purer cognitivism about means–end coherence, in response to worries about false beliefs about one's intentions.

V

Perhaps the best hope for a purer cognitivism lies in a strategy that Harman himself once sketched.[29] The idea is that if you accept the *identification* of intention with belief you can argue that one's false belief that one intends M really does bring with it incoherence *in belief*. After all, according to the theory intention *is* belief. So one's false belief about what one intends is a false belief about what one believes: on the theory, if one has such a false belief then "one believes one believes something which in fact one does not believe."[30] And such a false belief about one's own beliefs is, arguably, an incoherence within one's beliefs.

This response tries to find an incoherence *within* one's beliefs by exploiting the identification of intention with a certain kind of belief. This contrasts with Wallace's effort to see intention as different from (though involving) belief, but to appeal to a further principle that sees false

29. In a footnote to his comments on my "Intention and Means–End Reasoning" at the 1980 Eastern Division Meetings of the American Philosophical Association.

30. Here is the text of what Harman said: "In 'Practical Reasoning' I assumed that to intend to do B is to have a certain sort of self–referential belief. So in this case [that is, the case of falsely believing one intends the necessary means] one believes one believes something which in fact one does not believe, and this might count as a kind of incoherence in one's beliefs." In my discussion here of Harman's effort to block concerns about false beliefs about what one intends, I simply accept, for the sake of the present argument, this suggestion from Harman that this would "count as a kind of incoherence in one's beliefs." I then argue that even given this assumption, means–end incoherence is not incoherence in belief. In Bratman 2009 [this volume, essay 3] I say a bit more about why one might accept this suggestion from Harman. And at the end of section VII of the present essay I briefly consider a cognitivist view that need not accept this suggestion from Harman.

belief about what one intends as irrational (when one's intention is "accessible"). I have argued that Wallace's strategy is problematic and may lead to a compromised cognitivism. Harman's strategy is the more promising strategy for defending a purer cognitivism about means–end coherence.

However, even if we accept, for the sake of argument, both the basic outlines of Harman's 1976 theory and the idea that false belief about one's own beliefs is a form of incoherence of belief, there are two reasons to be skeptical about Harman's strategy for responding to my objection. The first is that there still remain cases of means–end incoherence that are not cases of incoherence of belief. To see why, recall that even on Harman's 1976 identification of intention with belief, two beliefs can have the very same content and yet one be an intention and the other not be an intention. This is because, on the theory, a belief is an intention only if it is a conclusion of practical reasoning. Suppose then, to use an example that derives from Harman's paper, that there are two people who believe they will remain awake all night. Alice believes she will remain awake, and that this will happen because she believes it. And Bill has the analogous, purportedly self-fulfilling belief. Suppose that Bill's belief is based, by way of practical reasoning, on his desire to stay awake; whereas Alice is the believed self-fulfilling but reluctant insomniac that, as Harman tells us, Derek Parfit once described.[31] Bill intends to stay awake; Alice does not intend to stay awake. But the difference is not a difference in content of belief.

Suppose now that Alice falsely believes that she intends to stay awake. Perhaps she believes that staying awake is a necessary means to something she intrinsically desires—finishing an essay she is writing, say. And she believes—albeit, incorrectly—that this is why she believes she will stay awake as a result of this very belief. She believes she intends to stay awake even though she does not intend to stay awake. But it is not true that she "believes [she] believes something which in fact [she] does not believe," since she does in fact believe she will stay awake by way of this very belief. It is just that this belief is, in fact, not based on practical reasoning, and so is not an intention (on Harman's 1976 view of intention). So Harman's identification of intention with a kind of belief does not support the claim that all cases of false belief about what one intends are cases of believing one believes something that in fact one does not believe.

It follows that pure cognitivism about means–end coherence remains vulnerable to counterexample. To see this, suppose that Alice intends to finish her essay, believes that this requires staying awake and that staying awake requires intending to stay awake. Suppose further that she believes

31. Harman 1999: 61–5; and see also Harman 1986b: 375.

she intends to stay awake but in fact, though she does believe that she'll stay awake because of this very belief, she does not, strictly speaking, intend to stay awake, since that reflexive belief is not in fact an issue of practical reasoning. Alice is means–end incoherent, for she intends the end but does not intend what she believes to be necessary means even though she believes so intending to be necessary. But this means–end incoherence is not incoherence in belief.

VI

A second reason to be skeptical about Harman's defense of pure cognitivism about means–end coherence is that the identification of intention with belief leads to a further problem about the distinction between intending means and expecting side effects.[32]

Suppose—to take a much discussed example—that in wartime one intends to bomb a munitions factory as a means to promoting the war effort, knows that one will thereby destroy a school that is nearby, but does not intend to destroy the school.[33] I think we want our theory to allow for such cases in which, while one believes one will X by way of one's intention, one does not intend X. The problem is that it is not clear how we can say this if intention is belief.

Let's see how this problem emerges within Harman's theory.[34]

The bomber intends to drop the bombs, and his intention is (according to Harman) an appropriate belief that is the issue of practical reasoning. What practical reasoning? If we assume that the bomber is thoughtful about the various costs and benefits, it seems that his reasoning will consider various overall scenarios:[35]

(a) bomb the factory, thereby promote the war effort but also destroy the school;

32. So there is, in effect, a dilemma: if we say that intention is, so to speak, belief-plus, then problems about false beliefs about one's own intentions loom; but if we identify intention with belief then problems loom concerning the distinction between intention and foresight. My concern in the present section is with the second horn of this dilemma.

33. See Walzer 1977, Jonathan Bennett 1980, and Bratman 1987: ch. 10.

34. I discuss these matters under the guise of what I call "the problem of the package deal" in Bratman 1987: 143–55 (a discussion from which I draw here). In "Cognitivism About Practical Reason" (1999: 257–61), I argue that Velleman's theory faces an analogous problem.

35. See Sellars 1966 (esp. 131–6).

(b) don't bomb, and thereby bypass an important means for promoting the war effort.

And it seems that the bomber concludes in favor of (a), and so arrives at the intention—that is, the reflexive belief—in favor of bombing. What exactly is the belief-conclusion of his practical reasoning? It seems it should be—at least if he is thoughtful about his options—the conclusion that he will bomb and thereby promote the war effort, but also destroy the school, and that this will come about by way of this very belief. But then the bomber not only intends to bomb, he also intends to destroy the school.[36] So it is not clear how, on this theory of intending, a thoughtful agent in this example can merely expect, and not intend, that he will destroy the school.

What Harman needs to explain is why it can be reasonable for the bomber instead to reach, by way of practical reasoning, the more limited conclusion:

(a*) bomb the factory, thereby promote the war effort;

and then go on, by way not of practical but of theoretical reasoning, to the further conclusion:

(c) I will thereby destroy the school.

The bomber would then believe (c), but this belief would not be an intention since it would not be a conclusion of practical reasoning.

But why think that the bomber should not rather arrive at (a) as a conclusion of practical reasoning?

There are two different responses to this problem in Harman's work, one in his 1976 paper, and another in his 1986a book. In his 1976 paper Harman acknowledges that he needs an explanation of why a rational bomber may draw the two different conclusions (a*) and (c), rather than the single practical conclusion (a).[37] He then offers the following solution:

We must assume that there is a requirement on reasoning that favours theoretical reasoning over practical reasoning. If a conclusion can be reached by

---

36. I am helping myself here to what I have called the principle of "intention division." See Bratman 1987: 145–8.
37. See Harman 1999: 66.

theoretical reasoning alone, it is not to be reached as a conclusion of practical reasoning. Let us call this the minimality requirement on practical reasoning.[38]

The idea is that this minimality requirement says that the bomber's practical reasoning should arrive at the more minimal practical conclusion (a*), rather than the less minimal conclusion (a). So the bomber may reasonably intend to bomb but only expect to destroy the school.

As Harman notes, this does make it unclear why the bomber's practical reasoning does not simply arrive at the even more minimal conclusion:

(a**) bomb the factory

and leave the impact on the war effort to further theoretical reasoning. At this point Harman appeals to "the requirement of not predicting decisions that one can make instead."[39] But for present purposes I want to focus on the minimality requirement itself.

In appealing to the minimality requirement Harman is supplementing his cognitivism with a principle about the relation between practical and theoretical reasoning. So this is a supplemented cognitivism. I do not mean this as a criticism, but only as a point about the kind of theory Harman has put on the table. But now we need to reflect on this minimality requirement.

As Reuben Veek has noted (in conversation), one idea that may be at work here is that we normally want first to figure out what the world is like, and then, in light of that knowledge, decide what to do. So theoretical reasoning gets priority.

The problem is that this does not explain the kind of priority at issue in the minimality requirement, as Harman is understanding that requirement. Veek's rationale for the minimality requirement concerns cases in which one first reasons theoretically and then, in light of one's theoretical conclusion, reasons practically. But in the cases of present interest, the relevant reasoning begins as practical reasoning about what to do. The issue is the extent of the conclusion of this practical reasoning and when, so to speak, theoretical reasoning takes over. Concerning this issue the cited rationale for a priority for theoretical reasoning does not seem forceful.

The next point is that the minimality requirement conflicts with a plausible ideal of practical clear-headedness and honesty, an ideal that supports

38. Harman 1999: 66.
39. Harman 1999: 66. There is also a question, which I put to one side here, about why the bomber does not simply conclude: (a***) push the bomb button. See Harman's remarks at 1999: 67–8.

a kind of full disclosure in one's practical conclusions. According to this ideal, if the bomber really does consider in his practical reasoning various important pros and cons, including the destruction of the school, then these considered pros and cons should be represented in a conclusion of the bomber's practical reasoning. If the bomber does conclude in favor of bombing, and does consider these important pros and cons in his practical reasoning, then a conclusion of the bomber's practical reasoning should indeed be (a). So in the absence of a further defense of the minimality requirement in the face of such pressure for full practical disclosure we are without an adequate explanation of the possibility of reasonably expecting an upshot of what one intends without intending it, when that expected upshot is something that one considers seriously in one's practical reasoning.

If we reject the minimality requirement we need a different account of why, consistent with a defensible model of practical reasoning, it can be reasonable only to expect, and not to intend, relevant side effects of what one does intend.[40] So let us turn to the different approach that Harman takes in his 1986 book.

Now, as noted, in this book Harman pulls back from identifying intention with belief, while holding on to the idea that intending to act involves a belief that one will. And I have argued that the absence of the identification of intention with belief exacerbates the problem for cognitivism about means–end coherence that is posed by the possibility of error about one's own intentions.[41] But we still need to consider Harman's alternative treatment, in his 1986 book, of the distinction between intending and expecting, since that treatment might also be used to defend the identification of intention and belief against the objection that that identification does not do justice to that distinction.

Harman's target in his 1986 book is 'a holistic view of decisions':

In a holistic view, when one decides what to do, one must consider all foreseeable effects . . . and must evaluate them as a total package . . .

Once this much is accepted, it becomes difficult to see how there could be a real distinction between what one intends and what one merely foresees as

---

40. I sketch an alternative approach in Bratman 1987, one that involves rejecting what I called the "choice-intention principle" (see esp. 152–60). The basic idea is that the backward-looking pressures for a holistic conclusion apply primarily to choice, but the forward-looking pressures to function in characteristic ways in further reasoning and action apply primarily to intention; and these phenomena can come apart. This strategy is not available to a theory that identifies intention with belief.

41. And recall that the response to this problem that Harman suggested in his 1980 APA comments did appeal to the identification of intention with belief.

consequences and side effects of one's action, because it is natural to suppose that (A) one's intention comprises the conclusion one reaches as a result of practical reasoning. But in a holistic view of practical reasoning, (B) one's conclusion should include the acceptance of everything one knows about one's action.[42]

Harman proceeds to argue against the "holistic" idea that "when one decides what to do, one must consider all foreseeable effects . . . and must evaluate them as a total package." His argument is that this is not a realistic requirement on agents with limited resources of attention and reasoning. Such agents reasonably limit what they consider in their practical reasoning primarily to ends and means, rather than side effects: they begin with their ends and determine means; they do not consider in this reasoning expected side effects (Harman 1986a: 106). Rules for such agents need "to keep things simple"; and "[t]he rationale for this way of proceeding lies in its cost-effectiveness" (1986a: 107). Such considerations of cost effectiveness block "holistic" inputs into practical reasoning, and thereby the need for a "holistic" practical conclusion. This contrasts with the earlier appeal to the minimality requirement directly to block, not holistic inputs, but rather holistic conclusions. And this strategy for blocking holistic inputs supports the distinction between intending means and expecting side effects.

One aspect of this change from the 1976 view is that the cognitivism is now not supplemented merely by a principle—the minimality requirement—that concerns the priority of theoretical over practical reasoning. The cognitivism is now compromised; for it depends on an appeal to considerations of "cost-effectiveness," and so of a form of instrumental rationality for resource limited agents like us. Again, I intend this not as a criticism of Harman's account, but rather as an effort to make explicit what kind of account is in the offing.

However, it does seem to me that this compromised cognitivism does not accomplish what we need.[43] It does explain why certain kinds of expected but unimportant side effects—the movement of air molecules as a result of one's walking to the store, say—are reasonably excluded from consideration in practical reasoning. But it does not explain why side effects of acknowledged significance, such as the destruction of the school, should be excluded from consideration. Indeed, it seems that normally such important, anticipated side effects *should* be considered. In any case, we are supposing that the bomber *does* consider the cited, expected side effect, so the costs of attention and the like have already been incurred. And now

42. Harman 1986a: 98.
43. See Bratman 1987: 148–52.

we need to know how he can—and reasonably so—still not intend that side effect even while intending the means which have that side effect. Harman's strategy here does not answer this question, so far as I can see.

VII

What should we say, then, about the prospects for a defensible cognitivism about consistency and coherence demands on intention? Well, if we embrace only a weak belief-condition (c), the cognitivism will need to be supplemented with an intention-agglomeration principle even to account for consistency demands on intention. If we embrace a stronger belief-condition along the lines of (a) or (b) our cognitivism about consistency demands can be pure, though at the price of defending some such stronger—and, as I see it, controversial—claim about belief-involvement. When we turn to means–end coherence, and the problem posed by the possibility of false beliefs about one's intentions, matters get even more complex. If we do not identify intention with a kind of belief but only subscribe to a belief-condition along the lines of (b)—or perhaps even only (c)—the account will be problematic and will likely become a compromised cognitivism that makes essential appeal to a form of instrumental rationality. If we were instead to follow Harman (in 1976) in identifying intention and belief then we might try to stick with a pure cognitivism specifically in response to the possibility of false belief about one's intentions. Here, however, I have raised a worry by appeal to a version of Parfit's example: I have argued that even if we identify intention with belief in the way that Harman does in 1976, false belief about one's own intentions need not be false belief about what one believes. Further, such an identification of intention with belief will be challenged by the distinction between intending means and expecting side effects.

A final cognitivist move might be to bite the bullet and reject the formulation of the demand for means–end coherence that has shaped our discussion. The idea would be that what means–end rationality requires is only coherence within the agent's own beliefs about herself; and in the cases highlighted in which the agent mistakenly believes that she intends necessary means there is no incoherence in these beliefs, though there is error. But it seems to me that this would be a high price to pay to defend cognitivism. In these cases the agent does, in fact, fail to intend a necessary means that, by her own lights, she needs to intend in order to achieve her intended end. It would be good to have a theory of the rational demands on one's intentions and plans that saved the commonsense idea that such an agent is means–end irrational; and that is what the favored formulation of the demand for means–end coherence does.

I conclude that the defense of cognitivism about consistency and coherence demands on intention is at best a complex and delicate matter, may well be led to compromise, and faces significant problems in its response to our fallibility about our own intentions and in response to the distinction between intended means and expected side effects. This gives us reason to look elsewhere.

VIII

So let us return to the planning theory. The planning theory does not require (though it is consistent with) the assumption that intending to act involves a belief that one will so act. And the planning theory does not try to ground the demands for consistency and coherence of intention in theoretical demands for consistency and coherence of involved belief. Instead, the planning theory tries to see these norms as basic to our planning agency in a way that does not depend on a derivation from theoretical demands on involved beliefs.

The planning theory can allow both that in many cases one does believe that one will act as one intends, and that this belief, when present, helps simplify and support relevant practical reasoning and planning. It can even allow that it might turn out that linguistic intuitions about the verb "intend" support the idea that we do not talk of intending to act unless we suppose that there is, as well, a belief that one will so act (though I am skeptical about this). The basic claim is not about the *word* "intend" but about how best to make sense of the characteristic norms on intentions and plans. The planning theory, in contrast with cognitivism, sees these norms as fundamentally practical.

At this point, however, it might be asked whether we really can account for the demands for consistency and coherence of intentions without supposing that intention involves corresponding belief. Indeed, this challenge has recently been brought to the fore in a probing discussion by J. David Velleman. There are difficult issues here, but let me try to take some tentative steps.

Velleman claims that in the absence of a strong belief-requirement on intention my account of the roles and norms characteristic of intention is "unmotivated."[44] He writes:

44. Velleman 2007: 205. Velleman sounds a similar theme, though more briefly, in his "The Centered Self," in Velleman 2006: 253–83, at 271. In my discussion of Velleman's

that for many of the purposes that Bratman assigns to intention, knowledge of one's forthcoming actions is what actually does the work . . . Intention would be ill-suited to serve these purposes if it were compatible with agnosticism about one's forthcoming actions.[45]

The challenge is that if intention "were compatible with agnosticism about one's forthcoming actions" we would have no account of why such intentions are subject to the demands of consistency and means–end coherence.

Note that the issue is not whether, in the many cases in which intending to A does bring with it a belief that one will A, that belief also engages relevant demands for consistency and coherence. The issue, rather, is whether intention is subject to its own demands of consistency and coherence, demands that do not derive from these demands on associated belief and that would be in force even in the absence of that belief.

Begin with consistency. Velleman asks: "why should my intentions be subject to a requirement of consistency if I can remain cognitively uncommitted to their truth?" (2007: 206). Velleman also indicates, though, that there would be an explanation of this consistency requirement if we could suppose that intentions "are agglomerative, in the sense that rationality favors combining an intention to A and an intention to B into a single intention to A and B" (2007: 206). This is because, as Velleman grants,[46] we do not need cognitivism to explain why it is not rational to intend something one believes not to be possible. But what is important here is that, according to Velleman, while we do not need cognitivism to explain why there is a norm that eschews intending what one believes impossible, we do need cognitivism to explain the agglomerativity of intention. Is that right?

Well, I agree with Velleman that there is here a basic issue: what explains the rational agglomerativity of intention? Indeed, it was a version of this issue that led me to argue that Wallace's cognitivism needed, because of its weak belief-condition, to be supplemented in order to explain the requirement for intention consistency. The issue now is whether the agglomerativity of intention needs to be grounded in a strong belief-requirement on intention, so that in the absence of such a belief-requirement an agglomerativity condition is "unmotivated." Here is what Velleman says:

views in this and the next section I have benefited from discussions with Jennifer Morton and Gideon Yaffe.

45. Velleman 2007: 208.
46. Velleman writes: "Surely I cannot rationally intend to be in Chicago and have dinner with you here at the same time" (2007: 206).

Beliefs are agglomerative because they aim to fit the world, of which there is just one . . . The rational pressure to conjoin beliefs is a pressure to fuse them into a single characterization of the single world that all of them aim to fit. An agglomerativity requirement would be equally appropriate for intentions if they had to be jointly executable in a single world . . . the question is why my intentions must be jointly executable, if I can be agnostic as to whether they will be executed. If I can have a plan without believing that it will be carried out in this world, why should I confine myself to planning for a world in which it is carried out?[47]

When Velleman says that "[b]eliefs are agglomerative" he means that they are subject to "rational pressure" in the direction of agglomeration. What does he mean when he says that beliefs "aim to fit the world"? Well, his precise understanding of this idea has been changing a bit. In his "Introduction" to his 2000 book he argued that belief "aims at truth descriptively, in the sense that it is constitutively regulated by mechanisms designed to ensure that it is true." This appeal to the design of a regulating mechanism is, I take it, an appeal to the idea that it is, descriptively, a function of belief to track truth.[48] And Velleman also averred that it is "only because" belief aims at truth in this descriptive sense that it "aims at the truth in the normative sense"—that it is subject to a norm of truth.[49] More recently, Velleman has to some extent pulled apart the descriptive truth-tracking function from the applicability of a norm of truth. He no longer claims that that norm applies only because it is descriptively a function of belief to be truth-tracking. But he still sees this descriptive aim of belief as supporting a norm of truth. He says, following Nishi Shah, that "the norm of truth is a norm we apply to cognitions that are largely regulated for truth already but become more intelligible to us by virtue of being consciously and more thoroughly regulated under that norm."[50] And his point in the present passage from "What Good is a Will?" is that, given that norm of truth, and given that there is just one world, it follows that beliefs are also subject to a norm of agglomerativity. The idea is that *each* belief, taken individually, has the aim of truth of *its* content.[51] But, since all of an agent's beliefs are

47. Velleman 2007: 206.
48. This leaves it an open (and big) question exactly how to understand this talk of design and function.
49. Velleman 2000: 16–17. And see also "On the Aim of Belief," in Velleman 2000 (esp. 247–55).
50. Velleman 2004: 294. Velleman refers to Nishi Shah 2003.
51. See "On the Aim of Belief," in Velleman 2000, at 279–80.

accountable to *one and the same world*, there is rational pressure for agglomeration of those beliefs.

Velleman is skeptical that there is an analogous argument for agglomeration of intention, in the absence of a strong belief-condition on intention. But let's try. After all, it seems that if we are willing to say that belief aims at truth—at fitting the world—we should also be willing to speak of the (or, anyway, an) aim of intention.[52] And perhaps this aim will support a norm of agglomeration of intention in a way that to some extent parallels the theoretical case.

Indeed, appeal to an aim of intention seems broadly in the spirit of the planning theory. That theory tries to articulate both characteristic functions of intentions—typically as elements in larger planning structures—and associated norms. So the theory will want to appeal both to a description of what intentions have it as a function to track, and to norms associated with that function; and these are the two central elements in Velleman's conception of an aim of an attitude. One might still wonder whether this talk of an aim of an attitude is the best way to get at such interrelated phenomena of function and norm. But for present purposes I will follow Velleman in talking about such an aim, without trying here to settle this further issue.

What then should we identify as an aim of intention? Well, an intention for the future normally brings with it a future-tense description of action. And Velleman interprets me as seeing these "intentions as conative commitments to *making* these future-tense descriptions true but not as cognitive commitments to their *being* true" (2007: 205). This may suggest that a view like mine should say that the aim of each intention is making its content true—or, more carefully, making its content true in the world as one believes it to be. This would help explain why, as Velleman grants, there is, even without cognitivism, a rational demand not to intend something one believes is not possible. And Velleman's challenge is: if each intention has that aim, why is it that "my intentions must be jointly executable, if I can be agnostic as to whether they will be executed"?

But now the point to make is that if we are going to talk this way about the aim of intention we should say of each intention not simply that its aim is to make *its* specific content true in the world as one believes it to be, but

52. When Velleman turns to the practical he appeals to what he sees as the aim of action, or agency—on his view (as I discuss below), this is a theoretical aim of self-understanding. In contrast, I appeal here only to an aim of intention. Stalzer also explores an appeal to an aim of intention in "On the Normativity of the Instrumental Principle," 2004: ch. 5.

rather that its aim is to make its content true *as an element in a coordinated realization of one's system of intentions*, in the world as one believes it to be.[53] Each intention includes in its aim a reference to the agent's overall system of plans.

Why say this? Because our intentions and planning attitudes are elements in a *coordinating system*. The central role of this system is to guide practical thought and action by way of a coordinated representation of our practical future in the world as we find it.[54] A system of attitudes that were not responsive to pressures for coordination within that system would not be a planning system. This is a basic way in which intentions differ from ordinary desires. So I do not agree with Velleman's remark that "the coordinating role of intentions would itself come into doubt if intentions did not involve a cognitive commitment" (2007: 206).

Velleman thinks of the aim of belief atomistically—*each* belief aims at *its* truth—and then appeals to the idea that "there is just one" world to explain the rational pressure for agglomeration of belief. If we think of the aim of each intention in a correspondingly atomistic way—*each* intention aims at making *its* specific content true in the world as one believes it to be—it is not clear why one intention should agglomerate with a second intention in the absence of belief in success of both intentions. But I think we should see the aim of each intention more holistically: each intention aims at making its content true as a part of a *coordinated* realization of one's planning system, in the world as one believes it to be. Responsiveness to such coordination is a defining characteristic of the functioning of a planning system, and of its elements, just as responsiveness to the world is a defining characteristic of belief. On Velleman's view, the unity of the world helps explain the rational pressure toward agglomeration of belief. On my view, a projected unity of agency helps explain the rational pressure toward agglomeration of intention. And once this demand for agglomeration of intention is in place we have an explanation of the demand for consistency of one's various intentions. So we have an explanation of the norm of consistency of intention that has the same structure as Velleman's explanation of the norm of consistency of belief—an explanation that appeals to an aim of intention in a way that parallels Velleman's appeal to the aim of

53. Dana Nelkin has raised the question of whether we should say, rather, that the aim is to make the content true in a coordinated realization of one's intentions in the world as one *relevantly* believes it to be. I will not try to sort out this issue here.

54. This is in the spirit of Harman's remarks about "an evolving system of plans" in "Practical Reasoning" (1999: 60); though, of course, I am not endorsing Harman's interpretation of this as an evolving system of beliefs.

belief. And this explanation of the norm of consistency of intention does not appeal to cognitivism.

Turn now to means–end coherence. Velleman asks: "Why . . . should an agent be rationally obliged to arrange means of carrying out an intention, if he is agnostic about whether he will in fact carry it out?" (2007: 205). My initial answer is that, in the cases at issue, while one may be agnostic about the ultimate success of one's intention for the end, one is not agnostic about the need to intend the means. Even if I am not confident that I will stop at the bookstore on my way home, given my absent-mindedness, I do know that a necessary means to stopping there is, say, starting on the path home that goes by the bookstore, rather than an alternative path that does not. My doubts about whether, in the end, I will remember to stop do not block the demand that, given that I do intend to stop, I start out on the appropriate path.

Granted, my uncertainty about the efficaciousness of my plan for stopping at the bookstore might reasonably lead me not to bother with that plan, especially if I find the alternative path home nicer in other respects. But if I am persuaded by this then what I should do is give up the intention to stop at the bookstore, not intend to stop there but still not intend known necessary means.

Velleman would not be satisfied with this answer, however. He writes:

> Part of the reasoning-centered function of intention, in Bratman's view, is to cut through such cost-benefit calculations by generating a categorical requirement to identify means of doing what is intended. But why should I be categorically required to invest in means whose benefits I am not yet prepared to believe in?[55]

Now, what is "categorically required" is not "to invest in means" but, rather, either to intend the necessary means or to give up the end.[56] But Velleman will ask: why is *that* "categorically required" if it is not a matter of theoretical coherence of belief?[57]

55. Velleman 2007: 205.
56. See Broome 1999: 398–419.
57. Why, on Velleman's view, is coherence of *belief* "categorically required"? Given Velleman's strategy of appealing to the truth-aim of belief, it might seem that the answer is that incoherence of belief undermines the aim of truth of belief. But beliefs can be explanatorily incoherent, in the sense that they include things believed that have no explanation within the system of beliefs, and yet still turn out to be true. So it may be that to explain the requirement for belief coherence Velleman would appeal also to the aim, of certain forms of thinking, of understanding. I discuss this purported aim below.

Well, as I have said, if we are willing to appeal to the aim of belief in supporting norms on belief, we should also be willing to make an analogous appeal to the (or, an) aim of intention. And if we are trying to specify such an aim, it is plausible to suppose that intentions aim at coordinated control of action *that achieves what is intended*. Further, it is a fundamental fact about agents like us that such effective control[58] normally depends on a process of filling in partial plans with intentions concerning needed means. If I intend that there be light in the room I need to intend some means if there is going to be light; unlike God, I cannot just think "let there be light!" At least for non-divine agents like us, intentions for ends normally cannot reach their hands over end–means connections and directly control the world. If our intentions in favor of ends are to be effective, they normally need to function by way of our intending needed means. Granted, sometimes no means need be intended, since what one intends is directly in one's power, or the means will occur in a way that does not depend on one intending them. Nevertheless, it is common that to achieve what is intended as an end one in fact needs to intend means. So if one is to achieve the characteristic aim of one's intention—an aim in favor of coordinated control of action that is effective in the pursuit of what is intended—one needs, in such cases, to intend the means. So, given that the agent knows relevant facts about his own causal powers, means–end *in*coherence of his intentions will normally undermine the aim of effective control. So if we can see norms on belief as grounded in the aim of belief,[59] we can, in an analogous way, see a norm of means–end coherence as grounded in this aim of intention.

More would need to be said in a full defense of this approach to the norms of consistency and coherence of intention. But I do think these remarks make it plausible that the planning theory can see these norms as, at bottom, practical norms that are characteristic of the planning system and associated with the basic coordinating and controlling functions of that system. Looked at this way, these practical norms need not derive from demands for consistency and coherence on associated beliefs.

---

58. Note that the effective control at issue here, in specifying the relevant aim of intending, is effectiveness with respect to what is *intended*. At this point we are not appealing to the broader notion of effectiveness with respect, broadly, to the agent's practical perspective—a broader notion noted earlier and to which I return below.

59. And perhaps also in the aim of theoretical reasoning. See above note 57.

I want to conclude by considering one further form of philosophical pressure in the direction of cognitivism, and the way in which the planning theory seeks to respond. As we have seen, according to Velleman, belief aims at truth. It is also Velleman's view that reflective thinking and reasoning—both theoretical and practical—has its own characteristic aim, namely, an aim of understanding. In the case of practical reasoning the aim is, in particular, understanding *oneself*. In the absence of this aim what thinking there is does not constitute the relevant form of reasoning. This aim helps support norms of consistency and coherence of belief[60]—and so, given that intention involves belief, the corresponding demands on intention. And, as Velleman sees it, this aim of understanding is not escapable:

> You can dissociate yourself from other springs of action within you, by reflecting on them from a critical or contemplative distance. But you cannot attain a similar distance from your understanding, because it is something that you must take along, so to speak, no matter how far you retreat in seeking a perspective on yourself.[61]

Since Velleman sees practical reasoning as a species of theoretical reasoning, he takes himself to be arguing that one's aim of self-understanding is an inescapable element of *practical* reasoning. Call this idea of an inescapable, theoretical aim of practical reasoning *Velleman's intellectualism*. This intellectualism is not yet cognitivism about norms of consistency and coherence on intention, since by itself this intellectualism does not impose a belief-requirement on intention. Nevertheless, this intellectualism does provide philosophical pressure in the direction of cognitivism, since taken together they promise to explain a kind of inescapability of fundamental norms on intention.

My response is to highlight fundamental pressures toward planning agency that are independent of intellectualism and that lend support to demands on intention independently of cognitivism. Our recognition of the deep role in our lives of planning agency—and so of associated norms on intention—need involve neither intellectualism nor cognitivism.

60. This raises the question—which I will not pursue here—of how this aim of understanding interacts, in its support for these theoretical norms, with the truth-aim of belief.
61. Velleman 2000: 30–1. See also Velleman 2004: 293–4 for more recent complexities.

Begin by asking: why should we (continue to) be planning agents? Being a planning agent is not inescapable in the strong, metaphysical sense Velleman has in mind in his remarks about understanding. There are, after all, agents who are not planning agents—cows, perhaps.

I think the initial answer to this concern will have a structure that is to some extent similar to one Peter Strawson famously observed in responding to an analogous question about the system of reactive emotions.[62] First, that we are at least to some extent planning agents does not seem to be something that is in fact within our direct voluntary control (even if it is metaphysically possible to be agents who are not planning agents). Granted, various kinds of deprivation can thwart the development of capacities needed for planning agency.[63] And it may perhaps be that humans in certain radically different cultural and social contexts would not be planning agents. But this does not mean that we who are planning agents have it in our power to give up, at will, all structures of planning.

Second, our planning agency is organically interwoven into the fabric of our lives, both individual and social. Completely to give up our planning agency—if we suppose for the moment that we could—would be to opt for a radically different form of life. And, third, if we had a choice (which we do not) about whether or not to be planning agents it seems that the richness of lives made possible by this planning agency would be a determinative consideration (which is not to deny that there are costs associated with planning). Our successful pursuit of many of the complex and temporally extended ends and values that are most important to us depends on forms of planning: our planning capacities are universal means.[64] And structures of cross-temporal and interpersonal planning are partly constitutive

---

62. Peter Strawson, "Freedom and Resentment," *Proceedings of the British Academy* 48 (1962): 1–25; reprinted in Watson (ed.) 2003: 72–93. Strawson sees the reactive emotions as responses to "quality of will." As I understand Strawson, this involves both a tendency to withdraw the emotion when one discovers there was not the relevant quality of will (as when you discover that a person bumped into you only because of an involuntary seizure), and a norm that says the reactive emotion in such a case would be "inappropriate" (2003: 77–8). And Strawson's response to the question, why participate in the framework of the reactive emotions?, has the three-part structure I go on to exploit in discussing an analogous question about our planning agency (see esp. 83).

63. This is analogous to the point that various deprivations can thwart one's capacities to participate in the system of reactive emotions. An extreme case is a sociopath.

64. Bratman 1987: 28. I see this aspect of the Strawsonian response I am here fashioning as continuous with the broadly pragmatic approach I take in Bratman 1987. The next point I go on to make in the text—concerning integrity, autonomy and sociality—is in the spirit of my approach in that book but goes beyond it in ways that draw on my more recent work on autonomy and sociality. See Bratman 2007, and the quartet of essays on shared agency in Bratman 1999.

of, in particular, forms of cross-temporal integrity, cross-temporal self-government, and sociality that we highly value.[65]

This last point is important, and I will return to it below. For now let me just briefly note two ideas that are involved in this last point. One idea is that the cross-temporal integrity and self-government that we value highly involves forms of cross-temporal organization of the thought and action of a temporally persisting agent, forms of organization that are, for us, to a large extent attributable to our planning capacities. A second idea is that important forms of sociality involve, for us, structures of interlocking, interdependent, and potentially meshing intentions and plans.[66] In each case, then, fundamental practical structures that we highly value involve our planning capacities.

To return to the main idea, we can put it this way: though planning agency is not essential to agency, for planning agents like us the question of whether to continue to be planning agents seems not to be realistically up for grabs. Nevertheless, we can explore rationales for being planning agents. And this leads us to various contributions of planning agency to the richness of our lives.[67] Finally, such planning agency involves, according to the argument of the previous section, attitudes of intention that are subject to norms of consistency and means–end coherence.[68]

The next step is to confront the worry that there is a circularity here. After all, part of our story is a broadly instrumental rationale for the planning system. But one of the issues on the table is the status of the demand for means–end coherence within that system. How can an appeal to instrumental reason be part of a non-circular explanation of the significance of means–end coherence?

Here we need to return to the earlier point that instrumental reason comes in two forms: (i) means–end coherence of, in particular, intentions and plans; and (ii) a concern with the conditions of broadly effective agency—where effectiveness is assessed with respect to the agent's practical standpoint. Our Strawsonian strategy should appeal, in the first

65. My talk of cross-temporal self-government derives from Velleman's talk of "diachronic autonomy" in his "Deciding How to Decide," in Velleman 2000 (at 240–1), though my treatment of this phenomenon differs from Velleman's. My appeal to cross-temporal integrity is to some extent similar to Stalzer's appeal to "self-fidelity" in his "On the Normativity of the Instrumental Principle," ch. 5.

66. See, e.g., my "Shared Cooperative Activity" in Bratman 1999.

67. One way to articulate the idea that there are deep pressures that lead from barebones agency to planning agency is to exploit Grice's methodology of "creature construction," as I do in my "Valuing and the Will," reprinted in Bratman 2007.

68. In her "Practical Reasoning and the Varieties of Agency" (Stanford University PhD thesis, 2008) Jennifer Morton also explores a broadly pragmatic approach to these norms. Morton highlights caring as providing the ends that are relevant to her broad pragmatic argument.

instance, to (ii) in its account of the contribution of planning agency to the richness of our lives.[69] The idea is that planning agency is deeply embedded in our lives and makes essential contributions to the broad effectiveness of our agency; and such planning agency involves a commitment to a demand for means–end coherence in the sense of (i).

So there need not be a circularity. Nevertheless, it remains true that a broad form of instrumental reason is one of the elements at the bottom of our Strawsonian strategy. Perhaps this broad form of instrumental reason—and its view that the support of broadly effective agency is practically justifying—has an even deeper ground.[70] But we need not settle this further matter in order to appeal to this form of instrumental reason as one element in our understanding of the significance of planning agency in our lives.

A final step appeals to the idea of agential authority. As we have learned from the work of Harry Frankfurt, we need an account of what it is for an agent to identify with a certain thought or attitude—of what it is for a thought or attitude to speak for the agent, to have agential authority.[71] And this issue is implicit in several of the rationales for planning agency I have been sketching. I have supposed that our answer to the question "why be a planning agent?" will appeal to structures involved in cross-temporal integrity and autonomy. And in both cases those structures involve guidance by basic attitudes that speak for the agent, that have agential authority. I have also supposed that our answer to the question "why be a planning agent?" will appeal to the role of planning agency in broadly effective agency— effective, that is, in the support of the values, cares, ends, and concerns that constitute the agent's practical standpoint. And the question "what constitutes the *agent's* practical standpoint?" is a question about agential authority.

Now, in a series of papers I have argued that for an attitude to have agential authority for agents like us is in significant part for it to play central roles in the Lockean cross-temporal organization of thought and

---

69. When in Bratman 1987 I said that the "two-level structure of practical reasoning has a pragmatic rationale" (1987: 35)—where one level is that of intentions and plans that pose problems (by way of concerns with means–end coherence) and filter options (by way of concerns with consistency)—I was making a point about the contribution of planning structures to our effective, temporally extended agency, a point that draws on instrumental reason in the form of (ii).

70. This is where Joseph Raz (2005: 18) ties the value of being "an effective agent" to "the value of rational agency."

71. See, e.g., Frankfurt 1988; and for the terminology of agential authority see Bratman, "Two Problems About Human Agency," as reprinted in Bratman 2007.

action. And I have argued, further, that certain plan-type attitudes—in particular, policies concerning what to treat as justifying in practical reasoning—are central cases of attitudes with such authority.[72] These authoritative policies of reasoning need to be embedded in structures of planning agency: policies of deliberative significance are themselves plan-like commitments concerning practical reasoning, and these policies function in part by way of plan-like commitments to action. So structures of planning agency are an essential element in this solution to the problem of agential authority.

Further, norms of consistency and coherence of intention are aspects of the capacity of planning structures to solve this problem of agential authority. Agential authority involves a more-or-less unified framework that has that authority; and consistency of intention helps ensure that there is such a single, more-or-less unified framework. Agential authority also involves some degree of actual control of action; and means–end coherence helps ensure, given basic features of our non-divine agency, that our plans for ends do indeed tend effectively to shape our action.

This does not show that these planning structures are strictly inescapable, even for agents who have, in the relevant sense, an agential standpoint; for there may be, for all that I have said, alternative solutions to this problem of agential authority. But when we see this potential role of planning structures in constituting agential authority for agents like us, and when we bring that insight together with a Strawsonian pragmatism about these structures, we can make sense to ourselves of a basic feature of ourselves, namely, that we are planning agents. And since part of being a planning agent is to be committed to the cited norms of consistency and coherence on intention, we can make sense to ourselves of our commitment to these norms. Our commitment to these norms makes sense as an element in a broadly universal means, as an element in structures of integrity, autonomy, and sociality that we value, and as an element in a basic aspect of (at least one form of) agential authority—where such agential authority is itself partly constitutive of integrity, autonomy, and the agential standpoint implicated in the appeal to effective agency.

What do I mean in saying that our commitment to these norms makes sense to us? Well, the considerations adduced involve a broad form of instrumental reason; appeals to integrity, autonomy and sociality; and an

---

72. See, in particular, "Reflection, Planning, and Temporally Extended Agency," "Planning Agency, Autonomous Agency," and "Three Theories of Self-Governance," all reprinted in Bratman 2007. My thinking about these Lockean themes has benefited greatly from extended interactions with Gideon Yaffe. And see Yaffe 2000 (esp. ch. 3).

appeal to conditions of agential authority, where such authority is itself implicated in integrity, autonomy, and agential effectiveness. But there is also a theoretical aspect: we understand how planning creatures like us function and why these modes of functioning can be expected to be stable under our practical reflection. We understand why there is not, so far as we can see, an inherent instability in the psychological economy of planning agency, an instability that might be expected to lead, on reflection, to the demise of that economy.[73] What makes sense in this complex way—a way that involves both practical and theoretical reason—involves basic norms on intention. Since this does not depend on deriving those norms from corresponding theoretical norms on associated beliefs, we can in this way avoid the forms of cognitivism whose difficulties I have tried to chronicle.[74]

REFERENCES

Bennett, Jonathan (1980). "Morality and Consequences," in *Tanner Lectures on Human Values*, ed. Sterling M. McMurrin. Cambridge: Cambridge University Press (1980), 45–116.

Binkley, Robert (1965). "A Theory of Practical Reason," *The Philosophical Review* 74: 423–48.

Bratman, Michael E. (1981). "Intention and Means–End Reasoning," *The Philosophical Review* 90: 252–65.

_____ (1987). *Intention, Plans, and Practical Reason*. Cambridge, MA: Harvard University Press; reissued by CSLI Publications (1999).

_____ (1999). *Faces of Intention: Selected Essays on Intention and Agency*. Cambridge: Cambridge University Press.

_____ (2007). *Structures of Agency: Essays*. New York: Oxford University Press.

_____ (2009). "Intention, Belief, and Instrumental Rationality," in *Reasons for Action*, eds. D. Sobel and S. Wall. Cambridge: Cambridge University Press, 13–36.

73. So we understand our planning agency as in what Harman calls "rational equilibrium." See Harman 1986a: 112.

74. Thanks to Gideon Yaffe for very helpful comments on an earlier draft, to Jennifer Morton for a series of helpful discussions, and to Simon Robertson and John Skorupski for helpful comments on the penultimate draft. Thanks also to Gilbert Harman, Dana Nelkin, and Jeffrey Seidman. Versions of this paper were presented at the University of Michigan April 2005 Colloquium on Action Theory; at the April 2005 Conference on Practical Reason at the University of Maryland; at the June 2005 Conference on the Unity of Reason at the University of St Andrews, at Vassar College; at the University of Syracuse, at the May 2006 Inter University Center, Dubrovnik, Conference on "Regulating Attitudes with Reasons"; and at the University of Warwick December 2006 Mind Grad Conference. In each case I learned a great deal from the discussions. I want especially to thank my commentator at the Maryland Conference, Kieran Setiya, for his extremely thoughtful, probing, and insightful comments.

Broome, John (1999). "Normative Requirements," *Ratio* 12: 398–419.

_____ (2007). "Is Rationality Normative?," *Disputatio* II: 161–78.

_____ (2009). "The Unity of Reasoning?," in *Spheres of Reason*, ed. S. Robertson. Oxford: Oxford University Press, 63–92.

Brunero, John (2005). "Two Approaches to Instrumental Rationality and Belief Consistency," *Journal of Ethics and Social Philosophy* 1/1: <http://www.jesp.org>.

Feigl, H. (1958). "The 'Mental' and the 'Physical,'" *Minnesota Studies in the Philosophy of Science* 2: 370–497.

Frankfurt, Harry (1988). "Identification and Wholeheartedness," in his *The Importance of What We Care About*. Cambridge: Cambridge University Press.

Harman, Gilbert (1976). "Practical Reasoning," *Review of Metaphysics* 29 (3): 431–63.

_____ (1986a). *Change in View: Principles of Reasoning*. Cambridge MA: MIT Press.

_____ (1986b). "Willing and Intending," in *Philosophical Grounds of Rationality: Intentions, Categories, Ends*, eds. R. Grandy and R. Warner. Oxford: Oxford University Press (1986), 363–80.

_____ (1999). *Reasoning, Meaning, and Mind*. Oxford: Oxford University Press.

Morton, Jennifer (2008). PhD thesis: "Practical Reasoning and the Varieties of Agency." Stanford, CA: Stanford University.

Railton, Peter (1997). "On the Hypothetical and Non-Hypothetical in Reasoning about Belief and Action," in *Ethics and Practical Reason*, eds. G. Cullity and B. Gaut. Oxford: Clarendon Press, 53–80.

Raz, Joseph (2005). "The Myth of Instrumental Rationality," *Journal of Ethics and Social Philosophy* 1/1: <http:www.jesp.org>.

Sellars, Wilfrid (1966). "Thought and Action," in *Freedom and Determinism*, ed. Keith Lehrer. New York: Random House, 105–39.

Setiya, Kieran (2003). "Explaining Action," *The Philosophical Review* 112/3: 339–94.

Shah, Nishi (2003). "How Truth Governs Belief," *The Philosophical Review* 112/3: 447–82.

Stalzer, Kenneth (2004). PhD thesis: "On the Normativity of the Instrumental Principle." Stanford, CA: Stanford University.

Strawson, Peter (2003). "Freedom and Resentment," reprinted in *Free Will*, ed. G. Watson. Oxford: Oxford University Press (2nd ed.), 72–93.

Velleman, J. David (1989). *Practical Reflection*. Princeton, NJ: Princeton University Press.

_____ (2000). *The Possibility of Practical Reason*. Oxford: Oxford University Press.

_____ (2004). "Replies to Discussion on *The Possibility of Practical Reason*," *Philosophical Studies* 121: 277–98.

_____ (2006). *Self to Self: Selected Essays*. New York: Cambridge University Press.

_____ (2007). "What Good Is a Will?," in *Action in Context*, ed. A. Leist. Berlin: Walter de Gruyter: 193–215.

Wallace, R. Jay (2001). "Normativity, Commitment, and Instrumental Reason," *Philosophers' Imprint* 1/3: 1–26.

Walzer, Michael (1977). *Just and Unjust Wars*. New York: Basic Books.

Williams, Bernard (1973). *Problems of the Self*. Cambridge: Cambridge University Press.

Yaffe, Gideon (2000). *Liberty Worth the Name: Locke on Free Agency*. Princeton, NJ: Princeton University Press.

_____ (2004). "Trying, Intending, and Attempted Crimes," *Philosophical Topics* 32: 505–32.

CHAPTER 3

Intention, Belief, and Instrumental Rationality*

1. TWO APPROACHES TO INSTRUMENTAL RATIONALITY

Suppose I intend end E, believe that a necessary means to E is M, and believe that M requires that I intend M. My attitudes concerning E and M engage a basic requirement of practical rationality, a requirement that, barring a change in my cited beliefs, I either intend M or give up intending E.[1]

* This essay is a sequel to my "Intention, Belief, Practical, Theoretical," in Simon Robertson, ed., *Spheres of Reason* (Oxford: Oxford University Press, 2009) [this volume, essay 2]. Some of the ideas developed here are also in that earlier essay, but I hope in this present essay to go somewhat beyond that earlier work. I do, however, see my overall argument in favor of (to use terminology to be introduced in the main text) the practical commitment view, in contrast with cognitivism, as drawing on both of these essays (as well as on the basic account presented in my *Intention, Plans, and Practical Reason* [Cambridge, MA: Harvard University Press, 1987; reissued by CSLI Publications, 1999]). The present essay was motivated in part by Kieran Setiya's "Cognitivism about Instrumental Reason: Response to Bratman" (2005), which constituted his very thoughtful and helpful comments on "Intention, Belief, Practical, Theoretical," at the Conference on Practical Reason, University of Maryland, April 2005. My present chapter has also benefited from conversation with John Perry, Jennifer Morton, and Sarah Paul; detailed comments from Gideon Yaffe and John Broome on earlier drafts; and very helpful comments from George Wilson, David Sobel, and Steven Wall.

1. Concerning the need for the belief that M requires that I intend M, see Robert Binkley, "A Theory of Practical Reason," *The Philosophical Review* 74 (1965): 423–48, at 443. The language of "requirement" comes from John Broome; see "Normative Requirements," *Ratio* 12 (1999): 398–419.

Call this the *Instrumental Rationality* requirement—for short, the *IR* requirement.[2]

Suppose now that I believe that E, and I also believe that E will only occur if M. My beliefs engage a basic demand of theoretical rationality, a demand that, roughly, either there be a change in at least one of these two beliefs or I believe M. Call this the *Belief Closure* requirement—for short, the *BC* requirement. BC, note, is not a consistency demand on my beliefs: failure to add the further belief that M need not involve inconsistency in the way that adding a belief that not-M would. Nevertheless, something like BC seems a basic rationality constraint on belief.[3]

Both IR and BC express constraints on the coherence of the agent's relevant attitudes; and these constraints are aspects of the normal rational functioning, in the psychic economy of believing-and-intending agents, of the cited attitudes. The intentions and beliefs of such agents will tend to be responsive to these constraints. But the requirements differ in important ways. IR is engaged only if I intend E; whereas BC is engaged if I believe E, whether or not I intend E. And a central way of meeting the demands of IR involves intending M; whereas a corresponding way of meeting the demands of BC involves, rather, believing M. Further, if we ask why these principles—IR and BC—are, indeed, aspects of the rational functioning of the cited attitudes, we arrive, I believe, at importantly different answers. Roughly: In the case of BC we will appeal, I think, to something like a general need for coherence of one's beliefs if one is to understand the world. In the case of IR we will appeal, I think, to something like a general need to intend necessary means if one is to be an effective agent and if one is to

2. In other work I have focused on what I have called a requirement of means-end coherence of one's intentions and plans. I see IR as a central aspect of that requirement, though the requirement of means-end coherence goes beyond IR, strictly speaking, in requiring that an agent fill in her plans with one or another sufficient means when what is needed is that the agent settle or some such means or other. And the requirement of means-end coherence allows for delay in filling in plans with means when there remains sufficient time. (For some of these complexities see *Intention, Plans, and Practical Reason*, 31–5.) But IR is at the heart of the requirement of means-end coherence, and it will simplify my discussion here to focus on it. Note that both IR and the requirement of means-end coherence specifically concern means-end rationality with respect to *intended* ends; there remain further issues about means-end rationality concerning things one wants, prefers, or values.

3. There are important issues, in understanding BC, about what Gilbert Harman calls "clutter avoidance": as Harman emphasizes, we do not suppose one must add *all* beliefs entailed by other beliefs one already has. See Gilbert Harman, *Change in View* (Cambridge, MA: MIT Press, 1986): 12. These issues do not arise in the same way for IR. Given that the agent believes that intending M is itself necessary for E, forming that intention will not be mere "clutter." I return to this matter briefly below in n. 21.

have a practical standpoint that has the kind of efficacy characteristic of self-government.[4]

These last claims about what lies behind IR, on the one hand, and BC, on the other, are, of course, sketchy; and I cannot pursue these matters in detail here. I do think, though, that there is here a general and plausible idea. This is the idea that these stories will differ, and that one will cite basic theoretical concerns—with understanding, for example—and the other will cite basic practical concerns—with effective agency and self-governance, for example. When we put this very general idea together with our initial observations about the differences between IR and BC—the focus on intention, in one case, and belief in the other—we are led to the view that these are importantly different demands of rationality—in one case practical, in the other case theoretical—though these demands will, of course, significantly interact in many cases.

There are, however, philosophical pressures that have led a number of philosophers to draw principles along the lines of IR and BC much more closely together. Their idea, roughly, is to see IR, or something close to it, as, at bottom, a special case of the theoretical requirement expressed in BC, or something close to it, together perhaps with some further principle of theoretical rationality. There are different versions of this idea, as we shall see. But what they share is the idea that IR is, at bottom, a theoretical demand on beliefs. This is *cognitivism* about instrumental rationality.[5]

Cognitivism about instrumental rationality identifies what had seemed to be a basic element of practical rationality with theoretical rationality. It need not, however, say that all demands of practical reason are, at bottom, demands of theoretical reason.[6] So, for example, I see John Broome, Wayne Davis, Gilbert Harman, Kieran Setiya, J. David Velleman,

---

4. That is, the concerns and commitments that constitute the practical standpoint with which one identifies need to be ones that are effectively in control of one's intentional conduct, if one is to be self-governing. One aspect of such effective control will be conforming, in general, to IR when one's beliefs about what is required are accurate and when the intended ends are elements in, or in other ways endorsed by, the practical standpoint with which one identifies. I try to deepen this connection between central norms on intention and self-government in "Intention, Belief, Practical, Theoretical."

5. More precisely, this is cognitivism about that aspect of instrumental rationality that IR, and closely related principles, aims to capture. For this use of the term "cognitivism" (in contrast with its standard use in meta-ethics), see my "Cognitivism about Practical Reason," as reprinted in my *Faces of Intention* (New York: Cambridge University Press, 1999); and my "Intention, Belief, Practical, Theoretical." Kieran Setiya also uses this term in this way in his "Cognitivism about Instrumental Reason," *Ethics* 117 (2007): 649–73.

6. Setiya makes this point in his "Cognitivism about Instrumental Reason: Response to Bratman."

and R. Jay Wallace as, in different ways, cognitivists about instrumental rationality;[7] but whereas Velleman is, quite broadly, a cognitivist about practical reason—he sees practical reason as grounded in a theoretical concern with self-knowledge and self-understanding—the cognitivism defended by the others is more limited: it extends at least to IR but does not purport to extend to all of practical reason. I do think that it would be difficult to be a cognitivist about IR but not about certain other rationality requirements on intention. This is clearest with respect to the consistency requirement on intentions. This is the requirement that one's overall set of intentions be consistent as well as consistent with one's beliefs: one needs to be able to put one's various intentions together—to agglomerate them—into an overall plan that is internally consistent and consistent with one's beliefs.[8] A marriage of cognitivism about IR with a rejection of cognitivism about these consistency demands is likely to be unstable, since the alternative story about the consistency demands will threaten to spill over to a story about IR. It is a hard question what a cognitivist about IR should say about norms of cross-temporal stability of intention. In any case, my primary focus here will be on cognitivism about IR.

Here is one way to look at it. Suppose you now prefer A at some later time to its envisaged alternatives. This is not yet to intend A. After all, while you do now prefer A, you may still see the issue as not yet settled and be engaged right now in further deliberation about whether to A. Now suppose that this further deliberation does issue in an intention to A. In what, precisely, does this transition from a preference to an intention

7. See John Broome, "The Unity of Reasoning?," in Simon Robertson, ed., *Spheres of Reason* (Oxford: Oxford University Press, 2009); Wayne Davis, "A Causal Theory of Intending," *American Philosophical Quarterly* 21 (1984): 43–54; Gilbert Harman, "Practical Reasoning," reprinted in Gilbert Harman, *Reasoning, Meaning, and Mind* (Oxford: Oxford University Press, 1999): 46–74; Setiya, "Cognitivism about Instrumental Reason"; J. David Velleman, *Practical Reflection* (Princeton, NJ: Princeton University Press, 1989); *The Possibility of Practical Reason* (Oxford: Oxford University Press, 2000); and "What Good Is a Will?," in Anton Leist and Holger Baumann, eds., *Action in Context* (Berlin and New York: de Gruyter and Mouton, 2007); R. Jay Wallace, "Normativity, Commitment, and Instrumental Reason," *Philosophers' Imprint* 1 (3) (2001). Setiya's cognitivism about instrumental rationality goes directly by way of his version of BC. My strategy in this essay of focusing on the role of BC in such cognitivism follows Setiya in this respect.

8. Note that this demand for consistency is not just that each intention have a consistent content; it includes, as well, the demand that one be able to agglomerate one's various intentions into an overall intention that has a consistent content. I will sometimes emphasize this way in which this demand for consistency involves an implicit agglomerativity demand; but sometimes, for ease of exposition, I will simply speak of consistency, leaving the idea of agglomeration implicit. As this formulation of the consistency demand suggests, there are puzzles here that parallel puzzles about consistency of belief and the "preface paradox"; but I put these aside here.

consist? In particular, in now intending to A you come to be under the rational pressure of IR: you now need, roughly, to intend known necessary means, or give up your intention to A. In contrast, the mere preference for A did not, by itself, engage IR. What about the transition from preference to intention explains why IR is newly engaged?[9]

A cognitivist about IR will see the transition from preference to intention as at least in part a matter of belief. And a cognitivist about IR will appeal to the belief aspect of this transition to explain why IR is newly engaged. In contrast, on the view I would like to defend—and the view suggested by our preliminary remarks about the differences between IR and BC—the step from preference to intention is a practical step, a step to a distinctive kind of practical commitment that is not itself a belief. And it is that, not belief, that is at the heart of the new applicability of IR. So we can contrast cognitivism with such a *practical commitment* view of instrumental rationality.

A basic idea that underlies the kind of practical commitment view I would want to defend is that intentions are elements of a planning system, one that has fundamental roles in the coordination and control of action. Planning agents like us normally need to intend means if we are to achieve our intended ends. We are not gods who can simply and effectively will "let there be E!" (If I were simply to will "let there be light!" it would not work: I need to flip the switch.) And insofar as one fails to intend means intending which is necessary for intended ends, this planning system will fail to be effective.[10] Further, insofar as one's intentions are inconsistent with each other and/or with one's beliefs, this planning system will fail in its coordinating role, a role that is at the heart of the cross-temporal effectiveness of that system. So, in general, conformity to norms of consistency and means-end rationality are—at least for non-divine planning agents with reliable beliefs about the world—conditions for the successful operation of this system of coordinated control. Further, a full-blown planning agent will not just happen to conform to such norms: she will think in ways that are at least implicitly guided by these norms; and this will be part of the explanation of the successful functioning of her planning agency. In

9. Cf. R. Jay Wallace: "there must be something about the attitude of intending to do *x* that goes beyond the attitude of desiring that one do *x*, in a way that brings a distinctively rational requirement into play." ("Normativity, Commitment, and Instrumental Reason": 18) (Though note that I allude to preference whereas Wallace appeals to desire.) As my remarks below indicate, though, I think we need to be careful here, since the step from preference to an attitude that engages something like IR might be only a step to a "settled objective" and not a step all the way to intention, strictly speaking.

10. Here I am in agreement with Joseph Raz, "The Myth of Instrumental Rationality," *Journal of Ethics and Social Philosophy* 1 (1), [www.jesp.org], (2005): 17.

particular, she will be responsive in her thinking to the need to intend means intending which is needed for her intended ends; and she will be responsive in her thinking to a demand for consistency of intentions and beliefs. Norms of means-end rationality and consistency will be, for her, internal norms.[11] Her intention in favor of E is a practical commitment in part in the sense that it engages these internal norms.

There is a complexity here, however. IR is tied to the normal, successful functioning of the planning system as a system that effectively controls action in pursuit of intended ends. A norm of consistency of intention is tied to the normal, successful functioning of the planning system as a coordinating system. Intentions are elements of a planning system whose central roles are those of effective coordinating control. However, we are also capable of commitments to ends that we do not treat as subject in precisely the same way to the sorts of coordinating pressures that impose a demand for agglomeration and consistency. I might try to get into Harvard Law, and try to get into Stanford Law, while knowing that these law schools coordinate admissions and so that, while I have a shot at getting into each, it is not possible to get into both.[12] As I see it, I do not, strictly speaking, intend to get into Harvard Law, or intend to get into Stanford Law. This is because if I intended one I would, by the symmetry of the case, intend the other; so I would thereby have intentions that violate rational demands for agglomeration and consistency. Nevertheless, I do have getting into Harvard Law as what Hugh McCann calls a "settled objective";[13] and similarly concerning getting into Stanford Law.

Such examples seem to show that, while each settled objective needs to be internally consistent, not all settled objectives engage agglomeration and consistency demands in precisely the way characteristic of intention. In some cases a settled objective is not embedded in the standard intention-like way within the overall coordinating role of one's planning system, though the pursuit of the settled objective does impose more localized coordination pressures. (I need, for example, first to get the Harvard application, then fill it out; if I try to proceed in the reverse order it won't work. And I need to ensure that my plan for filling out the application meshes with my other plans for the day.) The conclusion I draw is that not all settled objectives are intentions, strictly speaking[14] (though

---

11. For this terminology see *Intention, Plans, and Practical Reason*: 109.

12. This example is modeled on the video games example I discuss in *Intention, Plans, and Practical Reason*: chapter 8.

13. Hugh McCann, "Settled Objectives and Rational Constraints," *American Philosophical Quarterly* 28 (1991): 25–36.

14. It is in this conclusion that I disagree with McCann, though I will not here try to respond to his arguments against this conclusion.

they may be associated with intentions—say, to get into some law school or other, or intentions about means to the objective). Nevertheless, settled objectives do engage a requirement that is something like IR: after all, in the envisaged case, I am under rational pressure to settle on means to get into Harvard Law, pressure I would not be under if I merely desired to get into that school. Rational pressures of means-end rationality can be engaged even if one's attitude does not engage pressures of agglomeration and consistency in precisely the way characteristic of intention.

Now, it seems that certain non-planning agents can still have settled objectives. Perhaps a squirrel can have getting the nuts as a settled objective even though it does not have sufficient structure in its thinking about the future to be a planning agent.[15] However, when a planning agent like us has certain settled objectives that are not, strictly speaking, intentions, pressures of means-end rationality engaged by such settled objectives will normally be met by forming *intentions* about means. Even if my commitment to getting into Harvard Law is a settled objective but not an intention, my sub-plans for pursuing this end will normally be intended, strictly speaking. This is because those sub-plans still need to mesh with my sub-plans for getting into Stanford Law. After all, the plan is for one and the same agent—namely, me—to carry out both sub-plans even though they are in pursuit of objectives that are, given the special features of the case, not co-possible.[16]

An implication of these reflections on settled objectives is that the two different norms on intention highlighted here—IR and a norm of consistency—have a slightly different status. A norm of means-end rationality that is similar to IR will be engaged by settled objectives, whereas the cited norm of agglomeration and consistency will not be engaged in the same way by settled objectives as by intentions, strictly speaking. But, having noted this complexity, I will focus primarily on the account of IR for intentions, since it is here that cognitivism about instrumental rationality has its best chance.

---

15. So the step from such a non-planning agent with settled objectives to a full-blown planning agent would be an important step in a Gricean "creature construction" model of agency. See Paul Grice, "Method in Philosophical Psychology (From the Banal to the Bizarre)," (Presidential Address), *Proceedings and Addresses of the American Philosophical Association* (1974–5): 23–53; and Bratman, "Valuing and the Will," reprinted in *Structures of Agency: Essays* (New York: Oxford University Press, 2007).

16. In this last sentence I have benefited from discussions with Luca Ferrero and Michael Nelson. And see *Intention, Plans, and Practical Reason*: 137–8 (though there I proceed in the language of "guiding desire" rather than McCann's language of "settled objective").

As I have said, I envisage an account of IR that ties it to the proper functioning of the planning system as a system of coordinated, effective control. And in other work I have also emphasized an even broader significance of this planning system in our lives as an element both in our self-governance and in our sociality.[17] By itself, however, this picture of our planning agency, and of the central roles in it of norms of agglomeration, consistency and means-end rationality, does not show that cognitivism is false. A cognitivist can agree with all this and then argue that these norms turn out, on examination, to derive from theoretical norms on associated beliefs. What these appeals to the proper functioning of the planning system do indicate, though, is that there is an initial plausibility to the idea that these norms are practical norms grounded in the practical roles of the planning system of coordinated control. If we are to be led to cognitivism we need some further arguments, ones that goes beyond noting that we do, indeed, appeal to and depend on these norms insofar as we are planning agents. We need arguments for thinking that we should see these norms as, at bottom, theoretical; and we need a defense of the idea that theoretical norms really can do the requisite work. So let's see.

2. HARMAN'S BASIC IDEA

We can begin with what I will call *Harman's basic idea*, since it derives from his groundbreaking 1976 paper "Practical Reasoning" (though the way I will present it here goes a bit beyond that paper). Harman, like many cognitivists about IR,[18] supposes that intending E necessarily involves believing E. Further,

> since intention involves belief, theoretical and practical reasoning overlap.

17. "Intention, Belief, Practical, Theoretical."
18. There are important qualifications. Wallace endorses only a weak belief condition: intending to A requires believing A is possible. (As I note in "Intention, Belief, Practical, Theoretical," this weak belief condition does not on its own explain the rational agglomerativity of intention.) Broome says only that if you believe you intend A then you believe A. I will return to this view of Broome below. In his 1976 paper Harman *identifies* intention with a kind of belief that one will A; whereas in a later paper ("Willing and Intending," in Richard Grandy and Richard Warner, eds., *Philosophical Grounds of Rationality* (Oxford: Oxford University Press, 1986): 363–80. Harman only says that intending A requires believing A. The argument for cognitivism I am now sketching is neutral as between these two ways of understanding the connection between intending A and believing A—though below, in section 4, the purported identification will matter.

In theoretical reasoning, one seeks to increase the coherence of one's overall view of the world . . . Since intention involves belief, and theoretical and practical reasoning overlap, coherence must be relevant to any sort of reasoning about the future, theoretical or practical. . . .

The thesis that intention involves belief associates practical reasoning about means and ends with theoretical reasoning. It brings these two sorts of reasoning under a single principle.[19]

Given the emphasis on the claim "that intention involves belief," it seems that the "single principle" to which Harman alludes is a principle of coherence on one's beliefs. It is because "intention involves belief" that this principle of coherence on belief extends to one's intentions. And—though at this point I go beyond what Harman says—it seems plausible to see something like BC as an aspect of belief coherence that is importantly relevant in this way to IR. A violation of BC would normally be a form of belief incoherence,[20] and it is this form of incoherence that may seem to be at stake in violations of IR. After all, if I intend E (and so believe E) and believe M is a necessary means to E, BC requires that, if I do not change those two attitudes, I believe that M. If I also believe that M will obtain only if I intend M,[21] BC requires, if I do not change those two attitudes, that I believe I intend M. And it can seem that to believe I intend M I need actually to intend M (though this is a matter to which I will return). So the demand to satisfy BC—a demand that seems to be a central element in the requirement for belief coherence—seems to issue in a demand to satisfy IR. And that is cognitivism about IR.

As I am understanding it, then, Harman's basic idea is that we arrive at cognitivism about instrumental rationality in two steps: we begin by noting that intention involves corresponding belief; we then reflect on the nature of the theoretical pressures on those involved beliefs—where, as I have developed this idea here, these pressures include BC. And now I want to point to two problems for this route to cognitivism about IR.[22] The first concerns

19. *Reasoning, Meaning, and Mind*: 49–50. In the original essay, Harman had said that "[I]n theoretical reasoning, one seeks to increase the explanatory coherence of one's overall view of the world." In this more recent version of his essay he appeals broadly to coherence, where explanatory coherence is one kind of coherence (though the appeal specifically to *explanatory* coherence remains: 56 and 63).

20. Putting to one side issues of "clutter avoidance." See n. 21.

21. Setiya argues that a cognitivist may appeal to something like this belief to block, for such cases, Harman's worries about "clutter avoidance." ("Cognitivism about Instrumental Reason") In order to give the cognitivist a sympathetic hearing, I am following Setiya here.

22. I also believe a third problem looms, a problem concerning the distinction between intending X and merely expecting that X will be a result of something one intends.

the idea that intention involves corresponding belief. Suppose, to take an example I have discussed elsewhere, I intend to stop at the bookstore on the way home.[23] Still, I know that I am forgetful; so I am not confident that I will stop—after all, once I get on my bicycle I do have a tendency just to pedal on home. About this case I am inclined to say: I intend to stop, but I do not believe I will stop (though I do not believe I will not stop).[24] Many think, though, that it is a misuse of the word "intend" to say that I intend to stop but do not believe I will. Concerning this issue about the word "intend" there seems not to be a consensus one way or the other.[25] What matters for our present discussion, though, is not primarily what we would say using this word, but whether my attitude toward stopping, however labeled, engages the basic demand at the bottom of IR. And it seems to me that it does.

My attitude toward stopping is not a mere preference to stop: I have, rather, settled on stopping. If there were two routes home, only one of which went by the bookstore, my commitment to stopping at the bookstore would require that I take the route that goes by the bookstore. It would also require that I not settle also on another alternative known by me to be inconsistent with my stopping.[26] So my attitude toward stopping

See "Intention, Belief, Practical, Theoretical"; and for a discussion of this problem as it arises for Velleman's theory, see "Cognitivism about Practical Reason," reprinted in *Faces of Intention*. I put this potential third problem to one side here. My own discussion of this distinction is in *Intention, Plans, and Practical Reason*: chapter 10.

23. *Intention, Plans, and Practical Reason*: 37, and "Practical Reasoning and Acceptance in a Context," in *Faces of Intention*: 31–2. My use of this example in the present context benefited from discussion with John Perry.

24. As I note in "Practical Reasoning and Acceptance in a Context": 32, I may nevertheless accept, in the context of relevant deliberation, that I would stop if I were to decide to stop. As I explain in that essay, acceptance in a context is not the same as belief. Wallace also alludes to something like this idea in "Postscript" to "Normativity, Commitment, and Instrumental Reason," in *Normativity and the Will: Selected Essays on Moral Psychology and Practical Reason* (Oxford: Oxford University Press, 2006): 116. But Wallace seems to suppose that such acceptance is itself a kind of belief, whereas I would balk at this. These observations about acceptance in a context do raise the question of whether there is available to us a kind of cognitivism that goes by way of acceptance in a context, rather than belief. I have my doubts that what will emerge is really a kind of cognitivism, since the connection between intending and accepting in a context seems itself to be grounded in practical rationality; but I cannot pursue these matters here. Both Facundo Alonso and Olivier Roy have been pursuing this and related issues in unpublished work.

25. For a lively sense of the disagreement here, see Paul Grice, "Intention and Uncertainty," *Proceedings of the British Academy* 57 (1971): 263–79; Donald Davidson, "Intending," reprinted in *Essays on Actions and Events*, 2nd ed. (Oxford: Oxford University Press, 2001): 83–102; Gilbert Harman, "Willing and Intending."

26. So my commitment to stopping is not a mere "settled objective," in the sense in which my commitment to the end of getting into Harvard Law, in the example described earlier, is. In contrast with such mere settled objectives, my commitment to

engages demands of consistency and means-end rationality that are characteristic of intention. And it does this even in the absence of a belief that I will stop. This suggests that we should seek an account of, in particular, IR that applies to my commitment to stopping at the bookstore, whether or not I also believe I will stop, contrary to Harman's basic idea.

My second reason for being skeptical about Harman's basic idea can allow, for the sake of argument, that if you intend A you believe A. What this second reason for skepticism involves is the idea that you can misidentify what you intend: you can falsely believe you have a certain intention. The mind, after all, is not an open book, even to the person whose mind it is. However we understand our special first-person access to our minds in general and, more specifically, to our intentions, it does not ensure incorrigibility about our own intentions.

In particular, there can be cases in which one believes one intends a means but does not intend that means. Perhaps I get confused and believe I intend to go shopping next Tuesday, though in fact I do not intend this but intend, rather, to go shopping next Thursday.[27] So there can be cases in which one intends E, believes that E requires both M and one's intending M, believes both M and that one intends M, but still does not, in fact, intend M. Though one believes one intends M, one is mistaken about this. One's beliefs satisfy BC; but this does not ensure satisfaction of IR, since, in the case envisaged, one does not in fact intend M. So it seems that we should reject cognitivism about IR.

These, anyway, are two concerns about Harman's basic route to cognitivism. In each case there are complexities we need to examine; and I will proceed to some of these complexities below. This will put me in a position to reflect on several related ideas that others have offered in defense of a version of cognitivism about IR. But first I want to note, and try to defuse, a line of argument that can seem to make cognitivism attractive.

3. CONSTITUTIVE AIM: VELLEMAN

Belief aims at truth. Or so it seems plausible to say.[28] Let me note three aspects of this idea. The first is that beliefs are embedded in a psychic

---

stopping at the bookstore not only requires settling on means, it also needs to be consistent with my other intentions.

27. For this example, see my "Intention, Belief, Practical, Theoretical." I first discussed this objection to Harman's cognitivism in "Intention and Means-End Reasoning," *The Philosophical Review* 90 (1981): 252–65, at 255–6, n. 4.

28. A classic discussion of this idea is Bernard Williams, "Deciding to Believe," in *Problems of the Self* (Cambridge: Cambridge University Press, 1973): 136–51.

economy that tends, in belief-formation, to track the truth, though of course it can on occasion fail. An attitude embedded in a psychic economy that, in its formation of that attitude, tracked instead the pleasant-to-think-of, would be a candidate for fantasy, not for belief. A second and closely related aspect of this idea is that, as Bernard Williams puts it, "truth and falsehood are a dimension of an assessment of beliefs."[29] Beliefs are criticizable if they are false, if they fail to track what—given the kind of attitudes they are—they tend to track. And, third, part of the explanation of how, for agents like us, beliefs track the truth will appeal to an internal norm that assesses beliefs in terms of their truth.[30]

That said, it is a hard question precisely how these three aspects of the truth-directedness of belief are related. So, for example, at one point J. David Velleman thought that the second, normative aspect derived from the first, descriptive aspect.[31] In later work with Nishi Shah, however, Velleman has come to a more complex view of the relation between these two aspects.[32] These are difficult issues, and I will not try to sort them out here. It suffices for my purposes here simply to include all three, interrelated aspects in the idea that belief aims at truth.[33] Following Velleman, we can express this idea by saying that a "constitutive aim" of belief is truth.[34] And it seems plausible to say that demands on belief of consistency and coherence are closely related to this purported truth-aim.

29. *Problems of the Self*: 137.

30. Something like this seems implicit in Williams's remarks about the underlying problem with believing at will. See *Problems of the Self*: 148.

31. In "Introduction" to *The Possibility of Practical Reason*, Velleman claimed that "belief aims at the truth in the normative sense only because it aims at the truth descriptively" (2000: 17). Velleman discusses these matters further in "On the Aim of Belief," in *The Possibility of Practical Reason*. His most recent discussion is in Nishi Shah and J. David Velleman, "Doxastic Deliberation," *The Philosophical Review* 114 (2005): 497–534.

32. "There is both a descriptive and a normative component to belief's truth-directedness." "Doxastic Deliberation": 530, n. 10. See also Nishi Shah, "How Truth Governs Belief," *The Philosophical Review*, 112 (4) (2003): 447–82. Shah, and Velleman in this joint work, are concerned with the issue of how "to explain the fact that the deliberative question *whether to believe that p* is transparent to the question *whether p*" ("Doxastic Deliberation": 497). I do not try to address this issue here.

33. As does Williams, who also includes the further idea that in *saying* one believes p one is *claiming* that p is true. "Deciding to Believe": 137.

34. For the language of "the constitutive aim of belief," see "Introduction": 16. Since Shah and Velleman say that "there is both a descriptive and a normative component to belief's truth-directedness," I am assuming that talk of constitutive aim carries over to include, in this new work, both the descriptive and the normative component, even though the latter is no longer seen as derivable from the former.

So far, all this is neutral with respect to cognitivism. But one might think that the availability of such a story about various normative demands on belief supports the idea that these very same demands account for the cited normative demands on intention. Or at least this may seem plausible given the assumption that to intend A is, at least in part, to believe A. After all, if belief aims at truth there is, on this assumption, a story about the demand for consistency of intention: consistency is needed for the associated beliefs all to achieve their constitutive aim. Granted, even given the assumed connection between intention and belief, cognitivism about IR is more delicate, since failure of one's associated beliefs to conform to BC does not ensure that any of them are false (though it does ensure that if one's actual beliefs do achieve their constitutive aim then one's set of beliefs do not maximally achieve this aim—since the failure of closure would be a failure to add a true belief). Still, there may seem to be some close connection between the truth-aim of belief and BC.[35] So if we could see IR as grounded in BC, we would then have the beginnings of an account of IR that grounds it in the purported constitutive aim of belief. So there may seem to be philosophical pressure in favor of cognitivism.[36]

I think, however, that it is important to see that if we are attracted to this idea that norms on belief are tied to its constitutive aim of truth, then we can argue, in parallel fashion, that norms on intention are tied to the (or anyway, a) constitutive aim of intention. And this parallel argument is independent of cognitivism. So appeal to constitutive aims of relevant attitudes does not, on its own, provide support for cognitivism.

In particular, if we are attracted to the appeal to constitutive aims of attitudes we can interpret the planning model of intention as articulating a constitutive aim of intention, namely: coordinated, effective control of action. Each intention aims at its realization in coordination with one's overall system of intentions. Coordination involves consistency among one's intentions, given one's beliefs; effective control requires that one intend means intending which one knows to be needed to achieve intended ends. So it is plausible that we can see norms of consistency and means-end rationality—norms characteristic of intention—as related to the (or, an) aim of intention in a way that parallels the relation between analogous norms on belief and the truth-aim of belief.

35. It may be that we should here appeal instead to a concern with understanding; but I put this complexity to one side here.

36. An argument broadly in this spirit is in J. David Velleman, "What Good is a Will?" I discuss this essay in "Intention, Belief, Practical, Theoretical," where I also develop further the ideas to follow about the aim of intention.

We can put the idea this way: The planning theory of intention articulates characteristic roles of intention in coordination and effective agency: intentions are embedded in a planning system that tracks coordination and effective control and systematically adjusts, when need be, in their direction. The planning theory sees the achievement of coordinated effectiveness as, to return to Williams's remark, "a dimension of an assessment" of intentions.[37] And the planning theory supposes that the explanation of how plans support coordination and effectiveness will involve associated internal norms. So the planning theory provides resources that parallel the trio of ideas I have included within talk of the aim of belief. So we seem to have as much reason to appeal to an aim of intention as we do to an aim of belief—though, of course, the aims are different.

This does not require that it is essential to *agency*, quite generally, that one be a planning agent, one who forms intentions that have—or so we are now supposing—the constitutive aim of coordinated, effective control of action. Planning agency is a distinctive form of agency, one that contributes substantially to the pursuit of complex, temporally extended aims, to structures of self-governance, and—though I have not emphasized this here—to forms of sociality.[38] There can be agents who are not planning agents,[39] and these agents can even act intentionally in an attenuated sense that doesn't bring with it planning structures. But if you are, as we are, a planning agent[40] your intentions and plans have—we are now assuming—characteristic aims, aims associated with norms of consistency and means-end rationality. And this does not require cognitivism about IR.

This possibility of appealing to an aim of intention, in contrast with the aim of belief, tends to be obscured from within Velleman's cognitivist theory because, when he turns from belief to intention, he turns not to a distinctive aim of intention (other than—since intention is, on Velleman's

37. Though, of course, not all failures of coordination or effectiveness will be cases of irrationality.
38. Concerning this connection to forms of sociality, see essays 5–8 in *Faces of Intention*.
39. This is implicit in the general strategy of Gricean "creature construction" in the philosophy of action (see above, n. 15). In unpublished work, Jennifer Morton pursues further implications of, as she puts it, the "varieties of agency."
40. I discuss the question, why (continue to) be a planning agent?, in "Intention, Belief, Practical, Theoretical," where I emphasize the roles of planning agency in cross-temporally effective agency, in self-governance, and in our sociality. In these ways there are distinctively practical pressures in the direction of a kind of planning agency within which intentions have (or so we are now supposing) the cited constitutive aims. Note that this does not entail that we actually have a choice about whether to be planning agents. Nor does it rule out the possibility of cases in which things go better if one's planning system does not on that occasion function properly.

view, a kind of belief—the aim of belief) but to a purported aim of, most generally, agency.[41] His central idea is that agency itself has an intellectual constitutive aim—namely, self-knowledge and self-understanding. And this leads to Velleman's overall cognitivism about practical reason. But we can seek a practical parallel to the appeal to the aim of belief, without appeal to a purported aim of agency. We can talk, rather, of the aim of intention. And the planning theory gives us a plausible way to do that, a way that avoids cognitivism.

Now, one might think that we need to appeal to cognitivism to explain the special nature of the demand expressed in IR. In particular, we need to explain why violations of IR are a kind of *incoherence*.[42] The cognitivist will say that this is because the demand expressed in IR just is the demand for a kind of belief coherence. And the cognitivist sees this demand of coherence on belief as tied to the very nature of belief—where this includes the way it must be embedded in a system that tracks truth. But we can say something similar about intention without being cognitivists. We can say that the demand of coherence on intention (taken together with belief) is tied to the very nature of intention—where this includes the way it must be embedded in a planning system that tracks coordinated and effective control of action. And we can say this while acknowledging that not all agents are planning agents.[43]

4. MISTAKES ABOUT ONE'S OWN INTENTIONS: HARMAN AND SETIYA

Let me turn now to the complexities I promised concerning my two objections to Harman's basic idea. Begin with the second objection:[44] I might falsely believe I intend a certain means intending which is, I know, needed for my intended end. In such a case I might satisfy BC but not IR. So IR is not grounded in BC. Or so I have averred. What might a cognitivist say in reply?

Well, a cognitivist might argue that such a false belief about one's own intention ineluctably violates a further basic theoretical demand on one's beliefs. So the theoretical demands on one's beliefs—where these

41. See *The Possibility of Practical Reason*.
42. Setiya raises this issue in his comments on my "Intention, Belief, Practical, Theoretical."
43. In this last sentence I am in disagreement with Setiya.
44. I discuss the first objection in the context of my discussion, in the next section, of views of John Broome.

theoretical demands include those necessarily violated by one's false belief about one's intention—really do, taken together, fully account for the rational force of IR. So my appeal to the apparent possibility of false belief about one's own intentions does not work as an objection to cognitivism about IR, so long as that cognitivism is allowed to appeal not only to BC but also to broad theoretical constraints against false belief about one's own intentions.[45]

For this to work there must be a form of theoretical irrationality—and not just fallibility—whenever one misidentifies what one intends. What could that be?

One idea here—once suggested by Harman[46]—is that in falsely believing I intend M I falsely believe I *believe* M. And a false belief about what one believes involves a set of beliefs that are incoherent. After all (though here I go beyond Harman's explicit remarks), if I believe I believe p I should be willing to use p as a premise in my ordinary reasoning; but if I do not believe p I should not.[47] And the claim is that this incoherence within one's beliefs is ineluctably triggered by a false belief about what one intends.

But why say that in falsely believing I intend M I falsely believe I *believe* M? Well, as noted, cognitivist theories see intention as at least involving corresponding belief; and some see intention as itself a special kind of belief. So perhaps it will seem that, on such assumptions about the connection between intention and belief, when I falsely believe I intend M I do falsely believe I believe M. But, on reflection, we can see that this need not be so.

Suppose we say only that to intend A is, in part, to believe A, though it also involves other elements as well—perhaps intention involves both such a belief and, as well, a preference for A.[48] Well, then, I might falsely believe I intend M and yet still in fact believe M; it is just that, as a matter of fact, I do not satisfy the further condition for intending M—in the example, a preference for M. I believe I intend M but I do not intend M—though I do

45. Wallace offers a version of this reply. I discuss it in "Intention, Belief, Practical, Theoretical." Here I focus on versions of this reply due to Gilbert Harman and to Kieran Setiya.

46. In a footnote to his 1980 APA comments on "Intention and Means-End Reasoning," Harman wrote:

> In "Practical Reasoning" I assumed that to intend to do *B* is to have a certain sort of self-referential belief. So in this case [that is, the case of falsely believing one intends the necessary means] one believes one believes something which in fact one does not believe, and this might count as a kind of incoherence in one's beliefs.

I also discuss this suggestion of Harman in "Intention, Belief, Practical, Theoretical."

47. Here I put to one side complexities involved in the possibility of acceptance in a context that is not belief.

48. See Davis, "A Causal Theory of Intending."

believe M I do not, unbeknownst to me, satisfy the further condition for intending M. So it is not true in this case that in falsely believing I intend M I falsely believe I believe M.

Now suppose we identify intending with believing. Well, we cannot plausibly say that intending to M is simply believing one will M. If we identify intending with believing it must be with a special kind of believing. To intend M is, in this special way, to believe M. Harman's 1976 theory has this form: to intend M is to believe you will M by way of this very belief, where this belief is a conclusion of practical reasoning. Intentions are reflexive beliefs[49] that are, as well, the output of practical reasoning. Well, then, I might believe I intend M and, indeed, reflexively believe M, and yet not actually intend M. This could happen if my reflexive belief that M is not, in fact, the conclusion of practical reasoning. So I might falsely believe I intend M even though I do in fact reflexively believe M.

Indeed, Harman himself provides an example (one he attributes to Derek Parfit) in which one's reflexive belief is not a conclusion of practical reasoning, and so is not an intention. An insomniac might believe that he will stay awake because of his very belief that he will; yet he does not intend to stay awake. On Harman's 1976 theory, the insomniac's reflexive belief is not an intention because it is not a conclusion of practical reasoning.

Suppose now that the insomniac somehow mistakenly thinks his reflexive belief is the conclusion of practical reasoning—reasoning that is concerned, perhaps, with his desire to stay awake in order to write his paper for a conference on practical reason. He thereby mistakenly thinks he intends to stay awake. His belief that he intends to stay awake is false, though he does (reflexively) believe that he will stay awake. So, again, it is not true in such a case that in falsely believing one intends x one falsely believes one believes x.

I conclude that if misidentification of one's own intentions is always a form of theoretical irrationality, it will need to be for a reason different from that alluded to by Harman. And, indeed, Kieran Setiya has sketched a different argument for thinking there will always be a form of theoretical irrationality.[50]

Setiya begins with a theory of intention that is close to Harman's 1976 view: to intend to A is to have a self-referential belief that one will A by way

---

49. That is, intentions are beliefs whose contents have the form: I will M in part because of this very belief.

50. An initial formulation was in his comments on "Intention, Belief, Practical, Theoretical"; a more detailed version is in "Cognitivism About Instrumental Reason."

of this very belief, where this belief is itself motivating.[51] Setiya thinks that if this is what intention is, then false belief about what one intends is always a form of theoretical incoherence in which one violates "the epistemic 'should'."

In defense of this last claim, Setiya begins with an idea he derives from work of Richard Moran: "In the epistemic sense of 'should', one should never make an inference"—where Setiya is focusing on non-deductive inference "on the basis of evidence"—that is of a kind that "could never be both sound and ampliative."[52] But, given Setiya's theory of intention,

> An inference to the conclusion that I intend to x, from *any* premise, will instantiate a pattern that cannot be both sound and ampliative. For suppose that I infer that I intend to x on the ground that p. If the conclusion is false, the inference is unsound. But if the conclusion is true, the self-reference of intention ensures that the inference is redundant. If I intend to x, I already believe that I am going to x because I so intend. . . .
>
>   It follows . . . that there is something incoherent about the belief that I intend to x, unless it is constituted by the intention to x. It is an inherently defective belief.[53]

Is it really true, on Setiya's theory of intention, that "If I intend to x, I already believe that I am going to x because I so intend"? If this were true it would be surprising, since it seems at least *possible* to have intentions one does not believe one has (which is not yet the possibility of mistakenly believing one has an intention one does not have). So if Setiya is accurately representing an implication of his theory we should be wary of that theory. The theory combines the idea that (a) intention is a kind of belief, with the idea that (b) intention involves reflexivity. Each of these ideas has a certain plausibility, though I myself would want to resist at least (a). And—it is important to note—these ideas are independent: one could accept (a) without (b), and vice versa.[54] But, if Setiya is accurately representing an implication of his theory, then what has happened is that when we put these two ideas together we get a surprising conclusion that one *never* intends something

51. In saying that the belief itself is motivating, Setiya may be going beyond what Harman claims in his 1976 paper, though Harman does sketch a similar view in his 1986 essay "Willing and Intending."

52. "Cognitivism About Instrumental Reason": 670. Setiya is here extending talk of soundness to non-deductive inference.

53. "Cognitivism About Instrumental Reason": 671 (I have changed the action variable).

54. John Searle, for example, accepts (b) but not (a). See *Intentionality: An Essay in the Philosophy of Mind* (Cambridge: Cambridge University Press, 1983): chapter 3.

without believing that one so intends. By my lights, this should lead us to go back and re-examine the proposed merger of (a) and (b).

But perhaps Setiya is not accurately representing an implication of his theory. To be sure, on the theory, if I intend x then I believe I will x because of this very *belief*. But not all such reflexive beliefs—even true ones—are intentions; that is the lesson we learn from Parfit's insomniac case. So perhaps, even on Setiya's theory, I can in fact intend x without believing I *intend* x, though in intending x I reflexively believe I believe x, and this reflexive belief is, in fact, my intention. If so, I might newly come to believe, on the basis of evidence, that I do indeed intend x and do not merely reflexively believe I will x. If I do in fact intend x then the reasoning that leads me to this new belief about my intention could be both sound and ampliative. So it would not violate Setiya's epistemic prohibition of inference that is of a kind that "could never be both *sound* and *ampliative*." If I do not in fact intend x then I will have a false belief about what I intend even though the reasoning leading to that false belief is of a kind that *could* be both sound and ampliative (though, of course, it is not in this case).

My conclusion, then, is that Setiya has not convincingly shown that a false belief about one's own intentions ineluctably violates an epistemic "should." If we interpret his theory of intention in a way that does seem to show this, the theory is problematic; if we interpret the theory in a less problematic way, it does not show this.

5. BROOME ON PRACTICAL REASONING

Both of my objections to Harman's basic idea interact with recent work by John Broome on practical reasoning, work that leads Broome to a version of cognitivism about IR. Broome's views are complex; but for present purposes we can understand the relevant aspects of his view in terms of the following claims:[55]

(1) Intention is not belief.
(2) It is not in general true that if you intend E you believe E.

This last is because (and here Broome and I agree)

55. In this discussion I focus on Broome's "The Unity of Reasoning?" I quote from the manuscript of August 2008. [Where possible, I have added, in brackets, the corresponding page numbers to the published version (the full citation of which can be found in n. 7, above).]

(3) You can sometimes intend E but fail to believe you intend E; and in such cases you may well not believe E.

(4) But, if you do believe you intend E then you will believe E.

(5) And for your intention to E to enter into practical reasoning about means to E, you need to believe you intend E.

(6) So when your intention to E enters into your practical reasoning about means to E, you believe E.

(7) And it is this belief that E that provides the premise for your reasoning, namely: E.

(8) If you also believe that E only if M, and if these beliefs do not change, BC requires that you believe M; and that is where your reasoning can lead.

(9) But if in the "background" you believe that M will obtain only if you intend M, then if you do arrive at the belief that M this will normally be by way of intending M. In satisfying BC in this way you will satisfy IR.

This, then, is Broome's broadly cognitivist picture of reasoning from intended ends to intended means. Broome wants to acknowledge, though, that it remains possible to intend E, believe that this requires both M and that you intend M, but falsely believe that you intend M. Broome grants that in such a case you fail to satisfy IR, though you may well satisfy BC. But, says Broome,

(10) In such a case "your false belief blocks any reasoning that can bring you to satisfy" IR.[56] So,

(11) Insofar as IR is a rational demand *that can be satisfied by reasoning* it is a demand that derives from BC. Insofar as IR seems to impose demands that go beyond what is imposed by BC, these are not demands that can be satisfied by reasoning.

In this sense, it is BC that is fundamental for a theory of practical reasoning from ends to means.

Let me focus here on two ideas. The first is that my intention to E enters into my means-end reasoning by providing the believed premise that I will E. I will believe this premise since, for my intention to enter into my reasoning I need to believe I so intend; and if I believe I intend E then I believe E. The second idea is that a false belief that I intend M blocks the possibility of arriving at an actual intention to M by way of practical reasoning that

56. "The Unity of Reasoning?": msp. 17 [p. 87 in published version].

begins with my intention to E. The first idea is that the relevant practical reasoning that can lead me to satisfy IR is theoretical reasoning concerning the contents of my associated beliefs. The second idea is that insofar as IR may seem—in cases of false belief about what one intends—to impose a rational demand that goes beyond what such theoretical reasoning can satisfy, it imposes a rational demand that no reasoning can satisfy. Taken together, these ideas amount to a kind of cognitivism about IR. And I think that both of my reasons for objecting to Harman's basic idea also suggest challenges to this form of cognitivism.

Broome supposes, in claim (5), that my intention to E can enter into my practical reasoning only if I believe I so intend. This seems delicate. On the one hand, it seems that we do not suppose that the belief that p can enter into theoretical reasoning only if one has the second-order belief that one believes p. It seems, for example, that a child might reason theoretically without having the concept of belief, and so without having a belief that she believes.[57] (Though perhaps, if her reasoning is *conscious*, she needs some higher-order thought that is in fact about her belief.[58]) So why should we think that intention is different from belief in this respect? On the other hand, a reasoning system needs to keep track of whether an attitude involved in reasoning is a belief or an intention. And one way to do this is to have second-order beliefs—or perhaps some other sort of higher-order thought—about which attitude is in fact involved.

Since I do not want to try to sort out this matter here, I will proceed by bracketing this complication and simply granting claim (5) for present purposes. Note though that Broome also needs claim (4), the claim that if you believe you intend E then you believe E. Claim (4) assumes that the only breakdowns between intending E and believing E occur when you fail to believe you intend E. But there is reason to be skeptical about this assumption: that is the point of the example of my commitment to stopping at the bookstore while being aware of my absent-mindedness, an example I offered as part of my first objection to Harman's basic idea.

Broome notes the possibility of such examples, and he acknowledges that we sometimes call the agent's attitude toward his action in such examples "intention." Broome says that in the case of such a non-confident

---

57. Example courtesy of John Broome, in correspondence.
58. See David Rosenthal, "A Theory of Consciousness," in Ned Block, Owen Flanagan, and Guven Guzeldere, eds., *The Nature of Consciousness: Philosophical Debates* (Cambridge, MA: MIT Press, 1997): 729–53.

intention in favor of E will not provide, as a premise for one's practical reasoning, the believed proposition E. Since Broome's story of the role of an intention to E in providing a premise for such practical reasoning is that it provides the believed proposition that E, he must grant—as he does—that his story of practical reasoning from ends to means does not apply to the case of a non-confident intention in favor of E: such non-confident intentions are "beyond the scope" of his account.[59]

But even if my intention to stop at the bookstore is non-confident it involves a distinctive kind of practical commitment that goes beyond mere preference: I have, in some practical sense, settled on stopping there. This returns us to the basic question of whether it is this practical step that newly engages a requirement like IR, or whether the relevant requirement of instrumental rationality is only engaged once one actually believes one will do as one intends. If we say the former—that even non-confident intention engages a requirement along the lines of IR—then we should worry that Broome's account of practical reasoning from ends to means is inappropriately limited in scope. Broome identifies such practical reasoning with a form of theoretical reasoning that is commonly—though, it seems, not necessarily—associated with practical reasoning from ends to means. And that identification seems problematic.

What about Broome's claim (10), the claim that in a case in which you knowingly intend E and know that this requires your intending M, but you falsely believe you intend M, "your false belief blocks any reasoning that can bring you to satisfy" IR? Broome's view here is that

[t]here is simply no way you can reason your way to an actual intention, past your belief that you have an intention.[60]

This leads to Broome's idea that insofar as IR goes beyond what is required by BC—since IR requires that you actually intend M in cases in which BC is satisfied by your false belief that you so intend—it does not require something you can achieve by reasoning. This is Broome's strategy for responding to the issues raised by my second objection to Harman's basic idea. What to say?

Well, consider reasoning in which one aims to *reconfirm* what one in fact already believes. I believe I locked the door when I left home earlier today. But I find myself engaged in reasoning that aims at reconfirmation:

59. "The Unity of Reasoning?": msp. 13 [p. 80 in published version].
60. "The Unity of Reasoning?": msp. 16 [p. 86 in published version].

Susan was there. She would have seen whether I locked it. If she had seen that I had failed to lock it she would have said something. She didn't say something. So, I locked it.

Granted, in many such cases I suspend my belief that I locked it, once I embark on the reasoning. But I don't see that this is necessary. A concern with reconfirmation need not begin with doubt about what is to be reconfirmed; it might be focused, rather, on articulating the precise grounds for one's belief.

Suppose now that I didn't really believe I had locked the door, though I somehow believed I believed that. It seems that I could engage in the cited reasoning—reasoning that I mistakenly thought of as merely reconfirming my belief—but which, in fact, leads to my newly believing I locked the door. As a matter of fact, this reasoning finally fully convinces me that I locked the door. My earlier false belief that I already believed I locked the door need not block this.

Return now to the case of a false belief about what one intends. Suppose I intend E (and I know this), I know that E requires M by way of intending M, I do not in fact intend M, but I falsely believe I intend M. Though I satisfy BC (in the relevant respect) I am in violation of IR, though I do not know that I am. Suppose I aim to go through the practical reasoning in favor of intending M as a way of articulating the rational support for the intention in favor of M that I falsely believe I already have. (Perhaps, for example, M is my engaging in unpleasant physical therapy, and I seek to reconfirm the grounds for doing this unpleasant thing as a means to my intended end of recovery from my accident.) It seems I can go through the relevant means-end reasoning and thereby in fact be led newly to intend M, though by my own (false) lights my intention to M is not new and this reasoning merely reconfirms an intention I already have. My earlier false belief that I already intend M need not block this way of newly coming into conformity with IR by way of reasoning. So—though I grant that such cases are unusual—I do not think we should accept Broome's claims that "[t]here is simply no way you can reason your way to an actual intention, past your belief that you have an intention" and that "your false belief blocks any reasoning that can bring you to satisfy" IR. So we need a version of IR that goes beyond BC in order to understand how reasoning your way to an intention in favor of necessary means despite a prior false belief that you already so intend can newly bring you into conformity with a requirement of instrumental rationality. And that means that we should not be cognitivists about IR.

6. CONCLUSION

What conclusion should we draw from these reflections? Well, cognitivism seems beset by difficulties associated with the possibility of mistaken beliefs about what one intends; and many versions of cognitivism do not sufficiently come to terms with the way in which non-confident intentions seem to engage a basic demand of instrumental rationality even in the absence of a belief in success. Further, it seems plausible that we do not need cognitivism to see the relevant norms as tied to a constitutive aim of intention, or thereby to explain their special nature. So, though there remain important unresolved problems that arise both for cognitivism and for the practical commitment view, the weight of these reflections seems so far to argue in favor of the practical commitment view as a better model of this fundamental aspect of reason.[61]

61. As noted, I am including in these reflections the arguments in both this present essay and in "Intention, Belief, Practical, Theoretical." Let me note, however, an issue I have not tried to address in either of these essays. One might conjecture that cognitivism about IR is needed in order to avoid the kind of unacceptable bootstrapping described in "Intention and Means-End Reasoning" and in *Intention, Plans, and Practical Reason:* 24–7. The idea, in a nutshell, is that it is only by seeing IR as, at bottom, a theoretical requirement on belief rather than a requirement of practical rationality on intention, that we can avoid seeing intending E as always providing a kind of practical reason for M that constitutes unacceptable bootstrapping. Setiya develops an idea along these lines in "Cognitivism About Instrumental Reason." I hope to address this issue on another occasion. [See this volume, essay 4.]

CHAPTER 4

Intention, Practical Rationality, and Self-Governance*

The planning theory of intention and of our agency highlights the fundamental coordinating and organizing roles of structures of planning in the temporally extended and social practical thought and action of agents like us.[1] Intentions are elements of plans of action, plans that are normally hierarchically structured, partial, and at least in part future directed. And these planning structures help to support and to constitute forms of agency that we value highly.

* Much of this article was initially written when I was a fellow at the Stanford Humanities Center, to which I am grateful for the wonderful support. Versions of this article were presented and usefully discussed at the 2008 OSU-Maribor-Rijeka Conference in Moral Philosophy in Dubrovnik, Croatia; at Rutgers University; at UCLA; at the UNC 2008 Colloquium (at which Kieran Setiya provided insightful comments); at Princeton University; and at Harvard University. In addition, John Broome, Sarah Paul, Jeffrey Seidman, Yonatan Shemmer, and Gideon Yaffe have all provided extremely helpful comments on earlier drafts. Final revisions were aided by extremely helpful comments from Bruno Verbeek, John Fischer, and an anonymous referee.

1. See my *Intention, Plans, and Practical Reason* (Cambridge, MA: Harvard University Press, 1987; reissued by the Center for the Study of Language and Information, 1999), esp. 14–35 and 50–3, where I lay out some of the main ideas that are my concern here. (An earlier effort is in my "Intention and Means-End Reasoning," *Philosophical Review* 90 [1981]: 252–65.) I have also tried to rethink some of these ideas in two other recent articles: "Intention, Belief, Practical, Theoretical," in *Spheres of Reason: New Essays on the Philosophy of Normativity*, ed. Simon Robertson (Oxford: Oxford University Press, 2009), 29–61 [this volume, essay 2]; and "Intention, Belief, and Instrumental Rationality," in *Reasons for Action*, eds. David Sobel and Steven Wall (Cambridge: Cambridge University Press, 2009), 13–36 [this volume, essay 3]. Roughly speaking, these articles leave off at the point at which the current article begins.

Planning agency involves characteristic norms of practical rationality. However, when we try to understand these norms, and their relation to practical reasons, we are led to a hard problem. In this essay I try to say what this problem is and to solve it in a way that is responsive to the recent literature. Some (I call them "cognitivists") see these rationality norms as, at bottom, norms of theoretical rationality. Some instead see the idea that these rationality norms have a distinctive normative force as a "myth." I seek a path between, one that highlights connections between practical reason, planning structures, and the metaphysics of self-governance: for planning agents like us, our reason for conforming to these norms of practical rationality derives in part from our reason to govern our own lives.[2]

I. RATIONALITY AND REASONS

The norms of rationality at issue here are "wide-scope" norms on sets of attitudes: they are, roughly, norms that enjoin or reject certain combinations of attitudes.[3] These include norms of theoretical rationality that enjoin both consistency and coherence within one's beliefs. And these include norms of practical rationality that apply to intentions. In particular, there are norms of consistency and of means-end coherence of intentions and plans.[4] There is a rational demand that one's intentions, taken together with one's beliefs, fit together into a consistent model.[5] And there is a

2. Although I said in *Intention, Plans, and Practical Reason* that "intentions enable us to avoid being merely time-slice agents" (35), it is primarily in more recent work—much of which is included in my *Structures of Agency* (New York: Oxford University Press, 2007)—that I have been able to articulate the connection between planning structures and the metaphysics of an important kind of self-governing agency. The current effort to provide a sturdier foundation for the views in *Intention, Plans, and Practical Reason* about rationality and reasons depends on connections between planning and self-governance that only came clearly into view after that book.

3. See John Broome, "Reasons," in *Reason and Value*, ed. R. Jay Wallace et al. (Oxford: Oxford University Press, 2004), 28–55; and "Does Rationality Give Us Reasons?," *Philosophical Issues* 15 (2005): 321–37. For a recent debate about this, see Niko Kolodny, "Why Be Rational?" *Mind* 114 (2005): 509–63; John Broome, "Wide or Narrow Scope?" *Mind* 116 (2007): 359–70; and Niko Kolodny, "State or Process Requirements?" *Mind* 116 (2007): 371–85.

4. I also think there is a norm of rational stability of intentions over time, but I postpone to another occasion an examination of the implications of my discussion in this article for our understanding of this norm [see this volume, essays 5, 6, 10, 11].

5. In "Intention, Belief, Practical, Theoretical," esp. sec. 8, I tease apart two elements of this norm: a norm of agglomeration and a norm of consistency of contents of an intention. However, it will make the discussion more manageable here to build both these ideas into the norm of intention consistency under consideration.

rational demand that one's intentions be means-end coherent in the sense, roughly, that it not be true that one intends E, believes that E requires that one now intends necessary means M, and yet not now intends M.[6] In both respects intentions are subject to rationality norms that do not apply in the same way to ordinary desires.

We can express these norms of practical rationality roughly as follows:

Intention Consistency: The following is always pro tanto irrational: intending A and intending B, while believing that A and B are not co-possible.

Means-End Coherence: The following is always pro tanto irrational: intending E while believing that a necessary means to E is M and that M requires that one now intend M, and yet not now intending M.[7]

Such norms figure in our interpretative practices and in our assessments of agents.[8] But my focus here is on their role in a planning agent's first-personal practical reasoning. According to the planning theory, the (perhaps, implicit) acceptance of these norms is operative in such reasoning. Given prior but partial plans of action, threats of means-end incoherence pose deliberative problems. Given demands for intention consistency, prior intentions provide a filter on options to be considered in deliberation. In these ways guidance by our (implicit) acceptance of these norms is central to the proper functioning of planning in our agency.

Turn now to the idea of a reason—that is, a normative reason—for action. We can begin with T. M. Scanlon's remark that "a reason for

6. This is a more narrowly focused version of the demand for means-end coherence than the one I formulated in *Intention, Plans, and Practical Reason*, 31–5. The version there adumbrated sufficient as well as necessary means (see 35). However, the problems of this article concern more specifically the case of necessary means.

7. Why "pro tanto"? Well, there can be practical analogues of the paradox of the preface. There can be cases of rational triage in which, given limits of time and attention, one must focus on some proper subset of threatened violations. And there can be cases of psychological compulsion in which the response that is on balance rational involves a limited violation of one of these norms. (I return to this last sort of case in my discussion below of views of Kieran Setiya.) In cases such as these, we may sometimes want to say that good practical reasoning leads the agent to a psychological profile that involves a pro tanto (not merely prima facie) irrationality. So we need to allow that to be guided solely and exclusively by a single such rationality requirement can sometimes be a failure in one's practical thinking. (I discuss this last point in my "Setiya on Intention, Rationality, and Reasons," in *Analysis Reviews* 69 [2009]: 510–21.)

8. The point about interpretation is familiar from work of Donald Davidson. I discuss the assessment of agents in *Intention, Plans, and Practical Reason*, chaps. 4–6.

something . . . [is] a consideration that counts in favor of it."[9] Once we try to go beyond this remark, however, controversy looms.

Begin with two fundamental ideas. The first is that a normative reason for action must be able to connect up with motivation of action. Bernard Williams puts it this way: "if it is true that A has a reason to φ, then it must be possible that he should φ for that reason." And this leads Williams to the claim that "A has a reason to φ only if he could reach the conclusion to φ by a sound deliberative route from the motivations he already has."[10]

The second idea is that to judge that something is a reason for action is appropriately to endorse it. One version of this idea, for example, is at the heart of Allan Gibbard's expressivist metanormative theory.[11]

A full theory of the nature of normative reasons for action, if we could have one, would need to do justice to both of these ideas, although perhaps not in the shape they are given by Williams and Gibbard.[12] Perhaps in the end, in the effort to do justice to both of these ideas, the very idea of a normative reason for action will fall apart under our philosophical microscopes. But here I proceed on the optimistic assumptions both that there is an important and coherent idea of a normative reason for action that lies behind current debates and that both Williams and Gibbard are pointing to important aspects of that idea.[13] My concern is with the question of how some such idea of a normative reason for action—assuming both its coherence and its importance for practical philosophy—needs to be connected to the idea of practical rationality. As the discussion develops, I will make some comments about "internal

9. T. M. Scanlon, *What We Owe to Each Other* (Cambridge, MA: Harvard University Press, 1998), 17.

10. Bernard Williams, "Internal Reasons and the Obscurity of Blame," in his *Making Sense of Humanity* (Cambridge: Cambridge University Press, 1995), 35–45, 39, and 35.

11. Gibbard aims to "pursue the element of endorsement that full-information accounts leave out." This leads him to the claim that "when a person calls something—call it *R*—a reason for doing *X*, he expresses his acceptance of norms that say to treat *R* as weighing in favor of doing *X*" (Allan Gibbard, *Wise Choices, Apt Feelings* [Cambridge, MA: Harvard University Press, 1990], 22, 163). And see Allan Gibbard, *Thinking How to Live* (Cambridge, MA: Harvard University Press, 2003), 188–91; Simon Blackburn, *Ruling Passions: A Theory of Practical Reasoning* (Oxford: Oxford University Press, 1998). For a normative realist understanding of such endorsement, see Scanlon, *What We Owe to Each Other*, 55–64.

12. Compare Scanlon, *What We Owe to Each Other*, 372.

13. For example, I think it is natural to see Michael Smith's theory of reasons for action as responding to both pressures, although I am not hereby endorsing that theory. See Michael Smith, "Internal Reasons," *Philosophy and Phenomenological Research* 55 (1995): 109–31. In contrast, both Simon Blackburn and Barbara Herman have each suggested (in correspondence or discussion) some skepticism about the very idea of a normative reason for action.

reasons"—normative reasons grounded in what Williams calls the agent's "subjective motivational set."[14] And I will take it for granted that to judge that something is a reason for action is, at least in part, to endorse its role of having justifying weight in relevant practical deliberation. I will, however, leave open the question of exactly how to interpret this endorsement. And I will leave open exactly how to put together these two aspects of the idea of a reason for action. My hope is to articulate interrelations between rationality and reasons that will be a part of any fully developed theory.

We can now ask: Do intentions generally provide normative reasons for means? This is not the question: Do states in the agent's subjective motivational set ever ground internal reasons for action? As I see it, certain kinds of agential commitments and concerns can ground internal reasons for action, although a judgment in a particular case that there is such a reason needs to be defended in normative reflection.[15] My question here, however, differs from this general question in two ways. The first is that my question specifically concerns intention, not the agent's subjective motivational set quite generally. To explain the second difference, I need to make a distinction. One way an intention might provide a reason for means is by being a ground of a corresponding internal reason. But an intention might provide a reason for action without itself being such a ground. This would happen if there is in the background a practical reason that together with the intention induces a reason for action that is not induced by that background reason by itself. And my current question concerns this broader idea of providing a reason for action.

That said, I think that intending E does not in general provide a reason for (intending) means to E.[16] My reason for saying this appeals to the possibility of certain kinds of failures in intending E.

14. However, I leave it open whether we need, in all cases of normative reasons for action, an essential relativity to the agent's actual "motivational set" of the sort that Williams sees as a necessary condition for being a reason for action. See Bernard Williams, "Internal and External Reasons," in his *Moral Luck* (Cambridge: Cambridge University Press, 1981), 101–13, and "Internal Reasons and the Obscurity of Blame." (For Williams's focus specifically on necessary conditions for a reason for action, see 35 of the latter.) For a development of Williams's concerns that tries to avoid this kind of relativity, see Smith, "Internal Reasons."

15. The relevant norms might include the idea that the commitments and concerns that ground such internal reasons do not favor things that are unqualifiedly bad. See my "A Thoughtful and Reasonable Stability," comments on Harry Frankfurt's 2004 Tanner Lectures, in Harry G. Frankfurt, *Taking Ourselves Seriously and Getting It Right*, ed. Debra Satz (Stanford, CA: Stanford University Press, 2006), 77–90, 81–4.

16. In putting the idea this way, I am supposing that all reasons for intending the means are reasons for the means. In this way I am putting to one side the issue raised by Gregory Kavka in "The Toxin Puzzle," *Analysis* 43 (1983): 33–6.

Suppose, that my decision in favor of end E is irrationally akratic: my stable best judgment about the balance of reasons favors an alternative end F over E. If my intention in favor of E were in general to provide a further reason for means to E, then such a reason would favor the means to E even when my intention in favor of E is akratic. Such a reason might then tilt the balance of reasons in favor of the means to E over the means to F. This would be an odd kind of bootstrapping of the case in favor of the means to E over the case in favor of the means to F. After all, from my own point of view the intention in favor of E is ill-advised. Why would I, in general, suppose that this intention nevertheless provides yet one more reason in favor of the means to E over the means to F?[17]

Now suppose, in a second case, that the end is a very bad end— ethnic cleansing, say—and yet the agent wholeheartedly intends that end. This intention may well motivate the performance of terrible means. Should we also say that in such a case one's intending that end provides a normative reason for those means? Well, recall that in seeing something as a normative reason, one endorses its role of having justifying weight in relevant practical deliberation. So long as we retain this idea, I think that we will, in the absence of some special consideration, want to resist the claim that this intention in favor of ethnic cleansing provides a reason in favor of the terrible means.[18]

So I think we should deny that an intention in favor of an end quite generally provides a normative reason for the means. So—limiting our attention to necessary means—we are led to

Intentions × Reasons: Intending E does not in general provide a practical, normative reason for necessary means to E and so does not in general provide a practical, normative reason for intending those necessary means.[19]

Intentions × Reasons does not say that intentions never provide reasons for necessary means.[20] But it does say that intentions do not always do this.

17. This kind of example was a main concern of mine in *Intention, Plans, and Practical Reason*, 24–7. See also my "Intention and Means-End Reasoning."

18. For an expressivist version of this thought, see Allan Gibbard's remarks about Caligula in "Morality as Consistency in Living," *Ethics* 110 (1999): 140–64, 145. The reason for my qualification—"in the absence of some special consideration"—will become clear below.

19. The intended interpretation of *Intentions × Reasons* is that it entails that intending E does not in general provide a reason for intending necessary means to E even when the agent has the relevant beliefs about means.

20. Indeed, I take it that certain kinds of non-akratic intended projects that do not aim at unqualifiedly bad ends do normally ground internal reasons for action. When,

Consider now the relation between such reasons and rationality. If you intend E but do not now intend known necessary means intending which you know is now necessary, then it follows from *Means-End Coherence* that you are pro tanto irrational. This follows even if your intention is akratic, or favors a bad end. But we are also saying that it is not in general true that the intention in favor of E provides a corresponding reason for the means. What then is the precise normative significance of norms of practical rationality like *Means-End Coherence*?

II. NORMATIVE SIGNIFICANCE OF INTENTION COHERENCE AND CONSISTENCY

Suppose you are a planning agent and you settle on an intention in favor of E. Since you are a planning agent, your further practical thinking will be guided by your (at least, implicit) acceptance of norms of means-end coherence and intention consistency. This is normal, rational functioning of a planning agent. Still, we can ask: What can you say to justify this, to explain why it matters that you be guided in this way?[21]

Well, the first thing you can say is that in being guided by (your acceptance of) a norm of means-end coherence, you are more likely to pursue E effectively. After all, you are not a god who can simply will "Let there

e.g., the boy in Sartre's famous case settles on a project of fighting for the Free French, he may thereby come to have normative reasons for certain actions that he did not have before. And when I settle on an academic career rather than a career in business, I may thereby come to have reasons for action that I did not have before. (Here I have been helped by Yonatan Shemmer, "Practical Reason: From Philosophy of Action to Normativity" [unpublished manuscript, University of Sheffield]. A related although somewhat different idea is in Ruth Chang, "Voluntarist Reasons and the Sources of Normativity," in Sobel and Wall, *Reasons for Action*, 243–71.)

I think that John Broome and Joseph Raz are sometimes understood as holding the view that intentions never provide reasons for means. Broome writes that "it is not credible that, just by adopting some end, you make it the case that you have reason to pursue it" ("Have We Reason to Do as Rationality Requires? A Comment on Raz," *Journal of Ethics and Social Philosophy* Symposium 1 [2005]: 1–8, 1). And Raz rejects the "blanket conclusion that having goals or intentions provides reasons" ("Instrumental Rationality: A Reprise," *Journal of Ethics and Social Philosophy* Symposium 1 [2005]: 1–19, 19). But immediately before saying this, Raz points to cases in which "intentions or their expression provide reasons." And Broome is careful to insert the important qualifier "just." So perhaps they would settle for my version of *Intentions × Reasons*.

The distinction between the idea that intentions never provide reasons for means and the idea that they do not always do so is noted by Kieran Setiya in his "Cognitivism about Instrumental Reason," *Ethics* 117 (2007): 649–73, 653.

21. In talking about why this "matters," I am following Garrett Cullity in "Decisions, Reasons, and Rationality," *Ethics* 119 (2008): 57–95, 82.

be E!" and expect the world to cooperate. You can also say that guidance by a norm of intention consistency makes it more likely that you will not trip over yourself. You can, then, say that guidance by these norms is likely useful in the particular case.

You can also note that the general mode of thinking involved in planning agency that is guided by these norms has much to be said for it. You can note that violations of norms of consistency and coherence will normally undermine effective agency and associated forms of coordination. In this sense, you can say, these planning capacities—where these include guidance by these norms—are universal means.[22] Further, you can say that the cross-temporal self-government that you value highly involves forms of cross-temporal organization of thought and action that are, for us, to a large extent attributable to these planning capacities.[23] And, finally, you can note that forms of sociality that you value highly involve structures of planning agency.[24] You can in this way cite a trio of interrelated ways in which structures of planning—where these include guidance by the cited norms—contribute quite generally to the richness of life and the effectiveness of agency.[25]

So there is a lot you can say to justify the way in which you are guided by these norms. But there is one thing you cannot yet say. In being guided by these norms, it may well seem to you that you are according intention coherence and consistency their own noninstrumental normative significance in the particular case, a significance that is distinctive in the sense that it is not merely a matter of the promotion of your particular intended ends. But, so far, this has not been justified. Granted, your first thought is about your particular case. But it sees consistency and coherence as tools for effectively pursuing your intended ends, tools whose normative significance derives instrumentally from whatever normative significance those

22. Bratman, *Intention, Plans, and Practical Reason*, 28.

23. This is a central theme of the essays in my *Structures of Agency*. I return to this idea below.

24. See esp. essays 5–8 in my *Faces of Intention* (New York: Cambridge University Press, 1999); and "Modest Sociality and the Distinctiveness of Intention," *Philosophical Studies* 144 (2009): 149–65.

25. For this general point, see my "Intention, Belief, Practical, Theoretical." This kind of pragmatic backing for these norms is broadly in the spirit of the work of David Gauthier and Edward McClennen. See, e.g., David Gauthier, "Commitment and Choice: An Essay on the Rationality of Plans," in *Ethics, Rationality, and Economic Behavior*, eds. Francesco Farina, Frank Hahn, and Stefano Vannucci (Oxford: Oxford University Press, 1996), 217–43; and Edward F. McClennen, "Pragmatic Rationality and Rules," *Philosophy & Public Affairs* 26 (1997): 210–58. Jennifer Morton pursues a related strategy in her "Practical Reasoning and the Varieties of Agency" (PhD diss., Stanford University, 2008).

ends have. And your second—three-part—thought concerns the benefits of a general mode of thinking, not specifically the benefits in the particular case. And one lesson from debates about rule consequentialism is that the step from justifying a general practice to justifying a specific instance of that practice is fraught and prone to worries about "rule worship."[26]

At this point you might conclude that the thought that such coherence and consistency have their own distinctive, noninstrumental normative significance in the particular case is a mistake. What can be said in favor of being guided by these norms has been said, and while this is substantial, it does not support this thought about normative significance in the particular case. The idea that intention coherence and consistency have a distinctive, noninstrumental normative significance in the particular case is, you might conclude, a "myth."

You would be in good company, for this is a view to which both Joseph Raz and Niko Kolodny have been led.[27] As they see it, what matters for deliberation are the specific reasons for the specific actions at issue. Coherence and consistency of intention can help us respond to those specific reasons. But it is a myth to think of coherence and consistency as themselves having a distinctive, noninstrumental normative significance in the particular case.

I myself do not think this idea is a myth. I do think that the grounds that support the role of our acceptance of these norms in our practical thinking go beyond—in ways just indicated—such a distinctive, noninstrumental normative significance. Nevertheless, I believe that there is, at least normally, some such distinctive, normative significance and that its recognition contributes to our understanding of our agency. To defend this, however, I need to solve a hard problem.[28]

---

26. J. J. C. Smart, "Extreme and Restricted Utilitarianism," in *Theories of Ethics*, ed. Philippa Foot (Oxford: Oxford University Press, 1967), 171–83.

27. Joseph Raz, "The Myth of Instrumental Rationality," *Journal of Ethics and Social Philosophy* 1 (2005): 1–28; and Niko Kolodny, "The Myth of Practical Consistency," *European Journal of Philosophy* 16 (2008): 366–402. Raz writes that "there is no *distinctive* form of rationality or of normativity that merits the name instrumental rationality or normativity" (24). Kolodny aims to extend Raz's view and rejects the "myth [that there is] a set of principles that enjoin formal coherence as such" (390). (As Kolodny notes—n. 12—an early version of a related idea occurs in Hugh McCann, "Settled Objectives and Rational Constraints," *American Philosophical Quarterly* 28 [1991]: 25–36.) And Kolodny notes the relevance of Smart-type worries about "traditional forms of rule utilitarianism" in "Why Be Rational?" 543–44. There may be subtle differences between what is being claimed by these two philosophers, but I take it that in both cases the underlying ideas lead to rejecting the claim that, quite generally, intention coherence and consistency has its own distinctive, noninstrumental normative significance in the particular case.

28. Questions from Nadeem Hussain, Jeffrey Seidman, and Yonatan Shemmer over the years have helped me focus on these issues. And specific questions from Aaron

III. THE PROBLEM

To reject a myth theory, we need an explanation of the purported distinctive normative force of these rationality norms. We should not be satisfied here with a kind of quietism.[29] We need an explanation of why the thought that these norms involve distinctive, noninstrumental normative demands on the particular occasion is not, as Kolodny has put it, an "outlandish" concern with "psychic tidiness."[30]

Let's focus on *Means-End Coherence*. To get the kind of account for which we are looking, we will want to say that there is in the particular case a practical reason to avoid means-end incoherence. We will also want to say that this reason to avoid incoherence within a cluster of intentions is not merely a matter of promoting the specific reasons one has for each of the specific intentions in that cluster, taken individually. The reason in question is a distinctive reason against such incoherence itself. And we will want to say that this is a noninstrumental reason against such incoherence itself.

The idea is not to see the role of means-end coherence in practical reasoning as primarily that of one more consideration to be weighed in favor of a specific action. According to the planning theory, the primary role in practical reasoning of our acceptance of a norm of intention coherence is, rather, to help structure deliberation by posing problems of means and the like. The current idea is that we have a distinctive, noninstrumental reason that supports this structuring role in the particular case by supporting the avoidance of the violation of this norm of coherence. When one intends the end but, so far, not the believed necessary means, this distinctive reason to avoid violating the norm of means-end coherence can help pose a problem about how to avoid this incoherence. This reason could thereby support certain transitions in thought over time that help solve this problem—although this reason to avoid incoherence does not by itself determine how exactly to do that.[31]

James, in response to a presentation of "Intention, Belief, Practical, Theoretical," convinced me of the need for a further step. My thanks to all. Aspects of Hussain's challenge are in "The Requirements of Rationality," ver. 2.4 (unpublished manuscript, Stanford University). An early formulation of aspects of my strategy in the current essay was sketched in my comments on Kolodny's "Myth of Practical Consistency" at the 2007 Syracuse Workshop on Practical Reason.

29. Here I was helped by a question from Jennifer Church.

30. Kolodny writes: "it seems outlandish that the kind of psychic tidiness that N [a requirement for belief consistency], or any other requirement of formal coherence, enjoins should be set alongside such final ends as pleasure, friendship, and knowledge" (Niko Kolodny, "How Does Coherence Matter?" *Proceedings of the Aristotelian Society* 107 [2007]: 229–63, 241). Elsewhere Kolodny likens such a concern with psychic tidiness to a fetish. See "Why Be Rational?" 546–7.

31. So in the terms of Niko Kolodny's discussions of these matters, we are seeing *Means-End Coherence* as concerned with "the state [the agent] is in at a given time"

Now, it is too strong to say that there is always an overriding reason to avoid such incoherence. What is more plausible is rather something roughly along the following lines—where I label this proposal "initial" to signal that we will arrive, in the end, at a more complex view:

Reason for Means-End Coherence—Initial: There is a distinctive, noninstrumental practical reason (although one that may be outweighed) to avoid the following: intending E, believing that a necessary means to E is M and that M requires that one now intend M, and yet not now intending M.

This is to see the demand of practical rationality in *Means-End Coherence* as linked to a distinctive, noninstrumental practical reason to avoid a correspondingly incoherent psychological complex.[32] And we can add this link to the ideas, already noted, that guidance by *Means-End Coherence* both is normally useful in the particular case and is central to a mode of thinking that quite generally enriches our lives. This would give us a three-track account of the normative significance of this norm of practical rationality.

However, even before we argue for something like *Reason for Means-End Coherence—Initial*, we can see a tension with *Intentions × Reasons*. Suppose that you intend E and also have the cited beliefs. You can conform to *Means-End Coherence* by intending M. According to *Reason for Means-End Coherence—Initial*, you have a distinctive practical reason to conform to *Means-End Coherence*. So it may seem to follow that you have a practical reason to intend M. So it seems that the intention in favor of E quite generally provides a practical reason for intending M whenever one has the cited means-end beliefs. But such a general connection to reasons for means is rejected by *Intentions × Reasons*.[33] Our problem then is can we account for the distinctive normative force of *Means-End Coherence* in a way that is in the spirit of *Reason for Means-End Coherence—Initial* but still coheres with *Intentions × Reasons* and with the considerations that led us to *Intentions × Reasons*?

but supposing that the cited reason can justify certain "transitions from one state to another over time." This is, however, not to say with Kolodny that the basic rationality constraint is itself a "process requirement" ("Why Be Rational?," 517).

32. Note that to assert such a link is not to claim to reduce *Means-End Coherence* to this claim about reasons.

33. Well, what this general connection to reasons for intending means is strictly incompatible with is *Intentions × Reasons* with the added qualification "even when the agent has the cited beliefs about means." But, as noted, I have been interpreting *Intentions × Reasons* to entail that.

IV. "FACTUAL DETACHMENT OF A REASON"

Let's suppose, and hold it fixed, that the agent has the cited beliefs about means and that these beliefs are true. And let's identify a reason to avoid not intending M with a reason to intend M. The argument just mooted involves the inference:

i) There is practical reason to avoid [Intend E but Not Intend M]
ii) Intend E

So,

iii) There is practical reason in favor of intending M.

John Broome calls such an inference a "factual detachment of a reason."[34] And Broome argues that this is not a deductively valid inference.

I agree. Even given i and ii, one will normally still have available, without intending M, a way of avoiding what i says one has reason to avoid, namely, by no longer intending E (thereby newly falsifying ii). After all, even if ii is in fact true, one normally retains the ability to make ii false. The claim in iii that there is a practical reason in favor of intending M involves an implicit comparison of intending M with its available alternatives. And premise ii still allows that one of the available alternatives involves giving up the intention in favor of E. Granted, it is true that, in the current circumstances, intending M is sufficient for avoiding what i says there is a reason to avoid. However, intending M is not (in the relevant sense) necessary for this, for one still has it in one's power instead to stop intending E, and it seems consistent with i and ii that that (i.e., no longer intending E) is what there is reason to do.

The purported conflict between *Reason for Means-End Coherence—Initial* and *Intentions × Reasons* depends, however, on seeing the inference from i and ii to iii as deductively valid. So perhaps we can retain *Reason for Means-End Coherence—Initial* and still hold on to *Intentions × Reasons*. We just need to follow Broome in rejecting factual detachment of a reason.

V. NONMODIFIABLE INTENTIONS AND THE TRANSMISSION OF REASONS

Matters are, however, more complicated. Kieran Setiya, to some extent following Patricia Greenspan, has pointed to special cases in which a closely

---

34. Broome, "Have We Reason to Do as Rationality Requires?," 5. Raz defends a version of such detachment in "Myth," 12.

related inference seems acceptable. These are, roughly, cases in which the agent does not have the psychological capacity to change the relevant end intention.[35] And the worry is that, if these inferences are indeed acceptable, then we will still be faced with a deep tension between *Reason for Means-End Coherence—Initial* and *Intentions × Reasons.*

Setiya's example is an intention to smoke that you do not have the ability to change. What Setiya says is that "there is no decision that would affect [your] intention to smoke."[36] But the example suggests further—although here I go beyond what Setiya says—that this is because your intention is grounded in something like a kind of psychological compulsion, one that is not just a momentary affliction. It is because of this underlying psychological incapacity that your intention is not modifiable by you in the ways in which we normally are able to modify our intentions.

When an intention is not modifiable by the agent because of some such underlying psychological incapacity, I will say that the intention is psychologically nonmodifiable.[37] And such cases of psychologically nonmodifiable intentions reintroduce the tension between *Reason for Means-End Coherence—Initial* and *Intentions × Reasons.* I proceed to explain why.

Return to Setiya's smoker. And suppose that her relevant beliefs about means are not changeable by her, given her obvious and abundant evidence for them. So, holding these beliefs fixed (as I will throughout this discussion) and given that her intention is psychologically nonmodifiable, the only way that is psychologically available to her to conform to *Means-End Coherence* is to intend M. Does it follow,

---

35. Setiya, "Cognitivism about Instrumental Reason"; Patricia Greenspan, "Conditional Oughts and Hypothetical Imperatives," *Journal of Philosophy* 72 (1975): 259–76. Setiya's explicit concern is with an inference that involves an all-in practical "should," whereas my focus is on an inference that concerns practical reasons. (See his principle *Transmission* below.) I am assuming, however, that Setiya would make analogous claims about practical reasons. After all, part of Setiya's case for his cognitivism about instrumental rationality (to be discussed below) is that if we were instead to give these rationality norms distinctive practical normative force, we would be led, by detachment, to unacceptable conclusions. For this line of argument to address the alternative to cognitivism (and to the myth theory) that I am sketching in this essay, it would need to make a claim about the detachment of practical reasons.

36. Setiya, "Cognitivism about Instrumental Reason," 661.

37. Tamar Schapiro (in conversation) has wondered whether this idea of a nonmodifiable intention is confused, given the tight connection between intention and choice between alternatives. But the agent's pro-attitude toward smoking may play major roles in organizing thought and action that are characteristic of intention. So I would not want a broad view about the relation between practical rationality and practical reasons to depend on insisting that, nevertheless, this attitude is not an intention.

given *Reason for Means-End Coherence—Initial*, that she has a reason to intend M?

Well, holding the cited beliefs fixed, the inference now has the form

  i) There is practical reason to avoid [Intend E but Not Intend M]
 ii*) Intend E, and this is psychologically nonmodifiable

So,

 iii) There is practical reason in favor of intending M.

And the Setiya detachment claim is that this is a valid inference.[38]

Should we agree? Well, support for this detachment claim needs to come from a principle about the transmission of reasons. In his discussion, Setiya appeals to:

> *Transmission*: If you should do E, all things considered, and doing M is a necessary means to doing E, you should do M, all things considered, too.[39]

However, given the way our problem has been set up, what we need is, rather, a principle about the transmission of reasons.[40] It will also facilitate discussion to change the variables. So consider the analogue:

> *Transmission Reasons—Initial*: If R is a practical reason in favor of X, and Y is a necessary means to X, then R is a practical reason in favor of Y.

What we want to know is whether this, or some close variant, supports the Setiya detachment claim for the case in which X is avoid [Intend E but Not Intend M], Y is intend M, and the relevant necessity is provided by the psychological nonmodifiability of intending E.

Begin with two preliminary observations. First, I take it that talk of "necessary means" to X should include talk of necessary constitutive elements

---

38. Setiya indicates ("Cognitivism about Instrumental Reason," 656, n. 17) that he sees this claim as in the spirit of work of Greenspan, who appeals to what is "unalterable by the agent" (Greenspan, "Conditional Oughts," 265). A similar claim is also made by Mark Schroeder, who also refers to Greenspan. See his "Means-End Coherence, Stringency, and Subjective Reasons," *Philosophical Studies* 143 (2009): 223–48. There are complex questions here about whether there are different notions of "unalterable" at work in these claims of these different philosophers. But I put these questions aside here.
39. Setiya, "Cognitivism about Instrumental Reason," 652.
40. And see n. 35.

of X. So I will make this explicit. Second, it seems that what matters are necessary means to, or constitutive elements of, an end that is itself attainable by the agent. A reason for an end that is not itself attainable by the agent may not transmit to a reason for a necessary (but insufficient) means or constitutive element.[41]

So let's consider:

> Transmission Reasons: If R is a practical reason in favor of X, X is attainable by the agent, and M is a necessary means to or necessary constitutive element of X, then R is a practical reason in favor of M.

Note that this is a principle about the transmission of reasons antecedently present; this contrasts with *Reason for Means-End Coherence—Initial* which cites a reason to avoid a certain incoherence (a reason that does not require that there be a reason for intending E). Note also that *Transmission Reasons* concerns the transmission of reasons across lines of necessity. It does not say that a reason for X transfers to sufficient means to X. It can instead allow that an inference to reasons for sufficient means will be defeasible.[42]

Does *Transmission Reasons* support the Setiya detachment claim? This depends on the kind of necessity that is needed. And the idea on the table is that if intending E is psychologically nonmodifiable, then intending M is indeed necessary in the relevant sense for the end for which i says that there is a reason, namely, avoiding [Intend E but Not Intend M]. Should we accept *Transmission Reasons* when interpreted in this way?

Well, suppose there is an unmovable boulder that prevents me from taking route A to the attainable goal I have reason to achieve. If, because of this boulder, taking route B is necessary for that goal, then a reason to achieve that goal transmits to a reason to take route B. And what is plausible, I think, is that the psychological nonmodifiability of intending E makes it appropriate to see that intention as an internal, nonmodifiable analogue of such an unmovable boulder, one that stands in the way of achieving means-end coherence by dropping that intention. So it is plausible that given this psychological nonmodifiability of intending E, a reason for avoiding [Intend E and Not Intend M] transmits to a reason

---

41. Which is not to say that the end must be one that the agent will in fact attain.
42. This is, pretty much, the point behind John Broome's criticism of Joseph Raz's facilitative principle. See Broome, "Have We Reason to Do as Rationality Requires?," 7; and Raz, "Instrumental Rationality: A Reprise," 3, esp. n. 8. And see Anthony Kenny, *Will, Freedom, and Power* (Oxford: Blackwell, 1975), 92–6.

for intending M.[43] Accordingly, I would like to develop my alternative to a myth theory in a way that is consistent with the Setiya detachment claim.[44]

Now, that claim, taken together with *Reason for Means-End Coherence—Initial*, is not strictly incompatible with *Intentions × Reasons*. It does not follow from the Setiya detachment claim, together with *Reason for Means-End Coherence—Initial*, that intending E (given relevant beliefs) always gives a reason for M. What follows is only that intending E (holding fixed relevant beliefs and given the attainability of conformity to *Means-End Coherence*) gives a reason for intending M, when the intention in favor of E is not psychologically modifiable.

Nevertheless, the Setiya detachment claim, taken together with *Reason for Means-End Coherence—Initial*, is in tension with the considerations that led us to *Intentions × Reasons*. After all, in a particular case the intention to commit ethnic cleansing might not be psychologically modifiable. Or an akratic intention might become compulsive.[45] In either case, if we were right before to say that the intention to commit ethnic cleansing, or an akratic intention, does not, in the absence of special circumstances, provide a reason for the means,

43. I do not thereby endorse an analogous claim about detachment in the realm of rationality. Suppose that an agent intends E and has the cited means-end beliefs. And suppose this end intention is psychologically nonmodifiable. Holding fixed the cited beliefs, we can ask whether the following is valid:

A. Intending E while not intending M is pro tanto irrational.
B. Intend E, and this is psychologically nonmodifiable

So,

C. It is pro tanto irrational not to intend M.

And the answer seems to be no. Rationality and irrationality are primarily matters of coherence and consistency within clusters of attitudes (or their absence). Norms like *Means-End Coherence* say that certain clusters are pro tanto irrational. If we were to go on to say that a single attitude, or even (as in C) the absence of a single attitude, is itself irrational, we would need to locate an incoherence within that very attitude or absence of attitude. But A and B together do not entail that this will be true about the absence of intending M, taken by itself.

If we are going to say that a certain attitude is itself, strictly speaking, irrational (and not mean only that it is part of a complex that is irrational), we need to locate some incoherence or inconsistency within that very attitude. In contrast, a reason for X is a consideration that bears directly on X but need not depend solely on the intrinsic features of X. A reason for X can depend on the fact that Y—where this is a fact about the relation of X to other things or the context within which X would obtain—without being merely a reason for the complex (X and Y). So we need to understand what to say about the transmission of a reason for Z to a reason for that which is in some sense necessary for Z, without assuming that our answer commits us to a corresponding view about detachment of rationality. (This footnote responds to extremely helpful correspondence from John Broome.)

44. And, as I will explain, I would like to develop in this way my alternative to cognitivist theories like Setiya's.

45. Since it is part of the definition of an akratic intention that it is not compulsive, we would no longer describe the cited intention as akratic. But that does not affect the current point.

then won't we also want to say that, in the absence of special considerations, a psychologically nonmodifiable intention in such cases also provides no such reason? But it is not clear how we can say this if we accept both the Setiya detachment claim and *Reason for Means-End Coherence—Initial*.

VI. COGNITIVISM ABOUT INSTRUMENTAL RATIONALITY

The myth theory—in rejecting the distinctive, noninstrumental practical normative force of *Means-End Coherence* and thereby problematic versions of premise i—is one response to this conundrum. A second response, in contrast, accepts that *Means-End Coherence* does have a distinctive normative force but offers a different account of this normative force. It sees *Means-End Coherence* as at bottom a norm of *theoretical* rationality engaged by the beliefs that are involved in intending. This is Setiya's view and the view of some others as well.[46] And this is the view I have called cognitivism about these norms on intention.[47]

Such cognitivism understands *Means-End Coherence* along the lines of

Theoretical Coherence: Intending E, while believing that a necessary means to E is M and that M requires that one now intend M, and yet not now intending M, taken all together, necessarily involves incoherence of belief. And there is a demand of theoretical rationality for coherence of one's beliefs.

For this to work, we would need a close connection between intending and believing. One idea would be that intending E is itself a special kind of belief that E.[48] An alternative idea would be only that intending E necessarily involves a belief that E.[49] With some such link between intending and believing in place, the idea is that when you intend E, have the cited beliefs about the need for M and intending M, but fail to intend M, your associated beliefs include a belief that E without a belief that a believed

46. See, e.g., R. Jay Wallace, "Normativity, Commitment and Instrumental Reason," *Philosopher's Imprint* 1 (2001): 1–26. An even more ambitious version of this idea is in the work of J. David Velleman. See, e.g., his "What Good Is a Will?" in *Action in Context*, eds. Anton Leist and Holger Baumann (Berlin: de Gruyter, 2007), 193–215. (I discuss this essay in "Intention, Belief, Practical, Theoretical.")

47. For this terminology, see my "Cognitivism about Practical Reason" as reprinted in my *Faces of Intention*, 250–64. (This use of the term "cognitivism" should be distinguished from its more standard use in metaethics.)

48. This is Setiya's view, according to which, roughly, intending E is a desire-like belief that E-because-of-this-very-belief.

49. See, e.g., Wayne Davis, "A Causal Theory of Intending," *American Philosophical Quarterly* 21 (1984): 43–54. In his "Normativity, Commitment and Instrumental

necessary condition for E will come to pass. And that is a kind of theoretical incoherence.

The central claim is that the rational demand for intention coherence is a demand of *theoretical* rationality. So even given a psychologically nonmodifiable intention in favor of E, and the cited beliefs, we cannot derive a conclusion that one has a *practical* reason in favor of M or intending M. But *Intentions × Reasons* concerns the relation between intending E and practical reasons for intending M. So *Intentions × Reasons* and our grounds for *Intentions × Reasons* remain compatible with *Theoretical Coherence*.[50]

As I see it, however, such cognitivism about *Means-End Coherence* runs into significant difficulties, even if we grant the cognitivist the cited close (and controversial) connection between intention and belief.[51] The basic problem arises from the possibility of falsely believing one intends the means.[52]

Suppose I intend E and know that E requires both M and that I now intend M. If I still do not intend M, my intentions suffer from means-end incoherence. But suppose that, while I in fact do not now intend M, I nevertheless falsely believe that I now intend M. My beliefs are that E, that E requires both M and that I now intend M, that I now intend M, and that M. There is no incoherence (although there is falsity) in this structure of beliefs. So means-end incoherence does not entail belief incoherence, contrary to *Theoretical Coherence*.

Reason," Wallace develops a version of cognitivism that uses a yet weaker belief condition, but I think that it is subject to the same worry I note in the text. (I also think it has a distinctive difficulty with *Intention Consistency*.) I discuss Wallace's essay in "Intention, Belief, Practical, Theoretical."

50. As Yonatan Shemmer has emphasized, we can still ask at this point whether (*a*) it follows from Setiya's view that a person with such an unchangeable intention and the cited beliefs has a theoretical reason to believe he will perform the means. If so, we can go on to ask whether (*b*) he thereby has a reason to intend the means since that is the only way he is going to believe, with justification, that he will perform the means. Setiya's response to *b* is that intending M, although it is, on his view, a kind of belief, "also consists in a motivational condition that theoretical reason cannot govern. So it won't make sense to claim that I should intend to do M, in the epistemic sense of 'should'" ("Cognitivism about Instrumental Reason," 672, n. 54). The idea, I take it, is that the theoretical or epistemic "should"—and, so, theoretical reasons—cannot coherently apply to the motivational aspect of intending and so cannot coherently apply to intending. But now my worry is that this is, in effect, close to the feature of cognitivism that I go on to criticize in the main text, namely, that the demands of theoretical rationality do not strictly speaking engage intentions—they only engage associated beliefs—and so that we have not captured the full force of *Means-End Coherence*.

51. For examples that give me significant pause about such a tight connection, see *Intention, Plans, and Practical Reason*, 37–8.

52. I first sketched this objection in "Intention and Means-End Reasoning," n. 4.

I have tried to assess some replies to this objection in other work.[53] Here let me just say that in my judgment this effort to understand the normativity of *Means-End Coherence* as a matter of theoretical rationality is unlikely to work. So I seek a path between a myth theory and cognitivism.

VII. SIMULTANEOUS SOLUTIONS

This returns us to our problem of accounting for the distinctive normative force of *Means-End Coherence* in the particular case, in a way that is in the spirit of *Reason for Means-End Coherence—Initial* but that also coheres with *Intentions × Reasons* and the considerations that support it. This problem has led us to two subproblems. First, we need to say what in particular the distinctive practical reason is that is cited in *Reason for Means-End Coherence—Initial*. Second, we are still faced with the worry that once we cite such a reason, a form of detachment of a reason for means will lead to a tension with our grounds for *Intentions × Reasons* in cases of a psychologically nonmodifiable intention in favor of the end.

Putting these subproblems together suggests a joint solution. The Setiya detachment claim is that we can strengthen premise ii:

ii)   Intend E

in a way that allows for detachment of a reason, given premise i:

i)   There is practical reason to avoid [Intend E but Not Intend M].

The idea is to strengthen ii by adding a nonmodifiability condition:

ii*)   Intend E, and this is psychologically nonmodifiable.

The thought is that we thereby get (by way of an appropriate transmission-of-reasons principle) a valid inference from i and ii* to iii:

iii)   There is practical reason in favor of intending M.

And the claim that we can reach this conclusion quite generally is in tension with our grounds for *Intentions × Reasons*.

---

53. See Bratman, "Intention, Belief, Practical, Theoretical"; and "Intention, Belief, and Instrumental Rationality."

But consider now the reason cited in i. Suppose that this reason depends on the presence of certain normal background conditions; i should then be replaced by

i*)   Given normal conditions C, there is practical reason to avoid [Intend E but Not Intend M].

We could then ask whether the further condition of nonmodifiability in ii* (a condition needed to support the detachment inference) precludes condition C in i* (a condition needed to support the relevant reason) and thereby blocks the relevant reason. If the answer is yes, then the relevant inferences would not be sound.

What account of the reason in i* involves a background condition that is, at least normally, incompatible with the nonmodifiability condition in ii*? It is here that I want to return to the idea, anticipated at the beginning of this essay, that what is central is our reason to govern our own lives: the relevant reason for intention coherence and consistency derives from a reason for self-governance.[54] However, at least normally, this reason only favors a structure of intentions that are appropriately modifiable since the capacity to be self-governing in a relevant domain normally involves an appropriate capacity to modify relevant intentions. And that capacity to modify is blocked by the nonmodifiability invoked in ii*. I proceed to develop and to defend this proposal.

VIII. SELF-GOVERNANCE AND PLANNING AGENCY

Return to the thought that our planning agency helps to constitute and to support our cross-temporal self-governance. In the background is Harry Frankfurt's insight that we need an account of what it is for an agent to

---

54. This thought is to some extent similar in spirit to David Copp's defense of the claim that "*rationality* is in the service of self-*government*" ("The Normativity of Self-Grounded Reason," in his *Morality in a Natural World* [Cambridge: Cambridge University Press, 2007], 309–53, 351). It may also be to some extent similar in spirit to efforts to ground these rationality norms in forms of integrity or the like. For example, Kenneth Stalzer explores the idea that we might ground such rationality norms in what he calls "self-fidelity" ("On the Normativity of the Instrumental Principle" [PhD diss., Stanford University, 2004], chap. 5). And Jonathan Dancy briefly considers an appeal to "integrity" and "self-respect" as a ground for a related wide-scope "ought" ("Replies," *Philosophy and Phenomenological Research* 67 [2003]: 468–90, 474–5). However, the appeal specifically to self-governance has a feature that will be important below, namely, the distinctive connection between self-governance and modifiability of attitude in the light of reasons and rationality.

identify with a certain thought or attitude—of what it is for a thought or attitude to speak for the agent, to be part of where the agent stands, to have agential authority.[55] We need this because cross-temporal self-governance consists, in part, in guidance by psychological structures that have agential authority. The problem of agential authority is, roughly, the problem of specifying psychological structures that are such that when they guide, the agent governs.[56]

Now, elsewhere I have argued that for an attitude to have agential authority for agents like us is in significant part for it to play central roles in the Lockean cross-temporal organization and integration of thought and action.[57] And I have argued, further, that certain plan-type attitudes—in particular, policies concerning what to treat as justifying in practical reasoning—are central cases of attitudes with such authority. These authoritative policies of reasoning need to be embedded in structures of planning agency. So structures of planning agency are an essential element in this solution to the problem of agential authority.

I do not say that such planning structures are the unique solution to the problem of agential authority. But they are one solution, and a solution that seems characteristic of us. And this role in our self-governance is part of a rationale for these planning structures—structures that involve guidance by norms of consistency and coherence of intention.

However, this does not yet explain why norms of intention consistency and coherence have their own distinctive normative force on the particular occasion. So far we have only concerned ourselves with the general significance of planning structures in our lives. Can we provide an explanation of such distinctive normative force by developing further these ideas about self-governance? I think we can.

Return to a Frankfurtian concern with where I stand. When I recognize inconsistency in my own intentions, I see that in this specific case there is

---

55. See, e.g., Harry Frankfurt's remarks about "where (if anywhere) the person himself stands" in his "Identification and Wholeheartedness," as reprinted in his *The Importance of What We Care About* (Cambridge: Cambridge University Press, 1988), 159–76, 166. My terminology of "agential authority" comes from my "Two Problems about Human Agency," in my *Structures of Agency*, 89–105.

56. More precisely, when psychological structures have agential authority, then when they guide, the agent directs, and the agent's direction of action is an essential feature of the agent's governance of action.

57. See, e.g., my "Reflection, Planning, and Temporally Extended Agency" and "Three Theories of Self-Governance," in my *Structures of Agency*, 21–46 and 222–53. (My talk here of "integration" draws from Luca Ferrero, "What Good Is a Diachronic Will?" *Philosophical Studies* 144 (2009): 403–30, sec. 7, DOI 10.1007/s11098-008-9217-1.) Drawing on an idea from Frankfurt, I also cite in these essays a condition of "satisfaction" that needs to be fulfilled if an attitude is to have agential authority.

no clear answer to the question, "Where do I stand?" This question about myself is, with respect to this domain, simply not settled; there is as yet no fact of the matter.[58]

We can say something similar about means-end incoherent plans. If I intend end E but I do not now intend known necessary means intending which now I know to be necessary, there is no clear answer to the question, "Where do I stand?" with respect to E. With respect to this end, there is as yet no relevant fact of the matter about where I stand.

The idea, then, is that inconsistency or incoherence of plan has an implication concerning the metaphysics of agency, namely, that in this particular case there is as yet no determinate answer to a relevant question about where the agent stands. This is because a central way that planning agents like us take such a stand—given the fundamental roles of planning structures in our practical thought and action—is to go beyond a conflicting stew of needs, desires, and considerations and settle on consistent and coherent plans and the like.

Granted, one can have incompatible desires, or desires for ends without desires for known necessary means, and yet there still be a clear answer to the question of where one stands on a relevant issue. Such conflict within, or incompleteness of, one's desires is a common feature of the human condition. But inconsistent or incoherent *plans*—where, as I am understanding them, plans are intentions writ large—do seem to baffle the kind of unity of stance needed for there to be a clear answer to that question.

The next point is that it is only if there is a place where you stand that *you* are governing in the corresponding domain, for in self-governance where you stand guides relevant thought and action. And this, together with the role of intention consistency and coherence in there being a place where you stand, implies that, in any particular case, relevant consistency and coherence of intention is a necessary constitutive element in the corresponding self-governance of planning agents like us. The necessity here is a kind of metaphysical necessity, relative to a type of agent: for planning agents like us, relevant consistency and coherence of intention is a necessary element in the metaphysics of corresponding self-governance. And this suggests that we understand the distinctive reason for conforming to *Means-End Coherence* in the particular case as tied to our self-governance.

58. I say "with respect to this domain" to indicate that I am not claiming that any inconsistency or incoherence blocks taking a stand on all matters. The claim I want to make is relativized to matters that are in the content of the intentions that are inconsistent or incoherent.

We suppose, that is, that we have an intrinsic reason to govern our own lives. We note that relevant conformity to *Means-End Coherence* (as well as *Intention Consistency*) is a necessary constitutive element in the corresponding self-governance of planning agents like us. On the assumption that such self-governance is available to the agent, we infer, by way of *Transmission Reasons*, that there is a reason of self-governance to avoid violating these norms of practical rationality. We note that this reason of self-governance for avoiding such irrationality is distinctive: it is not merely derived from the specific reasons one has for each of the specific intentions in the relevant cluster, taken individually. And we note that this is a noninstrumental reason for avoiding such irrationality since it derives from the fact that such avoidance is a necessary constitutive element in (rather than an instrumental means to) relevant self-governance. And that is why, in seeing *Means-End Coherence* as having distinctive, noninstrumental normative force in a particular case, we are not—to return to Kolodny's worry—guilty of an outlandish concern with psychic tidiness.[59]

That, anyway, is the basic idea. To this let me add three further comments. First, I want to allow that the cited reason in favor of self-governance may itself be an internal reason that is grounded in our normal concern with governing our own lives—although I do not say that every agent must care about self-governance.[60] To keep the discussion manageable, then, I will assume that if the reason of self-governance is grounded in this concern

59. Kolodny notes that my approach to self-governance (he calls it autonomy) "suggests that the value of autonomy itself might provide reason . . . to satisfy C [the constraint of intention consistency], at least where self-governing policies are concerned." Kolodny's main reply is that this "explains the normativity of C only insofar as C applies to self-governing policies, or to intentions that affect self-governing policies. But C applies to other intentions" ("Myth of Practical Consistency," 385). My claim in the text, however, is that my approach to "the normativity of C" by way of appeal to self-governance applies quite generally to the intentions of an agent for whom relevant self-governance is psychologically possible.

Kolodny also makes the point that "making self-governing policies consistent *as such* does not facilitate autonomy. If one achieves consistency by dropping *both* self-governing policies, one is no closer to autonomy" (ibid., 385). I agree, of course, that the mere absence of inconsistency and incoherence is not sufficient for there to be a relevant place where you stand. But my argument only requires that relevant consistency and coherence are necessary constitutive elements of taking a relevant stand.

60. I think, by the way, that it would be a plausible result that an agent who did not care about his own self-governance would not have a distinctive, noninstrumental reason in the particular case in favor of intention consistency and coherence—although consistency-and-coherence-constrained planning would still be for such an agent a universal means and an element in important forms of sociality.

with self-governance, then the agents we are discussing do indeed have that concern.

Second, I assume that the kind of self-governance that is favored by the cited reason is a garden-variety self-governance that can be embedded in a natural causal order. Planning structures support this kind of self-governance, not by pulling the agent out of the causal order but by supporting relevant forms of psychological guidance and control. Such self-governance can, however, be blocked by various kinds of psychological incapacities.

Third, in appealing to *Transmission Reasons* to support the transfer of the reason for self-governance to a reason for a necessary constitutive element of self-governance, we need to suppose that relevant self-governance is indeed psychologically possible.

I propose then that, for planning agents like us, if relevant self-governance is psychologically possible, then the reason for self-governance provides a distinctive, noninstrumental reason for conformity to *Means-End Coherence* in the particular case since such conformity is a necessary constitutive element of relevant self-governance. This reason will support the way in which the acceptance of *Means-End Coherence* helps pose problems for further deliberation, problems about how to fill in or modify one's plans so as not to violate *Means-End Coherence*.

We have arrived, then, at an adjusted version of our earlier *Reason for Means-End Coherence—Initial*:

> *Reason for Means-End Coherence*: When relevant self-governance is psychologically possible, there is a distinctive, noninstrumental practical reason (although one that may be outweighed)—a reason of self-governance—to avoid the following: intending E, believing that a necessary means to E is M and that M requires that one now intend M, and yet not now intending M.

This means that there is a background condition on the reason in *Reason for Means-End Coherence* in favor of conforming to *Means-End Coherence*—a condition of psychologically possible self-governance—that does not also qualify *Means-End Coherence* itself. To this extent we are agreeing with the myth theorist, since we are granting that there are cases to which *Means-End Coherence* applies, although there is not the cited reason for conformity to *Means-End Coherence*.[61] Nevertheless, our approach gives *Means-End Coherence* a strong link to a distinctive,

---

61. This point was emphasized in conversation by Nishi Shah. Note though that even in these cases the reasons in favor of the general modes of thinking that are guided by the acceptance of *Means-End Coherence* will remain forceful.

noninstrumental reason.[62] So long as the agent is capable of relevant self-governance, there is a reason of self-governance for conformity to *Means-End Coherence*.[63] We can now return to Setiya's objection.

IX. REPLY TO SETIYA: SELF-GOVERNANCE AND INTENTION MODIFIABILITY

Recall that the Setiya detachment claim focuses on a purported inference of the following form (where I continue to hold fixed the cited means-end beliefs):

i) There is practical reason to avoid [Intend E but Not Intend M]

ii*) Intend E, and this is psychologically nonmodifiable

So,

iii) There is practical reason in favor of intending M.

In the current case the relevant, purported inference is, roughly,

Given that relevant self-governance is psychologically possible, there is a practical reason of self-governance to avoid [Intend E but Not Intend M]

P intends E (and has the cited beliefs), and the intention in favor of E is psychologically nonmodifiable

So,

There is practical reason in favor of P intending the necessary means, M.

Setiya's idea, as I have understood it, is that, although Broome is right to reject simple factual detachment of a reason, the psychological

62. Although if the intentions concern mundane matters, the strength of the distinctive reason would be correspondingly weak.

63. Might the myth theorist accept this link but claim that the need for the background condition shows that there still is no reason for means-end coherence "as such" (to use Kolodny's formulation)? The purported myth would then be the idea that this distinctive reason for coherence applies without any assumptions at all about the underlying capacities of the agent. But then the supposed myth would turn out to be an overly simplified view of the relation between certain practical reasons and the underlying capacities of the agent. And it seems that the myth theorists see themselves as challenging considerably more than some such oversimplification. In particular, I take it that they would want to challenge the idea that there is, in general, a distinctive reason for means-end coherence when the agent is capable of relevant self-governance.

nonmodifiability of the intention in favor of the end does make the detachment work. However, if the nonmodifiability of intention cited in the second premise blocks the psychological possibility of relevant self-governance, then this inference will misfire: the second premise will block a background condition for the reason cited in the first premise.

And indeed, it does seem that if one has an intention that is not susceptible to modification in the light of reflection on reasons and rationality, then that would normally entail that in this specific domain one is not capable of being self-governing. To be self-governing is not only to have a relevant stand but, normally at least, for one's stand to be psychologically modifiable in the light of relevant reflection.[64] But it is the absence of such psychological modifiability that is crucial to Setiya's strategy for detaching a reason for means. So Setiya's inference in such cases will normally fail.

So once we turn to *Reason for Means-End Coherence*, we can block the objection that appeals to cases of psychological nonmodifiability like that of Setiya's smoker. The nonmodifiability that is appealed to in order to support the detachment of a reason for intending means from a reason for means-end coherence also blocks the attainability of self-governance that is part of the ground for that reason for coherence. We can thereby chart a course, in our understanding of *Means-End Coherence*, between a myth theory and cognitivism, and we can do this in a way that coheres with the grounds that led us to *Intentions × Reasons*. And that is what we wanted.

X. TAKING STOCK

Recall the two cases that led us to *Intentions × Reasons*: the case of a weak-willed intention and the case of intending a bad end. Now, according to

---

64. Granted, if one recognizes that certain of one's intentions—as in Setiya's example, the intention to smoke—are not psychologically modifiable, one might still be able to step back and figure out a strategy for responding to this feature of one's own psychology. One might, say, lock up the cigarette cabinet. And in figuring out and executing this strategy one may be self-governing. So nonmodifiability of an intention does not block all self-governance in the neighborhood. (A point emphasized in conversation by Gideon Yaffe and Larry Temkin.) And *Reason for Means-End Coherence*, taken together with the idea that self-governance normally requires relevant modifiability, seems to get the right result for such a case: one does not have a reason of self-governance to ensure that one's intention to smoke is supplemented with intentions about means to that, although one does have a reason of self-governance to ensure that one's intention to lock up the cigarette cabinet is supplemented with relevant intentions about means.

What about intention consistency? Well, in such a case one might intend to smoke, intend to lock the cabinet, and know that if one locks the cabinet one cannot smoke.

Reason for Means-End Coherence there is a distinctive, noninstrumental reason for intention coherence in the particular case so long as the planning agent is psychologically capable of relevant self-governance. And this is a distinctive practical reason. So in standard versions of these two cases there will be a distinctive practical reason for coherence of intentions. But Broome's objection to factual detachment of a reason blocks a deductive inference in either case to a reason in favor of means.[65]

Suppose, however, that these end intentions are psychologically nonmodifiable. Well, such nonmodifiability of intention is normally incompatible with the ability to govern one's life in the relevant subdomain. So there is no distinctive reason of self-governance in favor of relevant intention coherence in these cases—although we can still see a general disposition to seek intention coherence as useful. Since there is no such distinctive reason for relevant intention coherence in the particular case, there is no danger of arriving, by way of detachment from such a reason, at a reason specifically for the means.

Consider then the reflective thought of a planning agent with modifiable attitudes. Such an agent will be guided by her acceptance of practical rationality norms of consistency and means-end coherence of intention. She will be in a position to see such guidance as likely useful in the current case and as, in general, enriching our lives. Further, she will also be in a position to see the direct application of these norms to the particular case as having distinctive, noninstrumental normative force that is backed by a reason in favor of her self-governance. So she is in a position in these three ways to make justificatory sense of this central element of her practical thinking. Her guidance of her thought and action by these norms of practical rationality is, first, likely useful in the current case and is, second, generally supportive of the richness of our lives and the effectiveness of our agency. And, third, conformity to these norms is, in the particular case, a necessary constituent of a form of agency—namely, self-governance—for which she recognizes a reason.

It is time, however, to consider some important complexities.

So one violates *Intention Consistency*. But since the intention to smoke is not relevantly modifiable, one does not have a reason of self-governance to avoid this violation.

65. Granted, one way in which the agent can achieve relevant coherence is to intend the necessary means. But we have been supposing—with Broome—that practical reasons do not deductively transfer along lines of sufficient but not necessary means. And even though M is a necessary means to E, in the envisaged case intending M is not necessary for that for which *Reason for Means-End Coherence* says there is a reason, namely, means-end coherence.

XI. OTHER REASONS FOR MEANS-END COHERENCE?

I have argued that there is a distinctive, noninstrumental practical reason—a reason of self-governance—of the sort cited in *Reason for Means-End Coherence*. Our reason to govern our lives normally transmits to a reason for avoiding relevant means-end incoherence in the particular case since such coherence is a necessary constitutive element of relevant self-governance of planning agents. However, the transmission of this reason for self-governance to a reason in the particular case for means-end coherence normally requires that the relevant intentions be psychologically modifiable since such modifiability is normally needed for the self-governance to be psychologically available. So the incapacity in the case of Setiya's smoker blocks the transmission of the reason to govern oneself to a reason for means-end coherence.

Once we see that there is this distinctive practical reason for avoiding means-end incoherence, however, we need to consider the possibility that this reason is not unique, that there are other distinctive, noninstrumental practical reasons for avoiding means-end incoherence in addition to the reason that is grounded in the reason for self-governance. And we need to consider the possibility that some such further practical reason for avoiding means-end incoherence would not have the same background condition of intention modifiability. If there were such a further reason for avoiding means-end incoherence, we could not block the Setiya detachment in the way that we blocked it in the case of a reason of self-governance. So we would need yet again to worry about a potential incompatibility with our grounds for *Intentions × Reasons*.

A natural proposal here is that there is an intrinsic reason simply for the kind of psychic unity that is one aspect of self-governance.[66] For planning agents, means-end coherence of intentions would be an essential element in such psychic unity. So if such psychic unity were psychologically available, a reason for such unity would transmit, in the particular case, to a reason to avoid means-end incoherence. But such unity by itself would not preclude the possibility that certain intentions within that unity are not psychologically modifiable. So this proposed reason for psychic unity would induce a reason for avoiding means-end incoherence even for cases like that of Setiya's smoker. But then, if the Setiya detachment works, we are going to end up with reasons of psychic unity for terrible means to bad ends, when the intention for those ends is psychologically nonmodifiable. What to say?

66. Jeffrey Seidman, in correspondence, has emphasized this possibility.

Well, as they say, one philosopher's *modus ponens* is another's *modus tollens*. A theory along the lines I am sketching will, in this case, favor *modus tollens*. We do not think that, normally, a psychologically nonmodifiable intention in favor of a bad end provides a reason for the terrible means. But we are granting that a version of the Setiya detachment claim has force. So we will want to be skeptical of the conjecture that there is, quite generally, an intrinsic reason for psychic unity independent of the modifiability of the relevant intentions. And, indeed, it does seem plausible that the psychological nonmodifiability of the intention, although it does not block the psychic unity itself, does normally block the reason in favor of such psychic unity.

So even given the Setiya detachment claim, there are two ways in which the psychological nonmodifiability of the end intention—a nonmodifiability needed to make the detachment work—can nevertheless undermine the soundness of the purported reasoning to a conclusion about a reason for intending the means. (A) The psychological nonmodifiability of the end intention normally ensures that relevant self-governance is not attainable. But for the reason for self-governance to transmit to a reason for means-end coherence, in accordance with *Transmission Reasons*, it is required that the relevant self-governance be attainable. So in this case there is not a reason of self-governance for means-end coherence. (B) While we do not say that psychologically nonmodifiable intentions make relevant psychic unity itself unattainable, we do say that there is not in general a reason for psychic unity that involves such nonmodifiable intentions.

In *A* we grant the reason for self-governance generally, but we see the psychological nonmodifiability of a relevant intention as normally blocking the attainability of self-governance and thereby blocking transmission of the reason for self-governance to a reason for means-end coherence. In *B* we see the psychological nonmodifiability of the intention, not as blocking the attainability of psychic unity but rather as normally blocking the reason, in the particular case, for the psychic unity.

Now, in taking this position in *B* we are, in effect, applying Kolodny's skepticism about a reason for psychic tidiness to the idea of a reason for psychic unity quite generally. What Kolodny may miss, however, is the normal relation between psychic unity and governing your life. It is this relation—together with the idea that we do indeed have a reason to govern our own lives—that enables us to avoid a myth theory (as well as cognitivism) while sharing a version of Kolodny's skepticism about a reason for *mere* psychic tidiness. And once we appeal to this reason for self-governance, we can invoke the normal condition on self-governance that the relevant attitudes be psychologically modifiable and thereby block a reason for means-end coherence in the cases of psychologically nonmodifiable intention highlighted by Setiya.

Or, at least we can do this insofar as self-governance requires psychological modifiability of relevant intentions. We now need to consider a challenge to this.

XII. VOLITIONAL NECESSITY AND REASONS OF SELF-GOVERNANCE

Harry Frankfurt argues that certain special kinds of incapacities to modify basic commitments are not only compatible with self-governance; they are essential to self-governance.[67] Frankfurt calls these "volitional necessities." Such volitional necessities involve an incapacity to change a basic commitment right now and a higher-order approval of that incapacity, where that higher-order approval is itself not changeable at will. And in the case of a volitional necessity, the agent is wholehearted about all of this. For example, as Frankfurt sees it human beings almost always have a volitionally necessary commitment to their own physical integrity, and a parent may have a volitionally necessary commitment to promote the interests of his child. Frankfurt sees such cases as paradigms of love: we love our physical integrity, and the parent loves his child. In each case, although the relevant commitments are nonmodifiable, their guidance of the agent's thought and action can constitute self-governance.

If this is right then the idea that psychological nonmodifiability of intention precludes relevant self-governance is in need of qualification. What to say?

Well, I think that in many cases of self-governance the relevant commitments are not, strictly speaking, volitionally necessary. One is not incapable of change. It is just that one is wholehearted about a central commitment and sees no good reason for change. This is rational stability, not incapacity.[68]

Nevertheless, it is plausible that some special cases of self-governance do involve intended ends that are volitionally necessary. Perhaps Frankfurt's case of parental love will be such a case. Such volitional necessity requires, recall, not just an incapacity to change the intended end right now but also an

---

67. See Harry Frankfurt, *Necessity, Volition and Love* (Cambridge: Cambridge University Press, 1999), essays 9, 11, and 14; *The Reasons of Love* (Princeton, NJ: Princeton University Press, 2004), chap. 2; and *Taking Ourselves Seriously and Getting It Right*.
68. I make pretty much this point in "Thoughtful and Reasonable Stability," 88–90.

approval of that incapacity, an approval that itself is not changeable at will—where one is wholehearted about all of this. So the psychological incapacity involved in volitional necessity is distinctive. As Frankfurt says, "It is important to appreciate the difference between the necessities of love and various other deeply entrenched constraints upon the will, which are due to unwelcome and more or less pathological conditions such as compulsions, obsessions, and addictions."[69] In contrast, Setiya's smoker is faced with one of the latter sorts of "constraints upon the will."

Keeping in mind this special nature of volitional necessity, it does seem plausible that in cases of volitional necessity the nonmodifiability of the end intention need not block self-governance. So nonmodifiability of intention, in these special cases, will not block the reason of self-governance cited in *Reason for Means-End Coherence*. So in these cases of Frankfurtian self-governance by way of volitional necessities, Setiya's detachment can go through, and we can detach a reason for necessary means.[70]

Frankfurt says that "love is itself, for the lover, a source of reasons."[71] So perhaps he would call the just-noted reasons for means to what is loved "reasons of love." But that is not the idea I am now sketching. To be sure, the agent's love is, in these cases, essential to the reason for means. But

---

69. Frankfurt, *Taking Ourselves Seriously and Getting It Right*, 43.

70. In Setiya's smoker case, the psychological nonmodifiability of the end intention supports detachment of a reason for means but also blocks the reason of self-governance in the background of the detachment. What we have just noted is that the volitional necessity of the end intention can, in contrast, support the detachment without blocking the self-governance. In this sense, volitional necessities can differentially impact the detachment of a reason for intending means, on the one hand, and, on the other hand, the conditions that block the self-governance that grounds the reason for means-end coherence. This raises the question of whether there are other kinds of necessity that can have such a differential impact.

Consider, in particular, two kinds of necessity highlighted by John Fischer in comments on this essay. There is, first, the idea that intending E is causally determined by antecedent conditions. And there is, second, the idea that there is a Frankfurt-style counterfactual intervener hanging around to ensure that the agent not diverge from a path that includes intending E. (See Harry Frankfurt, "Alternate Possibilities and Moral Responsibility," as reprinted in his *Importance of What We Care About*, 1–10.) Do either of these kinds of necessity have such a differential impact? While a serious discussion of these issues is of course beyond the scope of this essay, it does seem plausible that the necessity involved in causal determination does not have such a differential impact. Such necessity of the end intention seems neither to block the kind of garden-variety self-governance a reason for which is playing a central role in this discussion nor to support the detachment of a reason for intending means. The second case—that of the Frankfurt-style counterfactual intervener—is harder, in part because of difficulties in understanding exactly what is involved in such cases. My tentative conjecture would be that here too there is not the kind of differential impact we have discovered in the case of volitional necessity. But this is not an issue I can pursue here.

71. Frankfurt, *Reasons of Love*, 37.

the basic ground for the reason I am highlighting is not the love itself but rather the reason for governing our own lives, as that reason applies to Frankfurtian cases of self-governance. The love provides a reason for means, but it is the reason for self-governance that grounds this reason for the means. So rather than call these reasons of love, it is more accurate to call them reasons of Frankfurtian self-governance.[72]

Recall *Intentions × Reasons*:

> *Intentions × Reasons*: Intending E does not in general provide a practical, normative reason for necessary means to E and so does not in general provide a practical, normative reason for intending those necessary means.

Will acknowledging such reasons of Frankfurtian self-governance be in tension with the considerations that led us to *Intentions × Reasons*?

Well, we can acknowledge such reasons of Frankfurtian self-governance while still insisting that normally intentions for ends are not volitionally necessary in Frankfurt's sense and so (for Broome-type reasons) do not in general induce (by way of detachment) reasons for means, even given a reason of self-governance for conformity to *Means-End Coherence* in the particular case. Further, if we suppose that the end intention is psychologically nonmodifiable in the way illustrated by Setiya's smoker, we block the background condition for the relevant reason of self-governance in favor of means-end coherence. And finally, in one basic case that led us to *Intentions × Reasons*—the case of weak-willed intention—the possibility that the weak-willed intention for the end is volitionally necessary is blocked by the wholeheartedness condition on volitional necessity since weakness of will precludes wholeheartedness.

This brings us, however, to the hard case. Suppose someone has a volitionally necessary commitment to a bad end—the personal destruction of a good and successful leader, say. This commitment is not modifiable, the person approves of this, this approval is not modifiable, and the person is

---

72. I do not say that there are no Frankfurtian reasons of love. These would be internal reasons grounded, at bottom, in the agent's love for something. Just when there are such reasons is a question for normative reflection. And such reflection might lead us to the view (one Frankfurt himself does not embrace) that love is the ground of a practical reason only if what is loved is not a bad thing. (See my "Thoughtful and Reasonable Stability," 81–4. Susan Wolf discusses related but somewhat different matters in "The True, the Good, and the Lovable: Frankfurt's Avoidance of Objectivity," in *Contours of Agency: Essays on Themes from Harry Frankfurt*, eds. Sarah Buss and Lee Overton [Cambridge, MA: MIT Press, 2002], 227–44.) But the reason for means I am here highlighting is not, at bottom, grounded in the agent's love but, rather, in the reason for self-governance, as that reason applies to cases of Frankfurtian love.

wholehearted about all of this. This is not compulsion; it is volitional necessity. Call this person Iago.

Is Iago capable of relevant self-governance? Well, his commitment is volitionally necessary, but we have granted that this special kind of incapacity need not block, and may help constitute, self-governance. But Iago's end is bad. Yes, but I take it that you can be self-governing in the pursuit of bad ends, just as a society can govern itself by way of a legal system that aims at bad things. So if there is in general a reason to govern our own lives, and if the Setiya inference is valid, then in this special kind of case the volitionally necessary bad end does induce a reason of Frankfurtian self-governance for the necessary means.

This reason for the means is not grounded in Iago's love: it is grounded in the reason for self-governance, taken together with Iago's volitionally necessary love. When we endorse this reason of self-governance, we do not thereby endorse what Iago loves; what we endorse is, rather, the justifying role of self-governance.[73] And we can still insist that in such cases this reason of self-governance can be overridden by other reasons.

Still, we have arrived at the somewhat unsettling conclusion that Iago may have a normative reason, grounded in the reason for self-governance, to pursue his terrible means. This has always been the risk of appealing to a reason for governing our own lives. The risk is that this reason will induce a reason for means to bad ends that are wholeheartedly embraced by a self-governing agent. We have significantly reduced this risk, in part by agreeing with Broome's rejection of factual detachment of a reason, in part by blocking much of the impact of the Setiya detachment claim by noting a background condition of the reason of self-governance for means-end coherence. But Frankfurt's reflections on the relations between volitional necessities and self-governance indicate that a risk remains that the reason for self-governance will, in cases of volitional necessity, induce reasons of Frankfurtian self-governance for actions we otherwise condemn. We might try to avoid this risk by building the goodness of the ends into the very idea of self-governance or by saying that volitional necessity blocks self-governance or by rejecting the Setiya detachment claim or by retreating to a myth theory or to cognitivism about the relevant rationality norms. However, although I have not argued conclusively against all of these

---

73. Gibbard writes, "Caligula, imagine, aims solely to maximize the suffering of others. That is a horrendous life policy, but it needn't be formally inconsistent. We decent people might recognize such a policy as consistent, but still disagree with it; we are coherent to do so" ("Morality as Consistency in Living," 145). I agree. If Caligula's aim is volitionally necessary, we may need to grant that he has an overridable reason of self-governance in favor of means. But this is not to endorse his "horrendous life policy."

alternatives, each does seem to me either philosophically risky or philosophically costly or both.

A final possibility would be to reassess the purportedly general reason to govern our own lives.[74] When we considered (in sec. XI) a purportedly general reason for psychic unity, I argued that we should resist overgenerality. So why not make a similar move here? Why not say that while volitionally necessary bad ends do not block self-governance itself, the reason for self-governance is blocked by such volitionally necessary bad ends? Indeed, why not say this precisely because, if we do not say this, we will be led to say that Iago has a reason of self-governance in favor of his terrible means? Why not, yet again, favor *modus tollens*?

This would still involve the idea that there is normally a distinctive, noninstrumental reason of self-governance for means-end coherence. But the further idea would be that this reason of self-governance for means-end coherence is blocked in the special case of volitionally necessary bad ends. This reason is blocked not because such volitionally necessary bad ends block self-governance; indeed, we are supposing that they need not block self-governance. The idea, rather, is that there is no intrinsic reason for self-governance that involves volitionally necessary bad ends.

The problem is that the idea that agents—at least, those agents who care intrinsically about governing their own lives—have quite generally a reason to govern their own lives, even given volitionally necessary bad ends, seems extremely plausible. So it seems much harder to insist that this reason does not apply when the self-governance involves volitionally necessary bad ends—much harder, that is, than it was to reject an overly general reason for mere psychic unity. Still, I do not see a way to settle this issue within the constraints of the current discussion. So let me just acknowledge that the conclusion that Iago has a reason of self-governance in favor of his terrible means depends on rejecting this, so to speak, *modus tollens* strategy in the case of the reason for self-governance: it depends on rejecting the claim that volitionally necessary bad ends quite generally block the reason for relevant self-governance even though they do not block the self-governance itself. I myself find it more plausible instead to conclude that Iago does indeed have a reason for the means. But at the least we now have a clearer understanding of the philosophical price of resisting that conclusion.[75]

74. A strategy suggested by Jeffrey Seidman (in correspondence) and by Kieran Setiya (in his comments at the UNC Colloquium).

75. I myself once tried to resist this conclusion, without paying the price, in "Thoughtful and Reasonable Stability," 83–4.

CHAPTER 5
Agency, Time, and Sociality

1.

There are many different kinds of agents, including spiders, dogs, and gorillas. In the philosophy of action, we are interested in agency quite generally; but we are also interested in the important features of, in particular, human agency.

If we begin by focusing on agency quite generally, I think we will be led, as a first step, to an idea that Harry Frankfurt, drawing on work of Ernest Nagel, once proposed.[1] Agency involves behavior that is under the control of a guidance mechanism; one that has the power to track a certain end and adjust the behavior in the light of that end; and one whose operation constitutes the activity of the agent, not merely of a subsystem. The last clause is delicate, and raises issues of circularity; but it is needed to distinguish the activity of the agent from the activity of the agent's stomach in digestion. But the point now is that these ideas about agency remain broadly generic.

When we turn specifically to human agency it is tempting to appeal to the central role of Reason. But I want to begin by highlighting two other important aspects of human agency, though I will return later to Reason.

The first concerns ways in which action is related to time. It might be that an agent persists over time and acts in the present in ways that influence the

1. Harry Frankfurt, "The Problem of Action," as reprinted in his *The Importance of What We Care About* (Cambridge: Cambridge University Press, 1988), 69–79. Frankfurt refers to Ernest Nagel, "Goal-Directed Processes in Biology," *Journal of Philosophy* 74 (1977).

future and are to some extent shaped by the past, and yet these actions do not involve that agent's own grasp of the larger temporal arc of his activity and the guidance of his activity by that grasp. The actions are goal-directed, but nevertheless primarily a reaction to present conditions. In contrast, in many cases of human agency the agent's present activity involves her grasp of how it is embedded in what she has earlier been doing and what she is on her way to doing.[2] Her grasp of the larger temporal arc of her activity is a central element in her guidance of that activity both at that time and over time. And this grasp is central to our understanding of her activity.

Think about writing an essay. If we were gods perhaps we could just will "let there be the essay!" and then, there it is. But, of course, our agency is not like that. For us writing an essay takes time, and it is crucial—both to the agent's guidance of the activity and to our understanding of that activity—that at various stages along the way the agent herself understand and guide her activity then in part by way of her understanding of and commitment to its relation to earlier and, if all goes well, later activities. Call this *temporally extended* agency. One striking feature of human agency as we know it is that it is quite frequently temporally extended.

Consider now ways in which an agent's actions are related to the actions of other agents. Agents will frequently act in a context that includes other agents in the vicinity, where each agent is aware of what the others are doing. In such contexts the actions of each of the agents might be mutually responsive: each adjusts to the actions of the others who are adjusting to each. And this might be out in the open, public. This is what happens, for example, when strangers in a crowd manage to walk together down the street without bumping into each other. In contrast—and as Margaret Gilbert has emphasized—sometimes agents walk together in an importantly stronger sense.[3] They each see their own activity as embedded in what *they* are doing together, and this understanding of their individual activity as embedded in their shared activity is a central element both in their guidance of that activity and in their and our understanding of what they are doing. Call this *shared intentional* activity. One striking feature of human agency as we know it is that it is many times a part of such shared intentional activities.

These reflections support the thought that among the important practical capacities involved in human agency are capacities both for temporally

---

2. For a similar contrast see Luca Ferrero, "What Good Is a Diachronic Will?," *Philosophical Studies* 144 (2009): 403–30.

3. Margaret Gilbert, "Walking Together: A Paradigmatic Social Phenomenon," *Midwest Studies* 15 (1990): 1–14.

extended and for shared intentional activity. A human life that did not significantly involve these capacities would be impoverished and difficult to understand. But what are these capacities, and how are they related to other important features of human agency?

In temporally extended agency, past, present, and (normally) future thought and action are tied together in distinctive ways. In shared intentional activity, the thoughts and actions of the participants are tied together in distinctive ways. We need to understand what these ties are, and what they tell us about mind and human agency.

In each case our concerns are conceptual, metaphysical, and normative. We seek conceptual resources that help us cut up these phenomena at their joints. We want to understand what there is in the world that constitutes these forms of agency. And we need to understand central normative elements.

I can now state a conjecture: a fundamental ground of these human capacities for temporally extended and shared intentional agency are human capacities for planning agency.[4] In saying that these planning capacities are a fundamental ground, I mean that the proper exercise of these planning capacities, given relevant contents of the plans, relevant contexts, and relevant interrelations with past, future, and others, will realize phenomena of temporally extended and/or shared intentional activity.[5] In this sense the conceptual, metaphysical, and normative resources in play in our planning agency provide a backbone of our temporally extended and shared intentional agency.

In saying this I do not mean directly to address larger, institutional forms of shared agency, such as, perhaps, law or democracy. My target is small-scale shared intentionality, in the absence of institutional authority relations. It is a further question how such small-scale and larger-scale cases are related.[6] I also do not mean to claim that the exercise of planning capacities is the only possible form of temporally extended or shared intentional activity. My conjecture concerns important forms of temporally extended and small-scale shared intentional activity, without being a claim to uniqueness. Nevertheless, this conjecture helps us answer basic questions

---

4. I offer a framework for thinking about our planning agency in my *Intention, Plans, and Practical Reason* (Cambridge, MA: Harvard University Press, 1987; reissued by CSLI Publications, 1999).

5. Note though that the effective exercise of planning capacities also involves a range of other capacities that are not essentially tied to planning, e.g., various perceptual and conceptual capacities, capacities for directing attention, and capacities for motor control.

6. For a systematic investigation into a possible extension to the case of law, see Scott Shapiro, *Legality* (Cambridge, MA: Harvard University Press, 2011).

about these phenomena and, as we will see, has implications about practical rationality and self-governance.

Before proceeding, a *caveat*. I will be discussing large matters, and I cannot hope in one lecture to argue conclusively for my approach, or to do justice to the many other efforts in the literature. But perhaps I can give you a sense of why it might be philosophically fruitful to see our planning agency as fundamental in these ways.

2.

Planning agency, as I see it, is a distinctive kind of goal-directed agency, one that involves attitudes of intention, many of which are future-directed. These intentions settle relevant practical matters and are normally embedded in larger plans. These larger plans normally have a hierarchical, end-means structure; and these plans will typically be partial in the sense that they do not yet specify all the steps needed for each intended end.

Intentions are plan states. Though they are subject to revision, these plan states nevertheless have a characteristic stability over time. And these plan states normally adjust in the direction of intention-belief consistency and means-end coherence of plans at a time. They are responsive to pressures for consistency of the many different things one intends with each other and with what one believes; and they are responsive to pressures to fill in hierarchically structured partial plans as needed with specifications of means and the like. These tendencies toward diachronic stability and synchronic consistency and coherence correspond to associated norms, ones whose at least implicit acceptance is at work in the psychic functioning of a planning agent. These norms have a claim to be norms of practical rationality, though this is not fully to answer the question—one to which I turn below—why it matters whether we conform to these norms.

Given the rational pressure to fill in partial plans to avoid means-end incoherence, prior plan states tend to pose problems for further deliberation, problems of means and the like. Given my intended end of writing the essay, for example, I am faced with a problem about how to do this. And given the rational pressure for consistency, these plan states tend to filter out from practical reasoning options intending which would not be consistent with one's other intentions and beliefs. Given that I already plan to teach my seminar on Tuesdays, for example, my plan for writing my essay is under rational pressure to be compatible with that—though I might, of course, instead change my seminar. And when the time for action is recognized to have arrived, these plan states tend to guide and control relevant conduct.

These roles and associated norms help distinguish intentions from ordinary desires and beliefs. Roughly, and partially: Ordinary desires are not subject to the same rational pressures for consistency. Desiring things that are not by our lights co-possible is all too human. And a belief that one will be doing something later—in contrast with an intention to do it—need not require that one settle on means to doing it; just think of your prediction that you are about to trip.

If all goes well, planning structures induce cross-temporal referential connections that are both forward and backward looking. My present plan to go to Boston next week at least implicitly refers to my later, then-present-directed intention to go by getting on the airplane; and my later intention at least implicitly refers back to my earlier intention. Further, the normal stability of such intentions over time helps support a coordinated flow of activity over time. These cross-temporal constancies and referential connections help support a temporally extended structure of partial plans that can provide a background framework for further deliberation aimed at filling in these plans as need be and as time goes by. And this further deliberation is shaped in part by rational pressures in the direction of means-end coherence and intention-belief consistency. In these ways, a planning agent's purposive activity over time is typically embedded within interwoven structures of partial, referentially interlocking, hierarchical, and more or less stable plan states, and in modes of further deliberation and planning that are motivated and framed by these plan states.

This idea of cross-temporally stable and referentially interlocking attitudes is familiar from the Lockean tradition of reflection on personal identity over time.[7] A central idea of that tradition has been that such identity over time—or, anyway, as Derek Parfit avers, "what matters" in such identity[8]—essentially involves overlapping strands of continuities of attitude and broadly referential connections across attitudes. And what we have seen is that the standard functioning in planning agency of attitudes of intending involves such Lockean cross-temporal ties. I'll return to this point below.

We now need to say more about stability.

Begin by noting three initial forms of support for stability of intention over time.[9] First, acting on an intention normally changes the world, and these changes may make it increasingly sensible to continue to act on that intention. There can be such a snowball effect because in acting on

---

7. John Locke, *An Essay Concerning Human Understanding*. Bk. 2, chap. 27.
8. Derek Parfit, *Reasons and Persons* (Oxford: Oxford University Press, 1984), at 217.
9. I discuss the following trio of ideas in *Intention, Plans, and Practical Reason*.

an intention one gets closer to its target and further from the target of a competing plan. But there can also be a social snowball effect. Once it is public that one has certain intentions, there may be—given the importance of predictability in our social interactions—distinctive social costs in later abandoning those prior intentions.

Second, reconsidering a prior intention takes time, uses various mental resources, and may require re-thinking other courses of action on which one had earlier settled as part of a package that includes the intention being reconsidered. So there is frequently reason not to reconsider, both because of the costs of reconsideration and because of risks of undermining coordination previously forged. And in the absence of reconsideration, a prior intention will tend to persist.

Third, given our limited mental resources,[10] we frequently depend on general—and typically non-deliberative—habits and strategies about when to reconsider. And it seems that general habits and strategies that to some extent favor non-reconsideration would tend to be conducive to the overall effectiveness of our resource-limited agency.

So there is this initial three-pronged support for the stability of the intentions of planning agents like us. I will argue below that there is also a further, diachronic constraint at work here. The idea will be that one's prior intentions rationally have a default status in later practical thinking, a status that goes beyond the cited three-pronged support for stability. For now, however, we have said enough about planning agency to see in outline how the rational functioning of planning structures will normally realize a strong form of temporally extended agency.

3.

The capacity for temporally extended agency is the capacity to guide one's activities in light of one's grasp of their location in a larger, temporally extended structure of what one has been doing and what one is on one's way to doing. In temporally extended agency, one's grasp of the location of present activity in a larger temporally extended structure to which one is committed, and one's grasp of the relation between one's temporally extended activities and their temporal sub-elements, is an essential element

10. See Herbert Simon, *Reason in Human Affairs* (Stanford, CA: Stanford University Press, 1983). For an application of these ideas to issues in artificial intelligence see M. Bratman, D. Israel, and M. Pollack, "Plans and Resource-Bounded Practical Reasoning," *Computational Intelligence* 4 (1988): 349–55.

in the explanation and understanding of what one is doing. And the important point now is that the psychic economy of a planning agent will realize this capacity for temporally extended agency. The interwoven, interlocking, and more or less stable structures of partial and hierarchical plan states will normally guide present activity as an element in larger activities favored by these plan states, and it will normally involve an explanatorily relevant grasp of salient relations between temporally larger activities and their temporal sub-parts. Actions that are guided by such plan states will include actions that the agent grasps as embedded in larger planned activities, as well as actions with salient temporal sub-parts; and this plan-shaped understanding and guidance will be an essential part of the explanation of those actions. And these explanatorily relevant, relatively stable plan states will involve referential connections to relevant earlier plans and, if all goes well, later plans and actions. Following through with prior plans is in these ways fundamentally different from following through with a golf swing.

So this planning psychology is a realization of the capacity for temporally extended agency. And this will come as no surprise. When we reflect on why we bother with planning—why we do not just cross our bridges when we come to them—the commonsense answer will appeal to the way in which it supports the cross-temporal organization of our agency. What we have briefly explored is the deep structure of this way in which the human mind supports the cross-temporal organization of human activity.

Turn now to shared intentional activity.

4.

When I noted Gilbert's example of walking together, I drew a contrast with a case of publicly interdependent intentional activities of each, as when you and a stranger walk down the street without colliding. But there is also a second contrast we need to draw, this time with a case in which you and I exchange promises that we will each walk with the other, thereby incurring mutual obligations to perform. Such exchanges, and their associated obligations, are not sufficient for shared intentional activity: just think of a case in which each promises insincerely and has no intention in favor of a shared walking. Nor are such promises necessary, as Hume observed about those who row the boat together "tho' they have never given promises to each other."[11]

11. David Hume, *A Treatise of Human Nature*, ed. L. A. Selby-Bigge (Oxford: Oxford University Press), 490.

What we want is a model of shared intentional activity that threads a path between walking with strangers and a web of promissory obligations. And here I propose to appeal again to our planning agency.

We begin with planning agents. We give their plan states contents of a sort that are characteristic of shared intentional activity. We locate these agents in a context in which their relevant plan states are appropriately interrelated. And we describe central ways in which these intentions of each interdependently work their way through to joint action. We try thereby to provide a plan-theoretic construction that is sufficiently rich to be a realization of shared intentional activity. And we can then go on to ask when and in what ways these plan-theoretic interrelations, and their normal etiologies and upshots, induce associated obligations.

Let me sketch how I would proceed with such a plan-theoretic construction.

5.

Suppose that you and I are going to San Francisco together, and that this is a shared intentional activity. What plan-theoretic construction can realize what is essential here?[12]

We need, as the basic step, five ideas. First, we need the idea that each of us intends not just to go *to* San Francisco, but *that we* go to San Francisco.[13] Second, we need the idea that each intends that we go to San Francisco in part *by way of* the *other* person's intention that we go. Third, we need the idea that we each intend that we go to San Francisco by way of sub-plans of each of us that *mesh* in the sense of being co-compatible. Fourth, we need the idea of *interdependence* in the persistence of these intentions of each. And fifth, we need the idea that these intentions of each lead to our going to San Francisco by way of *mutual responsiveness* of each to each, mutual responsiveness that tracks the intended joint activity.

In short, we need the ideas of each intending that we go, of each intending that we go in part by way of the other's corresponding intention, of each intending that we go by way of meshing sub-plans, of interdependence

---

12. The answer that follows is drawn from my quartet of essays on this subject in my *Faces of Intention* (Cambridge: Cambridge University Press, 1999); my "Shared Agency" [in *Philosophy of the Social Sciences: Philosophical Theory and Scientific Practice*, ed. Chris Mantzavinos (Cambridge: Cambridge University Press, 2009), 41–59]; and my "Modest Sociality and the Distinctiveness of Intention," *Philosophical Studies* 144 (2009): 149–65.

13. My initial thinking about this idea was aided by comments from Philip Cohen.

in persistence, and of relevant mutual responsiveness. I proceed to reflect briefly on this quintet.

First: I intend *that we* go to San Francisco, and so do you. It is not just that I intend to go while expecting you to go. But must this appeal within the content of my intention to *our* activity involve the very idea of our shared intentional activity? No, it need not. The concept of our activity, as it is involved in the content of my intention, can be a weak concept that includes cases like that of strangers walking together down the street without colliding. We then depend on the appropriate explanatory role of relevant, interdependent intentions to distinguish between such a weak form of acting together and shared intentional activity.

But can I really *intend* our activity? Isn't what I can intend limited to my own actions? Well, if we use the infinitive construction—intend to—then we are limiting what is intended in this way. But we also have the idea of intending *that*. And I can, normally, intend that *p* if I believe that whether or not *p* will depend on whether or not I so intend.

But we are supposing that *each* of us intends that we go to San Francisco. How can *both* of us sensibly think that whether *we* go is dependent on *his* own intention? The answer appeals to our fourth idea: interdependence in persistence. Each can think that our going depends on his own intention in part by way of the support that intention provides for the persistence of the other person's intention that we go, where our going also depends on that intention of the other person.[14]

This brings us to the second idea, that each intends that we go to San Francisco in part *by way of the intention of the other*. There is, within the content of the intention of each, reference to the role of the intention of the other. This contrasts with a case in which each intends that we go to San Francisco by way of throwing the other into the trunk of his car. The intentions characteristic of shared intentional activity, unlike such "mafia" intentions, referentially interlock with each other. The intentions of each refer to each other in ways that parallel the semantic interconnections over time of the intentions of an individual planning agent.

Third—and again in contrast with the mafia case—each intends that there be the cited *mesh in sub-plans*. This does not mean that there is yet such a mesh, only that each has a plan-like commitment to there being such mesh, where achieving that mesh may require relevant bargaining or shared deliberation. And such interlocking intentions in favor of mesh

---

14. In these last two paragraphs I am responding to challenges posed by, among others, Annette Baier, Frederick Stoutland, and David Velleman. For references and further discussion, see my "I Intend that We J" in my *Faces of Intention*, 142–61.

in sub-plans can motivate and frame such further bargaining or shared deliberation.

These second and third ideas appeal to interrelations between the intentions of each that are built into the contents of those intentions. In contrast, the final two ideas—interdependence in persistence, and mutual responsiveness that tracks the intended joint activity—primarily concern not the contents of these intentions but ways in which these intentions interact in their functioning. Note, though, that the interaction in functioning involved in mutual responsiveness will be in part explained by the contents of the intentions of each. It is because I intend that we go in part by way of your intention that we go, that I will adjust my relevant activity so as to help support the efficacy of your intention. And, as we have seen, interdependence in persistence helps support the very coherence of each intending the joint activity.

There is more to say. In particular, I would want to add that this structure of interrelated intentions is out in the open: that is why the participants can engage together in reasoning that uses the premise that *they* intend so to act together. But here let me just highlight the initial quintet of ideas. A basic conjecture is that these interdependent and interlocking intentions of each will, in responding to the rational pressures involved in individual planning agency, function together in ways that, if all goes well, constitute shared intentional activity.

In partial support of this conjecture recall that if you and I are involved in such an interpersonal planning structure, I do not just intend to do my part while expecting you to do yours, as I might intend to walk to my left knowing that the stranger is walking to my right. Rather, I intend that we act in part by way of your analogous intention and meshing sub-plans of our intentions; and intending is not merely expecting. This means that the rational pressure on me to make my plans means-end coherent and consistent—pressure built into individual planning agency—ensures rational pressure on me to mesh with and, as needed, support *your* relevant plans. And vice versa. This will frequently involve rational pressure on each of us to help the other, if such help is needed. In this way, rational pressures on the *individual* planning agents—given suitable contents of, and interrelations between their plans—induce rational pressures in favor of forms of *social* coherence and consistency that are characteristic of shared intentional activity. These pressures of social rationality depend on the presence of relevant intentions of each participant, intentions whose continued persistence is supported, though not ensured, by pressures for stability. And there will be these normative pressures even when—as is common—each participates in the shared activity for different reasons.

Suppose that we can in this way articulate a plan-theoretic construction that realizes an important form of shared intentional activity. Such a construction would bring to bear conceptual resources drawn broadly from the domain of individual planning agency[15] and argue that these conceptual resources are adequate to the task of theorizing about small-scale shared intentionality. It would aim to see the metaphysics of shared intentional activity as a construct of metaphysical resources already in play in the case of individual planning agency. And it would aim to see basic normative pressures characteristic of shared intentionality as rooted in normative pressures central to individual planning agency.

This plan-theoretic construction uses as its basic building block intentions of the sort that are central to individual planning agency, though intentions that have distinctive contents and interrelations. This contrasts with a view like that of John Searle, according to which the kind of intention of individuals that is needed for shared intentionality is not ordinary intention with a special content, but a fundamentally different attitude: a so-called we-intention.[16] The plan-theoretic construction to which I am alluding can draw directly from what our theory of individual planning agency tells us about the nature of intending, while also bringing to bear appeals to special contents, contexts, and interrelations. And that is what I have been doing. But if we see the building blocks of shared intentionality not as ordinary attitudes of intending with special contents, but rather as distinctive attitudes of we-intending, then we cannot do this.

Another contrast returns us to mutual obligation. Our plan-theoretic construction ensures that rational pressures for social coherence and consistency apply to shared intentional activity. But it does not say that it is essential that the parties have distinctive obligations of performance *to* each other, obligations grounded in the specific shared activity.[17] Nevertheless, we can expect such obligations to be common given that there will frequently be, in shared intentional activity, forms of assurance, intentional creation of expectation, or (as Facundo Alonso has emphasized[18]) intentionally reinforced reliance that ground moral obligations. And when the

15. Though questions remain about the idea of being out in the open.
16. John R. Searle, "Collective Intentions and Actions." In *Intentions in Communication*, eds. Philip R. Cohen, Jerry Morgan, and Martha E. Pollack (Cambridge, MA: MIT Press, 1990), 401–15.
17. Here I am disagreeing with Margaret Gilbert. See Margaret Gilbert, "Shared Intention and Personal Intentions," *Philosophical Studies* 144 (2009): 167–87.
18. Facundo Alonso, "Shared Intention, Reliance, and Interpersonal Obligations," *Ethics* 119 (2009): 444–75.

parties are guided by their recognition of those obligations there will be a corresponding increase in the stability of the sharing.

This plan-theoretic proposal highlights conceptual, metaphysical, and normative continuities between the individual and the shared case, continuities that depend on a rich model of individual planning agency. Both Searle and Gilbert take a different tack. They each see the step from individual to shared agency as involving a basic new metaphysical resource. In Searle's view what is needed is a new attitude of we-intention. In Gilbert's view what is needed is a new relation of "joint commitment" between the participants, a relation that necessitates mutual obligations.[19] And both philosophers try to understand larger institutions in large part in terms of the new element that they cite as central to small-scale shared agency.[20] In contrast, my plan-theoretic approach begins by distinguishing, in the individual case, between simple goal-directed agency and planning agency. Once individual planning agency is on board, the step to small-scale sociality need not involve a fundamental discontinuity—which is not to say that all planning agents have the capacity for shared intentional activity.[21] But this planning approach leaves it open how best to move from small-scale shared intentional activity to larger institutions.

6.

We have been exploring ways in which the human mind supports the cross-temporal and social organization of human activity. The basic idea is that our capacity for these forms of organization is grounded in our capacity for planning agency. And we have explored the conceptual, metaphysical, and normative structures that underlie this grounding relation.

Central to this story are rationality constraints on individual planning agency. I have highlighted synchronic constraints of intention-belief consistency and means-end coherence; and I have also alluded to a diachronic constraint that sees one's prior intentions as a rational default. But I have

19. Margaret Gilbert, "Shared Intention and Personal Intentions."
20. John R. Searle. *The Construction of Social Reality* (New York: The Free Press, 1995). Margaret Gilbert, *A Theory of Political Obligation* (Oxford: Oxford University Press, 2006).
21. Indeed, a central conjecture of Michael Tomasello's is that the great apes are planning agents who nevertheless do not have a capacity for shared intentional activity. See Michael Tomasello, *Why We Cooperate* (Cambridge, MA: MIT Press, 2009).

so far not directly addressed the question why it matters whether we conform to these constraints.[22]

Begin with the synchronic norms of consistency and coherence of intention. Some—for example, J. David Velleman and Kieran Setiya, following a path explored earlier by Gilbert Harman—propose that these norms are, at bottom, theoretical norms of consistency and coherence of belief.[23] This is because, or so it is claimed, to intend to A is, at least in part, to believe you will A—where this is seen by Velleman and Setiya as part of an explanation of the purportedly non-inferential self-knowledge said to be involved in our intentional agency.[24] On this view, inconsistent intentions bring with them inconsistent beliefs; and a structure of intentions that fails to include intentions to perform known necessary means will involve a structure of beliefs that is incoherent in the sense that certain beliefs remain explanatory danglers. It matters that we conform to these synchronic norms on intention just because and insofar as it matters that our beliefs conform to theoretical norms of consistency and coherence. Call this *cognitivism* about these norms of intention rationality.[25]

I am skeptical about such cognitivism. One reason for my skepticism is that even if we were to agree, for the sake of argument, that intending to A involves believing one will A,[26] it would remain possible to believe one intends a necessary means even though one does not in fact intend that means. In such a case one's beliefs may be consistent and coherent, and yet one's intentions may, in failing to include relevant necessary means, be means-end *in*coherent. So theoretical coherence of belief does not ensure means-end coherence of intention.[27]

22. For this way of putting the question see Garrett Cullity, "Decisions, Reasons, and Rationality," *Ethics* 119 (2008): 57–95, at 82.

23. J. David Velleman, "What Good Is a Will?" In *Action in Context*, ed. Anton Leist (Berlin: de Gruyter/Mouton, 2007), 193–215; Kieran Setiya, "Cognitivism about Instrumental Reason," *Ethics* 117 (2007): 649–73; Gilbert Harman, "Practical Reasoning," *Review of Metaphysics* 29 (1976): 431–63.

24. A classic source of this conjecture about self-knowledge is G. E. M. Anscombe, *Intention* (Ithaca, NY: Cornell University Press, 1963). For an importantly different approach to our knowledge of our own agency, see Sarah K. Paul, "How We Know What We're Doing," *Philosophers' Imprint* 9 (11) (2009).

25. For this label see my "Cognitivism about Practical Reason," as reprinted in my *Faces of Intention*, 250–64.

26. I challenge this assumption in *Intention, Plans, and Practical Reason*, 37–8.

27. I first sketched this argument in my "Intention and Means-End Reasoning," *The Philosophical Review* 90 (1981): 252–65, at note 4. I develop it further in my "Intention, Belief, Practical, Theoretical," in *Spheres of Reason: New Essays on the Philosophy of Normativity*, ed. Simon Robertson (Oxford: Oxford University Press, 2009), 29–61 [this volume, essay 2].

In contrast with such a cognitivism, I think we should see these norms of intention rationality as norms of practical rationality that need not piggyback on analogous theoretical norms on belief. At bottom is the thought that it is the complex of *practical* roles of intentions that lies behind these norms.

How might we appeal to these practical roles to explain why it matters whether we conform to these practical norms? Well, in the particular case conformity to these norms will frequently make it more likely that one will not trip over oneself and will achieve one's particular ends. Further, it seems plausible—especially given our limited mental resources—that a general disposition of responsiveness to these norms will tend to support the effective pursuit of one's ends. And insofar as planning agency is deeply involved in forms of agency that we appropriately value—for example, forms of sociality and, as we will see, our self-governance—there will be reason for a general disposition to conform to these norms insofar as such a disposition is part and parcel of being a planning agent.

So far so good. But there is an important further idea that we need to examine. This is the idea that in the particular case there is a non-instrumental practical reason to conform to these practical norms, a reason that is distinctive in the sense that it is not merely a matter of the reasons for the agent's particular ends in that case.[28] That there are reasons for general dispositions to conform does not in general get us to such a reason in the particular case; that is a lesson we learn from J. J. C. Smart's reflections on rule worship.[29] And the reasons that have been cited so far for conformity in the particular case derive from the specific reasons for the agent's specific ends.

It is here that Joseph Raz and Niko Kolodny, following a path sketched earlier by Hugh McCann, have argued that this idea of a distinctive practical reason in the particular case for conformity to these norms is a "myth."[30] Without trying to address the details of their arguments, let me describe a theoretical alternative, one that defends the thought that there is, barring special circumstances, such a distinctive reason in the particular case. To do this I need to return to the idea that our capacity for planning agency is

28. A defensible version of this idea would be a partial response to John Broome's query in his "Is Rationality Normative?" *Disputatio* vol. II, no. 3 (2007).
29. J. J. C. Smart, "Extreme and Restricted Utilitarianism." In *Theories of Ethics*, ed. Philippa Foot (Oxford: Oxford University Press, 1967), 171–83.
30. Joseph Raz," The Myth of Instrumental Rationality," *Journal of Ethics and Social Philosophy* 1, no. 1 (2005); Nico Kolodny. "The Myth of Practical Consistency," *European Journal of Philosophy* (2008): 366–402; Hugh McCann, "Settled Objectives and Rational Constraints," *American Philosophical Quarterly* 28 (1991): 25–36.

a ground for other basic practical capacities. Earlier I focused on capacities for temporally extended and shared intentional activity. I now want to consider, as anticipated, our capacity for self-governance—though this will also lead us back to the temporal extension of our agency.

7.

R. E. Hobart tells the story of the coming of the railroad to a nineteenth-century village unfamiliar with locomotive engines.[31] The villagers listened patiently to an explanation of how the engine works, but then asked: "but there is a horse inside, isn't there?" Now, we are too sophisticated to think there is a horse in the machine; but when we turn to self-governance we can still be tempted by the image of a little person inside who weighs considerations and moves the levers of action. But that would be a mistake. Instead, we should see self-governance as a distinctive kind of nonhomuncular psychological functioning. What kind? Well, we can suppose that an agent has a practical standpoint, one that consists of attitudes that constitute her stance with respect to relevant practical issues and in that sense speak for her.[32] And when that practical standpoint appropriately guides, the agent governs. In contrast, there can be activities—certain kinds of weakness of will, for example—that, while intentional, are not relevantly guided by this practical standpoint.

But what can constitute an agent's practical standpoint?

One idea is to appeal to the agent's judgments about value or reasons. But this Platonic idea—an idea in the spirit of work of Gary Watson[33]— faces a trio of related challenges. First, sometimes such judgments do not seem to be part of the agent's relevant standpoint. A plausible example, highlighted by Nomy Arpaly and Timothy Schroeder, is Huck Finn's judgment that it would be best to return the runaway slave Jim.[34]

Second, there seem to be practical commitments that are part of the agent's standpoint but are not themselves judgments about value or reasons. Think of cases of love of the sort that have been highlighted

31. R. E. Hobart. "Free Will as Involving Determination and Inconceivable Without It," *Mind* 93 (1934): 1–27.

32. See Harry Frankfurt's reflections on "where (if anywhere) the person himself stands" in his "Identification and Wholeheartedness," as reprinted in his *The Importance of What We Care About* (Cambridge: Cambridge University Press, 1988), 159–76, at 166.

33. See esp. Gary Watson, "Free Agency," *Journal of Philosophy* 72 (1975), 205–20.

34. Nomy Arpaly and Timothy Schroeder. "Praise, Blame and the Whole Self," *Philosophical Studies* 93 (1999): 161–88.

by Harry Frankfurt.[35] A parent's love for his children may, according to Frankfurt, not be itself a judgment about reasons or value, though it may ground a judgment about reasons and, I would add, be constrained by some such judgments.

Third, we commonly see the need for choice among ends that we take to be equal or incomparable in value,[36] or think we simply do not know which is better. We see our choice as underdetermined by our prior judgments of reasons and value. A classic example is Sartre's case of the boy who must choose between the Free French and staying with his ill mother.[37] Once the boy settles on one of these ways of life, he has a commitment that is central to his practical standpoint but that goes beyond his judgments of reasons and value that do not themselves depend on that commitment.

So we cannot characterize the agent's standpoint simply by appeal to her judgments about value or reasons. What we need to appeal to are attitudes that can anchor deliberation but that need not involve value judgment in ways that would re-introduce this trio of problems. And I think a basic step here is to embed this potential role in deliberation in a wider role of knitting together the agent's practical thought (including deliberation and practical reasoning) and action both at a time and over time, thereby helping to constitute the agent for whom these attitudes would thereby speak. We appeal, in particular, to the role of knitting together thought and action by way of the kinds of Lockean continuities and connections highlighted earlier.[38] Tying practical thought and action together in these Lockean ways need not be—to use an expression from David Velleman—"the role of the agent"[39]: it need not be what the agent herself does. What it needs to do is help constitute the agent over time, the agent for whom these attitudes thereby speak. The thought, then, is that it is primarily in playing this broadly Lockean role in organizing practical thought and action over time, in the absence of relevant conflict with other such attitudes, that an attitude gets a prima facie

35. Harry G. Frankfurt. *Taking Ourselves Seriously and Getting It Right* (Stanford, CA: Stanford University Press, 2006).

36. Or, if this is a further possibility, "on a par" in the sense of Ruth Chang, "The Possibility of Parity," *Ethics* 112 (2002): 659–88.

37. Jean-Paul Sartre. "Existentialism Is a Humanism." In *Existentialism from Dostoevsky to Sartre*, ed. W. Kaufmann, rev. and expanded (New York: Meridian/Penguin, 1975), 345–69, at 354–56.

38. See my "Reflection, Planning, and Temporally Extended Agency," as reprinted in my *Structures of Agency* (New York: Oxford University Press, 2007), 21–46; and see Gideon Yaffe, *Liberty Worth the Name: Locke on Free Agency* (Princeton, NJ: Princeton University Press, 2000), chap. 3.

39. J. David Velleman, "What Happens When Someone Acts," *Mind* 101 (1992): 461–81, at 475.

claim to speak for the agent it thereby helps constitute, and so to be such that its guidance can help constitute that agent's self-governance.

Now, if this is how we approach self-governance then it will be plausible that central among the attitudes that constitute an agent's practical standpoint will be policy-like commitments to give weight in deliberation to certain considerations—for example, the success of the Free French, or the interests of one's beloved.[40] Such policy-like commitments may well be associated with value judgment; but they need not correspond to a prior judgment of the best, and may settle matters in response to underdetermination by prior value judgment. These policy-like commitments may also involve various forms of emotion and affect; but at their core they are plan states, plan states whose contents are appropriately general. So these commitments need to be embedded within the agent's planning system. And it is, quite generally, a central role of the plan states in this system to settle matters in response (many times) to a conflicting stew of needs, desires, and considerations, and in ways that tie together the agent's practical thought and action at a time and over time. In this way our model of self-governance returns us to the connection between planning and temporally extended agency: this connection helps explain why certain forms of plan-infused guidance of thought and action can be self-governance.[41]

The next point is that if an agent's plan states are to be a central part of the psychological structures whose guidance constitutes his self-governance, then these plan states will be under corresponding pressure to be consistent and coherent. After all, what is needed for self-governance is guidance of thought and action by a practical standpoint that constitutes where the agent stands. But if relevant plan states are inconsistent or incoherent, then there will not be a fact of the matter about where the agent stands on the relevant practical issue. If I intend A, see A and B as incompatible, and also intend B, then I have no clear stance on the issue of

40. As I see it, such policies about weights will normally be reflexive and involve higher-order attitudes about the role of relevant first-order attitudes; and these hierarchical aspects of these policies will help support their Lockean cross-temporal roles. See my "Three Theories of Self-Governance," as reprinted in my *Structures of Agency* (Oxford: Oxford University Press, 2007), 222–53. In "Shared Valuing and Frameworks for Practical Reasoning"—reprinted in *Structures of Agency*, 283–310—I argue that when we bring together such policies about weights with the structures of sharing discussed above in section 5, we arrive at a model of an important form of shared valuing.

41. For this approach to self-governance, see my "Three Theories of Self-Governance." For the application of these ideas to the problem of why it matters whether one conforms to the cited synchronic norms—a matter to which I turn below—see my "Intention, Practical Rationality, and Self-Governance," *Ethics* 119 (2009): 411–43 [this volume, essay 4].

whether A or B. And if I intend E but refrain from intending what I know to be necessary means to E, intending which now I know to be necessary for that means, then I have no clear stance with respect to E.

This means that for planning agents like us, self-governance in the particular case requires consistency and coherence of relevant plan states. On the assumption that we have a reason to govern our own lives, a reason that applies to the particular case, and on the assumption that relevant self-governance is attainable by the agent, we can infer that we have a reason of self-governance, in the particular case, to conform to the synchronic norms of intention consistency and coherence. (This inference depends on the principle that reasons for attainable ends transmit to reasons for necessary constitutive elements of those attainable ends.[42]) Though there is more to say,[43] this is, roughly, my response to the myth theorists' view of these synchronic norms.

8.

What about the purported diachronic norm of intention stability?

We cannot simply say that there is a rational demand not to change your prior intentions: diachronic intention rationality is not stubbornness. What we want, rather, is the idea that an intention at which you have sensibly and confidently arrived earlier is a rational default, though a default that is normally overridden if—perhaps by way of new information—you newly come to take your grounds, as specified by your practical standpoint, strictly to favor an incompatible alternative.[44]

To develop this idea, return to choice that is underdetermined by prior grounds. Consider cases in which you intend A and confidently take your relevant grounds adequately to support A, and yet also confidently take your relevant grounds adequately to support an incompatible alternative, B. This can happen in "Buridan" cases in which one sees one's conflicting, relevant

---

42. Which is not to say that reasons for attainable ends always transmit to what is entailed by those ends.

43. One further question is whether this approach lends support to inappropriate bootstrapping of new reasons for action. See my "Intention, Practical Rationality, and Self-Governance"; and see also my Intention, Plans, and Practical Reason at 24–27.

44. In saying that this default is "normally" overridden I leave room for the possibility that judgments about one's grounds might themselves be distorted by temptation, and that such distorted judgments might not override. In the discussion to follow, however, I bracket issues raised by this possibility. For an approach to some of these issues see my "Toxin, Temptation, and the Stability of Intention," as reprinted in my Faces of Intention, 58–90; and "Temptation Revisited," in my Structures of Agency, 257–82.

grounds as equal in weight, or in cases in which one sees one's conflicting, relevant grounds as incomparable. Suppose now that at t1 you intend to A at t2; and suppose that throughout t1-t2 you confidently take your relevant grounds adequately to support A. As noted, you might nevertheless at t2 also judge that your relevant grounds adequately support an alternative to A. The idea that your prior intention is a rational default entails that in such a case there remains rational pressure against abandoning at t2 your prior intention to A: there is a *pro tanto* diachronic rational breakdown if one intends at t1 to A at t2, throughout t1-t2 confidently takes one's relevant grounds adequately to support A at t2, and yet at t2 newly abandons one's intention to A at t2. The thought, then, is that once you have settled on an option compatibly with your confident assessment of your relevant grounds, there is rational pressure to retain your intention in the absence of relevant change in your assessment of grounds. And this idea promises to capture a distinctive rational pressure, in the particular case, for the stability of one's plan states—rational pressure that supplements the three-pronged support for intention stability noted earlier.

But why does it matter whether we conform with this diachronic norm?

9.

It does seem plausible, especially in light of our limited mental resources, that there are benefits to be derived from a general strategy of treating one's prior intentions as a default: one is thereby likely better to retain forms of cross-temporal coordination that support complex, temporally extended projects.[45] But, as we have seen, this kind of general consideration does not yet ensure that the agent has a distinctive reason to conform in the particular case.

In discussing the synchronic norms of consistency and means-end coherence we said that we have, in the particular case, a reason of self-governance to be consistent and coherent in this way, given that we have reason in the particular case to govern our own lives, and given that relevant self-governance is attainable. Can we make a corresponding claim about the idea of prior intention as rational default?

Well, is there a kind of self-governance *over* time for which we have reason and which involves a kind of cross-temporal stability of intention? If there were, we might have an explanation of why it distinctively matters whether we conform to our diachronic norm of intention stability.

---

45. This is where I left this matter in "Temptation Revisited," at 276.

What is it to govern one's life *over* a period of time and not just *at each* time within that period? Even if the person governing at each time is one and the same person, that person might lurch erratically from one standpoint to another, thereby undermining self-governance *over* the time period. So: What else is needed?

Our self-governance at a time involves, I have said, guidance by plan states that play Lockean cross-temporal organizing roles, and that are sufficiently consistent and coherent so as to constitute where the agent stands at that time. Consider, then, these potential, Lockean diachronic ties between those plan states whose guidance helps constitute the agent's self-governance at the various times. My proposal is that the diachronic "glue" needed for self-governance over time involves actual Lockean diachronic ties between the plan states whose guidance helps constitute self-governance at each time. [For further developments, see this volume, essay 11.]

These cross-temporal ties include interlocking referential connections and a form of constancy. What form of constancy? Well, self-governance over time need not involve stubbornness. But it is plausible that self-governance over time does involve constancy of relevant plan states given constancy in confident, relevant judgment in support. It seems plausible, that is, that a breakdown in such default constancy would block self-governance *over* the time, though it might still allow for self-governance *at* the various times. And this supports the thought that self-governance over time involves both self-governance at each time, and the further condition that the plan states whose guidance helps constitute the agent's self-governance at the various times both semantically interlock over that time, and are stable over that time given constancy in relevant supporting judgment.

In this way our approach to self-governance at a time supports a model of our self-governance over time within which constancy over time of intention sensibly and confidently arrived at is a default. So if we suppose that we have a reason in favor of such diachronic self-governance, a reason that applies in the particular case, and if we suppose that such self-governance is attainable, we can see this reason as supporting conformity to the cited diachronic norm in the particular case.[46] And once this reason is on board it provides yet further support for a mode of functioning in which self-governance at a time segues into self-governance over time.

---

46. Which is not to say that the earlier intention quite generally provides a new practical reason for later intention and action. And here, as in the synchronic case, a fuller treatment would need to address concerns about inappropriate bootstrapping of reasons.

The idea, then, is that in both the synchronic and the diachronic case we appeal to a connection between intention rationality and a kind of self-governance for which we have reason.[47] We conclude in each case that, if such self-governance is attainable, we have a reason of self-governance to conform to these rationality constraints (though a reason whose strength can vary with the significance of the projects at issue). In this way our plan-theoretic philosophy of action helps support basic norms of practical rationality.

This view of prior intentions as rational defaults is a kind of practical conservatism. It should be distinguished from an epistemic conservatism according to which one's prior *belief* is an *epistemic* rational default.[48] Default constancy of relevant intention over time is an element in the cross-temporal unity of practical stance that is characteristic of our self-governance over time. And it is plausible that we have practical reason for governing our lives over time, a reason that applies to the particular case. This is why, given that relevant self-governance is attainable, there is a distinctive practical reason at stake once one has decided, say, to pursue a certain career, and so long as one does not come to see some alternative as strictly superior, or simply lose confidence in one's relevant judgments of grounds. But it does not follow that there is a distinctive epistemic value in cross-temporal coherence of belief.[49] The practical conservatism to which the planning theory points as an element in its view of practical rationality is distinct from epistemic conservatism as a view about theoretical rationality.

10.

Let's take stock. The step from goal-directed to planning agency supports important forms of temporally extended agency. This step to planning agency

47. There is a parallel here with Lon Fuller's appeal to "the internal morality of law." As we might say, the appeal here is to the internal rationality of our self-governance. In each case, certain constraints are tied to the relevant mode of governance. See Lon Fuller, "Positivism and Fidelity to Law: A Reply to Professor Hart," *Harvard Law Review* 71 (1958): 630–72, at 645.

48. For a critical discussion of epistemic conservatism see David Christensen, "Diachronic Coherence versus Epistemic Impartiality," *The Philosophical Review* 109 (2000): 349–71.

49. This is compatible with the thought that the application of justified epistemic practices at each time would normally issue in a kind of cross-temporal stability of belief. It might be that, in contrast with the practical case, this cross-temporal epistemic stability, if such there were to be, would only be a spin-off without its own distinctive epistemic value.

also provides—given appropriate contents, contexts, and interrelations—a backbone for shared agency. Basic norms of individual intention rationality—norms of consistency, coherence, and stability—frame much of our practical thinking, and thereby also help induce associated norms of social rationality. In part because of their roles in temporally extended agency, planning structures can help constitute our self-governance. And this role of planning structures in self-governance— both at a time and over time—helps explain the distinctive significance in the particular case of basic norms of individual intention rationality. In these interconnected ways, the fact that we human agents are not simple goal-directed agents but, rather, planning agents helps shape the temporality and sociality of our agency, our governance of our lives, and basic norms of practical rationality.[50]

Call this the *fecundity of planning structures*. This fecundity is both theoretical and practical. It is theoretical in providing resources— conceptual, metaphysical, and normative—for understanding broad aspects, both descriptive and normative, of our human agency. It is practical in highlighting ways in which our planning capacities support aspects of our lives that we highly value. And this latter, practical fecundity supports an affirmative answer to a question inspired by Peter Strawson's work on the reactive attitudes[51]: if we had a choice (though we probably do not) whether to continue to be such planning agents, should we?[52]

50. And this model of our planning agency is, in effect, a model of the will. See "Shared Valuing and Frameworks for Practical Reasoning," section 9.

51. Peter Strawson, "Freedom and Resentment," as reprinted in *Free Will*, 2nd ed., ed. Gary Watson (Oxford: Oxford University Press, 2003), 72–93. I discuss this Strawsonian, practical fecundity of planning structures in my "Intention, Belief, Practical, Theoretical," section 9.

52. Many thanks to Facundo Alonso, Joshua Cohen, Jennifer Morton, Carlos Núñez, Sarah Paul, Manuel Vargas, and Gideon Yaffe; and to audiences at Stanford University, University of Regensburg, University of Buffalo, the 2010 St Louis Annual Conference on Reasons and Rationality, and the 2010 Reykjavik Conference in Moral Philosophy. Special thanks to Ruth Chang for extremely detailed and wide-ranging written comments.

CHAPTER 6
Time, Rationality, and Self-Governance

1.

Much adult human activity is temporally extended. It involves distinctive forms of cross-temporal guidance and organization. And the agent's plan-like commitment to these cross-temporal forms of organization is a central element in the explanation and understanding of her practical thinking and action.

Think about building a house. For us, building a house is a complex temporally extended activity, one in which the agent's acceptance of an overall (though partial and revisable) plan is central to the guidance of relevant thought and action, and one in which the various sub-parts are, if all goes well, related to each other in ways that we understand by appealing to the guiding plan. For us, such activities are cross-temporally organized largely because they are the output of accepted plans and planning. In this sense this cross-temporal organization is mind-infused.

An agent in the midst of such plan-structured, temporally extended activity will have a web of intentions that focus on the present and the future, and also refer back to relevant earlier intentions and actions. She now intends, let's suppose, to install the windows after having earlier framed the walls, and later to paint the room. These intentions are subject to characteristic norms of consistency and means-end coherence. Roughly, she is rationally required not both to intend A and intend B if she believes that A and B are not co-possible; and, again roughly, she is rationally required to be such that if she intends E and believes M is a necessary means to E then she intends M. These are norms that she at least implicitly accepts, and her acceptance of these norms helps guide her relevant thought and action.

These norms impose constraints on her intentions at a given time. These are synchronic constraints, ones that do not directly concern relations between intentions at earlier times and intentions at later times. Granted, an agent's intentions may develop over time in ways that aim at conformity to these synchronic norms: one might, say, add a new intention concerning means. But, so far, the conformity aimed at consists in a certain synchronic structure of attitudes.

Fundamental to planning agency, however, are characteristic relations between an agent's intentions *over* time. And this raises the question of whether there are further, *diachronic* rationality constraints on an agent's intentions. In particular, are there rationality norms that concern the stability of intentions over time?

Begin with a trio of ideas. First, once one begins to act on an intention the world may, as a result, change in relevant ways; and it may be that these changes make it increasingly sensible to continue to act on that intention. This is the snowball effect.[1]

Second, we normally retain our prior intentions unless we reconsider them. Reconsideration, however, takes time and uses other mental resources; and reconsideration may require, in the pursuit of coordination, re-thinking various other, related courses of action on which one had earlier settled. So there is frequently reason not to reconsider, both because of the risks of undermining coordination previously forged and because of the direct costs of such reconsideration.

Third, so as not to use deliberative resources inefficiently we frequently depend on general (and often non-deliberative) strategies about when to reconsider. And strategies that to some extent favor non-reconsideration are likely, in the long run, to be conducive to the overall effectiveness of our temporally extended and resource-limited agency.

So there are these three initial forms of support for the stability of intention over time.[2] Is there more to say? Is there some further, diachronic rationality constraint on an agent's intentions over time, a constraint that favors a kind of stability of intention over time? Or is this thought just a way of clothing the dead hand of the past with the cloak of purported rationality?

My conjecture is that there is some such diachronic rationality constraint of intention stability, that a plausible approach to this matter

---

1. Michael E. Bratman, *Intention, Plans, and Practical Reason* (Cambridge, MA: Harvard University Press, 1987; reissued by CSLI Press, 1999) at 82. As indicated there, I owe this phrase to John Etchemendy.
2. This is pretty much where I left this matter in *Intention, Plans, and Practical Reason*.

draws on our understanding of self-governance, and that these reflections support the idea that our prior intentions provide a rational default for present deliberation.

2.

The idea of a rationality constraint with which I am working here is the idea of a "wide scope" constraint on combinations of attitudes (or their absence).[3] Such a rationality constraint says that certain combinations of attitudes, or of attitudes taken together with the absence of other attitudes, constitute violations. Further, I will here understand such constraints as constraints of "local" rationality. The idea is that any violation really is a rational breakdown; it is not merely a prima facie indicator of a breakdown. Nevertheless, there remains a further question whether in a particular case one's local irrationality rises to the level of overall, "global" irrationality.[4]

This idea of a wide-scope constraint of local rationality contrasts with two other ideas: the idea of a normative reason and the idea of the transmission of normative reasons.

First, you might claim that there is a reason—a normative reason—for an agent to act in a certain way. On the surface, anyway, you are not making a claim about how certain attitudes of the agent should hang together. You are, rather, claiming that something is a consideration in favor of a certain action.[5]

3. See, e.g., John Broome, "Wide or Narrow Scope?," *Mind* 116 (2007): 359–70.
4. For this distinction between local and global rationality see Michael Smith, "The Structure of Orthonomy," in John Hyman and Helen Steward, eds., *Agency and Action* (Cambridge: Cambridge University Press, 2004), 165–93, at 190. Smith's concern is with norms of belief and desire; here I extend his approach to norms on intention. John Brunero also highlights a distinction between local and overall rationality in his "Instrumental Rationality, Symmetry, and Scope," *Philosophical Studies* 157 (2012): 125–140, at 129–30. However, it is not clear from Brunero's discussion whether he would allow that sometimes overall rationality involves local irrationality. In earlier work I tried to get at the underlying idea here by talking about "pro tanto" (in contrast with all-in) rationality. (See Michael E. Bratman, "Intention, Practical Rationality, and Self-Governance," *Ethics* 119 (2009): 411–443, at 413 [this volume, essay 4, at 78].) Here I adjust my terminology to fit with Smith's, which now seems to me more apt.
5. T. M. Scanlon, *What We Owe to Each Other* (Cambridge, MA: Harvard University Press, 1998), 17. For different but related ideas see Pamela Hieronymi, "The Wrong Kind of Reason," *Journal of Philosophy* 102 (2005): 437–57; and John Broome, *Rationality Through Reasoning* (unpublished manuscript, version of July 2011, "complete26") [published as *Rationality Through Reasoning* (Wiley Blackwell, 2013)], Chap. 3 [Chap. 4 in published version]. [My references below will be to the unpublished manuscript;

That said, there are deep issues here about the relation between normative practical reasons and attitudes of the agent. Bernard Williams has argued that all such reasons are "internal" in the sense that they are grounded in the agent's "subjective motivational set,"[6] and that in making judgments about your reasons I am thinking in "the 'if I were you . . .' mode."[7] The deep idea here, I think, is the idea that there is a tight connection between normative practical reasons and considerations that have force from the practical perspective of the agent herself. But there is also an important idea that normative judgment involves distinctive forms of endorsement: in particular, when I judge that you have a reason for action I am not merely describing the relation between that action and your motivational set; I am in some way endorsing that purported reason.[8]

We need a theory of the nature of normative practical reasons that does justice to both of these ideas, broadly understood. For present purposes, however, I will work with the idea of a normative practical reason without addressing this foundational issue. I will however assume that many times we sensibly judge that an agent's practical commitments, when they do not depend on false factual belief or involve commitments we find seriously unacceptable, ground such normative reasons.

The next point is that we sometimes appeal to principles that say when certain reasons for action transmit to or induce other reasons for action. One common idea here is that a reason for an end transmits to a reason for a means to that end. There are complex issues here.[9] For now, I just want to mark the difference between such a transfer principle and a wide-scope, local rationality constraint on combinations of attitudes. The former concerns the transmission of normative reasons; the latter concerns the coherence, or the like, of combinations of attitudes.

where possible, I have added, in brackets, the corresponding page numbers to the published version.] But these are complexities we can safely ignore here.

6. Bernard Williams, "Internal and External Reasons," in his *Moral Luck* (Cambridge: Cambridge University Press, 1981), 101–13.

7. Bernard Williams, "Internal Reasons and the Obscurity of Blame," in his *Making Sense of Humanity* (Cambridge: Cambridge University Press, 1981), 35–45, at 36.

8. See Allan Gibbard, *Wise Choices, Apt Feelings* (Cambridge, MA: Harvard University Press, 1990) at 163. And see also Simon Blackburn, *Ruling Passions: A Theory of Practical Reasoning* (Oxford: Oxford University Press, 1998).

9. For a recent, trenchant discussion see Niko Kolodny, "Instrumental Reasons," in Daniel Star, ed., *The Oxford Handbook of Reasons and Normativity* (Oxford: Oxford University Press, forthcoming).

Consider now the synchronic constraint of means-end coherence. A rough formulation[10] would be along the lines of

Means-end coherence. The following is locally irrational: Intending at t that E, believing at t that M is a necessary means for E, yet not intending at t that M.

Given a threatened violation of *means-end coherence*, one can satisfy this norm either by intending M, or by giving up one's intention in favor of E, or by revising one's cited belief.

Why think that this is a constraint of practical rationality? Well, it certainly has a pre-theoretical plausibility as a claim about rationality.[11] And something like this constraint is tightly connected to the very nature of intending, an attitude that plays basic roles in our agency. Intentions (in contrast with wishes or ordinary desires or preferences) are attitudes that are responsive to some such end-means pressures, where that responsiveness is itself explained in part by the agent's at least implicit acceptance of a norm roughly along the lines of *means-end coherence*.

These remarks provide part of a defense of the idea that something like *means-end coherence* is a constraint of practical rationality. They do not, however, fully answer the question of why it matters whether one conforms to this constraint.[12]

Consider two lines of response to this question. Both seek reasons for conformity to this constraint that are *distinctive* in the sense that they go beyond the particular reasons the agent has in the particular case for the specific end intended. But these responses proceed at different levels of generality.

The first considers the advantages of being an agent of a certain kind, namely: one who has intentions and plans, and generally guides her thought and action with an eye to conforming, inter alia, to *means-end coherence*. Here I would emphasize two kinds of considerations. First, such modes of practical thinking support our capacity for complex forms of cross-temporal organization of our temporally extended intentional agency, and these forms of diachronic organization are central to a wide range of our ends. Second, these modes of thinking are part of a kind of

10. A more precise formulation would refer to the need, by a certain time, for an intention to M if one is to M.

11. In his "The Requirements of Rationality," (unpublished manuscript version 2.4; August 2007). Nadeem Hussain emphasizes the relevance of a method of reflective equilibrium to our assessment of such claims about rationality.

12. In putting the question this way I am following Garret Cullity, "Decisions, Reasons, and Rationality," *Ethics* 119 (2008): 57–95, at 82.

planning agency that helps constitute important forms of sociality and of self-governance. I have argued for versions of these ideas in other places;[13] and below I will return to self-governance. But the point now is just that the relevant claim is a claim about the virtues of certain *general* strategies of practical thought.

Such claims contrast with a second response to our query about why it matters whether we conform *to means-end coherence*. Here the idea is not primarily about the merits of a general strategy of practical thought, but instead a claim that for a planning agent like us there is in each *particular* case (perhaps barring certain special conditions) a distinctive practical reason for conformity. And to develop this idea we would need to go on to provide an account of what that reason is.

Both responses are significant; and they are potentially mutually supporting. But the second response has an important feature: it can be directly addressed to the agent who is wondering in a particular case why she should care about conforming to the cited norm in that case. In contrast, the first response does not fully address this concern. This is because—as we have learned from J. J. C. Smart's reflections on "rule worship"—an agent might acknowledge the general advantages of a strategy of conforming to a norm but still wonder whether there is reason to conform in her particular case.[14]

My primary concern here will be with responses of this second sort. These try to articulate a distinctive practical reason for conforming to the cited synchronic, wide-scope, local rationality constraints, a reason that, in the absence of special conditions, applies in each particular case. Such responses can be directly addressed to the planning agent who is reflecting about why she should care about such constraints in her particular case. And such responses will be central when we turn later to a proposed diachronic rationality constraint.

13. For the first idea see my *Intention, Plans, and Practical Reason* (Cambridge, MA: Harvard University Press, 1987; reissued by CSLI Publications, 1999). For the connections to sociality see the essays on shared agency in my *Faces of Intention* (New York: Cambridge University Press, 1999), and my *Shared Agency: A Planning Theory of Acting Together* (Oxford: Oxford University Press, 2014). For the connections to self-governance see the essays in my *Structures of Agency: Essays* (New York: Oxford University Press, 2007).

14. J. J. C. Smart, "Extreme and Restricted Utilitarianism," in Philippa Foot, ed., *Theories of Ethics* (Oxford: Oxford University Press, 1967). For some complications see my "The Interplay of Intention and Reason," *Ethics* 123 (2013): 657–72. [this volume, essay 8]

3.

Is there, in the absence of special conditions, a distinctive practical reason, in the particular case, to conform to *means-end coherence*? In an earlier effort to answer this question, I appealed to the idea that we have a normative practical reason in favor of governing our own lives.[15] Why think that? Well, I take it that it is at the least extremely common to care significantly about whether one is governing one's own life,[16] and that such caring need neither depend on false factual belief nor target an end that is itself a bad thing. Such a concern is a prime candidate for grounding a normative practical reason. So I will assume that given such a concern, one does have a normative reason to govern one's life. And I will limit my discussion to those who do have some such concern.

The next idea is that self-governance at a time involves, as a necessary constitutive element, relevant forms of coherence and consistency of practical standpoint at that time. The argument for this does not itself appeal to a rationality norm of consistency or coherence, since if that were how we argued here we would not have a non-circular account of the normative significance of these norms. The argument for this is, rather, an appeal to the metaphysics of self-governance at a time. The idea is that such self-governance essentially involves, not the intervention of a little person in the head, but rather guidance and control by attitudes that help constitute a sufficiently unified point of view, a point of view that constitutes the agent's relevant practical standpoint. And for planning agents like us—agents whose intentions and plans settle practical matters—such practical unity at a time involves, in particular, relevant forms of intention coherence and consistency at that time.[17] If your plans are inconsistent or incoherent then there will not be, in the relevant sense, a place where you stand on the relevant practical issue; and this will block the possibility of guidance of your thought and action by where you relevantly stand.[18]

Consider now a transmission principle that says that a reason for X induces a reason for a necessary constitutive element of X so long as X is attainable by the agent. While principles along these lines can be challenged, this principle seems to me sufficiently plausible to use in our argument

15. See my "Intention. Practical Rationality, and Self-Governance," *Ethics* 119 (2009): 411–43.

16. Which is not to deny that we also sometimes want to give up control over aspects of our lives.

17. I defend this thought further in section 6.

18. For talk of where the person stands see Harry Frankfurt, "Identification and Wholeheartedness," as reprinted in his *The Importance of What We Care About* (Cambridge: Cambridge University Press, 1987), 159–76, at 166.

here.[19] And given this transmission principle, together with our observation about the role of means-end coherence in self-governance, we can infer that in cases in which relevant self-governance is attainable by the agent, the cited reason for self-governance induces a reason to conform to *means-end coherence*. This is a distinctive reason to conform to *means-end coherence*, one that goes beyond reasons for the specific ends in question, and one that applies to all particular cases in which relevant self-governance is attainable by the agent. We will also be able to make an analogous claim about a reason of self-governance for conforming to the demand for intention consistency. And in each case the strength of this reason can vary with the importance of the project at issue.

The idea, then, is that these norms of synchronic intention rationality are associated with conditions of self-governance. Given the assumption that we have normative practical reason to govern our own lives, and given the cited transmission principle, this connection with self-governance explains why, when relevant self-governance is attainable, we have a distinctive reason of self-governance (though one whose strength can vary with the significance of the involved project) to conform to these synchronic norms. We have, in particular, a reason of self-governance for conforming to *means-end coherence*.

4.

It is tempting to think that such synchronic rationality constraints are on more secure ground than are constraints of diachronic rationality. In particular, inconsistency at a time seems more clearly a rational failure than inconstancy over time. Indeed, change of mind over time is many times what is required by rationality. I think, nevertheless, that we can develop an approach to a diachronic rationality constraint of intention stability that is broadly parallel to the approach just sketched to synchronic constraints.

The synchronic constraints of consistency and coherence preclude certain patterns of attitudes at a time. How might we extend this strategy to the diachronic case?

19. One challenge concerns cases in which, while the end is attainable, the agent will in fact not perform all of the other necessary means or constitutive elements. [For a version of this challenge that concerns "ought" see John Broome, *Rationality Through Reasoning*, at p. 207 [p. 201 in published version].] Now, I grant that even if you ought to E (where E is attainable by you) and M is a necessary means to or constitutive element of E, if in fact you are not going to perform other necessary means to E then it does not follow that you ought to M. But it seems to me that reasons work differently than "ought" in such cases.

We of course do not want to say that it is in general irrational to revise a prior intention. Many times there is no irrationality at all in changing one's mind in response, for example, to new information that undermines one's earlier grounds for one's intention, or to one's recognition that one's earlier intention formation was flawed. Instead, a plausible version of a pattern strategy for the diachronic case would focus on changes of intention over time in the face of both initial, supposed support for that intention and constancy of view of the grounds for that intention. The idea would be, roughly, that if there is, by the agent's lights, adequate initial, confident support for the intention, and if there is constancy over time in this support, then there is rational pressure for constancy of intention over time.

So consider:

(D) The following is locally irrational: Intending at t_1 to X at t_2; throughout t_1–t_2 confidently taking one's relevant grounds adequately to support this very intention; and yet at t_2 newly abandoning this intention to X at t_2.[20]

(D) is wide scope in the sense that it concerns a pattern (albeit, a diachronic pattern) of attitudes together with the absence of an attitude. (D) states a local demand that concerns a specific sub-cluster of attitudes within an overall cross-temporal psychic economy. (D) does not say that the intention at t_1 provides a new normative reason for a later intention at t_2. Rather, what it says is that there is a rationality constraint that concerns the cited cross-temporal pattern of attitudes. When one arrives at t_2 with the cited history of thought prior to t_2, one can satisfy (D) either by sticking with one's prior intention or by revising in relevant ways one's assessment of one's relevant grounds. (I take it that, since the past is fixed, one cannot at t_2 satisfy (D) by changing the fact that at t_1 one intended to X at t_2.[21])

In interpreting (D) it is important to keep in mind that one might take one's grounds adequately to support X and yet also take one's grounds adequately to support some alternative, incompatible option. This can happen in "Buridan" cases in which one thinks that one's grounds equally support each of two incompatible alternatives. This can also happen in cases in which one sees the grounds for each of several conflicting options as

---

20. I limit my attention here to cases in which grounds support an intention to X by supporting X; and I also put to one side cases in which the agent's relevant thinking about her grounds is itself distorted in some way.

21. See Andrew Reisner, "Unifying the Requirements of Rationality," *Philosophical Explorations* 12 (2009): 243–60, at 250. And John Broome notes that the fixity of the past supports what he calls "necessary detachment." (John Broome, *Rationality Through Reasoning*, at pp. 130, 145 [pp. 124, 144 in published version].)

incomparable.[22] In such cases, intention formation differs from belief formation. Faced with equally strong evidential support for p and for not-p, epistemic rationality will normally call for withholding judgment. But in a Buridan case, or a case of incomparable conflicting considerations, practical rationality will frequently allow, and sometimes require, decision. And if one does make such a decision at t_1, principle (D) is then engaged.

In particular, suppose that at t_1 one takes one's relevant grounds adequately to support X at t_2, one also takes one's relevant grounds adequately to support Y at t_2, and one knows that X and Y are not co-possible. And suppose that at t_1 one settles in particular on X at t_2. According to (D), if these assessments of one's grounds remain confident and constant all the way through t_2, and yet one at t_2 newly abandons this intention to X at t_2 in favor of a new intention in favor of Y at t_2, then one is locally, cross-temporally irrational. And this is so even though it need not in general be locally, synchronically irrational at t_2 to take one's relevant grounds adequately to support X at t_2 and yet to intend instead to Y at t_2. In this way (D) confers on the prior intention in favor of X a kind of default status. To avoid violating this constraint, one is not to abandon this prior intention if one only comes to see a competing alternative as no worse supported by relevant grounds:[23] once you have settled on an option in conformity with your confident assessment of your relevant grounds, there is rational pressure, in the particular case, to retain your intention in the absence of relevant change in your assessment of grounds.[24]

22. I borrow the terminology of "incomparable" from Allan Gibbard, "Reply to Critics," *Philosophy and Phenomenological Research* 72 (2006): 729–44, at 735–7.

23. There is a parallel here with the judicial doctrine of *stare decisis*, though this is not to prohibit what Cheshire Calhoun calls "trading up." See her "What Good Is Commitment?" *Ethics* 119 (2009): 613–41, at 627.

24. Here I am in disagreement with Luca Ferrero. See his "Decisions, Diachronic Autonomy, and the Division of Deliberative Labor," *Philosophers' Imprint* 10, no. 2 (2010): 1–23, section 6. This rational default status also goes beyond John Broome's proposed principle of "persistence of intention." According to Broome's proposal (in its "special form"), "rationality requires of N that, if N intends at t_1 to F, and no canceling event occurs between t_1 and t_2, then either N intends at t_2 to F, or N considers at t_2 whether to F." (See John Broome, *Rationality Through Reasoning*, at p. 185 [p. 178 in published version]. For a related discussion of the case of Abraham and Isaac, see John Broome, "Are Intentions Reasons? And How Should We Cope with Incommensurable Values?" in Christopher W. Morris and Arthur Ripstein, eds., *Practical Rationality and Preference: Essays for David Gauthier* (Cambridge: Cambridge University Press, 2001), 98–120, esp. 114–119.) Without going into the details, it suffices here to note that, having so intended at t_1, one satisfies Broome's requirement simply by reconsidering that intention at t_2, at which point the cited principle describes no further rational pressure to retain that intention. (In this respect, Broome's approach here is similar in spirit to the approach I took in *Intention, Plans, and Practical Reason*.) According to (D), in contrast, even when one reconsiders one's prior intention it remains, in the absence of a relevant change in assessment, a rational default.

That said, the needed change in assessment might be fairly minimal. Perhaps one comes to think that Y would be a nice change of pace from earlier X-type activities, and variety is, after all, a good thing; and perhaps one concludes from this that Y is now slightly superior to X. (D) allows for a change of intention in such a case.

Further, it is not a violation of (D) if one's prior intention was an intention to engage in X-type activities for awhile, and one now thinks that the time is up and changes to an intention in favor of an equally attractive or incomparable alternative.[25] Nor is it a violation of (D) to have a plan for sampling, over time, a number of equally attractive alternatives—for example, a plan for sampling various restaurants, or the different tunes on one's I-pod, or different kinds of writing projects. In sampling these different alternatives over time one is not, as time goes by, abandoning one's prior intentions in a way that violates (D); one is simply following through with one's sampling plan. In certain cases (for example, cases involving close personal relations) such a sampling plan may well be ill advised; but this is not because, in following through with the sampling plan, one is violating (D).

With these clarifications in hand, (D) does seem initially plausible. But now we need to ask why it matters—if it does matter—whether we conform to (D).

5.

Well, it seems likely that there are benefits to be derived from a general strategy of treating one's prior intentions as a default: one is thereby likely better to retain forms of coordination that support complex, temporally extended ends and important forms of sociality. For resource-limited agents like us, starting from scratch will frequently be inefficient and baffle forms of reliability central to shared activity. But while this general consideration

25. In a case suggested by Chrisoula Andreou, one intends to pursue a career in philosophy and has been acting on that intention for awhile, but then shifts to a career in creative writing, which one sees as an incomparable alternative. In one version of this case, what one has been intending is to pursue philosophy for awhile, one has indeed been pursing philosophy for awhile, and one now thinks that it is a good time to switch to creative writing. This switch need not violate (D). In a second version of this case your earlier intention was an intention to pursue philosophy for your entire adult life, or anyway for an extended period that includes and goes beyond your present circumstance. In this case your switch would violate (D). (Chrisoula Andreou, "Incommensurable Alternatives and Rational Choice," *Ratio* 18 (2005): 249–61, at 257. I say only that Andreou suggests such a case because she describes her case as one involving "choosing preferences"; and it may be that choosing preferences are not, strictly speaking, intentions. See below note 33.)

is important, and does support a rule of thumb in favor of intention stability, it does not by itself ensure that the agent quite generally has a distinctive reason to conform to (D) in the particular case.

In discussing the synchronic norm of *means-end coherence* I said that if relevant self-governance is attainable, one has in the particular case a reason of self-governance to be means-end coherent. Can we make a corresponding claim about (D)? Can we say that conformity to (D) is an element in a form of self-governance for which we have reason?

The relevant form of self-governance would need to be self-governance *over* time.[26] And that does seem to be something that we care about in ways that make it plausible that we do indeed have reason for such self-governance over time.

But what exactly is self-governance over time? What is it to govern one's own life not just *at each* of a series of times,[27] but *over* that time?

A partial answer is that it is necessary that it be the same person who is governing at each of the times (though perhaps we could weaken this to require only that there be, as Derek Parfit says, "what matters" in personal identity over time).[28] But sameness of person over time is not sufficient to take us from self-governance at each time to self-governance over the entire period of time. After all, one and the same person can lurch, willy-nilly and for no good reason, from one plan-like commitment to another, in ways that seem to block that person's self-governance *over* that entire time.

Such a person would live what Richard Kraut (in conversation) once called a "shuffle" life. But we need to be careful here. As noted, one might have a plan that enjoins sampling over time various different, equally attractive alternatives. Given such a sampling plan, each of one's intentions in favor of an alternative is constrained in such a way that when one moves on to the next alternative one is not abandoning one's earlier intention; one is simply continuing with one's sampling plan. There is no general incompatibility between such sampling plans and diachronic self-governance, though—as noted—certain sampling plans may well be ill advised. What is in tension with diachronic self-governance is lurching from one plan-like commitment to another incompatible commitment seen as equal or incomparable, in a way that involves abandoning one's prior intentions. Call

26. See Jed Rubenfeld, *Freedom and Time* (New Haven, CT: Yale University Press, 2001) part II; and see J. David Velleman's appeal to "diachronic autonomy" in his "Deciding How to Decide," as reprinted in his *The Possibility of Practical Reason* (Oxford: Oxford University Press, 2000), 221–43, at 238–40.

27. We can suppose that these relevant times themselves have some temporal thickness.

28. Derek Parfit, *Reasons and Persons* (Oxford: Oxford University Press, 1984).

this *brute shuffling*. Something that is central to self-governance over time seems to be blocked by such brute shuffling. We need to say what that is.

6.

Return to self-governance at a time. Self-governance at a time involves guidance by a synchronic structure of attitudes that is sufficiently unified so as to constitute where the agent stands at that time, and so as to be such that its guidance can constitute the agent's self-governance. But not just any coherent and consistent framework of attitudes has this connection to self-governance. A coherent and consistent set of fantasies, for example, does not. Earlier I highlighted the significance to synchronic self-governance of consistency and coherence of, in particular, plan states. But why do plan states have this special standing?

The answer, I think, is that plan states play certain fundamental, interrelated roles in a planning agent's psychic economy. First, they settle relevant practical matters. This supports their capacity to help constitute where the *agent* stands and to be such that their guidance is the agent's direction (where agential direction is an essential element in agential self-governance). Second, and relatedly, they play certain characteristic roles over time. The planning system involves characteristic continuities of plan states over time, continuities that are supported, in the first instance, by the initial three-pronged support (noted earlier) for intention stability. And these plan states characteristically refer forward to later plan states involved in their execution; and those later plan states characteristically refer back both to those earlier plans. These roles help knit together practical thought (including practical reasoning and deliberation) and action over time. And these cross-temporal continuities and semantic interconnections contribute to what is, on a broadly Lockean view, constitutive of the identity of the person over time.[29]

The proposal, then, is that it is because these plan states play these interrelated roles that, in the absence of relevant conflict, their guidance of thought and action helps constitute the agent's self-governance.[30] And this is why a planning agent's self-governance at a time involves guidance, at

29. Or anyway, "what matters" in personal identity over time. Of course, the agent can persist over time even when some of these plan states fail to play these roles.

30. This is a development of a view I discuss in my *Structures of Agency*, and in my "Agency, Time, and Sociality," *Proceedings and Addresses of the American Philosophical Association* 84, no.2 (2010): 7–26 [this volume, essay 5].

that time, by a consistent and coherent structure of, in particular, relevant plan states of the agent.

This view ties a planning agent's self-governance *at* a time to planning attitudes whose roles include the organization of thought and action *over* time in ways that involve cross-temporal connections and an appropriate constancy over time. Of course, this constancy needs to be sensitive to the fact that sometimes an agent supposes there are conclusive reasons for change. So it needs to be a defeasible constancy: constancy in the absence of supposed conclusive reason for an alternative.

Would a weaker form of defeasible constancy—in particular, constancy in the absence of supposed adequate reason for an alternative—suffice? Well, such a weaker form of constancy is compatible with a brute-shuffle life in which one keeps lurching from one commitment to a different and incompatible commitment seen as equal or incomparable. But a central role of plan-type commitments (in contrast, for example, with ordinary desires and preferences) is to settle practical matters in a way that protects us from such brute shuffling. That is one of their characteristic jobs in the psychology of planning agency; and it is in part because plan states have this settling role that they are such that their guidance can constitute the *agent's* self-governance. So such plan-like commitments will, when functioning properly, play a role that involves the cited, stronger form of constancy.

This suggests that a planning agent's self-governance over time involves two conditions. The first is that there is self-governance at the relevant times along the way. And the second is that the intentions whose guidance helps constitute the agent's self-governance at each time along the way are, over time, both

(a) semantically interconnected, and
(b) stable in the absence of supposed conclusive reason for change.

In satisfying (a) and (b) the intentions involved in the self-governance at each time actually do play the roles over time that are central to the significance of those attitudes to the planning agent's self-governance at each time.

Sydney Shoemaker observes that the "psychological continuity" central to broadly Lockean theories of personal identity over time "is just the playing out over time of the functional natures of the mental states characteristic of persons."[31] I am making a parallel proposal about a planning

---

31. Sydney Shoemaker, "Personal Identity," in Sydney Shoemaker and Richard Swinburne, *Personal Identity* (Oxford: Basil Blackwell, 1984) at 95.

agent's diachronic self-governance. A planning agent's self-governance over time involves the "playing out over time" of functional roles that are characteristic of her self-governance at a time. The actual cross-temporal "playing out" of those functional roles—and so the satisfaction of (a) and (b)—helps "glue" together self-governance at different times when there is self-governance over time. In this way we get from a view about the proper functioning of the plan states involved in a planning agent's synchronic self-governance to a view about the nature of her diachronic self-governance, and thereby to a view about the diachronic "glue" that is missing from a brute-shuffle life.

Consider now an example from John Brunero:

> Candice decides to go to the post office this afternoon to send out some mailings, but on the way there, she gives up on this end and decides to go buy groceries instead. But on the way to the market, she yet again trades in this end for another: going to hang out with her friend David. But on the way to David's house, she once more changes her mind and intends to spend a relaxing afternoon at home, but by the time she gets home the afternoon is gone and she's accomplished nothing.[32]

We have seen that in such a case there is a breakdown in the "glue" needed for diachronic self-governance. It is also true that Candice's changes over time are self-defeating in the sense that she "accomplished nothing."[33] But not all cases of brute shuffling will be cases of self-defeat in this sense. Perhaps one accomplishes a bit with respect to each of several incompatible projects as one brute-shuffles from one to another. Still, we have seen reason to think that such brute shuffling stands in the way of self-governance over time.

---

32. John Brunero, "Instrumental Rationality, Symmetry, and Scope," at 136. As Brunero notes, there is a similar example in Christine Korsgaard, "The Normativity of Instrumental Reason," as reprinted in her *The Constitution of Agency* (Oxford: Oxford University Press, 2008), 27–68, at 59 n. 52.

33. A similar point holds for Korsgaard's cited case. In talking here about self-defeat I am drawing on a related but somewhat different use of this term by Chrisoula Andreou in her comments on an earlier version of this essay. See also Chrisoula Andreou, "Incommensurable Alternatives and Rational Choice," at 255–57. In this latter essay Andreou rejects a "default presumption in favor of one's initially favored choosing preferences" (257). If "choosing preferences" are, strictly speaking, intentions that are not qualified by a relevant sampling plan, this rejected "default presumption" will be similar to principle (D). However, it may be that "choosing preferences" do not have it as a characteristic role that they settle relevant practical issues, and so are not intentions of the sort of interest here. If so, there need be no disagreement between us about (D).

Given this approach to the metaphysics of self-governance over time, we can go on to argue from a reason to govern one's own life over time to a reason to conform to (D), for those plan states whose guidance helps constitute self-governance. Examples will include important decisions (e.g., career decisions) in the face of supposed equality or incomparability. But almost any plan-like commitment can potentially play this role. Once I decide at t_1 which of several equally desirable concerts to go to at t_2, I am self-governing *over* t_1–t_2, with respect to this particular matter, only if my relevant plan states during this interval conform to (D). (Though my reason for self-governance with respect to this relatively mundane matter may accordingly be quite minimal.) And this gives us an account of why it distinctively matters whether we conform to (D).

In both the synchronic and the diachronic cases, then, we appeal to the connection between wide scope, local rationality constraints on intention, and a form of self-governance for which we have pro tanto reason. In each case our account of the metaphysics of self-governance has the implication that conforming to the cited rationality constraint is an aspect of relevant self-governance. And we conclude that, if relevant self-governance is attainable, we have a reason of self-governance to conform to these constraints (though a reason whose strength can vary with the importance of the projects at issue). In particular, in the diachronic case we have:

(R) If relevant self-governance over time is attainable, there is a practical, pro tanto reason of self-governance to conform to (D).

Suppose then that you have at t_1 formed the intention to X at t_2; that from t_1 to just up to t_2 you have confidently taken your relevant grounds adequately to support your X-ing at t_2; and that relevant diachronic self-governance is attainable by you. At t_2, you have a reason of self-governance to conform to (D). So, given that your past prior to t_2 is not changeable by you at t_2, you have at t_2 a reason of self-governance either to retain your prior intention to X, or relevantly to change your mind about the strength of your grounds for X. However, it does not in general follow that you have a reason of self-governance simply to retain your prior intention, since you might have conclusive reason instead to change your assessment of your grounds for X.[34] Nor does this preclude the possibility that the reason

34. Recall Broome's principle of persistence of intention (in its special form): "rationality requires of N that, if N intends at t_1 to F, and no canceling event occurs between t_1 and t_2, then *either* N intends at t_2 to F, *or* N considers at t_2 whether to F" (emphasis

against such local, diachronic irrationality in a particular case might, in certain circumstances, be overridden.

7.

I conclude that considerations about self-governance that support the synchronic norm of means-end coherence can be developed in a way that supports the diachronic norm (D). As planning agents, we normally have, in the particular case, a reason of temporally extended self-governance to conform to (D) and in this way to treat our prior intentions as a rational default.[35]

added). Note that Broome's principle also highlights a second disjunct, though a different second disjunct from the one to which I am here appealing. (The second disjunct implicit in (D) involves relevant change in assessment of grounds for X, not just reconsidering whether to X.) Both Broome and I aim to avoid in this way an implication from the fixity of one's past formation of the intention at t_1, directly and simply to a reason later to retain and act on that intention at t_2. But, as indicated in note 24, the combination of (D) and (R) does this in a way that provides for a stronger diachronic constraint than does Broome's principle of intention persistence. (See John Broome, *Rationality Through Reasoning*, pp. 184–90 [pp. 177–85 in published version].)

35. Thanks to Luca Ferrero and Chrisoula Andreou, thoughtful commentators on an early version of this paper at the January, 2010 SOFIA workshop, to the audiences at Rice University and at the SOFIA workshop; and to John Broome, Garrett Cullity, Carlos Núñez, Sarah Paul, and Michael Titelbaum.

CHAPTER 7

Temptation and the Agent's Standpoint

I. DIACHRONIC RATIONALITY FOR PLANNING AGENTS

A planning agent forms future-directed intentions that settle relevant matters in advance in ways that normally support cross-temporal organization. Sometimes these intentions concern specific options on a specific, envisaged future occasion. I might decide in advance to spend this evening working on my essay rather than watching a movie. Sometimes these intentions are general policies that concern patterns of activity over time. I might decide in advance in favor of a policy of drinking only a single glass of wine at dinners, despite the attractions of a second glass.[1] And in each case—intention for a specific future action, and intention for a pattern—one may form such an intention while recognizing that, when the time (or times) of action arrives (or arrive), one will be tempted to act contrary to one's prior intention. Indeed, one may form the intention in part because one expects to be tempted.

In such cases of prior intention we can ask: how will or may a rational planning agent think and act from the time of her initial intention formation to the time (or times) of follow-through? Intentions are, I think, best understood as plan-like commitments. A major role of such plan-like commitments is to settle practical matters in a way that structures temporally downstream thought and action. We need to know how this cross-temporal settling and structuring would or might work if the agent were

---

1. Classic studies of such cases are Ainslie, *Picoeconomics, Breakdown of Will*. I discuss and criticize Ainslie's views in my "Planning and Temptation." And see also Ainslie, "Precis."

proceeding rationally. A theory of planning agency needs to shed light on the nature of such diachronic rationality for planning agents.

This would be, in part, a theory of norms of rational temporally extended planning agency, norms that potentially guide the thought and action of a planning agent over time. We want to know what these norms are, what roles their acceptance plays in temporally extended planning agency, and why it matters (if it does matter) whether or not one guides one's thought and action in conformity with these norms. We might also appeal to such norms in a third-person assessment of an agent; but the main focus here is on norms that potentially guide the thinking of the agent herself.[2]

My own initial proposal for such a theory was in my 1987 book, *Intention, Plans, and Practical Reason*.[3] In that book I sketched an approach to diachronic plan rationality in which a central role is played by the agent's rational non-reconsideration of her prior intentions. If one does not reconsider one's prior intention, one normally will follow through with that prior intention. Further, given our cognitive limits, and the risks of undermining important forms of coordination previously forged, it will many times be quite sensible, in the absence of relevant new information, not to reconsider certain prior intentions. And that is the key to the rational stability of prior intentions over time. Or so I argued.

This is an outline of what I will call the *rational non-reconsideration model of diachronic planning agency*. A sophisticated development and extension of aspects of this model can be found in recent, important work of Richard Holton.[4] And I myself continue to believe that a theory of planning agency will need to highlight the significance of rational non-reconsideration. However, I have also come to believe that we need to introduce further resources.

There are at least two kinds of case that point toward the need for such additional resources. First, there are cases of prior decision and intention in favor of a temporally extended course of action in the face of underdetermination by one's recognized grounds, perhaps because of

2. Nomy Arpaly distinguishes two different approaches to practical rationality. We might "see the ideal theory of rationality as providing us with a manual of sorts" for the guidance of the agent herself in her thinking and acting. Or we could see such a theory as providing standards for assessment, from a third-person perspective, of the extent to which a certain agent was rational in her thought and action. My primary concern is in the neighborhood of the former, though, as noted, there will also be associated forms of third-person assessment. Arpaly, *Unprincipled Virtue*, 33.

3. And see also Bratman, Israel, and Pollack, "Plans."

4. John Broome's approach to diachronic rationality is also broadly in the spirit of the RNR model, though his focus is primarily on the kind of normatively underdetermined case to be noted below. Here I focus on Holton's work. Holton, *Willing, Wanting, Waiting*; Broome, *Rationality through Reasoning*, ch. 10.

important forms of non-comparability of those grounds. Perhaps, to take an example from John Broome, Abraham recognizes that the options of sacrificing his son and of disobeying God are non-comparable, but he nevertheless decides to go to the mountain and sacrifice Isaac.[5] Or the young man in Sartre's example decides to engage in a course of action of aiding his mother rather than fighting for the Free French, despite recognizing that the central considerations favoring these conflicting alternatives are non-comparable.[6] In each case we can ask whether, as the course of action develops over time, the prior intention in favor of that course of action has rational significance even though, as expected, the non-comparability and underdetermination reappear at each stage of action.

Second, there are cases of the sort with which I began this essay in which one forms a prior intention in anticipation of later temptation to act contrary to that prior intention. And here we can ask what rational significance, if any, that prior intention has at the time of the anticipated temptation and in the absence of relevant new information.

I discussed the first kind of case in a recent essay in which I argued that there is, at least for many, a pro tanto reason of diachronic self-governance in favor of a kind of constancy of prior intention in such underdetermination cases.[7] Here I focus on the case of (potentially) resisting temptation in part by way of a prior intention or policy, and on the conjecture that such cases also point to the need for certain further resources.[8] At the bottom of the present discussion will be an effort to deepen our understanding of the potential role in the practical stance of a planning agent of certain expectations about herself in the future, and thereby to deepen our understanding of the temporally extended structure of rational planning agency. In the end, I would hope that this could be part of an overall adjustment to the rational non-reconsideration model, one that draws on the cited theoretical resources in ways that systematically address both kinds of case, and perhaps others as well;[9] but I do not try to do that here.

5. Broome, "Are Intentions Reasons."
6. Sartre, "Existentialism Is a Humanism."
7. Bratman, "Time, Rationality, and Self-Governance" [this volume, essay 6]. See also Bratman, "Agency, Time, and Sociality" [this volume, essay 5].
8. My discussion draws on, and aims to improve upon, ideas from my "Toxin, Temptation, and the Stability of Intention" and my "Temptation Revisited."
9. I do not claim that these are the only difficult cases for a theory of diachronic plan rationality. There are puzzles about cases of slippery slope intransitivities discussed by Warren Quinn. (See Quinn, "Puzzle of the Self-Torturer"; Tenenbaum and Raffman, "Vague Projects." I discuss such cases in Bratman, "Toxin, Temptation.") There are puzzles about potential forms of "dynamic inconsistency" that are threatened when an agent has a preference structure that violates an important independence axiom.

II. RATIONAL NON-RECONSIDERATION MODEL

The first step is to spell out the rational non-reconsideration (RNR) model in some more detail.

Suppose that Anne decides at t1 to A at t2; suppose that Anne's decision at t1 is supported by her assessment, at t1, that there are adequate grounds—grounds that matter to her—that favor A at t2; and suppose that Anne continues so to intend up to t2. On the RNR model there are at this point in the temporal progression two basic cases of rational functioning at t2. There is, first, the case of rational non-reconsideration at t2. In this case Anne rationally does not reconsider her prior intention and straightway follows through at t2. In a second case, Anne rationally reconsiders at t2, taking into account relevant new information, if such there be. What Anne goes on to do is then a function of the new assessment at t2 in which her reconsideration issues. This new assessment will take the form of a judgment that assesses how her different options are supported by those considerations that matter to her. It will be a judgment of what, in the light of those considerations that now matter to her, it would be best to do at t2.

There are, of course, other possible cases. Anne might not reconsider even though she should have; Anne might reconsider even though she should not have; or Anne might reconsider and yet act contrary to her new judgment of what it would be best to do. But the initial two cases are those in which Anne is, according to the RNR model, in this respect diachronically rational.

This is not yet to say how we are to assess the rationality of (non-) reconsideration. In my 1987, book I argued that here it was appropriate to have a two-tier theory for a wide range of cases: we assess general habits and strategies of (non-) reconsideration pragmatically and with an eye to our resource limits, our susceptibilities to short-term distortions in our attitudes, and the advantages to coordination of leaving previously settled matters settled.[10] We then assess a wide range of specific cases of (non-) reconsideration by seeing how they relate to relevant, pragmatically justified

These puzzles have framed discussions of so-called sophisticated and resolute choice. (For helpful discussions see Rabinowicz, "To Have One's Cake," Rabinowicz, "Wise Choice.") And there may also be other challenging cases. My hope here and in "Time, Rationality, and Self-Governance" is not to sort out all these challenges but rather to articulate theoretical resources that can help us with the present cases and promise to help us as well with such further complexities concerning diachronic plan rationality.

10. Bratman, *Intention, Plans, and Practical Reason.*

general habits or strategies. And part of my reason for saying this was that (non-) reconsideration is many times not itself the issue of explicit deliberation but is non-deliberative and the issue of general habits and strategies that are in the background. (Holton's approach to these matters is also in the spirit of such a two-tier theory.)

Let me highlight three important features of this picture of diachronic planning agency. First, it allows for what I have called (following John Etchemendy, in conversation) the snowball effect. Once Anne decides at t1 to A at t2 she may well take relevant steps between t1 and t2, and these steps may well go some way toward making A the best option at t2. If option A is, say, traveling to Boston, and if Anne goes ahead between t1 and t2 and gets a ticket to Boston, then, even if she reconsiders at t2 whether at t2 to go to Boston or to New York, her actions in the interim will have tilted the scale in favor of Boston.

Second, this RNR model allows for the possibility that it will be rational at t2 for Anne not to reconsider even though it is also true that were she to reconsider she would sensibly judge that a different, alternative option would be best at t2. If she had reconsidered and reached that judgment, and if she had been functioning rationally, then, according to the RNR model, she would have given up her intention to A at t2 and proceeded with this alternative option at t2. Nevertheless, she may have been functioning rationally in refraining from reconsidering at t2 and so going ahead with A at t2.

Each of these two aspects of the RNR model provide a way in which the prior intention, formed at t1, can help shape the rationality of action at t2. Nevertheless, the model retains the idea that if, when the dust settles, the agent does indeed have a relevant judgment at t2 concerning which alternative would be strictly best at t2, then, if that agent is functioning rationally, she will opt for that alternative (if she opts for any alternative at all). Though the introduction of prior intentions and plans complicates the model of rational agency, there remains this basic rational connection between the agent's evaluation at t2 of present options and what she intends at t2 to do at t2. Call this the *rational priority of present evaluation*.[11]

Thus the outlines of the RNR model. I now turn to second thoughts.

---

11. Holton also aims to develop a theory that is compatible with something like this priority of present evaluation. Note that this priority of present evaluation can allow that one's present evaluation is responsive to the normative or evaluative significance, if such there be, of the specific prior history leading up to this moment of assessment. Holton, *Willing, Wanting, Waiting*, ch. 7.

III. TEMPTATION

Return to my general intention to have only one glass of wine at dinners despite the expected attractions, on each evening, of a second glass. My intention is grounded in my assessment that a general pattern of stopping with a single glass is far superior to a two-glass pattern, given how important it is to me to be able to work well after dinner. I know, however, that on each occasion I will be tempted at dinnertime to have a second glass just this once. I know, also, that this temptation will not just be a motivational push in the direction of a second glass; instead, I will at dinnertime come to value a second glass just this once more highly than the option of sticking with my one-glass policy this time. Putting to one side a distinction between valuing and value judgment (a distinction that is important, but that I bracket here[12]) my temptation will, I know, involve my judgment at dinnertime that it would be better on this particular occasion to have a second glass—better in light of those considerations that now matter to me.[13] My case will not just be one of a preference shift in favor of a second glass this time; it will involve what Holton calls a "judgment shift."[14] Finally, I know that this judgment shift will be temporary: at the end of the day I will stably revert to my judgment that what would have been best at dinnertime would have been to stop with a single glass of wine.

This raises a problem for my prior, one-glass intention. Given the priority of present evaluation, if I do judge at the time of follow-through that it would be strictly better to have the second glass this time, then it will be rational of me so to act—even if I expect to revert to my earlier evaluative assessment at the end of the day. And in forming my general, one-glass intention, I know that when the time for follow-through comes, I will indeed judge that it is strictly better to act contrary to that intention. But how can I rationally form the prior intention while knowing that when the time comes to do as I intend it will be rational for me not to follow through with that intention?[15]

---

12. In "Temptation Revisited" I appeal to what the tempted agent values, rather than her judgments of value. But by framing the problem here in terms of judgments of value I can more directly illuminate differences between my approach and Holton's. I do not try here to assess how to extend the proposal I go on to make to cases of valuing that is not a judgment of value.

13. That is, the judgment at dinnertime purports to bring to bear those relevant considerations that matter to me then, and says that these considerations favor a second glass of wine.

14. Holton, *Willing, Wanting, Waiting*, 137.

15. See my discussion of the "linking principle" in Bratman, "Toxin, Temptation," 64. In that essay I also discuss the relation between this principle and cases like Kavka's toxin puzzle. See Kavka, "Toxin Puzzle."

To make room for the rationality of such a general, one-glass prior intention, given expected temptation in the form of a judgment shift, it seems we will want to find a way to say that, having formed that intention, if things go as expected, it will be rational to follow through with that intention. But given the principle of the priority of present evaluation, it is unclear how we can say that.

Can we respond to this challenge by appealing to the role of rational non-reconsideration in the rational progression from prior intention to action? This is what Holton aims to do.[16] On his view, what is needed to allow me rationally to follow through each night with my prior one-glass intention is a kind of blinder: I need, rationally, to refrain from reconsidering that prior intention. After all, if I were to reconsider I would judge it strictly better to have the second glass; and so, given the priority of present evaluation, what would then be rational to do is not to follow through with my one-glass intention. So the key is somehow rationally to block the reconsideration that would lead to this judgment shift. And Holton thinks a two-tier pragmatic approach to rational non-reconsideration will tend to support the idea that it will be in such cases rational not to reconsider. So, he argues, we can in this way provide, within the RNR model, a plausible account of diachronic rationality and rational willpower in temptation cases.

A problem here, as Sarah Paul has emphasized,[17] is that it is going to be psychologically difficult, when offered the second glass of wine, to be vividly aware of one's option and yet not in effect reconsider one's intention to stick with one glass. Granted, sometimes there is a need for fast reaction that precludes reconsideration. Consider one's prior plan for what to do if the tiger attacks. But you might be offered the second glass at the beginning of the dinner and it might remain on offer throughout the dinner. Granted, it might be that a general habit of non-reconsideration in such cases would pay off pragmatically, in the long run. But, as we have learned from J. J. C. Smart, the inference from the advantages of the general habit directly to a specific conclusion about what to do on the present occasion, once the question of what to do on the present occasion is raised, is fraught.[18] Given that I know that I am inclined to think that it would be better to have the second glass, and given that I have ample time to reconsider, why not this time go ahead and reconsider my one-glass intention?

16. Holton, *Willing, Wanting, Waiting*, ch. 7.
17. Paul, "Review."
18. And see also Michael Thompson's discussion of a "transfer principle." Smart, "Extreme and Restricted Utilitarianism"; Thompson, *Life and Action*, ch. 10.

In any case, sometimes agents do reconsider in such cases. In Holton's view such reconsideration defeats the practical rational significance of the prior intention.[19] And we can ask whether this is, at least in certain cases, an overly weak view about the rational significance of prior intention.

Holton and I agree that the phenomenon of rational non-reconsideration is important; and we agree that sometimes it might be rational not to reconsider even if one would sensibly change one's mind if one were to reconsider. But if we try to explain rational follow through in the face of temptation by appeal primarily to these ideas about rational non-reconsideration, we are led to a rather weak model of diachronic plan rationality and rational willpower. And this leads me to ask whether, and if so how, we should strengthen this model.

To strengthen our account of diachronic rationality for planning agents in the face of such temptations, we would need to explain a way in which such an agent might rationally follow through with her general one-glass policy despite her judgment shift in the direction of a second glass just this once. But the problem is that it is not clear how to do this. We might allow that from a third-person perspective someone evaluating the agent who faces the temptation might see that it really would be better—better from the point of view of what matters to that tempted agent—to stick with the prior policy.[20] But here we are interested in norms of practical rationality that can guide the agent herself in her practical thinking; and it is hard to see how such a norm might endorse acting contrary to what you yourself judge best to do.[21]

So we have a dilemma. If we stick with the resources of the RNR model as so far described, we are led to put most of the theoretical weight, in our treatment of temptation cases, on the phenomenon of rational non-reconsideration; and this yields a fairly weak account of diachronic rationality for planning agents in temptation cases. However, if we seek to strengthen our model of such diachronic rationality, we face an objection grounded in the priority of present evaluation. What to say?

19. Broome's view has a similar structure.
20. Something like this thought lies behind the idea that certain forms of akrasia can be in a sense rational. On "inverse akrasia," see, for example, Arpaly, *Unprincipled Virtue*. (My thinking about inverse akrasia has benefited from work by Samuel Asarnow.)
21. This is broadly in the spirit of Arpaly's observation that "'Act against your best judgment' is . . . an absurd piece of advice." [*Unprincipled Virtue*, at 34]. However, I would want to express this idea in terms of the agent's judgment of the best, rather than the agent's "best judgment."

IV. ANTICIPATED REGRET

I want to explore the idea that a key to our response to this dilemma is the potential relevance of anticipated future regret to the rationality of resisting temptation.[22]

Suppose Anne knows she will be tempted at dinnertime. She begins the day with her one-glass policy. At dinner she experiences, as anticipated, a judgment shift and judges that a second glass would be superior to sticking with her one-glass policy this one time. But later that night, and also as anticipated, she stably reverts to her judgment that having only one glass that evening would have been the superior option then—superior in the light of those considerations that matter to her. If she had, at dinnertime, acted on her shifted judgment and drunk the second glass, her assessment at the end of the day would amount to a kind of regret.[23] And at dinnertime she anticipates this later regret. The idea I want to consider is that such anticipated future regret can sometimes make it rational for Anne to stick with her one-glass policy at dinnertime.

I think this is, in broad outline, a fairly commonsense idea. We are familiar with and recognize the force of advice along the lines of "Watch out, you will regret this." But it is not clear exactly how to develop this idea in the present context.

One thought is that Anne might see her future regret as evidence that her present judgment that it would be best to have a second glass of wine is faulty, and so be led to revise that judgment. A second, related thought is that Anne might seek a kind of cross-temporal coherence of judgment, see that to achieve this she needs to adjust her present judgment to cohere with her anticipated future judgment, and so revise her present judgment. In this way she comes to judge at dinnertime that it would be best not to have the second glass.

This second thought involves a parallel with Bas van Fraassen's "Reflection" principle. According to Reflection, rationality requires that your degree of credence at t1 in p, given that your degree of credence in p at t2 will be n, is n. And what we are now envisaging is that Anne seeks to conform to a principle that says, roughly and defeasibly, that her judgment at t1 of her best option at t1, given that her judgment at t2 is that A was her best option at t1, is that A is her best option at t1. Since, in each case,

---

22. This was a central idea in Bratman, "Toxin, Temptation."
23. In talking of regret I aim to refer to a fairly broad phenomenon of a later negative assessment of an earlier, significant decision. I am abstracting away from any specific emotional tone that may be involved in feeling regret.

in applying the norm at t1 the agent must depend on her expectation at t1 of her attitude at t2, we can say that in each case what is enjoined (perhaps defeasibly) is an alignment between attitude at t1 and anticipated attitude at t2.[24] And, as I see it, in each case there will need to be qualifications concerning cases in which the agent knows that her attitude at t2 will be significantly flawed.[25]

In each of the envisaged cases—anticipated regret as evidence, and the pursuit of cross-temporal epistemic coherence—Anne is led away from her initially shifted judgment and toward a judgment that coheres with her prior one-glass policy. Each of these forms of reflection treats the anticipated regret not as directly changing what it would be best to do, but rather as providing a kind of *epistemic* pressure to change one's present judgment about what it would be best to do. And there are, I think, contexts within which this will be a sensible form of reflection.[26] But I think it is important that there is also a different way in which, for a planning agent, anticipated regret can support rationally following through with one's prior policy, a way that involves forms of practical rather than epistemic coherence. The anticipated regret can affect the relative standing of one's present evaluative judgment in the structure of one's practical attitudes. Its direct impact can be *practical*, rather than epistemic; though once it has this practical impact it can indirectly affect relevant judgments of the best, by affecting what it would be, in the relevant sense, best to do. Or so I now want to argue.

V. AGENT'S STANDPOINT

A key is to examine interrelations between these issues about plan rationality and ideas about self-governance associated with work of Harry Frankfurt.[27] In particular, Frankfurt has highlighted the idea of the agent's

24. I am assuming here that these epistemic norms are to be applied by the agent herself; they are not just norms of third-person assessment.

25. van Fraassen, "Belief and the Will," "Belief and the Problem." And see also Evnine, *Epistemic Dimensions of Personhood*, ch. 5. For the worry about flawed later credence, see Christensen, "Clever Bookies." It is because of a corresponding worry about flawed future regret that I describe Anne's principle as defeasible.

26. Related forms of epistemic reflection are explored in Paul, "Doxastic Self-Control"; and Lau, "Temptation."

27. As I say in my "Temptation Revisited," "behind debates about instrumental practical reason lurk . . . broadly Frankfurtian issues about the constitution of the agent." Bratman, "Temptation Revisited," 26. For Frankfurt's discussions see, for example, Frankfurt, *Importance*. I discuss related issues about relations between normative reasons and the constitution of the agent in Bratman, "Constructivism."

practical standpoint—the idea of "where [the agent] stands."[28] The agent's governance of his own life consists in part in the guidance of his relevant thought and action by attitudes that constitute where he stands; and important aspects of his rational functioning will be a matter of such guidance by his practical standpoint.

The idea of the agent's standpoint is not the idea of a single, distinctive attitude of that agent. It is, rather, the idea of how the agent's various attitudes, and other relevant features of her psychology, come together (or perhaps fail to come together) to constitute a coherent, relevant standpoint. When Frankfurt attempts to say more precisely how the agent's standpoint is constituted, he appeals to higher-order desires. But he also appeals to phenomena of wholeheartedness and satisfaction, in which the latter is a matter, roughly, of "simply *having no interest* in making changes."[29] And Frankfurt sees these phenomena not as themselves further, distinctive attitudes of the agent but, rather, as more or less holistic properties of the agent's psychological economy. Without endorsing the specifics of these Frankfurtian proposals, we can agree with the background insight that, though certain attitudes may be especially salient, the agent's standpoint is not itself a specific attitude but a more or less holistic property of the agent's overall psychological profile.[30] In talking of the agent's standpoint we are alluding to a kind of function—as we might say, a *standpoint function*—from overall psychological profile to standpoint. And one of the lessons of the important exchange between Frankfurt and Gary Watson on these matters is that there are complex philosophical issues lurking in the decision as between different proposed standpoint functions.[31]

I return later to this idea of a standpoint function. For now I want to note that in the background here is a wide-scope norm roughly along the lines of

---

28. Frankfurt, "Identification and Wholeheartedness," 166.

29. Frankfurt, "Faintest Passion," 105. The initial appeal to higher-order desires is in Frankfurt's "Freedom of the Will."

30. It may be that the temptation to identify the agent's standpoint with a specific, distinctive attitude—say, an attitude of reflective endorsement—reveals a kind of homuncular picture of agential standpoint. And one of Frankfurt's insights, in appealing to ideas of wholeheartedness and satisfaction, is that we need an understanding of where the agent stands that does not see it as a single privileged reflective attitude, one that is held by a little person in the head.

31. For Watson's contributions see: Watson, "Free Agency," "Free Action and Free Will." I discuss these exchanges, and themes relevant to this present discussion, in Bratman, "Three Theories of Self-Governance."

Synchronic Standpoint Rationality: It is defeasibly rational of an agent that (If at t her practical standpoint is committed to X, and if she knows that this commitment to X argues conclusively in favor of a course of action A at t, and she knows that her A-ing then requires her intending then to A, then at t she intends to A.)[32]

And a ground for this rationality principle is that conformity to it is an element in synchronic self-governance; and, we can suppose, there is something to be said for such self-governance.

Return now to the potential relevance of anticipated regret. Here my thought is that this Frankfurtian conception of the agent's standpoint, and the associated norm of synchronic standpoint rationality, puts us in a position to articulate a *practical* role to be played by anticipated regret in our account of rational follow-through. The intuitive idea is that, given the anticipated regret, in certain cases the agent's standpoint does not favor the option favored by her shifted evaluative judgment, but favors, rather, following through with her general policy.[33] The direct impact of the anticipated regret is in this way practical, rather than epistemic.

Why think this? Well, it seems plausible that in engaging in planning agency we are committed to giving significance to how our planned activities will look to us as our plan progresses into the future.[34] If this is right, it suggests that anticipated future regret can sometimes undermine the normal status of present evaluative judgment in a planning agent's present practical standpoint. In this way, Frankfurtian ideas about where the agent stands make room for an associated interpretation of the practical significance of anticipated future regret. Anticipated future regret matters, according to this interpretation, because it can sometimes undermine the normal status of present evaluative judgment in a planning agent's present standpoint. Anticipated future regret does not simply provide

32. Manuel Vargas discusses a related idea of, as he calls it, "the agent's rational standpoint," and the relation of this idea to interpretations of "inverse akrasia." Vargas, "Some Doubts."

33. As I once said: "anticipated future regret can sometimes undermine the agential authority of that normally overriding evaluative ranking in favor of the second glass and, so to speak, delegitimize it." Bratman, "Temptation Revisited," 278.

34. In a fuller discussion we would need to ask in more detail whether and why this commitment really is embedded in our planning agency. Here I take the liberty of working with the supposition that it is. David Gauthier appeals to a related idea of a plan being "confirmed" as it is executed over time. See Gauthier, "Intention and Deliberation." I discuss this idea in Bratman, "Interplay of Intention and Reason" [this volume, essay 8].

evidence concerning one's standpoint; it helps shape the contours of one's standpoint.

A problem, however, is that we seem now to be saying that the relevant advice of rationality, advice that is to guide the agent's thinking, can be to act (i) in conformity with your general policy and (ii) contrary to what you now judge to be best. But, as noted earlier, (ii) would be puzzling as an element in a norm of rationality that is to guide the practical thinking of the agent herself. Can we exploit the insights of this Frankfurt-style interpretation of the significance of anticipated regret without a heroic insistence on rational advice in favor of (ii)?

VI. INDIRECT EPISTEMIC IMPACT OF ANTICIPATION OF REGRET

Recall that the relevant judgment about which option would be best is a judgment about which would be best in the light of the considerations that matter to the agent. But now we should note that insofar as anticipated regret changes where the agent stands, it changes what matters to the agent. However we understand the intuitive idea of the agent's standpoint, and however we understand the intuitive idea of what matters to the agent, we will want these to be linked: what matters to an agent is specified in part by where she relevantly stands. So, insofar as anticipated regret changes where the agent stands it can change which option is, in the relevant sense, best. So, once we recognize the potential impact of the anticipated regret on where the agent stands, we should allow that there will potentially be a corresponding indirect impact on the agent's judgment of the best. The primary impact of the anticipated regret is practical: it helps shape where the agent stands. This is not a version of the epistemic strategy in which the anticipated regret is evidence of an epistemic error made in present evaluation, or in which what leads to change in present evaluation is a concern for epistemic coherence over time. Nevertheless, this direct impact on where the agent stands indirectly supports an associated change in relevant evaluative judgment. So in acting in accord with her cited view of where she stands, Anne need not be violating the priority of present evaluation.

We provide then for the possibility of a direct practical impact of anticipated regret on the agent's stance. This can then help shape what matters to the agent, and so what it would be, in the relevant sense, best to do. So there is a potential indirect impact on judgment of the best. And this allows us to retain the priority of present evaluation.

This supposes that anticipated regret can indeed have this (defeasible) impact on where the agent stands. We need now to reflect further on this supposition.

VII. STANDPOINT FUNCTIONS

Return to Anne at dinnertime. Simplifying, her psychology at that time includes:

(1) Her general one-glass policy, one she knows was formed earlier in the light of her earlier evaluative judgment.
(2) Her shifted evaluative judgment in favor of a second glass this one time.
(3) Her anticipation that she would later regret acting on 2 rather than 1.

How do we get from these attitudes of her psychology to where Anne relevantly stands at dinnertime?

Here we need to return to the idea of a *standpoint function*: a function from the agent's overall psychological profile to where she stands. Let us say that a *time-slice evaluative* standpoint function is one that simply reads off the agent's relevant present standpoint from that agent's present evaluative judgment of her options (in this case, 2). By contrast, a *cross-temporally structured* standpoint function also gives defeasible significance, in determining the agent's present standpoint, to the agent's present expectation of how she will see relevant matters in the future (in this case, 3) and/or to her present grasp of how she has seen relevant matters in the past (in this case, an aspect of 1).

Both a time-slice evaluative standpoint function and a cross-temporally structured standpoint function will be *present focused* in the sense that, for each, it is, at bottom, present attitudes that shape present standpoint. Where they differ is on the question of whether present recognition or expectation of relevant past or future attitudes can matter. And this difference induces another difference. A time-slice evaluative standpoint function will not itself exert rational pressure in the direction of revision of the relevant evaluative judgments. It will be, in this sense, *conservative*. By contrast, a cross-temporally structured standpoint function may, for reasons noted in the previous section, exert rational pressure in the direction of revision of present evaluative judgment. It will be, in this sense, *potentially revisionary*.

The conjecture that Anne's anticipated regret can shape her present standpoint entails that Anne's relevant standpoint function is, in this future-directed respect, cross-temporally structured rather than time-slice evaluative. But why think that? What determines the appropriate standpoint function for an agent?

As I see it, the standpoint function that is apt for a given agent is a feature of the kind of agent that agent is.[35] And here it is important that, as noted earlier, it seems that a planning agent is committed to shaping present thought and action with an eye to how her planned activities will stably look as they develop over time. So it seems plausible that it is a constitutive feature of being a planning agent that one's standpoint function gives defeasible significance to one's present expectations of how one will see relevant matters as one's plans and policies unfold over time. This means that a planning agent's standpoint function will be, at least in this future-directed respect, cross-temporally structured, and so potentially revisionary.[36]

This idea that the standpoint function for a planning agent is, in the cited future-directed way, cross-temporally structured, and so potentially revisionary, is my proposed addition to the RNR model of diachronic plan rationality. It allows for a distinctive practical role that may be played by the expectation of future regret. And when we make this addition to our theory we can go beyond the thought of the RNR model that the fundamental source of diachronic stability of prior plan-like commitments is the rational pressure not to reconsider.[37]

This proposal supplements but does not supplant the potential role of rational non-reconsideration in diachronic plan rationality. Indeed, the two

35. Aspects of Vargas's discussion in his "Some Doubts" suggest that he would be skeptical here.

36. This argument for the relevance to the agent's present standpoint of the anticipated later assessment applies to cases in which one is carrying out a relevant plan or policy. I put aside the question whether also to include within an apt standpoint function an appeal to expected future assessments that are not tied in this way to the ongoing execution of plans and policies. I also put aside the question whether an apt standpoint function will also give defeasible significance to the agent's present recognition of how she has seen relevant matters in the past. (Here one might try to argue for an affirmative answer by arguing that a planning agent characteristically seeks a cross-temporal plan-structured coherence, one that incorporates both the past and the future.) In both respects my discussion here is partial and preliminary. [For further developments see this volume, essays 10, 11, and 1 (esp. note 25).]

37. In discussing my earlier efforts to understand the potential significance of anticipated regret, Holton says that we could understand this as "providing an extra reason to be factored into any reconsideration" or we could understand it "as working within a two-tier account [of non-reconsideration], providing a constraint on the kinds of tendencies it would be rational to have." Holton, *Willing, Wanting, Waiting*, 157. The practical role I am trying to articulate for anticipated regret is closer to Holton's first option, but it is important that the anticipated regret is to affect the output of reconsideration in the distinctive way I have described, by way of its recognized impact on the agent's standpoint rather than by way of appeal to a distinctive new reason. In response to a view along the lines of his first option, Holton observes that sometimes we correctly see future regret as misguided, and in any case a person sufficiently in the grips of temptation may fail to anticipate the regret or may fail to appreciate its significance. And here I fully agree. But our job is not to provide a failsafe solution to

ideas can interact with a kind of synergy. The present proposal about the standpoint function of a planning agent helps make rational sense of the prior intention to resist the expected later temptation given the anticipation of regret in the yet further future. This helps support the initial formation of that prior intention. And once that prior intention is in place, rational pressures in support of non-reconsideration of that prior intention can also come to bear.

Return now to van Fraassen's Reflection principle. We can understand that principle as enjoining an alignment between attitude at t1 and expected (at t1) attitude at t2. And, if we assume that the agent's regret at t2 would determine her relevant standpoint at t2, we can see our proposal as in a way analogous to van Fraassen's. The idea would be, roughly, that a planning agent's standpoint function says that, defeasibly, the agent's standpoint at t1, given that her expected (at t1) standpoint at t2 stably favors X, favors X. This defeasibly induces an alignment between the agent's standpoint at t1 and the agent's expected (at t1) stable standpoint at later stages of plan execution. And that is the partial parallel with Reflection. We have, as it were, a (defeasible) Standpoint Reflection principle for planning agents. However, this Standpoint Reflection principle—in contrast with Reflection—is not itself a rationality norm, one that can be violated and whose purported normative force needs defense. It is, rather, a structural principle that is part of the metaphysics of planning agency: it says how the contours of a planning agent's present standpoint are potentially shaped by certain expectations of future attitudes. Nevertheless, with this structural principle in place there will be important implications about rationality, given the Synchronic Standpoint Rationality principle.

Return to Anne. Her standpoint function will be, in the cited future-directed way, cross-temporally structured in its treatment of the relevance to where she stands of her anticipation of regret. This allows that she may rationally stick with her one-glass policy because of the impact of her anticipation of regret on the contours of her present standpoint. And this may sensibly have an indirect impact on her present judgment of the best: her standpoint function is potentially revisionary. So in following through she may also conform to the priority of present evaluation.

In rationally resisting temptation in this distinctive way, Anne's solution to a threatened judgment shift is not to refrain from reconsideration

---

temptation, a kind of failsafe self-help guide. Our job, rather, is to articulate an important and sometimes available form of rational resistance to temptation, one that goes beyond the limited story of the RNR model. (Though, as I go on to note in the text, the proposal I am making does not supplant the possible role of rational non-reconsideration.) And our job is to understand the implications of this account for our basic model of temporally extended planning agency.

but to engage in more reconsideration.[38] (Though the question remains whether it is worth it to engage in such reconsideration.) When faced with the temptation of the second glass, she at first reconsiders and has a shift of judgment in its favor. But upon even further reflection she anticipates future regret, recognizes the impact on where she stands, and thereby arrives at an evaluative judgment that coheres with her one-glass policy.

Is it rationally required that Anne be a planning agent, in a sense that entails that her standpoint function is, in the cited future-directed way, cross-temporally structured, and so potentially revisionary? That is too strong. What does seem true is that there are very good reasons for her to (continue to) be a planning agent. So Anne's continuing to be a planning agent makes sense, and she can see this on reflection. (Which is not to say that Anne has a psychologically real option of becoming, at will, an agent who is not a planning agent.)[39] And so long as Anne continues to be a planning agent, her standpoint function will potentially support the rationality of her following through with her considered, prior one-glass policy.

Might Anne ask: "Can I stop being a planning agent for just long enough to have the second glass of wine, which I now judge to be the superior option?"[40] Here I think the answer will be: you probably do not have it in your power simply, at will, to stop being a planning agent. And it is even less plausible that you have it in your power to stop being a planning agent for just long enough to have the second drink, and then revert to planning agency given the general benefits of that form of agency. Being a planning agent involves a complex web of dispositions of thought and action, and these are not the sorts of things we plausibly have the capacity to turn off and then on again at will.[41]

Being a planning agent makes possible for Anne a distinctive kind of rational stability of intention in the face of temptation. This form of rational stability goes beyond (though it does not preclude, and can interact with) the stability that can be achieved by way of rational non-reconsideration of a prior

38. Compare with a common liberal thought that a solution to badly exercised free speech is not a restriction on speech but more speech.

39. I develop the ideas in these last three sentences, and note a parallel with P. F. Strawson's approach to the reactive attitudes, in Bratman, "Intention, Belief, Practical, Theoretical," section IX [this volume, essay 2]. [And see this volume, essay 1, section 4.]

40. A question from Krista Lawlor.

41. In a way this response is in the spirit of Harry Frankfurt's appeal to volitional necessities. But his idea is that certain substantive commitments—for example, who or what one loves—can be volitional necessities. By contrast, my thought here is only that certain basic dispositional structures, those that are involved in distinctive forms of agency, are not plausibly changeable at will. See Frankfurt, "On the Necessity of Ideals."

intention. And this potential role in supporting this further form of rational stability is itself another reason for her to (continue to) be a planning agent.

ACKNOWLEDGMENTS

An earlier version of this essay was presented at the August 2013 workshop on diachronic rationality at the Oslo Center for the Study of Mind in Nature. Thanks to all for extremely helpful discussions of these issues.

REFERENCES

Ainslie, George. *Breakdown of Will*. New York: Cambridge University Press, 2001.

Ainslie, George. *Pico-economics: The Strategic Interaction of Successive Motivational States within the Person*. Cambridge: Cambridge University Press, 1992.

Ainslie, George. "Precis of *Breakdown of Will*." *Behavioral and Brain Sciences* 28 (2005): 635–50.

Arpaly, Nomy. *Unprincipled Virtue*. Oxford: Oxford University Press, 2003.

Bratman, Michael E. "Agency, Time, and Sociality." *Proceedings and Addresses of the American Philosophical Association* 84, no. 2 (2010): 7–26 [this volume, essay 5].

Bratman, Michael E. "Constructivism, Agency, and the Problem of Alignment." In *Constructivism in Practical Philosophy*, eds. James Lenman and Yonatan Shemmer, 81–98. Oxford: Oxford University Press, 2012.

Bratman, Michael E. "Intention, Belief, Practical, Theoretical." In *Spheres of Reason*, ed. Jens Timmerman, John Skorupski, and Simon Robertson, 29–61. Oxford: Oxford University Press 2009 [this volume, essay 2].

Bratman, Michael E. *Intention, Plans, and Practical Reason*. Cambridge, MA: Harvard University Press, 1987. (Re-issued by CSLI, 1999. Stanford, CA: CSLI Publications.)

Bratman, Michael E. "The Interplay of Intention and Reason." *Ethics* 123 (2013): 657–72 [this volume, essay 8].

Bratman, Michael E. "Planning and Temptation." In *Faces of Intention: Selected Essays on Intention and Agency*, 35–57. Cambridge: Cambridge University Press, 1999.

Bratman, Michael E. "Temptation Revisited." In *Structures of Agency*, 257–82. New York: Oxford University Press, 2007.

Bratman, Michael E. "Three Theories of Self-Governance." In *Structures of Agency*, 222–53. New York: Oxford University Press, 2007.

Bratman, Michael E. "Time, Rationality, and Self-Governance." *Philosophical Issues* 22 (2012): 73–88 [this volume, essay 6].

Bratman, Michael E. "Toxin, Temptation, and the Stability of Intention." In *Faces of Intention: Selected Essays on Intention and Agency*, 58–9. Cambridge: Cambridge University Press, 1999.

Bratman, Michael E., David J. Israel, and Martha E. Pollack. "Plans and Resource-Bounded Practical Reasoning." *Computational Intelligence* 4, no. 3 (1988): 349–55.

Broome, John. "Are Intentions Reasons? And How Should We Cope with Incommensurable Values?" In *Practical Rationality and Preference: Essays for*

David Gauthier, eds. Christopher W. Morris and Arthur Ripstein, 98–120. Cambridge: Cambridge University Press, 2001.

Broome, John. *Rationality through Reasoning.* Chichester, UK: Wiley-Blackwell, 2013.

Christensen, David. "Clever Bookies and Coherent Beliefs." *Philosophical Review* 100 (1991): 229–47.

Evnine, Simon. *Epistemic Dimensions of Personhood.* Oxford: Oxford University Press, 2008.

Frankfurt, Harry. "The Faintest Passion." In *Necessity, Volition, and Love,* 95–107. Cambridge: Cambridge University Press, 1999.

Frankfurt, Harry. "Freedom of the Will and the Concept of a Person." In *The Importance of What We Care About,* 11–25. Cambridge: Cambridge University Press, 1988.

Frankfurt, Harry "Identification and Wholeheartedness." In *The Importance of What We Care About,* 159–76. Cambridge: Cambridge University Press, 1988.

Frankfurt, Harry. *The Importance of What We Care About.* Cambridge: Cambridge University Press, 1988.

Frankfurt, Harry. "On the Necessity of Ideals." In *Necessity, Volition, and Love,* 108–16. Cambridge: Cambridge University Press, 1999.

van Fraassen, Bas. "Belief and the Will." *Journal of Philosophy* 81 (1984): 235–56.

van Fraassen, Bas. "Belief and the Problem of Ulysses and the Sirens." *Philosophical Studies* 77 (1995): 7–37.

Gauthier, David. "Intention and Deliberation." In *Modeling Rationality, Morality, and Evolution,* ed. Peter A. Danielson, 41–54. New York: Oxford University Press, 1998.

Holton, Richard. *Willing, Wanting, Waiting.* Oxford: Clarendon, 2009.

Kavka, Gregory S. "The Toxin Puzzle." *Analysis* 43 (1983): 33–6.

Lau, Arthur. "Temptation, Resolution, and Epistemic Self-Trust." Unpublished manuscript, Stanford University, 2013.

Paul, Sarah. "Doxastic Self-Control." *American Philosophical Quarterly* 52 (2015): 145–58.

Paul, Sarah. "Review of Richard Holton's *Willing, Wanting,* Waiting." *Mind* 120 (2011): 889–92.

Quinn, Warren. "The Puzzle of the Self-Torturer." In *Morality and Action,* 198–209. Cambridge: Cambridge University Press, 1993.

Rabinowicz, Wlodek. "To Have One's Cake and Eat It Too; Sequential Choice and Expected Utility Violations." *Journal of Philosophy* 92 (1995): 586–620.

Rabinowicz, Wlodek. "Wise Choice: On Dynamic Decision-Making without Independence." In *Logic, Action, and Cognition,* eds. Eva Ejerhed and Sten Linstrom, 97–109. Dordrecht, The Netherlands: Kluwer, 1997.

Sartre, Jean-Paul. "Existentialism is a Humanism." In *Existentialism from Dostoevsky to Sartre,* revised and expanded, ed. Walter Kaufmann, 345–69. New York: Meridian/Penguin, 1975.

Smart, J. C .C. "Extreme and Restricted Utilitarianism." In *Theories of Ethics,* ed. Philippa Foot, 171–83. Oxford: Oxford University Press, 1967.

Tenenbaum, Sergio, and Diana Raffman. "Vague Projects and the Puzzle of the Self-Torturer." *Ethics* 123 (2012): 86–112.

Thompson, Michael. *Life and Action.* Cambridge, MA: Harvard University Press, 2008.

Vargas, Manuel. "Some Doubts about Inverse Akrasia." Unpublished manuscript, University of San Francisco, 2013.

Watson, Gary. "Free Action and Free Will." In *Agency and Answerability,* 161–96. Oxford: Oxford University Press, 2004.

Watson, Gary. "Free Agency." In *Agency and Answerability,* 13–32. Oxford: Oxford University Press, 2004.

CHAPTER 8

The Interplay of Intention and Reason*

I

My title comes from the last sentence of David Gauthier's essay "Assure and Threaten."[1] In this 1994 essay, together with a series of interrelated essays published shortly thereafter, Gauthier lays out a deep and important approach to the nature of practical reason.[2] I think we have yet fully to come to terms with the ideas in these essays, and what I want to do here is to take some tentative steps in that direction. This will lead me to propose

* Thanks for help (including written comments from Claire Finkelstein) from the participants at the conference on David Gauthier's work at York University in May 2011, a conference deftly organized by Susan Dimock. And thanks to Sarah Paul for written comments on an earlier draft. We all owe a great deal to David Gauthier for his groundbreaking contributions to this subject. On a more personal note, I want to thank David for conversations and exchanges over the years from which I have learned a great deal.

1. David Gauthier, "Assure and Threaten," *Ethics* 104 (1994): 690–721.

2. The further essays of particular interest to my discussion are David Gauthier, "Intention and Deliberation," in *Modeling Rationality, Morality, and Evolution*, ed. Peter A. Danielson (Oxford: Oxford University Press, 1998), 41–54; "Rethinking the Toxin Puzzle," in *Rational Commitment and Social Justice: Essays for Gregory Kavka*, ed. Jules L. Coleman and Christopher W. Morris (Cambridge: Cambridge University Press, 1998), 47–58; and "Commitment and Choice: An Essay on the Rationality of Plans," in *Ethics, Rationality, and Economic Behavior*, ed. Francesco Farina, Frank Hahn, and Stefano Vannucci (Oxford: Oxford University Press, 1996), 217–43. Other related essays include "Rationality and the Rational Aim," in *Reading Parfit*, ed. Jonathan Dancy (Oxford: Blackwell, 1997), 24–41; and "Resolute Choice and Rational Deliberation: A Critique and a Defense," *Noûs* 31 (1997): 1–25. Gauthier's approach in these essays is in the spirit of—though in certain ways it differs from and goes beyond—his account of "constrained maximization" in his *Morals by Agreement* (Oxford: Oxford University Press, 1986).

an adjustment in the theory, an adjustment that takes its cue from one of Gauthier's central ideas about temporally extended agency.

Gauthier's view of practical rationality in these papers involves two fundamental ideas. There is, first, the idea that the primary targets for rational assessment are not specific choices and actions, but rather "deliberative procedures."[3] In assessing these procedures, Gauthier proposes that "their underlying rationale must be found, not in some a priori conception of rationality, but pragmatically in their role in enabling the deliberating agent to realize her most favored prospects."[4] In "Assure and Threaten" this appeal to realizing one's most favored prospects is conceptualized as an appeal to the basic aim that one's "life go as well as possible."[5] And the proposal is that "deliberative procedures are rational if and only if the effect of employing them is maximally conducive to one's life going as well as possible, where this effect includes, not only the actions they determine, but also the actions they make possible."[6] And a specific choice or action is "rational if and only if it is adequately supported by rational deliberative procedures."[7]

Let me pause for two comments. The first concerns the idea of employing a deliberative procedure. Gauthier does not here speak simply of a disposition of action, or even simply of accepting a deliberative procedure. The phenomenon he is focusing on is that of employing a standard—where that involves accepting it and being guided by it in one's relevant practical thinking. And Gauthier supposes that if the general employment of the procedure passes his pragmatic test, then each employment will be rational.

Second, consider the aim that one's life go as well as possible. In "Assure and Threaten," Gauthier leaves this as a largely untheorized idea and intends thereby to ensure that his theory can work given very different specifications of what it is for one's life to go well. It is clear, however, that he thinks this is a matter of the agent's contingent and potentially idiosyncratic "concerns," concerns that may be more or less other-regarding.[8] This is a broadly subjectivist conception of one's life going well.

3. Gauthier, "Assure and Threaten," 701.
4. Gauthier, "Resolute Choice and Rational Deliberation," 10.
5. Gauthier, "Assure and Threaten," 690.
6. Ibid., 701. Gauthier qualifies this in a later paper ("Rethinking the Toxin Puzzle," 58 n. 5). In pursuit of the emendation he thinks is needed he says: "as a first approximation, we might say that deliberative procedures are rational if and only if they are effectively directed to making one's life go as well as possible." The idea is to substitute "effectively directed to" for the earlier "effect of employing them." For the purposes of our discussion here, however, I think we can safely put this complexity to one side.
7. Gauthier, "Assure and Threaten," 701. This slogan comes from an objection that Gauthier rejects, but Gauthier nevertheless endorses the slogan itself.
8. Ibid., 690–1.

Returning to the main thread: a guiding thought is that, to draw from *Morals by Agreement*, "a fully rational being is able to reflect on his standard of deliberation, and to change that standard in the light of reflection."[9] We ask what general standard such a fully rational agent would settle on and employ, and the rationality of a specific action or choice is then a function of that general standard of deliberation.

This pragmatic two-tier theory is Gauthier's meta-theory. His substantive theory of practical rationality in these essays—and this is his second fundamental idea—is a proposal concerning certain aspects of a standard of deliberation that would pass this pragmatic test. In particular, Gauthier's central interest in these essays concerns the standard of deliberation for cases of interaction between two or more rational agents. In the cases of interest, each is in a position to settle at t_1 on a plan of action that extends over time, from t_1 through t_3, and each knows that the resulting impact of his plan on his aim that his "life go as well as possible" depends both on his own plan and action and on the plan and action of the others.

Putting aside some complexities, and following Gauthier in making a fairly strong assumption about each person's knowledge of the other's mind, we can focus on two kinds of cases. There is, first, the case of *potential assurance*. I am faced with a choice whether sincerely to assure you at t_1 that if you help me at t_2, I will help you at t_3. If I do sincerely assure you at t_1 then, if you assume I would follow through if you were to help me, you can judge that your life goes best if you do indeed help me at t_2. But if I do not sincerely assure you at t_1 you will reasonably believe that you do better not to help me at t_2, since you then will reasonably not expect that I would reciprocate at t_3. My life goes better if we each help the other than if neither helps the other, and I can ensure that better outcome by sincerely assuring you. But it is also true (we are to suppose) that at t_3 if you have already helped me at t_2, my life goes even better if I then abandon my assurance and do not help you. So it is not clear that even if I settle on this assurance plan at t_1, and you do indeed help me at t_2, it will at t_3 be rational for me to follow through with my plan.[10] But if I know that if matters proceed as planned up to t_3 it will not be rational for me to follow through, then

9. Gauthier, *Morals by Agreement*, 183.
10. If we could appeal here to moral reasons to do as one has assured another, we could go some way toward explaining why I would, having assured you, have sufficient reason to follow through. But Gauthier's foundational project is to explore the rational structure of assurances and threats prior to the introduction of explicitly moral considerations. This is why he says that his "essay is about rationality, not morality" (Gauthier, "Assure and Threaten," 693 n. 7; and see also n. 17).

it seems that I cannot rationally and sincerely assure you at t_1.[11] So from doubts about rational follow through at t_3 we arrive at doubts about the rationality of sincere assurance at t_1.

The second case is that of *potential threat*. It is important to me that you do not X at t_2. I can make it unlikely that you will X at t_2 by issuing a sincere threat at t_1 that says: if you X at t_2 I will Y at t_3, where my Y-ing would be costly to you, though also costly to me. On natural assumptions, I can expect at t_1 that my life would go better if I sincerely threaten, in contrast with refraining from adopting a threat plan. However, in a case in which, though I threaten, you nevertheless X at t_2, I will be faced at t_3 with the issue of whether to follow through on my threat. Though the expected impact on my life of the sincere threat at t_1 was quite good, the known impact on my life of following through at t_3, given that you have gone ahead and X-ed, is quite bad. So it is not clear I can rationally follow through at t_3 with my threat plan. So it is not clear I can rationally and sincerely issue the threat in the first place, at t_1.

In each case I am faced with a choice at t_1 between different plans for the time t_1–t_3 (where to choose a plan is to form the corresponding intention), and am also faced at t_3 with the issue of whether to follow through with the plan I settled on at t_1. A substantive theory should help us say which temporally extended plans and which actions it would be rational of the agent to choose: it should thereby help us understand "the interplay of intention and reason." And here Gauthier distinguishes between three different theories.[12]

According to a sophisticated deliberative standard,[13] we look first at the decisions that loom at t_3. We ask which decision would be best—best with respect to the aim of one's life going as well as possible—as compared with the other alternatives at that time of action, t_3, given the plan adopted at t_1. A constraint on a rational decision at t_1 in favor of a plan of action for the period t_1–t_3 is that the options it specifies for t_3 pass the test of being

11. "I can't sincerely assure you that I shall do something that I know I shall have sufficient reason not to do, and believe that as a rational person, I therefore shall not do" (Gauthier, "Assure and Threaten," 693). And see what I call the "linking principle" in Michael E. Bratman, "Following Through with One's Plans: Reply to David Gauthier," in Danielson, *Modeling Rationality, Morality, and Evolution*, 55–66, at 55.

12. Gauthier, "Intention and Deliberation," 52–3, where Gauthier characterizes "three forms that a planning theory might take."

13. For the terminology of sophisticated and—to follow in the text—resolute, see Edward F. McClennen, *Rationality and Dynamic Choice: Foundational Explorations* (Cambridge: Cambridge University Press, 1990). Gauthier does not use these labels in the passage in "Intention and Deliberation" cited in the previous note, but they seem to me appropriate labels and their use here helps set the stage for Gauthier's own proposal.

as least as good as their alternatives *at t_3*, given the choice at t_1. This means I can rationally settle on a plan of assuring you at t_1 and conditionally reciprocating at t_3, only if in the reciprocation-requiring circumstance at t_3 reciprocating would be in the relevant way (at least, weakly) superior to not reciprocating at t_3. On present assumptions about our assurance case, an implication of this sophisticated standard is that it will not be rational to settle on the cited assurance plan. And a similar line of thought indicates that on such a sophisticated standard of deliberation, it will not be rational to settle on the cited threat plan.

Second, there is a resolute deliberative principle. We begin by asking which temporally extended plan for the period t_1–t_3 is best as compared, at t_1, with its alternative plans for t_1–t_3, on the assumption that the plans would indeed be executed. If you settle at t_1 on a temporally extended plan that is in this way expected-superior to alternative plans you might adopt at t_1, and if that plan tells you to Y at t_3 in circumstance C, then if you do indeed end up in C at t_3, where C is as you had supposed it would be, it is rational for you to Y then. On present assumptions, an implication of this resolute standard is that it will indeed be rational to settle on, and then to follow through with, both the cited assurance plan and the cited threat plan.

Gauthier defends a third theory. Sophisticated deliberation focuses at first on whether follow through at t_3 will be superior to abandoning one's prior plan at t_3, given the plan one has adopted at t_1. Resolute deliberation focuses at first on whether the expected benefits at t_1 of settling on a temporally extended plan for t_1–t_3 exceed the expected benefits at t_1 of settling on a different temporally extended plan for t_1–t_3—where in each case we take for granted follow through in relevant circumstances at t_3. For each standard the basic evaluative comparisons concern plans or options at the very same time. In the case of sophistication we compare follow-through at t_3 with non-follow-through at t_3; in the case of resoluteness we compare settling at t_1 on a temporally extended assurance or threat plan, with settling at t_1 on a nonassurance or nonthreat plan. In contrast, Gauthier's proposal has a cross-temporal and counterfactual structure. We compare follow-through of a plan at t_3, with what would have transpired if one had not settled on that plan at t_1.[14] And such a *counterfactual comparison*

14. Gauthier writes: "Within the context provided by a course of action, the reasons relevant to performing a particular action focus not on whether the action will yield the best outcome judged from the time of performance, but on whether it will yield a better outcome than the agent could have expected had she not undertaken that course of action" ("Intention and Deliberation," 48). And see Gauthier, "Assure and Threaten," 707 and 717.

deliberative standard is poised to treat differently the cases of assurance and of threat.

Suppose I sincerely assure you at t_1, and you do help me at t_2. At t_3 I can see that if I follow through with my assurance plan I do better than I would have done if I had not adopted my assurance plan at t_1 (since then you would not have helped me at t_2). So the counterfactual comparison deliberative standard will tend to support both adopting and following through with an assurance plan even though in following through I do worse than I would if I were instead at t_3 to abandon my prior plan and not reciprocate.

A threat plan will tend to fare differently. Suppose I threaten you and yet you still X at t_2. At t_3 I ask: if I follow through on my threat do I do as well as I would have done if I had not adopted the threat plan in the first place, at t_1? And on present assumptions, the answer is "no" since my threatened action, Y, is costly to me, and in Y-ing I do not change the fact that, despite my threat, you have earlier X -ed. Since all this will be clear at t_1, it will not be rational to settle on the threat plan at t_1. So on Gauthier's cross-temporal counterfactual comparisons standard, there is an asymmetry between rational assurance and rational threat.

An important complication is raised by cases in which you do not simply make a situation-specific threat but have a policy of following through with threats quite generally.[15] So when you consider following through with your threat you ask whether you thereby do better than you would have done if you had no such general policy. And the answer to this question may well be "yes," thereby adding support to the rationality of following through with the threat. There are complex issues here.[16] But for present purposes I put them aside and focus on the deliberative standard for single-situation threat plans. And in these cases, on present assumptions, you will correctly judge that if you follow through with your threat you do worse than you would have done if you had not made the threat in the first place.

What is crucial, then, is the cross-temporal counterfactual assessment: Do you thereby do better than you would have done had you not settled on that plan in the first place? Of course, when the time of plan follow-through arrives one can compare following through then—at t_3—with refraining at t_3 from following through then. The idea behind the counterfactual comparisons deliberative standard is not that one cannot make such comparisons with other options at the time of follow-through; the idea is, rather, that a deliberative standard that puts such time-of-follow-through

---

15. Gauthier, "Assure and Threaten," sec. 9.
16. For critical discussion, see Joe Mintoff, "Rational Cooperation, Intention, and Reconsideration," *Ethics* 107 (1997): 612–43, esp. 619–25.

comparisons aside, and focuses instead on the cited cross-temporal counterfactual comparisons, is a superior deliberative standard.

Why, exactly? The official answer, I take it, is that this feature of the deliberative procedure—this way of articulating what the relevant comparison is in assessing follow-through at t_3—is itself a matter of which deliberative procedures are such that (to return to a passage quoted earlier) "employing them is maximally conducive to one's life going as well as possible, where this effect includes, not only the actions they determine, but also the actions they make possible."[17] The official argument for a cross-temporal counterfactual comparisons deliberative standard, in contrast with a sophisticated or a resolute standard, is a pragmatic argument that appeals to the contributions of the general employment of these general standards to making one's life go as well as possible.

That said, I am not sure what the argument is for the pragmatic superiority of the counterfactual comparisons standard in contrast with the resolute deliberation standard. We are to ask which of these standards is such that its general employment would have a better impact on one's life going well. And given the assumptions we are making, it is not clear why the answer does not favor resolution. After all, the assumption is that, overall, the risks of having to follow through with threats are compensated for by the associated expectations of benefits.[18]

In "Intention and Deliberation," Gauthier briefly addresses a version of this worry and responds: "But against this one may note that according to [the resolute standard] it may be irrational for an agent to reconsider a plan even if she recognizes that she would have done better not to have adopted it."[19] And Gauthier thinks that precluding reconsideration and, indeed, abandonment, of a prior plan under these circumstances would be a mistake.[20]

If this is a mistake, what mistake is it? It is not clear how to answer simply by appeal to the pragmatic meta-theory. Instead, I think that Gauthier may here be responding to a further idea, namely: there is something significant about temporally extended agency in which one can, as time goes by, accurately see oneself as acting within a framework of plans that is proving itself to have the kind of cross-temporal mettle specified by the counterfactual

17. And see Gauthier, "Intention and Deliberation," 53: "the rationale of this account is pragmatic."
18. I note this concern in "Following Through with One's Plans: Reply to David Gauthier," 59.
19. Gauthier, "Intention and Deliberation," 52.
20. Though what he says is rather tentative: "*if* [my emphasis] this seems a decisive objection" (ibid., 52).

comparison test. Significant in what way? Well, on the theory the main aim is that one's life goes as well as possible. And an idea that may be at work here is that the temporally extended life of a planning agent normally goes better to the extent that she can, as she lives it, accurately see her temporally extended plans as, to use Gauthier's term, "confirmed" by how things are working out[21]—though given Gauthier's subjectivism about a life going well, this connection between cross-temporally confirmed agency and one's life going well may not hold for every agent.

To get at this thought it will be helpful also to introduce an idea of a disconfirmed temporally extended, planned course of action: this will be a planned course of action that has developed in a way such that one reasonably judges that one would have done better not to have adopted it in the first place. This is what can happen with a failed threat. Suppose, then, that the temporally extended life of a planning agent does indeed go better insofar as it involves diachronically confirmed planning agency and goes worse insofar as it involves diachronically disconfirmed planning agency. These assumptions about the relation between modes of temporally extended agency and how well one's life goes will help favor, within the two-tier pragmatic meta-theory, Gauthier's counterfactual comparison standard, in contrast with resolution. And that is the argument in favor of Gauthier's standard that we wanted to find.

This result depends, however, on the cited, substantive assumption about what contributes to a life's going well. And it is not clear how to fit such an assumption within Gauthier's subjectivism about a life's going well. I will return briefly to this matter below. But now I want to turn to a broader concern about the pragmatic two-tier theory.

Suppose my accepted deliberative procedure incorporates Gauthier's cross-temporal counterfactual comparisons view. Since I am reflective, it incorporates this view because I see that my general employment of this deliberative procedure is maximally conducive to my life going as well as possible. Suppose now that I have opted at t_1 for an assurance plan, you have indeed helped me at t_2, and I am now at t_3 thinking about reciprocating. I can see that my accepted deliberative procedure enjoins reciprocation. And I can see that there is—or so we are now supposing—a pragmatic rationale for my general employment of that deliberative procedure. But we are to suppose that I can also see that when I compare reciprocation at t_3 with my other option at this very time of action—the option of not

21. "A course of action is confirmed at a given time, if at that time the agent may reasonably expect to do better continuing it than she would have expected to do had she not adopted it" (ibid., 49).

following through with my assurance plan—it is that other option that is superior with respect to the end of my life going as well as possible. I seem, then, to be buffeted by two forms of rational pressure, one that goes by way of the (supposed) pragmatic rationale for a general procedure that involves the counterfactual comparison standard, and one that goes by way of applying pragmatic considerations directly to my action at t_3 in comparison with my other options at t_3. I face what Kieran Setiya has called, in a different but related context, a "fragmentation of practical reason."[22]

The point is not that Gauthier is mistaken in supposing that the pragmatic reasons that are relevant in assessing a general deliberative procedure are reasons for and against the general employment of that procedure. Rather, the point is that there remains also the possibility of the pragmatic assessment of a specific, particular employment of any such general procedure. The threat of "fragmentation" is the threat that these two forms of assessment—of general and of particular—will, in important cases, point in different directions.

What to say? Well, in the light of somewhat similar concerns about Gauthier's theory, David Velleman advises us to turn instead to what he calls the constitutive aim of action and find therein a substantive standard of "success for actions."[23] I am not, however, sanguine about this alternative strategy.

Action is a generic phenomenon, one that includes both human and, say, canine action. So I think it unlikely that we can get substantive norms of the sort that Gauthier seeks out of such a generic phenomenon. Granted, we ourselves are a special kind of agent: we are, as I see it— and I think this thought is Gauthier-friendly—planning agents. And I do think that to be a planning agent is, in part, to accept and employ certain synchronic norms of consistency and coherence of intention.[24] But

---

22. See Kieran Setiya, "Intention, Plans, and Ethical Rationalism," in *Rational and Social Agency: Essays on the Philosophy of Michael Bratman*, eds. Manuel Vargas and Gideon Yaffe (Oxford: Oxford University Press, 2014). I raise a version of this issue for Gauthier's view in "Following Through with One's Plans: Reply to David Gauthier," 60–1. I note an analogous issue for views of Edward McClennen in Michael E. Bratman, "Planning and the Stability of Intention," *Minds and Machines* 2 (1992): 1–16, esp. 8–13. In both cases I note the parallel with J. J. C. Smart's well-known critique of certain forms of rule utilitarianism as guilty of "rule worship" (J. J. C. Smart, "Extreme and Restricted Utilitarianism," in *Theories of Ethics*, ed. Philippa Foot ([Oxford: Oxford University Press, 1967], 171–83). Michael Thompson discusses similar concerns for Gauthier's views in his *Life and Action* (Cambridge, MA: Harvard University Press, 2008), chap. 10.

23. J. David Velleman, "Deciding How to Decide," as reprinted in *The Possibility of Practical Reason* (Oxford: Oxford University Press, 2000), 221–43.

24. Michael E. Bratman, *Intention, Plans, and Practical Reason* (Cambridge, MA: Harvard University Press, 1987; reissued by CSLI Publications, 1999).

it seems nevertheless in an important sense possible—though perhaps not psychologically in the cards—for us to cease being planners while remaining agents.[25] So it is not clear what the normative force is of the observation that to continue to be, in particular, a planning agent is in part to continue to accept these norms. Indeed, it is here that a natural idea is to appeal not to a constitutive aim of action but rather to the pragmatic advantages of continuing to be, in particular, a planning agent.[26] In any case, the norm that is of special interest in Gauthier's work—his cross-temporal, counterfactual comparison norm—goes beyond such synchronic norms. And even if we could argue that the acceptance of some such norm is somehow tied to being, in particular, a planning agent, we would still need to address the question: Why (continue to) be such a planning agent? Finally, when in his own work Velleman develops this idea of the constitutive aim of action, he appeals to the theoretical aim of self-knowledge and self-understanding. This leads to what I have called "cognitivism" about practical rationality. And for reasons I have discussed elsewhere, I am skeptical that such a cognitivism can be made to work: I am skeptical that practical rationality really does ride piggyback on theoretical rationality.[27]

So I am attracted to Gauthier's alternative strategy of assessing deliberative procedures not by appeal to a constitutive aim of action but rather in a broadly pragmatic way. But the problem is that it is then difficult to see how to avoid a version of the fragmentation against which Setiya warns us. What we need is an approach that exploits the insights of a broadly pragmatic approach to general deliberative procedures but has a different story of the relation between that approach and the rationality of specific choices and actions, a story that works against the cited fragmentation.

25. This idea is built into the version of Gricean "creature construction" that I employ in my "Valuing and the Will," as reprinted in Michael E. Bratman, *Structures of Agency* (New York: Oxford University Press, 2007), 47–67.

26. I discuss these pragmatic advantages in Michael E. Bratman, "Intention, Belief, Practical, Theoretical," in *Spheres of Reason: New Essays on the Philosophy of Normativity*, ed. Simon Robertson (Oxford: Oxford University Press, 2009), 29–61, sec. IX [this volume, essay 2].

27. For Velleman's cognitivism, see, e.g., J. David Velleman, "Introduction," in *The Possibility of Practical Reason* (Oxford: Oxford University Press, 2000), 1–31, esp. 20–31. (In "Deciding How to Decide," at 241, Velleman appeals to a constitutive aim of autonomy; but the appeal to a constitutive aim of self-knowledge and self-understanding is the dominant view in his work.) For my criticisms of such a cognitivism, see Michael E. Bratman, "Cognitivism about Practical Reason," *Ethics* 102 (1991): 117–28; and my "Intention, Belief, Practical, Theoretical."

I think that we can make progress here by explaining how the very acceptance of the deliberative standard itself engages further, distinctive considerations that can tip the scales in favor of the specific employment of that standard, even in cases in which there is, prior to these distinctive considerations, a threat of fragmentation. Let's see how this might work.

The claim in which Gauthier is most interested is along the lines of:

1. Your general employment of D makes your life go as well as possible.

The idea now is also to consider a claim along the lines of

2. If you do accept D, then employing D in a particular case makes a distinctive, positive contribution in that case to your life's going well.

If we had a claim along the lines of 2, we would have incremental, substantive support for

3. Employing D in this particular case makes your life go as well as possible (as compared with other options at the time of the particular case).

And this would promise to help defuse the threat of fragmentation.

Suppose that a deliberative standard has a pragmatic rationale that is broadly along the lines of 1.[28] How would the acceptance of this deliberative standard itself engage distinctive considerations of the sort to which 2 alludes? Well, the standards we are talking about are a fundamental aspect of an agent's practical life. Synchronic inconsistency with such an accepted standard is a serious psychological fracture. And such a psychic fracture is an impediment to forms of agency that we value. In particular, if you are split in this way, there will not be, in this case, a sufficiently consistent and coherent synchronic practical standpoint whose guidance of your thought and action can constitute your governance of your relevant thought and action.[29] So such a psychic fracture would stand in the way of your self-governance.

---

28. I make this more precise below, when I formulate my adjustment to Gauthier's theory.

29. See Michael E. Bratman, "Intention, Practical Rationality, and Self-Governance," *Ethics* 119 (2009): 411–43 [this volume, essay 4].

A response may be: once you arrive at the time for follow-through in the particular case you can, if need be, avoid such synchronic inconsistency by changing the standard you accept, thereby garnering the benefits now available in that particular case. But an initial reply to this is that self-governance over time—as Velleman puts it, "diachronic autonomy"[30]—is not just self-governance at each of a sequence of times. It also involves some sort of cross-temporal coherence. And such abrupt shifts in a basic, accepted standard seem in tension with such cross-temporal coherence.

A counterreply will be that such a shift in basic deliberative standard, even if abrupt, need not be arbitrary. After all, we are supposing that such a shift would, in the particular case, allow you to garner certain benefits. So why think that such a shift, in pursuit of those benefits in the particular case without synchronic inconsistency, blocks diachronic self-governance?

The answer to this counterreply is that the assessment of a deliberative standard is the assessment of a *general* structure of practical thinking. The pragmatic reasons that bear on that assessment are reasons for or against such a general structure.[31] So long as we keep our focus on pragmatic reasons for such a general structure, the envisaged shift in basic standard will not be supported by appeal to special benefits in the particular case. After all, we are supposing at this point in the argument that these pragmatic reasons for general structures support one's initially accepted standard. So a shift that is purportedly grounded in the special benefits in the particular case would not only be abrupt but also unsupported by the kind of pragmatic considerations that bear on the assessment of such a general structure of practical thinking: it would be unsupported by the right kind of pragmatic reasons.

But what if one's initial deliberative standard, while having pragmatic support, is no more supported (though also no less supported) by relevant pragmatic considerations than is some competing standard? Might one then simply switch standards without a threat to self-governance? I think not. After all, in such a case your life over time would involve (to borrow an apt phrase from Richard Kraut, in conversation) a kind of "shuffle" from one basic deliberative standard to the next, in the absence of a relevant judgment of pragmatic superiority. Perhaps in such a case you would be

---

30. Velleman, "Deciding How to Decide," 238.

31. In insisting that the pragmatic reasons that are relevant to the assessment of a deliberative procedure need to be reasons whose target is the general employment of that procedure, we do not solve the problem of fragmentation. We simply clarify the reasons that bear on one of the threatened fragments. (This contrasts with Velleman's proposed interpretation that the deliberative standard is seen by Gauthier as "self-supporting"; Velleman, "Deciding How to Decide," 225.)

self-governing at each time. But there seems little traction here for the idea that you would be governing your life *over* that time. So if one's initial deliberative standard has an appropriate pragmatic rationale, but one abruptly shifts to a different standard that one does not see as better supported by the right kinds of pragmatic reasons, one would then be cross-temporally incoherent in a way that baffles diachronic self-governance.[32]

Building on a reading of Gauthier's appeal to the significance of diachronically confirmed planning agency, we have been laying the groundwork for an appeal to another form of temporally extended agency, namely, diachronic self-governance. We can express the underlying idea within the framework of Gauthier's theory by saying that synchronic consistency with respect to, and diachronic coherence in, fundamental deliberative standards is an aspect of a kind of temporally extended self-governance that is, at least for most of us, an important element in our lives going well. So if one does accept a general deliberative standard that is pragmatically justified, then employing that standard in the particular case will support such self-governance and so promote the aim that one's life go as well as possible. This leads to a claim along the lines of 2, and thereby to incremental support for claims along the lines of 3. And this promises to help us formulate a pragmatic theory that avoids fragmentation.

The idea, then, is to seek a deliberative standard that satisfies a pair of constraints. First, it passes a pragmatic test as a general standard. Second it is self-reinforcing in the sense that its very acceptance provides, by way of considerations of self-governance, reasons that, in tandem with other relevant reasons, tilt the scales in favor of employing that deliberative standard in the particular case.[33] And this leads to my proposed adjustment in Gauthier's meta-theory: the potential general standards that we compare pragmatically are to be ones that would be, if accepted, sufficiently self-reinforcing (by way of considerations of self-governance) to block the threat of fragmentation. A deliberative standard is rational, on this proposal, just in case it is a standard that is among the pragmatically best supported deliberative standards each of which would be, if accepted,

32. I discuss closely related ideas in Michael E. Bratman, "Time, Rationality, and Self-Governance," *Philosophical Issues* 22 (2012): 73–88 [this volume, essay 6].

33. This image of considerations of self-governance tipping the scales in the particular case is in the spirit of Velleman's conception of how the purported constitutive aim of self-knowledge and self-understanding shapes action in interaction with specific first-order motives. (See, e.g., Velleman, "Introduction," at 22.) The difference is that, rather than appeal to self-understanding, I appeal directly to the role of an accepted standard of deliberation in self-governance. and I do not ground this appeal to the normative significance of self-governance in a purported constitutive aim of action.

sufficiently self-reinforcing.[34] And a chosen action is rational if it is enjoined by a rational, accepted deliberative procedure. This coordination of rational accepted deliberative procedure and rational action is supported in part by distinctive reasons of self-governance in the particular case, reasons that are engaged by the agent's acceptance of the deliberative standard. And this coordination defuses the threat of fragmentation.

If this were our meta-theory, would we arrive at something like Gauthier's counterfactual comparison theory? Well, I think that there would at least need to be some adjustment as the two-level coordination proceeds.

Consider Kavka's toxin case, and suppose, for a start, that you internalize Gauthier's counterfactual comparison standard.[35] You then consider whether to decide at t_1 to drink the toxin at t_3, after receiving the million dollars at t_2 in return for having formed this intention at t_1. You know that the effects of drinking the toxin at t_3 would be nasty, though you would be willing to undergo them for the million dollars. If the time to drink were to arrive you would know that you do not need to drink to get the money, though you also know that if you were to follow through with a plan to drink you would do better than if you had not adopted that plan in the first place. On the proposal I am making, if you did indeed plan at t_1 to drink at t_3, then a resource you would have at t_3 rationally to stiffen your resolve to drink is that if you were to abandon your drinking plan you would either be involved in a synchronic inconsistency with a basic standard you accept (as we are supposing, Gauthier's counterfactual comparison standard), or you would be abruptly changing that standard; and in either case there is an impediment to self-governance. But it is a delicate question whether that would be enough to outweigh the awfulness of drinking in the particular case. Recognizing this threat of fragmentation, and continuing with our two-level coordination procedure, we will be under pressure to qualify Gauthier's counterfactual comparison deliberative standard. We will be under pressure to include a clause in that standard that allows for non-follow-through in cases in which the costs in the particular case of follow-through, as compared with other options available at the time of action, would be quite high and would not be sufficiently counterbalanced by the cited considerations of self-governance.[36] Indeed, we might try to

34. This allows for ties or noncomparabilities in the pragmatic assessments of the standards.

35. Gregory S. Kavka, "The Toxin Puzzle," *Analysis* 43 (1983): 33–6. In "Rethinking the Toxin Puzzle," Gauthier takes a view different from the one I am about to sketch.

36. Michael Thompson proposes that "if the practice makes some action good, then any action the practice cannot make good does not express the practice" (*Life and Action*, 188). The second half of this proposal is in a way similar to the proposal I am

accomplish this by making the standard in a way reflexive: follow through at t_3 in accordance with Gauthier's counterfactual comparison standard so long as, taking into account the considerations of self-governance engaged by your acceptance of this very standard, there is not fragmentation at t_3.

This need for the deliberative standard to be sufficiently self-reinforcing constrains to some degree the extent to which the standard can support assurance and follow-through. The standard will support assurance for, but only for, those cases in which the significance of self-governance is enough—in tandem with other reasons—to counter the pressures for non-follow-through that arise in relevant particular situations. Just how limiting this is will depend on how much weight these considerations of self-governance have. But in any case this limitation, however exactly we understand its extent, is a consequence of our pursuit of a pragmatic but nonfragmented theory.[37]

That said, it may still be that something in the neighborhood of Gauthier's counterfactual comparison deliberative standard would survive such two-level coordination. But now the contrast between that standard and sophistication will be more nuanced. We would have arrived at the proposal that a rational standard of deliberation—at least for the kinds of interaction that are our focus here—is a qualified form of the counterfactual comparison standard, but one that is sufficiently self-reinforcing, by way of the significance of self-governance, to block the threat of fragmentation. In conforming to this accepted deliberative standard one is, in part because of the significance of self-governance, acting in a way that is not inferior to one's alternatives at the very time of action.

If this is right, then it may be unnecessarily heroic for Gauthier to insist that "an action may be rational even though at the time of performance it is not, and is not believed to be, part of a life that goes best for the agent."[38] After all, if our present line of thought were successful we would be in a position to explain, by appeal to an adjusted version of Gauthier's counterfactual comparison standard, the rationality of many (though not all) cases of following through with a relevant assurance plan; and we would be able to do this without insisting on the cited gap between rational and (believed) best action. And the key is the phenomenon of self-reinforcement grounded in the significance of self-governance.

---

making concerning coordination across the two levels: general and particular. But the sense in which the general standard "makes" the particular action rational, on the view I am sketching, is different from that envisaged by Thompson.

37. Moral considerations for doing as one has assured may still come to bear on cases for which the theory is unable to explain the rationality of follow-through in the absence of appeal to such moral considerations.

38. Gauthier, "Assure and Threaten," 701.

Return now to the Gauthier-inspired idea that one's life goes better to the extent that one's temporally extended planned activities are confirmed over time. The idea I have been sketching—that one's life goes better to the extent that one satisfies central elements of diachronic self-governance—is in a similar spirit. Each appeals to the role of certain modes of temporally extended agency in one's life going well. However, these purported connections to living well are poised to play different theoretical roles: On the one hand, the significance of diachronic self-governance, and the self-reinforcement it supports, is a key to blocking the fragmentation that threatens such two-tier pragmatic theories. On the other hand, we have seen that the argument for, in particular, (a version of) Gauthier's counterfactual comparison standard, in contrast with resolution, may depend also on the significance to living well of diachronically confirmed planning agency.

We now need to return, as promised, to the tension with Gauthier's subjectivism about living well. If the contribution of a mode of temporally extended agency to living well depends, at bottom, on the contingent and varying concerns of the particular agent in question, then the impacts to which we have alluded of modes of temporally extended agency on living well will need to be relativized to different subjective backgrounds. This is not how Gauthier conceives of his project: he seeks standards of deliberation that are robust across fundamentally different sets of concerns, concerns that ground claims about living well. But in the absence of such connections between certain forms of temporally extended agency and living well, we are back to the difficulties faced by a more straightforward two-tier pragmatic theory.

In any case, and putting to one side diachronic confirmation, a theory that draws on the significance of diachronic self-governance could be combined with some such subjectivism. But an implication would be that for agents who have no, or very minimal, concerns that favor their own diachronic self-governance, there may not be significant normative pressure, by way of self-reinforcement, in favor of a close connection between pragmatically attractive general modes of deliberation and specific chosen actions. Such an agent could not depend on a concern with self-governance to protect pragmatically attractive and accepted general deliberative procedures from the threat of fragmentation. In contrast, a planning agent with a significant concern with her own self-governance would be in a position to protect pragmatically attractive and accepted deliberative procedures from fragmentation, thereby supporting a pragmatically attractive "interplay of intention and reason" in her temporally extended, planned agency.

CHAPTER 9
Consistency and Coherence in Plan

Our agency is extended over time and socially interconnected. We seem to some extent to govern our own lives. And we are planning agents. A central conjecture of my work is that this last—our capacity for planning—in a way underlies our capacities for temporally extended, social, and self-governed agency.[1]

In what way? I do not seek a traditional analysis that purports to provide, by appeal to our planning capacities, both necessary and sufficient conditions for each of these target phenomena. My more modest focus is, instead, on sufficient conditions. I try to defend interrelated conclusions along the lines of: if this type of planning psychology were to function in these ways, that would constitute a robust form of this target form of agency (as it may be, temporally extended, shared, self-governed). And to establish

---

1. [This essay originally appeared as part of my "Rational and Social Agency: Reflections and Replies," in Manuel Vargas and Gideon Yaffe, eds., *Rational and Social Agency: The Philosophy of Michael Bratman* (New York: Oxford University Press, 2014): 294–343.] The relation between our planning agency and our temporally extended agency is explored in my *Intention, Plans, and Practical Reason* (Cambridge, MA: Harvard University Press, 1987; reprint, Stanford, CA: CSLI, 1999). The relation to shared intentional and shared cooperative activity is explored in a quartet of essays in my *Faces of Intention* (Cambridge, UK: Cambridge University Press, 1999); "Shared Valuing and Frameworks for Practical Reasoning," *Structures of Agency* (New York: Oxford University Press, 2007); "Shared Agency," in Chris Mantzavinos, ed., *Philosophy of the Social Sciences: Philosophical Theory and Scientific Practice* (Cambridge, UK: Cambridge University Press, 2009): 41–59; "Modest Sociality and the Distinctiveness of Intention," *Philosophical Studies* 144, no. 1 (2009): 149–165; and *Shared Agency: A Planning Theory of Acting Together* (New York: Oxford University Press, 2014). The relation to an individual's self-governance is a central concern of the essays in *Structures of Agency*.

such claims we need not insist that we have identified the uniquely possible realizations of each of the cited trio of practical capacities.[2]

But how should we understand our planning agency? Here I have focused on what seem to me to be characteristic roles of plan-states in the diachronic organization of our practical thought and action, on associated norms of plan rationality, and on the interrelations between these roles and these norms. The result is the *planning theory*. I turn to some general reflections on that planning theory, with a focus on central plan-theoretic norms.[3]

Mice, cows, gorillas, and young human children are all purposive agents. But in our world adult human agents—and perhaps others—are purposive agents of a distinctive sort: they are planning agents.[4] Distinctive modes of planning structure their practical thought and action in ways that tend to support complex, effective forms of coordination and organization over time and, normally, socially. Intentions are basic elements of such planning structures: intentions are plan-states.

These plan-states go beyond ordinary desires and beliefs and settle practical questions about what to do, frequently in the face of multiple and conflicting considerations and alternatives, and in response to needs for coordination at a time, over time, and socially. These plan-states frequently concern future action, and they are normally partial: they specify ends without fully specifying means and preliminary steps in ways that will eventually need to be specified. As time goes by these partial plans

---

2. For this focus on sufficient conditions for relevant forms of sociality see "I Intend that We J," in *Faces of Intention*, p. 144; for a focus on sufficient conditions for self-governance see *Structures of Agency*, p. 11.

3. Some of the ideas in this essay are in an earlier sextet of essays of mine: "Intention, Belief, Practical, Theoretical," in Jens Timmerman, John Skorupski, and Simon Robertson, eds., *Spheres of Reason* (Oxford: Oxford University Press, 2009): 29–61 [this volume, essay 2]; "Intention, Belief, and Instrumental Rationality," in David Sobel and Steven Wall, eds., *Reasons for Action* (Cambridge, UK: Cambridge University Press, 2009): 13–36 [this volume, essay 3]; "Intention, Practical Rationality, and Self-Governance," *Ethics* 119 (2009): 411–443 [this volume, essay 4]; "Intention Rationality," *Philosophical Explorations* 12 (2009): 227–241; "Agency, Time, and Sociality," *Proceedings and Addresses of the American Philosophical Association* 84:2 (2010): 7–26 [this volume, essay 5]; and "The Fecundity of Planning Agency," in David Shoemaker, ed., *Oxford Studies in Agency and Responsibility* (Oxford: Oxford University Press, 2013). In writing this essay I have benefited from Kieran Setiya's "Intention, Plans, and Ethical Rationalism" in *Rational and Social Agency*: 56–82, and from probing written comments from Facundo Alonso. Earlier versions of this essay were presented at a symposium at the meetings of the Central Division of the APA, March 2011, and at the Nebraska Conference on Ethics and Practical Reason, April 2012.

4. The idea that planning agency is one species of agency is central to the use that I have made of H. P. Grice's strategy of "creature construction." See, for example, my "Valuing and the Will" as reprinted in *Structures of Agency*.

structure further practical thinking in the pursuit of incremental specification and articulation of these plans, frequently in light of further information and with an eye on coordination.[5] And this further thinking will be shaped by these prior plans in three main ways. First, these prior plans pose problems about means and preliminary steps, problems that this further practical thinking aims to resolve. Second, these prior plans filter further options to be considered: once one is settled on E further options that are, taken together with one's other relevant beliefs, incompatible with E will tend not to be treated as salient alternatives. And third, once one is settled in this way on E there is a disposition not to reconsider or revise this plan to E: the plan to E has a characteristic diachronic stability. In this sense the plan on which one is settled is, as Richard Holton says, a kind of "fixed point."[6]

One is faced, for example, with a decision about whether to go to law school or to a PhD program. Bringing to bear the various considerations to which one gives weight, one settles on, say, law school. Settling on this option is not to be identified with judging that it is the uniquely best alternative. After all, we frequently choose among options we see as equally choice-worthy, or perhaps non-comparable in important ways. We frequently realize that we simply do not know which option would be best. And we sometimes settle on options that we think are not even among the best. Nor is this simply a matter of predicting how one will behave. I can be sadly confident that when I am faced with a certain predictable temptation I will succumb, without yet intending to succumb. Instead, in settling in the relevant way on an option one arrives at a distinctive kind of more or less stable practical commitment in its favor. One is then faced with problems about means, and one will now be set to filter out incompatible alternatives.

Further, a planning agent will not simply be disposed to think along the lines of these patterns. She will also see divergence from these patterns as breakdowns, in a sense of "breakdown" that involves a kind of normative force. If she notices that her plan-states are, given her beliefs, inconsistent, she will see this as a breakdown, and she will see herself as under pressure to revise in a way that brings her back into conformity with this consistency

---

5. John McDowell proposes that we "conceive an intention for the future as a potential action biding its time." ("Some Remarks on Intention in Action," *Amherst Lecture in Philosophy* 6, 2011, p. 15, http://www.amherstlecture.org/mcdowell2011/mcdowell2011_ALP.pdf). To see intentions as plan-states that play complex roles in plan-shaped thinking prior to the time of action is to reject as importantly misleading this metaphor of intentions waiting around for time to go by.

6. Holton, "Intention as a Model for Belief," in *Rational and Social Agency*: 12–37.

pattern—and similarly if she notices that she intends E, believes M—and so intending M—are necessary for E, and yet does not intend M. I also think we can say something similar about stability of plan-states over time; but I will not discuss this in detail here.[7] The conclusion that I draw is that it is part of being a planning agent that one's plan-states, together with one's beliefs, tend to conform to these patterns of consistency and coherence in part because they are potentially guided by one's at least implicit or tacit acceptance of relevant norms of consistency and means–end coherence.[8]

This is not yet a justification of these norms of consistency and coherence. What we have said is that it is part of being a planning agent that one at least implicitly or tacitly accepts norms that enjoin such consistency (a) and coherence and so that one is responsive to at least apparent normative pressures for conformity to these norms. These forms of functioning (b) support effective, coordinated agency. And it is theoretically fruitful, for a (c) theory of human agency, to understand intentions as plan-states in a sense specified by this nascent theory of planning agency. But this does not by itself explain why one ought or should or has normative reason to conform to these norms.[9]

That said, our view of what, if anything, gives these norms their normative force will be an important element in our overall understanding of our planning agency. This is in part because we ourselves are planning agents. Our theory of planning agency is a theory about our *own* modes of thinking

---

7. I discuss this in "Agency, Time, and Sociality," in "Time, Rationality, and Self-Governance," *Philosophical Issues* 22 (2012): 73–88 [this volume, essay 6], and in "Temptation and the Agent's Standpoint," *Inquiry* 57 (2014): 293–310 [this volume, essay 7].

8. See *Intention, Plans, and Practical Reason*. To keep things simpler, I am including within the norm of consistency a norm of agglomeration that says: only intend several different options if an intention in favor of the conjunction of those options would not itself violate the norm of intention–belief consistency. For this understanding of agglomerativity see Gideon Yaffe, "Trying, Intending, and Attempted Crimes," *Philosophical Topics* 32 (2004): 505–532. I briefly note complexities posed by practical analogues of the paradox of the preface in "Intention, Practical Rationality, and Self-Governance," n. 7 [this volume, essay 4, at 78]. My talk of acceptance of these norms draws from Allan Gibbard's appeal to "norm acceptances" in his *Wise Choices, Apt Feelings* (Cambridge, MA: Harvard University Press, 1990). See also Peter Railton, "Normative Guidance," in Russ Shafer-Landau, ed., *Oxford Studies in Meta-Ethics* 1(2006): 3–33. A tentative proposal would be to see such norm acceptances as special kinds of reflexive plans about how to plan; but that is not a matter that I will try to discuss here.

9. This point is in the spirit of Timothy Schroeder's distinction between a "categorization scheme" of a norm and a "force-maker" of that norm (although I put to one side Schroeder's specific use of this distinction in his interpretation of Donald Davidson's views). See Timothy Schroeder, "Donald Davidson's Theory of Mind Is Non-Normative," *Philosophers' Imprint* 3(2003): 1–14.

and doing: we are not just Martian anthropologists looking down on these charming creatures who happen to be planning agents. And these modes of thinking and doing that are elements of our own planning agency are themselves subject to our critical reflection. So we will want to know whether it makes normative sense for us to think and act in the ways that, according to the theory, are characteristic of such planning agency. Further, if we as theorists have reason to think these norms do have normative force and if we suppose that this normative force is more or less apparent upon reflection, we will have reason to expect that the operation of these planning structures will tend to be stable under the practical reflection of a reflective planning agent. And a view about such stability would be an element in our overall explanatory theory of planning agency. In particular, this would help defuse a worry that this explanatory model is itself misguided since it attributes to us the acceptance of norms that do not pass normative muster.[10] In this respect, our assessment of the normative force of these norms will be part of our epistemic justification for accepting the planning theory as an explanatory theory of agents like us.

How then should we address this issue about the force of these norms? Well, if we thought that to be an agent at all one must be a planning agent, then we would be able to say that so long as you are an agent you must accept these norms. And we might try to see this as a kind of justification of these norms. But this thought is not available to us here, since it is not true that to be an agent you must be a planning agent. After all, cows are agents but, probably, not planning agents.

This issue of normative force can arise within the practical reflection of a planning agent. Kate, a planning agent, intends end E. She would see a failure to intend a necessary means to E, coupled with her retention of her intention in favor of E, as a breakdown. And this tends to frame her further practical reasoning by posing problems about means to E. But she can nevertheless step back and ask: "Why continue to accept the norm of means–end coherence, the norm according to which this would indeed be a breakdown, the norm that is now set to help frame my further practical reasoning?" This is not directly a request for a justification of a specific action but rather a request for a justification of this basic structure of her practical thinking. Kate can see that if she were to abandon the norm of means–end coherence she would no longer be a planning agent; so, since intentions are states within a planning psychic economy, she would no longer, strictly speaking, intend E (although she could retain a different

---

10. For a version of this worry, see Niko Kolodny, "Reply to Bridges," *Mind* 118(2009): 369–376.

kind of pro-attitude toward E). But she can nevertheless ask why she should continue to be a planning agent.

Here is another way to put Kate's question. Intentions are plan-states; plan-states function in planning that is guided by accepted norms of consistency and coherence; and such planning tracks and supports effective coordination. So there is a sense in which intentions aim at effective coordination by way of tracking consistency and coherence: they are, by their nature, embedded in a psychic economy that adjusts in response to, and thereby supports, effective coordination, in part by way of guidance by accepted norms of consistency and coherence.[11] An attitude that was not embedded in this way in this sort of psychic economy would not be an intention. Kate and I both grant all this. But there remains the question of why she should continue to be the sort of agent who is characterized by this psychic economy.

Well, one thing Kate might say is that there is no realistic possibility of her ceasing to be such a planning agent, so the question why she should continue to be a planning agent is in an important way idle. This is a deeply entrenched feature of her practical architecture, one that is not directly subject to her will.

But even supposing that giving up planning agency is not a psychologically realistic option for Kate—and so that it is misleading to picture Kate as *deciding* to be a planning agent—we (and she) will still want to ask what is at stake. After all, there may be deeply entrenched features of human psychology that do not pass muster on reflection. Examples might include our tendencies to believe what we want to be true, to seek revenge, or to be susceptible to certain perceptual illusions or probabilistic fallacies or undue peer influence. What we want to know about planning structures is not only that they are deeply entrenched (if they are) but what would be gained or lost in retaining them or, if one could, giving them up. To answer we need to reflect on the myriad ways in which our lives are infused by such

---

11. This corresponds to an aim in what J. David Velleman calls a descriptive sense. The issue before us is how to understand the relation between such an aim in this descriptive sense and an aim in a normative sense that entails that there are associated, justified norms. In his "Introduction," in his *The Possibility of Practical Reason* (Oxford: Oxford University Press, 2000), Velleman sees the normativity of the aim as following from the aim in the descriptive sense (see pp. 17–19). But in later work with Nishi Shah, Velleman supports a more complex story about the relation between descriptive and normative aim. See Nishi Shah and J. David Velleman, "Doxastic Deliberation," *The Philosophical Review* 114(2005): 497–534. The view that I am describing here also involves a more complex account of this relation, although one that differs from the proposal of Shah and Velleman. I return to Velleman's views in section 2 of my "Rational and Social Agency: Reflections and Replies."

planning structures. And my conjecture is that when we do that we arrive at a view that does not resist the question, why continue to be a planning agent?, but instead/answers it by appeal to the ways in which our planning agency helps to constitute and to support much of what we value and care about.[12]

Begin by returning to the observation that planning structures help support effective coordination of thought and action over time. Getting into and successfully attending law school, to continue the example, requires complex forms of coordination. And a standard way in which we achieve such coordination is by stably settling in advance on certain ends as elements in partial plans and, as time goes by, filling in these plans with means and the like while being careful to avoid tripping over ourselves by settling on incompatible options. And now the point to emphasize is that much of what we value and care about in our lives involves such plan-shaped cross-temporal coordination of our agency.

Further, much of what we value and care about involves not just coordination within our own agency over time but also forms of acting together with others. We value singing duets, conversation, the successful pursuit of joint projects, and—to use Margaret Gilbert's example—walking together. We value these important forms of shared intentional and shared cooperative activity, and we value them both instrumentally and noninstrumentally. And one of the claims that I want to make is that structures of planning agency are, for us, partly constitutive of at least a central form of shared intentionality: such shared intentionality involves, for us, structures of interlocking, interdependent, and potentially meshing intentions and plans.[13]

Additional support for these points comes from reflection on our limits.[14] We are agents with limited mental resources. Planning agency helps us navigate these waters by enabling us to settle certain matters—both individual and social—in advance when there is opportunity for thoughtful reflection, while also leaving room for disciplined, manageable, reliable, and appropriately flexible further specification as time goes by and as further information becomes available.

12. There is a parallel between these remarks and an aspect of P. F. Strawson's treatment of the system of reactive emotions. See his "Freedom and Resentment," *Proceedings of the British Academy* 48 (1962): 1–25. I discuss this parallel in "Intention, Belief, Practical, Theoretical," section IX.

13. See the work on shared agency cited in note 1. Gilbert's example is in her "Walking Together: A Paradigmatic Social Phenomenon," *Midwest Studies* 15 (1990): 1–14.

14. See Herbert Simon, *Reason in Human Affairs* (Stanford, CA: Stanford University Press, 1983).

Finally, we value governing our own lives over time. I'll be turning below to more detailed remarks about self-governance. But for now what we need is just the idea that planning structures help us achieve a kind of unity of practical stance at a time and over time, a unity that is normally involved in such self-governance. When all goes well, planning structures help constitute where the agent stands on a relevant practical question, and such a stance is a central condition of relevant self-governance.[15]

So we have a broadly pragmatic answer to Kate's query, why continue to be a planning agent? in a sense of "pragmatic" that includes both instrumental and constitutive relations between our planning agency and things we value.[16] This answer exploits what we can call the *fecundity of planning agency*: structures of planning agency are a common core for a range of basic practical capacities that matter to us a great deal. In particular, our capacity for planning agency helps to support and to constitute—in ways that are responsive to our limits—a trio of fundamental practical capacities, namely, our capacities for temporally extended intentional agency, for shared intentional agency, and for self-governance.[17] Our planning capacities support this trio of capacities by functioning in ways that involve guidance of practical thought (both explicit and implicit) by (implicitly or tacitly) accepted norms of consistency and coherence. This general form of functioning, involving such norm guidance, is partly constitutive of such planning agency and, given the fecundity of planning agency, has much to be said for it. In this sense, when a planning psychic economy functions in ways that thereby conform to these norms, it is to that extent *functioning properly*.

The idea is that we can construct each of these practical capacities by beginning with our capacity for norm-guided planning agency and, in the case of sociality and self-governance, adding some further resources. In this way we can model this trio of capacities within a project of creature

15. See Harry Frankfurt's reflections on "where (if anywhere) the person himself stands" in his "Identification and Wholeheartedness," in his *The Importance of What We Care About* (Cambridge, UK: Cambridge University Press, 1988): 159–176, at p. 166. I discuss this role of our planning agency in our self-governance in "Intention, Belief, Practical, Theoretical," pp. 56–59 [this volume, essay 2, at 46–50], and it is a general theme in the essays in my *Structures of Agency*.

16. For a discussion broadly in the spirit of such a pragmatic approach, see Jennifer Morton, "Toward an Ecological Theory of the Norms of Practical Deliberation," *European Journal of Philosophy* 19 (2011): 561–584.

17. Scott J. Shapiro, in his *Legality* (Cambridge, MA: Harvard University Press, 2011), argues for a further dimension of this fecundity: planning structures are at the heart of legality. And Allan Gibbard, in his *Thinking How to Live* (Cambridge, MA: Harvard University Press, 2003), sees planning structures as at the heart of normative thinking itself.

construction, in roughly the sense introduced by Paul Grice.[18] And a key to responding to Kate's query about these norms is to appreciate the many ways in which these capacities are important to our lives.

This initial answer to Kate's query does draw on a form of instrumental reasoning, since it sees planning agency as, inter alia, a kind of universal means.[19] But this form of instrumental reasoning need not itself depend specifically on the norm of means–end coherence on, in particular, intentions. So there need be no circularity in this answer.

But now note that this pragmatic story does not yet respond to a different question, a question about the application of these norms to the particular case. Suppose that Kate thinks: "I can see that there are strong pragmatic considerations in favor of being, as I am, a planning agent. And being a planning agent involves acceptance of various norms on intention, norms that help frame downstream practical reasoning and planning. But my question now is not about the advantages of the general capacity of planning agency, but rather about the specific application of these norms on each particular occasion: Is there reason—normative reason—on each particular occasion to conform to these norms?"

And Kate might continue: "I grant that normally the kinds of pragmatic considerations adduced for being, as I am, a planning agent will also favor conforming to the cited norms on the particular occasion. Conforming on the particular occasion will normally help promote the coordinated, effective pursuit of ends that I value, including the specific ends presently intended. And a violation of these accepted norms in the particular case may well involve unreliable, error-prone forms of thinking. But it remains possible that in an unusual case these very same pragmatic reasons nevertheless support, on balance, violating one of these norms on the particular occasion.[20] Perhaps this time there are special and unusual costs associated with consistency and/or coherence, or perhaps there are special and unusual benefits of inconsistency or incoherence. So it is unclear how we are to go from the cited pragmatic considerations in favor of being a planning agent, to a reason to conform to these norms in each particular case. So we

---

18. Paul Grice, "Method in Philosophical Psychology (From the Banal to the Bizarre)," *Proceedings and Addresses of the American Philosophical Association* 48 (1974–1975): 23–53.

19. *Intention, Plans, and Practical Reason*, p. 28.

20. This is broadly in the spirit of worries about "rule worship" articulated by J. J. C. Smart in his "Extreme and Restricted Utilitarianism," in Philippa Foot, ed., *Theories of Ethics* (Oxford: Oxford University Press, 1967): 171–183. I discuss these issues in "Planning and the Stability of Intention," *Minds and Machines* 2 (1992): 1–16. And see Michael Thompson's discussion of a "transfer principle" in his *Life and Action* (Cambridge, MA: Harvard University Press, 2008), chapter 10.

do not yet have an answer to my question whether there is, in each particular case, reason to conform to these norms."

Now, on the one hand, I agree with Kate that it is difficult to see how to defend a direct and nonmediated inference from the pragmatic support for one's planning agency in general to support for each and every particular case of conforming to the norms that are internal to such planning agency.[21] On the other hand, it seems to me that if we are to provide an adequate answer to Kate's question about the particular case it should build, in part, on the cited pragmatic considerations in favor of being a planning agent. We want a way to tie together (a) the normative structures present in the particular case; and (b) the pragmatic rationale for the general structures of planning agency, but we want to do this without appeal to a direct and nonmediated inference from (b) to (a). And this leads me to a view according to which the planning structures supported by these pragmatic considerations are *self-reinforcing*.[22] I proceed to explain.

Begin by noting that these norms of consistency and coherence apply quite generally to the agent's intentions. They apply, for example, to weak-willed intentions; and they are not limited to cases in which the agent has normative reason to intend E. So the norm of means–end coherence is not a norm about the transmission of normative reasons from ends to means. It is, rather, what John Broome calls a "wide-scope" norm, one that concerns combinations of attitudes (including absences of attitudes).[23]

In reflecting on these norms, should we turn to a kind of quietism? Such norms on intention are, we might try saying, as fundamental as our normative commitments get. They have a primitive normative force in each particular case, and it is a mistake to try to appeal to yet something else to explain that force.

But this would be philosophically underwhelming. After all, other practical attitudes—ordinary desire, for example—do not seem subject to the same pressures for consistency and coherence. It seems that we sometimes sensibly desire various things that are not co-possible. And it seems there sometimes need be no breakdown in desiring certain things without desiring their necessary means: a guy can dream. So it seems fair to ask

---

21. In *Intention, Plans, and Practical Reason* I tried to finesse this concern by distinguishing internal and external judgments. But I agree with Kieran Setiya, in his "Intention, Plans, and Ethical Rationalism," that this is problematic. That is why in more recent years I have been trying to craft a somewhat different strategy.

22. I discuss a related but different form of self-reinforcement in my discussion of views of David Gauthier in my "The Interplay of Intention and Reason," *Ethics* 123(2013): 657–672 [this volume, essay 8].

23. See, for example, John Broome, "Wide or Narrow Scope?" *Mind* 116(2007): 359–370.

why, in contrast, *intentions* are subject to these norms of consistency and coherence.

At this point some—including Joseph Raz and Niko Kolodny[24]—would answer that the idea that these are distinctive norms with normative force in each case is a "myth." But given our present understanding of our planning agency, this would be to see the thinking that is partly constitutive of our planning agency as involving an illusion, and that is an implication that we would do well to avoid, if we can.

A response to this, anticipated earlier, might be that the mistake that is being made is in our explanatory theory of what is involved in ordinary planning agency, not in the actual thinking of ordinary planning agents.[25] The difficulty that we are having in supporting the idea that these norms of consistency and coherence have a distinctive normative force in the particular case should lead us to reconsider the claim, built into the planning theory, that the psychology of planning agents like us involves the acceptance of, and guidance by, some such norms. After all, if we can see on reflection that the application of these norms to the particular case does not in general pass normative muster, why think that we do indeed accept them in our ordinary practical thinking?

Now, I do think that the planning theory has many explanatory virtues, virtues that both support and are supported by the fecundity of planning agency. But I also agree that it would be an objection to that explanatory model if it attributed to us the acceptance of norms that we can see to be normatively suspect (which is not to say that there are no patterns of thought that are deep seated in our psychology but normatively suspect). So we need to come to terms with Kate's further question. And success in answering this question will help defuse this challenge to the explanatory model.

At this point others—such as, in different ways, J. David Velleman, Kieran Setiya, and (with qualifications) R. Jay Wallace—would shift our focus: these norms of means–end coherence and intention–belief consistency are, at bottom, norms of *theoretical* coherence and consistency.[26] These

24. Joseph Raz, "The Myth of Instrumental Rationality," *Journal of Ethics and Social Philosophy*, 1, no. 1 (2005), http://www.jesp.org/PDF/6863_Raz-vol-1-no-1-rev.pdf; Niko Kolodny, "The Myth of Practical Consistency," *European Journal of Philosophy* 16(2008): 366–402. There are related ideas in Troy Jollimore, "Why Is Instrumental Rationality Rational?" *Canadian Journal of Philosophy* 35 (2005): 289–308.
25. See, again, Niko Kolodny, "Reply to Bridges."
26. J. David Velleman, *Practical Reflection* (Princeton, NJ: Princeton University Press, 1989, reprint, Stanford, CA: CSLI, 2007); J. David Velleman, "What Good Is a Will?," in *Action in Context*, ed. A. Leist. Berlin: Walter de Gruyter: 193–215 (Reprinted in *Rational and Social Agency*: 83–105); Kieran Setiya, "Cognitivism about Instrumental Reason," *Ethics* 117 (2007): 649–673; R. Jay Wallace, "Normativity, Commitment, and

norms apply, in the first instance, to the beliefs (or belief-like attitudes) that are associated with (or, on some views, identical with) our intentions. The normative force of these norms on intention derives from the normative force of norms of theoretical coherence and consistency that apply to associated beliefs (or belief-like attitudes).

I have called this approach "cognitivism" about the normative force of these norms.[27] For this cognitivist strategy to work for the norm of intention consistency, we would need a strong claim that intending to A involves believing you will A.[28] And this cognitivist strategy is still going to need an account of the normative force of the cited theoretical norms. But even given such a robust (and, as I see it, overly strong) connection between intention and belief and even given an account of the normative force of these theoretical norms (a matter that I do not address here), I would be skeptical of such a cognitivism about, at the least, the norm of means–end coherence. This skepticism depends on the possibility of misidentifying what one intends. Assuming that such misidentification is possible, it will be possible to intend E, believe that M is a necessary means to E and that intending M is needed for M, and believe that one does indeed intend M and yet in fact not intend M. In such a case of a false belief about whether one intends the means, one's beliefs may be coherent, but one's intentions will not be means–end coherent. So theoretical coherence of belief does not ensure means–end coherence.[29]

What I seek then is a path between a myth theory and cognitivism about these norms. And to articulate such a path we need to do some more philosophy of action.[30]

Instrumental Reason," as reprinted with added postscript in his *Normativity and the Will* (Oxford: Oxford University Press, 2006): 82–120.

27. "Cognitivism about Practical Reason," as reprinted in my *Faces of Intention*.

28. For example, if the connection between intending A and belief were only a connection to a belief that it is possible that A, we would not have an explanation of the mistake that is involved in intending A and intending B while knowing that A and B are not co-possible.

29. I discuss these matters in "Intention, Belief, Practical, Theoretical" and in "Intention, Belief, and Instrumental Rationality." I first made this point about the significance of false beliefs about what one intends in my "Intention and Means-End Reasoning," *The Philosophical Review* 90 (1981): 252–265, n. 4.

30. So I agree with J. David Velleman that "the philosophy of practical reasoning cannot be purified . . . of considerations from the philosophy of action." But Velleman immediately goes on to say that "the correct principles of practical reasoning are determined by the constitutive aim of action." My view, in contrast, is that, while the relevant principles are associated with what we can call the (descriptive) aim of intention, the defense of the normative force of these principles needs to appeal to further normative considerations. See J. David Velleman, "Deciding How to Decide," as reprinted in his *The Possibility of Practical Reason*, 221–243, at p. 233.

A key is to return to an even more demanding form of agency: self-governance. Suppose you are a planning agent. What else needs to be true for you to be governing your own life?

In R. E. Hobart's story of the arrival of the railroad to a village unfamiliar with locomotive engines, the villagers are told how the engine functions, and yet they still think that there is a horse inside that does the work.[31] We, in contrast, feel no need to posit a horse in the machine. Nevertheless, when we consider an agent's self-governance we can still be tempted by the idea of a person inside who deliberates and moves the levers of action. We can avoid this mistake by seeing self-governance as a matter of the guidance of thought and action not by a little person inside but rather by appropriate agent-level psychological structures and processes. To draw from a related thought of Harry Frankfurt's, we can see our self-governance as the relevant "operation . . . of the systems we are."[32] In particular—and to return to an idea broached earlier—we can suppose that an agent has a practical standpoint, one that consists of attitudes that constitute her stance with respect to relevant practical issues. Such a standpoint speaks for her, with respect to these practical matters. And when that practical standpoint appropriately guides, the agent governs.

This raises the general question of what constitutes the agent's relevant standpoint, and what counts as its appropriate guidance. For present purposes, however, we only need to reflect on certain aspects of such a standpoint, in the case of planning agency.[33] In particular, we need the idea that there is a link between conforming to the norms of intention consistency and means–end coherence and having a kind of standpoint that is needed by a planning agent for relevant self-governance.[34] And here there is a broadly Frankfurtian thought: if you intend E know that M is a necessary means and that you won't M unless you now intend M, and yet you still do not intend M, then there is no clear stance that is where you stand with respect to E. So there is no clear stance whose guidance would constitute

31. R. E. Hobart, "Free Will as Involving Determination and Inconceivable Without It," *Mind* 93(1934): 1–27.

32. Harry Frankfurt, "The Problem of Action," as reprinted in his *The Importance of What We Care About*, pp. 69–79, at p. 74.

33. My fuller model of such a standpoint, in the case of planning agency, appeals to the further idea of plan-like commitments to weights in deliberation. See my "Rational and Social Agency: Reflections and Replies," section 2.

34. See my "Intention, Practical Rationality, and Self-Governance." The thought here is to some extent in the spirit of David Copp's idea that "*rationality* is in the service of *self-government*." See his *Morality in a Natural World* (Cambridge, UK: Cambridge University Press, 2007), p. 351; emphasis in original. The thought is also to some extent in the spirit of Kenneth Stalzer's idea that violating these norms is a failure of "self-fidelity." See his *On the Normativity of the Instrumental Principle* (PhD thesis, Stanford University, 2004), chapter 5.

your self-governance with respect to E. In such a case you might perhaps intentionally act—for example, by intentionally refraining from pursuing the needed means to the still intended end. But this would not be self-governed agency: you are too conflicted for that. And a similar thought is available for cases in which one's intentions violate the consistency norm. If you intend A and intend B and believe A and B are not co-possible, then there is no clear stance that is where *you* stand with respect to A, and there is no clear stance that is where *you* stand with respect to B. So there is no clear stance with respect to A whose guidance would constitute your self-governance with respect to A and similarly with respect to B. In such a case you might perhaps intentionally act—for example, by intentionally A-ing. But this would not be self-governed agency; you are too conflicted for that.

Analogous points do not hold for ordinary desire. I might have and retain conflicting desires concerning an important practical matter but still make a decision and be relevantly self-governing. But, for a planning agent, conflicting intentions are a different matter.

This means that the violation of the norms of intention consistency and means–end coherence precludes relevant self-governance in the particular case for planning agents like us. This is a point about the metaphysics of self-governance for a particular type of agent, namely, a planning agent. If you are a planning agent and you are going to be self-governing with respect to end E, then you had better not both intend E and yet violate the norm of means–end coherence with respect to that intended end.

And now the idea is to use this point about the metaphysics of plan-infused self-governance to make progress with our question about the normative force of intention consistency and coherence in the particular case.

Return to Kate. "Let's assume," Kate can now say "that I have normative reason in each particular case to be self-governing in exercising my planning agency in that case (although a reason whose strength may vary with the significance of the project at issue). After all, I care intrinsically about governing my own life; this does not depend on relevant false belief, and self-governance is a human good. What we have just learned is that when my plan-states violate the norms of consistency or means–end coherence these violations block relevant self-governance. But it is plausible that if I have a normative reason for X and if X is something I have the capacity to attain, then I have a normative reason for a necessary constitutive element of X.[35] So I have reason for a necessary constitutive element of my self-governance in the particular case if I have the capacity for relevant self-governance. But

35. This is not to say that *ought* works in this way. Given that one ought to X and can X, whether one ought to pursue a necessary means to or constitutive element of X

conforming to the norms of intention consistency and means–end coherence is, as we have seen, a kind of organization of mind that is a necessary constitutive element of my relevant self-governance. So, given a capacity for relevant self-governance, I have reason of self-governance to conform to these norms in this particular case. So it is not only true that there are pragmatic reasons for being a planning agent who internalizes these norms and so is disposed to follow through in the particular case. And it is not only true that conforming to these norms normally helps promote the specific ends that I am pursuing. It is also true that, given that I am a planning agent who cares intrinsically about and has a capacity for relevant self-governance, there is a distinctive, noninstrumental practical reason of self-governance (although a reason that may vary in strength) to conform to these norms in each particular case."

Kate's proposal is limited to those cases in which the agent is a planning agent who cares intrinsically about and has the capacity for relevant self-governance. And it allows that the cited reason of self-governance for conformity to these norms may vary in strength. Nevertheless, her proposal is sufficient to defend—in response to the challenge from the myth theorists—relevant aspects of the descriptive and explanatory contours of the planning theory, given the plausible assumption that we normally do care intrinsically about and have the capacity for relevant self-governance.

Against this a myth theorist like Kolodny might object that Kate's focus on the internal organization of her mind involves an "outlandish" concern with "psychic tidiness."[36] The agency-theoretic response to this, however, is that Kate's focus is on a distinctive and significant form of agency, namely, plan-infused self-governance. It is misleading to describe her attitude as a mere concern with psychic tidiness. And it is plausible that we care intrinsically about such plan-infused self-governance and that it has a corresponding normative significance—although a normative significance that may vary in strength depending on the importance of the practical matters at issue.

Recall that we wanted an account that builds on the pragmatic argument for continuing to be a planning agent without simply appealing to

---

may depend on the likelihood of one's performing other necessary means to X. But the claim here is about the transmission of reasons, not oughts.

36. Niko Kolodny says that "it seems outlandish that the kind of psychic tidiness that N [a requirement for belief consistency], or any other requirement of formal coherence, enjoins should be set alongside such final ends as pleasure, friendship, and knowledge." See his "How Does Coherence Matter?" *Proceedings of the Aristotelian Society* (2007): 229–263, at p. 241. And in his "Why Be Rational?" *Mind* 114 (2005): 509–563, at 546–547, Kolodny likens such a concern with "psychic tidiness" to a fetish.

a problematic, direct inference from reasons to be a planning agent who accepts the cited norms to reason to conform to those norms in the particular case. And that is what we now have. We are planning agents, and, given the fecundity of planning agency, we have pragmatic reasons for continuing to be. Given that we are—as we have reason to be—planning agents, our self-governance involves coherence and consistency of relevant intentions. That is a feature of the metaphysics of self-governing planning agency. So given a reason for self-governance in the particular case, and a capacity for that self-governance, we have reason of self-governance for intention consistency and coherence in the particular case. And this is the sense in which the pragmatic argument is for general norm-infused psychological structures that are self-reinforcing: if we do instantiate the planning structures that these pragmatic reasons support, then, on plausible assumptions, we have an associated reason of self-governance to conform in the particular case to the consistency and coherence norms acceptance of which is internal to these structures.[37]

Now, our ordinary understanding of the idea that a violation of these norms is a normatively significant breakdown appeals to a kind of peremptoriness.[38] Any such violation itself constitutes a breakdown: such a violation is not just a prima facie indicator of, or a merely pro tanto contributor to, a breakdown. This is one reason why the norms of intention consistency and coherence are not well understood simply by appeal to the (in any case, controversial) idea that an intention for X in general provides a pro tanto reason for X.[39] After all, when a pro tanto reason is outweighed, it is normally a matter of proper functioning to intend and act contrary to that reason. But a violation of these norms is quite generally a breakdown in proper functioning. So a violation of these norms seems not merely to be a matter of thinking and acting contrary to whatever pro tanto reason, if any, would be provided by an intention for X.

This raises a question about the account that we have given of our reason to conform to these norms in the particular case. This account appeals to a reason of self-governance to avoid violations of these norms. This is not a reason for a specific X that is intended: it is a reason for conforming

37. In "Intention, Belief, Practical, Theoretical," I was primarily interested in a broad pragmatic argument for general structures of planning agency. In "Intention, Practical Rationality, and Self-Governance," I was primarily interested in showing how a reason to be self-governing induced, for a planning agent, a distinctive reason for intention consistency and coherence in the particular case. The present appeal to self-reinforcement aims to clarify the relation between these two arguments.

38. See my *Intention, Plans, and Practical Reason*, p. 24, following Alan Donagan.

39. Ibid. And for a challenge to the very idea that an intention for X quite generally provides a reason for X, see pp. 24–26.

to wide-scope constraints on one's package of intentions and beliefs. Nevertheless, this reason is pro tanto and can be overridden by other substantive considerations. So have we lost the relevant peremptoriness?

Well, given that we are planning agents, any violation of these planning norms is ipso facto a divergence from proper functioning: it is a divergence from the norm-guided functioning that is both partly constitutive of planning agency and has much to be said for it. Further, any such divergence from proper functioning is ipso facto a barrier to relevant self-governance in the particular case. And, on present assumptions, there is a reason against such a barrier to self-governance in the particular case. This reason is *pro tanto*, not merely *prima facie*.⁴⁰ So any such violation of these planning norms is a divergence from proper functioning of a sort that in each case we have reason to avoid.

The relevant peremptoriness, then, consists in the tight connections, for a planning agent who cares about and has the capacity for relevant self-governance, between (i) a violation of the norms of consistency or coherence; (ii) a breakdown in proper functioning; and (iii) a real cost in the particular case, a cost associated with self-governance. This does allow that the pro tanto reason of self-governance in favor of consistency and coherence may be overridden in special cases.⁴¹ Perhaps an evil demon threatens great harm if you are not means–end incoherent. Nevertheless, if you are means–end incoherent, you are diverging from proper functioning of a sort to which you have reason of self-governance to conform. This is not a standard case of conflict in which in intending contrary to a pro tanto reason on the losing side of the conflict you would be functioning properly. This is, rather, a breakdown in proper functioning, one with an identifiable cost, although perhaps one for which there is, in such a special case, sufficient reason.⁴²

Now, in discussing Kate's concerns I have spoken of the practical norms of intention consistency and means–end coherence; and I have tried to

40. See Shelly Kagan, *The Limits of Morality* (Oxford: Oxford University Press, 1989), p. 17.

41. Let me say that I do not think that the video games case that I have discussed elsewhere is such a case. The agent in the video games case has available several strategies that avoid violating the intention-consistency constraint but still respond appropriately to the relevant reasons. See my *Intention, Plans, and Practical Reason*, chapter 8, and my "Rational and Social Agency: Reflections and Replies," section 2, where I discuss Alfred Mele's essay in that same volume.

42. In my "Time, Rationality, and Self-Governance," I develop a related idea about a norm of diachronic rationality in terms of Michael Smith's distinction between "local" and "global" rationality, although Smith would not highlight, as I do, a distinctive reason to avoid such local irrationality. See Michael Smith, "The Structure of

explain the force of these norms by interrelated appeals to the fecundity of planning agency and to reasons of self-governance. Given that acceptance of and guidance by these norms is partly constitutive of our planning agency, given the fecundity and pragmatic significance of this norm-shaped planning agency and given that the role of these norms in self-governance makes these planning structures self-reinforcing, it is plausible to go on to describe these norms as norms of, in particular, practical *rationality*.[43] These are not, however, norms of practical rationality for agents quite generally. After all, not all agents are planning agents. These are, rather, norms of practical rationality for, in particular, planning agents.[44]

Orthonomy," in John Hyman and Helen Steward, eds., *Agency and Action* (Cambridge, UK: Cambridge University Press, 2004): 165–193, at p. 190.

43. In his "Intention, Plans, and Ethical Rationalism," Setiya emphasizes that this question of whether these are norms of rationality is not settled just by arguing that we have reason to conform to these norms.

44. This idea that certain norms of rationality are relativized to a type of agency fits well within the Gricean methodology of creature construction that lies behind my development of the planning theory. Such relativized rationality norms are broadly in the neighborhood of what Kieran Setiya calls "pluralistic rationalism." See my "Rational and Social Agency: Reflections and Replies," section 2, where I discuss Setiya's essay in that same volume.

CHAPTER 10

Rational Planning Agency[1]

We are planning agents. In support of both the cross-temporal and the social organization of our agency, and in ways that are compatible with our cognitive and epistemic limits, we settle on partial and largely future-directed plans. These plans pose problems of means and preliminary steps, filter solutions to those problems, and guide action. As we might say, we are almost always already involved in temporally extended planning agency in which our practical thinking is framed by a background of somewhat settled prior plans.

In this plan-infused practical thinking we are guided by norms of plan rationality. These include norms of plan consistency, including plan-belief consistency and the possibility of agglomerating one's various plans without running into problems of consistency.[2] These consistency norms are in the background of the filtering roles of our prior plans. These norms also include a norm of means-end coherence—a norm, roughly, that mandates intending believed necessary means to ends intended.[3] This norm is in the background of the problem-posing roles of our prior plans. And these norms include a norm of stability of plans over time, one that is in the background of the default stability of our plans in the support

---

1. This is a substantially revised version of my talk at the Royal Institute of Philosophy in October 2015. A version of this essay was presented at the April 2016 Conference on Practical Reason and Meta-Ethics at the University of Nebraska. The ideas in this essay are developed in more detail in my 2016 Pufendorf Lectures, delivered at Lund University in June 2016. (See http://www.pufendorf.se/sectione195f.html?id=2864)

2. For this way of formulating a norm of agglomerativity see Gideon Yaffe, "Trying, Intending and Attempted Crimes," *Philosophical Topics* **32** (2004), 505–32, 510–12.

3. For a more precise formulation see my *Intention, Plans, and Practical Reason* (Cambridge, MA: Harvard University Press, 1987; reissued CSLI Publications, 1999), 31.

of cross-temporal and social organization. While these norms admit of qualifications, we do not simply treat them as rules of thumb: we normally see their violation as a mistake/a breakdown. And guidance by these norms helps frame practical thinking in which we weigh pros and cons with respect to specific decisions that are on the deliberative table.

In other work I have developed these ideas as part of what I have called the planning theory of our human agency.[4] In this essay I want to reflect on the way in which the status of these norms can seem puzzling. After all, it is common to desire non-co-possible things, or to desire an end without desiring means. Why are intentions and plans different? Further, there seem to be cases in which we can better pursue our basic ends by adopting plans that are not consistent with each other.[5] And we can wonder what the problem is in failing to intend believed necessary means to an intended end if that belief is false, or if we have no good reason for our intended end.

These reflections point to a fundamental challenge: in giving these norms their own independent significance, are we endorsing an unjustified fetish for "psychic tidiness"?[6] We can think of this as a challenge to the reflective stability of these norms.[7] According to this challenge, a planning agent who accurately reflects on these structures of her practical thinking will reject these as norms with independent normative significance, since she will reject a brute appeal to the significance of mere mental tidiness. She will come to see that appeal to these norms as basic norms of practical rationality is an indefensible "myth." So these norms will not be stable under her critical reflection.

Such a failure of stability under reflection would pose a challenge to the descriptive and explanatory ambitions of appeals to our planning agency. If the norms involved in such agency would not survive a planning agent's critical reflection, then it would be less plausible that thinking shaped by

---

4. Bratman, *Intention, Plans, and Practical Reason*.

5. This is the structure of the video games example I discuss in Chapter 8 of *Intention, Plans, and Practical Reason*.

6. An early version of this challenge is in Hugh McCann, "Settled Objectives and Rational Constraints," *American Philosophical Quarterly* **28** (1991), 25–36. It is developed further in Joseph Raz, "The Myth of Instrumental Rationality," *Journal of Ethics and Social Philosophy* **1:1** (2005); and in Niko Kolodny, "The Myth of Practical Consistency," *European Journal of Philosophy* **16** (2008), 366–402. Talk of "psychic tidiness" is from Niko Kolodny, "How Does Coherence Matter?" *Proceedings of the Aristotelian Society* **107** (2007), 229–63, 241. The worry about being "fetishistic" is from Kolodny, "Why Be Rational?" *Mind* **114** (2005), 509–63, 547.

7. Cp. Christine Korsgaard: "If the problem is that morality might not survive reflection, then the solution is that it might"—though my concern here is not with morality but with basic plan-theoretic norms. See Christine Korsgaard, *The Sources of Normativity* (Cambridge: Cambridge University Press, 1996), 49.

these norms is a basic feature of human agency.[8] And my aim in this essay is respond to this challenge.[9]

In doing this I assume that if we can show that these norms are both central to the basic structure of a planning agent's practical thinking and would survive a planning agent's critical reflection, then we can justifiably conclude that these are indeed norms of practical rationality for a planning agent. This is not yet to determine whether we should be in a strong sense realists about these norms. But for our purpose of defending the explanatory ambitions of the planning theory, we need not settle that metaphysical question.

So how might we establish the reflective stability of these norms? Focusing at first on synchronic norms of plan consistency and coherence, an initial idea might be to see these norms as riding piggyback on norms of theoretical rationality that enjoin consistency and coherence of associated beliefs. This is *cognitivism* about these aspects of plan rationality. In other work, however, I have argued that this is not going to work.[10] This is primarily (but not solely) because one might believe one intends the necessary means to an end one intends and yet not in fact intend those means. In such a case one's beliefs might be theoretically coherent even though one's intentions do not conform to the norm of means-end coherence.

A second idea might be to say that our acceptance of these norms is inescapable for agents, so there is no real problem about their reflective stability. And, indeed, it is a central feature of planning agency, as understood within the planning theory, that one's intentions and plans are guided by one's (perhaps, implicit) acceptance of these norms. But this would only show that the acceptance of these norms is inescapable for agents if planning agency were inescapable for agents. But it isn't. One can be a goal-directed agent who acts purposively and for reasons but is nevertheless not a planning agent. This is an aspect of the *multiplicity of agency*.[11]

8. This is to some extent in the spirit of Niko Kolodny, "Reply to Bridges," *Mind* **118** (2009), 369–76.

9. My hope is thereby also to respond further to trenchant challenges to my earlier treatments of these issues in J. David Velleman, "What Good Is a Will?" in Manuel Vargas and Gideon Yaffe, eds., *Rational and Social Agency: The Philosophy of Michael Bratman* (New York: Oxford University Press, 2014), 83–105; and in Kieran Setiya, "Intention, Plans, and Ethical Rationalism," in Vargas and Yaffe, eds., *Rational and Social Agency*, 56–82.

10. See Michael E. Bratman, "Intention, Belief, Practical, Theoretical," in Simon Robertson, ed., *Spheres of Reason: New Essays on the Philosophy of Normativity* (Oxford: Oxford University Press, 2009), 29–61 [this volume, essay 2]; and "Intention, Belief and Instrumental Rationality," in David Sobel and Steven Wall, eds., *Reasons for Action* (Cambridge: Cambridge University Press, 2009), 13–36 [this volume, essay 3].

11. An idea built into the strategy of creature construction in H. P. Grice, "Method in Philosophical Psychology (From the Banal to the Bizarre)," *Proceedings and Addresses of*

Granted, we may not have the capacity, just like that, to give up being a planning agent and become, instead, a non-planning agent. But even if there were this contingent incapacity, we would need to address the possibility that a planning agent would, on reflection, be alienated from these norms in a way that would threaten their longer-term stability and challenge their status as basic features of our agency.[12]

Donald Davidson's work on interpretation points to another kind of inescapability. Davidson treated norms of rationality as a single overall package. With respect to that package he wrote:

> It is only by interpreting a creature as largely in accord with these principles that we can intelligibly attribute propositional attitudes to it . . . An agent cannot fail to comport most of the time with the basic norms of rationality.[13]

Broad conformity to certain basic norms of consistency and coherence is a fundamental feature of the attitudes we ascribe in interpreting an agent.

Something along these lines seems right. But it does not solve our problem about plan rationality. First, this would not explain why a violation of these norms in the particular case is a breakdown. At most what is claimed to be inescapable for a person with a mind is failing to "comport most of the time" with relevant norms.[14] Second, Davidson sees the relevant norms of rationality as a single overall package, one involved quite generally in interpreting minds. But once we note the multiplicity of agency we need to be alive to the possibility of a minded agent who is not a planning agent. So Davidson's idea about interpreting minds does not establish the inescapability, for a minded agent, of conformity with the norms of plan rationality.

A fourth idea would highlight the large benefits to us of our planning agency. Given general features of our minds and our environments, our pursuit of our most basic ends will normally be made more effective by our plan-shaped practical thinking, practical thinking that supports both cross-temporal and social organization and, as I will discuss, our self-governance.

---

the American Philosophical Association **48** (1974), 23–53. And see my "Valuing and the Will," as reprinted in Michael E. Bratman, *Structures of Agency: Essays* (New York: Oxford University Press, 2007), 47–67; and Jennifer Morton, "Toward an Ecological Theory of the Norms of Practical Deliberation," *European Journal of Philosophy* **19** (2011), 561–84.

12. For helpful discussion of related issues see Luca Ferrero, "Inescapability Revisited'," unpublished manuscript, April 2016, section 6.

13. "Incoherence and Irrationality," as reprinted in Donald Davidson, *Problems of Rationality* (Oxford: Oxford University Press, 2004), 189–98, 196–7.

14. Niko Kolodny makes this point in his "The Myth of Practical Consistency," 386.

This fecundity of planning agency supports the idea that we have good reason to be planning agents. Since our planning agency involves the application of the cited norms to particular cases, we may then try to infer that we have good reason to conform to these norms in their application to particular cases. This would be a two-tier pragmatic justification of these norms.

But, as we have learned from J. J. C. Smart, there is a problem.[15] Even given the advantages of general patterns of thought guided by norms of plan consistency and coherence, there can be particular cases in which it is known that conformity to these norms would not be as effective, with respect to the very same benefits, as would divergence. Perhaps sometimes it is useful to have inconsistent or incoherent plans. But what we are seeking is not just a defense of a general tendency to conform to these norms. We are also seeking a justification of the application of these norms to the particular case.

There is an insight built into the two-tier pragmatic approach: the general capacity for planning agency is good in myriad ways. But what we learn from Smart is that we need also to provide a further rationale that, given that one is (as there is reason to be) a planning agent, supports the application of these norms to the particular case. Otherwise, we cannot be fully confident that the acceptance of these as norms with independent significance in application to the particular case will be reflectively stable.

Here we can learn from Gilbert Harman's suggestion that in theorizing about such norms we follow

> a process of mutual adjustment of principles to practice and/or intuitions, a process of adjustment which can continue until we have reached what Rawls (1971) calls a reflective equilibrium. Furthermore, and this is important, we can also consider what rationale there might be for various principles we come up with and that can lead to further changes in principles, practices, and/or intuitions.[16]

---

15. J. J. C. Smart, "Extreme and Restricted Utilitarianism," in Philippa Foot, ed., *Theories of Ethics* (Oxford: Oxford University Press, 1967), 171–83.

16. Gilbert Harman, *Change in View: Principles of Reasoning* (Cambridge, MA: MIT Press, 1986), 9. Harman is here focusing on what he calls principles of reasoning, whereas our focus is on principles of plan rationality. We can nevertheless apply the spirit of Harman's comments to our concerns about plan rationality. This is also to some extent in the spirit of Nadeem Hussain's emphasis on a strategy of reflective equilibrium in his "The Requirements of Rationality," vers 2.4. (unpublished manuscript, Stanford University), though Hussain would not be sympathetic to what I later call the reason desideratum.

Our concern is with the stability under reflection of planning norms. Following Harman's suggestion, we can understand such reflection on the part of a planning agent as "a process of mutual adjustment" and search for a "rationale" that underlies the norms that guide one's plan-infused practical thinking. We can suppose that this rationale will involve some sort of two-tier pragmatic support. But it will need to go beyond that. So we ask: Is there some further consideration appeal to which could supplement the two-tier pragmatic approach and enable the reflective planning agent to make good normative sense of her application of these norms in the particular case? This would enable the reflective planning agent to defend her norms by way of a kind of inference to the best normative explanation.

In pursuit of such a best normative explanation, I will frequently speak directly in my own voice. But in doing so I take myself to be speaking on behalf of a planning agent who is reflecting on her plan-infused practical thinking. It is the reflective stability for a planning agent of that practical thinking that is our main concern.

We can articulate three interrelated desiderata for a rationale that underlies these planning norms. First, and in partial response to the myth theorist's challenge, it should explain why the forms of coherence at stake in these norms are not merely a matter of mental tidiness. Second, it would be good if this rationale articulated a relevant commonality across these different norms, both synchronic and diachronic. And third, it should explain why there is a systematically present normative reason that favors conformity to these norms.[17]

How should we understand this talk about normative reasons? This is controversial territory. But I think that, given our concern with the stability of these planning norms in light of the agent's own reflection, it is reasonable for us to work with a model of reasons as anchored in ends of the agent where what those ends favor is desirable. Roughly: a consideration is a reason for S to A only if it helps explain why S's doing A is needed to promote relevant ends of S,[18] and only if what these ends favor is desirable. A planning agent reflecting on her own practical thinking will have a

17. For this broad issue see John Broome, *Rationality Through Reasoning* (Hoboken, NJ: Wiley-Blackwell, 2013), chap. 11. Broome, however, does not work with the model of normative reasons to which I turn in the next paragraph. Further, talk of a "systematically present" reason is mine, not Broome's; and I will have more to say about this idea below.

18. A classic source of this idea is Bernard Williams, "Internal and External Reasons," in his *Moral Luck* (Cambridge: Cambridge University Press, 1981), 101–13. My formulation follows, with important adjustment, Mark Schroeder, *Slaves of the Passions* (Oxford: Oxford University Press, 2007), 59.

keen interest in what is needed to promote her ends and in whether these ends favor what is desirable. So it makes sense, for our present purposes, to work within this dual framework in exploring the reflective stability of the planning norms.

Let me briefly clarify my talk here of an agent's ends. Roughly: to have E as an end is to have a non-instrumental concern in favor of E. Not all such ends are intentions since, in contrast with intentions, not all ends tend to diminish when they are not co-realizable in light of one's beliefs. It is common in our complex lives to have ends that we know are not jointly realizable even while we believe that each is realizable. Further, one may intend X even if X is not in this sense one of one's ends, since one's intention may favor X solely instrumentally. Nevertheless, an intention in favor of X solely as a means can still induce rational pressure for an intention in favor of a known necessary means to X. So we need to be careful to understand the idea of an intended end, as it appears in the norm of means-end coherence, in a way that does not require that what is intended is, strictly speaking, an end of the agent's.

The second desideratum seeks a commonality across synchronic and diachronic norms. What diachronic norm? The idea is that our planning agency involves a norm of stability of plans over time. What norm?

Note two preliminary ideas. First, a prior intention at t1 to A at t2 will frequently lead to change in the circumstances between t1 and t2 in ways that reinforce that intention. Think about buying, at t1, a non-refundable ticket in support of your intention at t1 to fly to London at t2. This is the snowball effect.[19] Second, having formed the prior intention it may not be rational to reconsider. After all, reconsideration has its own costs and risks, especially for resource-limited agents like us. And normally, if one does not reconsider one's rationally formed prior intention, then one continues rationally so to intend.

In my 1987 book I focused on these two aspects of the rational stability of intention over time. But I have come to think that there is more to say about this rational stability. My reasons for this primarily involve two cases of potential intention stability. I will focus first on a case involving potential willpower.[20] Later I will turn to a second case. In the end, a virtue of the account I will propose will be that it treats both cases within the same overall framework, one that also supports a significant commonality in the rationale underlying synchronic and diachronic plan rationality.

19. *Intention, Plans, and Practical Reason*, 82.
20. See Richard Holton, *Willing, Wanting, Waiting* (Oxford: Clarendon, 2009). And see my "Toxin, Temptation, and the Stability of Intention," as reprinted in my *Faces of Intention* (Cambridge: Cambridge University Press, 1999), and my "Temptation and the Agent's Standpoint," *Inquiry* **57** (2014), 293–310 [this volume, essay 7].

Suppose that you know you will be tempted to drink heavily tonight at the party. You now think that, in light of what matters to you, this is a bad idea. However, you know that at the party your evaluation will shift in favor of drinking more. You also know that if you did drink heavily your evaluation would later shift back and you would regret that. So this morning you resolve to drink only one glass tonight. The problem is that, as you anticipate, if you were to stick with your resolve at the party, you would act against what would then be your present evaluation. And we normally suppose that action contrary to one's present evaluation is a rational breakdown. So how could you rationally follow through with your resolve?

As Sarah Paul has emphasized (in conversation), cases with this structure are ubiquitous in our lives.[21] We many times face temporarily shifted evaluations with respect to continuing with an ambitious project when, as it is said, the going gets tough. And even in the case of more modest temporally extended projects, we frequently face issues of procrastination. In following through with planned temporally extended activities one will frequently be tempted to procrastinate just a bit. It will frequently seem that one could get the benefits of the planned activity plus a small incremental benefit of, say, reading just one more e-mail.[22] Problems of willpower and temptation pervade our planned temporally extended activities. If we are going to understand the deep ways in which our plans help support important forms of cross-temporal organization we will need to understand how those plan structures are responsive to such de-stabilizing pressures. So we will need to ask whether there is at work here a norm of diachronic plan stability that goes beyond snowball effects and issues of rational non-reconsideration.

I turn to this question below. But first we need to return to our general pursuit of a rationale that underlies the planning norms in a way that suitably supplements the two-tier pragmatic account.

Here I propose a *strategy of self-governance*: a basic rationale underlying these norms, one that supplements the two-tier pragmatic account, appeals to a planning agent's self-governance, both synchronic and diachronic.[23]

21. For Paul's approach to these matters see her "Doxastic Self-Control," *American Philosophical Quarterly* **52** (2015), 145–58, and her "Diachronic Incontinence Is a Problem in Moral Philosophy," *Inquiry* **57** (2014), 337–55. For a discussion of related phenomena see Jennifer Morton and Sarah Paul, "Grit" (unpublished).

22. See Sergio Tenenbaum and Diana Raffman, "Vague Projects and the Puzzle of the Self Torturer," *Ethics* **123** (2012), 86–112, esp. section III.

23. A related idea is in David Copp, "The Normativity of Self-Grounded Reason," in his *Morality in a Natural World* (Cambridge: Cambridge University Press, 2007), 309–53, 351. A somewhat related idea is Kenneth Stalzer's thought that a violation of these norms is a breakdown in "self-fidelity." See his *On the Normativity of the Instrumental Principle* (PhD thesis, Stanford University, 2004), chap. 5.

Planning norms, both synchronic and diachronic, track forms of coherence that are essential to a planning agent's self-governance, and such coherence is not merely mental tidiness. Further, a systematically present reason in favor of conformity to these norms is grounded in one's reason to govern one's own life. A planning agent with the capacity for self-governance will be in a position to conclude, on reflection, that the best rationale for her planning norms, one that supplements the two-tier pragmatic account, appeals in these ways to the significance of self-governance. And given this rationale, her acceptance of these norms will be reflectively stable. Or so I will argue.

This is to focus on planning agents with the capacity for self-governance. At some point we would need to consider planning agents who do not have the capacity for self-governance—3-year old humans, perhaps. But I put this issue aside here.

The idea is not to see self-governance as a constitutive aim of agency.[24] As I see it, an appeal to such a substantive constitutive aim would over-burden[25] our descriptive and explanatory theory of action: there are just too many cases of agency that seems not to be guided by such an aim. R. Jay Wallace gives us a lively sense of this point when he highlights "sheer willfulness, stubbornness, lethargy, habit, blind self-assertion, thought-lessness, and various actions expressive of emotional states."[26] Just as the legal positivists distinguished between law as it is and law as it ought to be, we should distinguish between agency as it is and as it ought to be.

Again, the idea is not to appeal to self-governance to convince a pur-posive but non-planning agent to try to become a planning agent. To be sure, there are strong pragmatic reasons for making such a transition, if one can. But that is not the main focus of the strategy of self-governance. Its main concern is, rather, directly to address an agent who is already a planning agent, one whose reasoning accords the cited planning norms an independent normative significance. In addressing such an agent the self-governance strategy aims to articulate a rationale to which that agent can appeal to make good normative sense of her plan-infused practical thinking.

24. J. David Velleman sees the constitutive aim of action as self-intelligibility. However, I take it that on his account this constitutive aim is, in effect, an aim of au-tonomy. See J. David Velleman, *How We Get Along* (Cambridge: Cambridge University Press, 2009) chapter 5, esp. 131–5. See also 26–27. (In his "The Possibility of Practical Reason," in his *The Possibility of Practical Reason* (Oxford: Oxford University Press, 2000), 170–99, 193, Velleman appeals explicitly to a constitutive aim of "autonomy" and notes the continuity of that appeal with his account in his *Practical Reflection* (Princeton, NJ: Princeton University Press, 1989.)
25. Thanks to Jon Barwise and John Perry (in conversation) for this apt term.
26. "Normativity, Commitment, and Instrumental Reason," as reprinted in R. Jay Wallace, *Normativity and the Will* (Oxford: Oxford University Press, 2006), 82–120, 91.

Such a rationale would need to be responsive to our three desiderata: articulate relevant forms of coherence that are not merely mental tidiness; articulate a relevant commonality across the different norms; and identify a systematically present reason in favor of conformity. While this last desideratum—as I will call it, the *reason desideratum*—is fundamental, I will for now put it to one side and try to articulate a structure of self-governance-based norms that is responsive to concerns with coherence and commonality. In this way I will try to construct an initial, *prima facie*, though not yet conclusive self-governance-based case for these norms. I will then return to the reason desideratum.

A first step is to sketch a broadly naturalistic model of self-governance at a time (or anyway, during a small temporal interval). And here we can learn from Harry Frankfurt's idea of "where (if anywhere) the person himself stands."[27] Self-governance involves guidance of thought and action by where the agent stands, by the agent's relevant practical standpoint. Such a standpoint will need to be sufficiently coherent to constitute a clear place where the agent stands on relevant practical issues. It will need to guide choice. And choice will need to cohere with that coherent standpoint.

So coherence of relevant standpoint and coherence of choice with standpoint are elements in our model of self-governance at a time. And now we can propose, as part of our pursuit of inference to the best normative explanation, that there is a close connection between these forms of self-governance-related coherence and practical rationality. In doing this we will want a somewhat qualified connection. Incoherence of standpoint with respect to trivial choices, or with respect to tragic conflicts,[28] may not be irrationality. And we will want to leave room for a *pro tanto* or local rational breakdown that, while it is not merely a potentially misleading, *prima facie* indicator of irrationality, nevertheless does not ensure all-in irrationality.[29] So consider:

> *Practical Rationality/Self-Governance (PRSG):* If S is capable of self-governance it
> is, defeasibly, *pro tanto* irrational of S either to fail to have a coherent practical
> standpoint or to choose in a way that does not cohere with her standpoint.

27. Harry Frankfurt, "Identification and Wholeheartedness," as reprinted in Harry Frankfurt, *The Importance of What We Care About* (Cambridge: Cambridge University Press, 1988), 159–76, 166. And see also Gary Watson, "Free Agency," *The Journal of Philosophy* **72** (1975), 205–20, 216

28. E.g., William Styron, *Sophie's Choice* (New York: Random House, 1979).

29. For a distinction between local and global rationality see Michael Smith, "The Structure of Orthonomy," in John Hyman and Helen Steward, eds., *Agency and Action* (Cambridge: Cambridge University Press, 2004), 165–93, 190.

PRSG says that if S is capable of self-governance and yet fails to satisfy the cited coherence conditions of synchronic self-governance then, defeasibly, S is *pro tanto* irrational. The connection it articulates between a breakdown in self-governance-related coherence and irrationality is doubly qualified: it is a defeasible connection to *pro tanto* irrationality. But such a breakdown in self-governance-related coherence is not merely a potentially misleading *prima facie* indicator concerning what really matters.

As noted, this is so far only an initial, *prima facie* case for PRSG. I will turn later to the reason desideratum; but first, let's see how this initial case can be extended to, more specifically, a planning agent.

A planning agent will have a web of plans that settle—frequently in the face of conflict—on certain projects, as well as on certain considerations that are to matter in the pursuit of those projects. These plans will normally cross-refer to each other: one's plan for today will typically involve a reference to one's earlier and later plans; and vice versa. These issue-settling, cross-referring plans will frame much of one's practical thought and action over time. They will pose problems about how to fill in so-far partial plans with sub-plans about means and the like, sub-plans that mesh with each other. And they will filter options that are potential solutions to those problems. In playing these roles these plans will induce forms of psychological connectedness and continuity that are familiar from Lockean models of personal identity over time.

This leads to a proposal about self-governed planning agency.[30] Given the settling, cross-referring, framing, mesh-supporting, and Lockean-identity-supporting roles of her plans, a planning agent's practical standpoints will involve her web of plans concerning both projects and considerations that are to matter in her practical thinking: her practical standpoints will be *plan-infused*. A planning agent's plans help constitute her practical standpoint at a time in part because of their roles in structuring her temporally extended practical thought and action over time. So the guidance of her thought and action by these planning structures will help constitute her relevant self-governance. In such self-governance, plan-infused standpoints will need to be both coherent and coherent with choice. And when we combine this point about a planning agent's self-governance with PRSG we arrive at

---

30. See my "Three Theories of Self-Governance" as reprinted in my *Structures of Agency* (New York: Oxford University Press, 2007), 222–53, and my "A Planning Theory of Self-Governance: Reply to Franklin," *Philosophical Explorations* **20** (2017): 15–20. For a deep challenge see Elijah Millgram, "Segmented Agency," in Vargas and Yaffe, eds., *Rational and Social Agency*, 152–89.

Practical Rationality/Self-Governance-Planning Agency (PRSG-P): If S is a planning agent who is capable of self-governance it is, defeasibly, *pro tanto* irrational of S either to fail to have a coherent practical plan-infused standpoint or to choose in a way that does not cohere with her plan-infused standpoint.

Again, what we have so far is only an initial, *prima facie*, case in favor of PRSG-P. Keeping this limitation in mind, however, we can explore the implications of PRSG-P concerning plan consistency and coherence. And the basic idea here is that inconsistency or incoherence in plan, given one's beliefs, normally baffles the coherence of plan-infused standpoint that is needed for there to be a clear place where the agent stands with respect to relevant issues. If you intend A and intend B, while believing that A and B are not co-possible, there is no clear answer to the question of where you stand with respect to this practical question. If you intend A but believe not-A then you will normally be buffeted by conflicting dispositions to plan on the assumption that A and to plan on the assumption that not-A.[31] In this way there will be no clear answer to the question of where you stand with respect to A. And if you intend E but do not intend believed necessary means to E even though you believe it has come time to (as we say) fish or cut bait, there will be no clear answer to the question of where you stand with respect to E. In each case there is a contrast with ordinary desire: desires for non-co-possible things, or for things one believes will not happen, or for ends in the absence of desiring the means, are a common feature of our lives and need not block relevant coherence of standpoint.

A complication is that there can be intention analogues of the preface paradox.[32] Perhaps one has a wide range of plans for one's vacation, but sensibly believes that one will not accomplish everything one plans. So it is not possible to realize all one's intentions in a world in which all of one's beliefs are true. Still, one may sensibly proceed to plan in the normal way with respect to each of one's intended ends.

This suggests that in certain preface-analogue cases plan-belief inconsistency may not induce a breakdown in coherence of plan-infused standpoint. So we have a double defeasibility. As noted earlier, coherence of plan-infused standpoint is, defeasibly, needed to avoid self-governance-grounded *pro*

---

31. See *Intention, Plans, and Practical Reason*, 38–9. Carlos Núñez develops a forceful challenge to a prohibition on intention-belief inconsistency. See Carlos Núñez, *The Will and Normative Judgment* (PhD thesis, Stanford University, 2016).

32. I note this complexity in my "Intention, Practical Rationality, and Self-Governance," *Ethics* **119** (2009), 411–43 at note 7 [this volume, essay 4, at 78]. It is the target of an extended discussion in Sam Shpall, "The Calendar Paradox," *Philosophical Studies* **173** (2016), 801–25.

tanto irrationality. To this we add that plan-belief consistency is defeasibly needed for coherence of plan-infused standpoint. We thereby arrive at:

> *Plan consistency and coherence (PCC):* If S is a planning agent who is capable of self-governance it is, doubly-defeasibly, *pro tanto* irrational of S to have plans that are inconsistent or means-end incoherent, given her beliefs.

What underlies this rational pressure against plan inconsistency or incoherence is not merely mental tidiness but the coherence of standpoint that is essential to a planning agent's synchronic self-governance.

Though this is so far only a *prima facie* case in support of PCC, we can go on to ask whether this approach to synchronic plan rationality could be extended to diachronic plan rationality. Does diachronic plan rationality track a kind of cross-temporal coherence that is central to a planning agent's diachronic self-governance?[33]

To explore this we need a model of a planning agent's self-governance not only at a time but also *over* time.[34] An initial idea is that a planning agent's self-governance over time involves her self-governance at times along the way while engaging in a planned temporally extended activity, where these forms of synchronic self-governance are appropriately interconnected. But what interconnections are these?

Here I propose that they involve the interconnections between plan-infused attitudes that are characteristic of planned temporally extended activity, all in the context of self-governance at times along the way. These interconnections will include forms of continuity of intention, cross-reference between intentions, intended mesh in sub-plans, and interdependence between intentions and/or expectations of intention.[35] Further, though I cannot defend this here, I think such cross-temporal intention interconnections within planned temporally extended activity will be significantly analogous to the interpersonal intention interconnections highlighted in the account of shared intentional action I have developed

---

33. In asking this question here I continue with my strategy of postponing the question whether there is, systematically, a reason that favors conformity with these norms.

34. This is the focus of my "A Planning Agent's Self-Governance Over Time" [this volume, essay 11].

35. Given the hierarchical structure of plans, there can be such interconnections at a higher level despite a breakdown in interconnection at a lower level. If the lower level breakdown in interconnections is grounded in a sensible reassessment of lower-level plans, perhaps in light of new information, the higher-level interconnections will, in the context, normally support a judgment of diachronic self-governance. But in some

elsewhere.[36] This is a version of an important parallel between the cross-temporal organization of an individual's activity and interpersonal, social organization. The idea that a planning agent's diachronic self-governance involves interconnections characteristic of planned temporally extended activity, taken together with this parallel between the individual and the social, supports the metaphor that in her self-governance over time a planning agent is "acting together" with herself over time.

Will willpower comport with a planning agent's diachronic self-governance, so understood? Well, in a temptation case involving evaluation shift, following through with one's prior resolution to resist the temptation, while it would involve the cited cross-temporal interconnections, would conflict with one's then-present evaluation. It seems to follow that sticking with one's prior resolution would be incompatible with synchronic self-governance, and so with diachronic self-governance. But it also seems an important commonsense idea that willpower can be a central case of diachronic self-governance.

In responding, we do not merely seek some sort of causal mechanism in the psychology that can explain why one sometimes sticks with one's resolve. We want to explain why, at least sometimes, sticking with one's resolve coheres with one's present standpoint and, in part for that reason, coheres with self-governance. And here we will want to appeal to some general feature of the agent's standpoint that helps explain how the prior resolve sometimes helps re-shift the standpoint in favor of willpower. But what feature?

We do not want simply to appeal to an end of constancy of intention,[37] since such an appeal would face familiar concerns about a fetish for (in this case, cross-temporal) mental tidiness. In a discussion of related matters, J. David Velleman proposes that we appeal to our interest in understanding ourselves: "my intellectual drives . . . favor fulfilling my past intentions."[38] Given the commonality desideratum, however, this will lead to a general cognitivism about planning norms, with all its difficulties.

cases a more complex judgment about the extent of diachronic self-governance will be apt.

36. Michael E. Bratman, *Shared Agency: A Planning Theory of Acting Together* (New York: Oxford University Press, 2014). I defend this analogy in my "A Planning Agent's Self-Governance Over Time."

37. For ideas broadly in this spirit see Jordon Howard Sobel, "Useful Intentions," in his *Taking Chances: Essays on Rational Choice* (Cambridge: Cambridge University Press, 1994), 237–54, and Wlodek Rabinowicz, "To Have One's Cake and Eat It Too: Sequential Choice and Expected-Utility Violations," *Journal of Philosophy* **92** (1995), 586–620.

38. J. David Velleman, "The Centered Self," in his *Self to Self* (Cambridge: Cambridge University Press, 2006), 253–83, 272.

So let me propose instead that we appeal to the end of diachronic self-governance—where such self-governance is understood in terms of the model we are hereby developing. This is not an appeal simply to an end of constancy of intention; but it is also not an appeal that leads to cognitivism. This end would sometimes support willpower in the face of temptation, since such willpower would involve the cross-temporal continuity and interconnection of plan structures that is an element in diachronic self-governance.[39] In this way this end would be poised to help stabilize the agent's temporally extended, planned activities. Further, the presence of this end would help explain why a planning agent's diachronic self-governance is, at least frequently, intentional under that description.

Granted, this end of diachronic self-governance, even if present, may be overridden by other ends in the agent's standpoint at the time of temptation. And if it is overridden then sticking with one's prior resolution will not comport with synchronic self-governance; and so it will not comport with diachronic self-governance. But sometimes this end of diachronic self-governance can indeed help re-shift the agent's standpoint at the time of temptation to favor willpower. So this end can sometimes support the co-ordination of synchronic self-governance and diachronic continuity in such cases. In this way, willpower in the face of temptation may comport both with synchronic and with diachronic self-governance, given the end of diachronic self-governance. This does not explain how willpower always comports with self-governance; but we do not need to explain that, since it is not true.

So let's model a planning agent's diachronic self-governance as involving this end of diachronic self-governance. A planning agent's self-governance over time involves coordination of two kinds of coherence within planned temporally extended activity: the synchronic coherence involved in self-governance at times along the way, and the coherence involved in relevant cross-temporal continuities and interconnections of intentions over time. And this coordination of these two forms of coherence is to some extent supported by standpoints that include the very end of diachronic self-governance.

Return now to diachronic plan rationality. In discussing synchronic plan rationality I argued that a reflective planning agent with the capacity for self-governance would be led to the idea that there is, defeasibly, *pro tanto* rational pressure in favor of the coherence that is partly constitutive of synchronic self-governance. This would be an inference to the best normative

39. A full story would also appeal to the agent's expected regret at giving into temptation, but I put that aside here. See my "Toxin, Temptation, and the Stability of Intention." [And see this volume, essay 11, section 8.]

explanation of her plan-infused practical thinking—though, as noted, the support for this is so far only *prima facie*, since we have so far not addressed the reason desideratum. So let us now, in the same spirit, ask whether a reflective planning agent with the capacity for diachronic self-governance would be led to the idea that there is, defeasibly, *pro tanto* rational pressure in favor of the forms of coordinated coherence that are partly constitutive of a planning agent's diachronic self-governance.

A basic thought here is that there is a natural generalization available to the reflective planning agent. Just as there is rational pressure for the coherence central to her synchronic self-governance, so there is rational pressure for the coherence central to her diachronic self-governance. In each case the underlying idea, supported by an inference to the best normative explanation of her plan-infused practical thinking, is that there is rational pressure for coherence that is partly constitutive of her self-governance. So there is, in particular, rational pressure in favor of the coordination of synchronic and diachronic coherence that is characteristic of a planning agent's diachronic self-governance. So consider:

> *Diachronic Plan Rationality (DPR)*: If S is a planning agent who is capable of diachronic self-governance then the following is, defeasibly, *pro tanto* irrational of S:
>
> (a) S is engaged in a planned temporally extended activity that has so far cohered with both synchronic and diachronic self-governance.
>
> (b) Given her present standpoint, a choice to continue with her planned activity would cohere with that standpoint and so cohere with her continued synchronic self-governance and, in part for that reason, with her diachronic self-governance. And yet
>
> (c) S makes a choice that blocks her continued diachronic self-governance.

Condition (a) is a historical condition: it matters whether the agent has been engaged in a relevant planned temporally extended activity. And condition (b) would not be satisfied if S's ends develop in a way such that a choice to continue with the planned activity would not cohere with then-synchronic self-governance.

Return to willpower. Suppose you resolve at t1 to have only one beer at the party at t2 while knowing you will at t2 at least initially think it better to have many beers, but also knowing that at t3 you would regret it if you did indeed have many beers at t2. How does DPR apply to this case?

Well, we do not yet know since we do not yet know whether at t2 condition (b) is satisfied. If the standpoint at t2 included the end of diachronic self-governance then perhaps it would favor willpower, and so (b) would be satisfied. Since abandoning the prior resolution would satisfy (c), DPR would then favor, instead, willpower. But we are not yet in a position to suppose that the standpoint at t2 does include this end of diachronic self-governance.

Granted, DPR focuses on a planning agent with the capacity for diachronic self-governance. This capacity includes the capacity for having the end of diachronic self-governance, since that end is involved in central cases of a planning agent's diachronic self-governance. But you could have the capacity for that end and yet not in fact have that end. So in order to understand how DPR would apply to cases of potential willpower, we need to reflect further on the status of this end of diachronic self-governance.

But first we need to address a different issue about DPR. Let's assume that the end of diachronic self-governance is present, and so that at least some cases of willpower would cohere with both synchronic and diachronic self-governance and so be favored by DPR. The idea is that in such cases the end of diachronic self-governance re-shifts the agent's standpoint at the time of temptation so that it now favors following though with her prior resolution. So a failure of willpower would now be a failure of synchronic plan rationality. But then we can ask whether we really need a distinctive norm of diachronic plan rationality, a norm along the lines of DPR. Why not simply work with a norm of synchronic plan rationality along the lines of PRSG-P? DPR does have the implication I have emphasized concerning temptation cases: given the end of diachronic self-governance, it can explain why a breakdown in willpower in such cases can sometimes be irrational. But our question now is whether we need DPR for this. Why not just work with synchronic plan rationality, given the way in which the end of diachronic self-governance may shift the agent's standpoint at the time of temptation?

To respond to this challenge we need to consider, as anticipated earlier, a second kind of case that poses a problem of plan stability. These are cases in which one makes a decision in the face of non-comparable temporally extended options and then, in the process of follow through, is later faced with continued non-comparability.[40] In Sartre's famous example, the young man needs to decide between staying with his mother and fighting with the Free French, where he (plausibly) sees this as a decision

40. For a seminal discussion of the case of Abraham and Isaac, see John Broome, "Are Intentions Reasons? And How Should We Cope with Incommensurable Values?" in Christopher W. Morris and Arthur Ripstein, eds., *Practical Rationality and Preference: Essays for David Gauthier* (Cambridge: Cambridge University Press, 2001), 98–120, esp. 114–9. My earlier discussion of such cases is in Michael E. Bratman, "Time, Rationality, and Self-Governance," *Philosophical Issues* **22** (2012), 73–88 [this volume, essay 6].

between non-comparable values.[41] Suppose he decides in favor of staying with his mother. Later he (sensibly) reconsiders and notes that the non-comparability remains. Is there any rational pressure for him to stick with his earlier decision?

One virtue of DPR is that it articulates a rational pressure in favor of constancy in such cases. Whether or not the young man has the end of diachronic self-governance, each option—the option of staying with his mother, as well the option of instead fighting with the Free French—is supported by his now-present standpoint. But what is crucial is that, if the young man does stick with his prior decision to stay with his mother, his intentions over the relevant time will have the interconnections characteristic of a planning agent's diachronic self-governance. In contrast, if he changes his mind in favor of the Free French then his intentions over the relevant time will not have these interconnections. So DPR will favor his sticking with his decision.

In this way DPR can help us understand the rational pressure for constancy in such cases of decision in the face of ongoing non-comparability.[42] And once we are led in this way to DPR we can note that it promises to contribute to an overall treatment of the rational stability of plans in both such non-comparability cases and, to return to our earlier discussion, temptation cases. But, as noted earlier, the relevant implications of DPR concerning willpower depend on the presence of the end of diachronic self-governance. So we need to return to our question: What is the status of this end of diachronic self-governance?

In discussing synchronic plan rationality I argued that a reflective planning agent would be led to the thought that the best normative explanation of her plan-infused practical thinking draws on the significance of the coherence involved in her synchronic self-governance. I then generalized: the best normative explanation of her plan-infused practical thinking will draw on the significance of the coherence involved in her self-governance, both synchronic and diachronic. This led us to DPR. And this suggests yet a further generalization: we appeal to constitutive conditions of a planning agent's self-governance, where these include, but may not be limited to, coherence conditions. To this we then add our conjecture that diachronic self-governance, at least in (ubiquitous)

---

41. Jean-Paul Sartre, "Existentialism Is a Humanism," in *Existentialism from Dostoevsky to Sartre*, edited by Walter Kaufmann, rev. and expanded. (New York: Meridian/Penguin, 1975), 345–69.

42. This is to disagree with the Sartrean theme of "the total inefficacy of the past resolution." *Being and Nothingness* (Hazel Barnes translation) (New York: Washington Square Press, 1984), 70.

cases of temptation, involves the end of diachronic self-governance. We thereby have an argument for a norm that supports an end of diachronic self-governance:

> *Rational End of Diachronic Self-Governance (REDSG)*: If S is a planning agent who is capable of diachronic self-governance then it is *pro tanto* irrational of S to fail to have an end of diachronic self-governance.[43]

The argument for REDSG involves three ideas. First, there is the general idea, in the spirit of inference to the best normative explanation, that there is rational pressure in favor of satisfying constitutive conditions of self-governance. Second, there is the idea that a planning agent's diachronic self-governance, at least in cases of temptation, involves her end of diachronic self-governance. And third, there is the idea of the ubiquity of forms of temptation as potential destabilizers of planned temporally extended activities.[44]

So, the self-governance-based rationale for norms of plan coherence, both synchronic and diachronic, leads, on further reflection, to a rationale for a rationally supported end. In reflecting on our planning agency we are led to the self-governance strategy in order to support norms of plan coherence, both synchronic and diachronic, and in response to the challenge that these norms express a fetish for mere mental tidiness. This promises a significant commonality of rationale underlying synchronic and diachronic norms. And it leads us to an argument for a norm that supports the end of diachronic self-governance.

REDSG is a weak principle in at least two ways. First, it does not require, even *pro tanto*, that the end of diachronic self-governance be preeminent within the agent's standpoint. Different agents might satisfy REDSG by way of ends of diachronic self-governance that have different relative weights within their standpoints. Second, REDSG does not address the issue of how to respond in cases in which there is a tension between what is called for by diachronic self-governance over different temporal intervals.[45]

Nevertheless, it remains true that REDSG, together with DPR, can sometimes induce rational pressure in favor of willpower; and DPR on its own induces rational pressure for constancy in non-comparability cases.

43. I take it that concerns with trivial cases, tragic cases, and preface-analogue cases do not apply here; so we can express REDSG without the appeal to defeasibility that appears in our earlier principles.

44. This is an argument for rational pressure in favor of a certain end, given capacities for planning agency and diachronic self-governance; it is not an argument for rational pressure in favor of the introduction of a new basic capacity.

45. A point made by Gideon Yaffe.

So when we combine DPR with REDSG we arrive, *prima facie*, at a modest plan conservatism, one that includes but goes beyond the support of plan stability that is traceable to snowball effects and the rationality of non-reconsideration.

So we have an initial *prima facie*, self-governance-based case in favor of seeing PRSG-P, PCC, DPR, and REDSG as norms of plan rationality. These norms are, plausibly, central to the basic structure of a planning agent's practical thinking. They track forms of coherence central to self-governance, both synchronic and diachronic, and—in the case of REDSG—a basic form of support for the coordination of such synchronic and diachronic coherence. So these norms do not merely track mental tidiness. And this self-governance-based case promises to provide a common justificatory framework for this package of norms of synchronic and diachronic plan rationality.

We can now return, as promised, to the question whether for a planning agent with the capacity for self-governance there is a systematically present normative reason that favors conformity to these norms. I take it that if we could defend an affirmative answer to this question we would then be justified in going beyond the cited initial case for these norms and concluding that they are indeed norms of practical rationality for a planning agent. But how can we defend such an affirmative answer?

An initial observation is that a planning agent will have such a reason if she has a reason for her self-governance and that self-governance is attainable. After all, these norms track necessary constitutive features of a planning agent's self-governance. And a reason for self-governance will transmit to a reason of self-governance for those necessary constitutive features if the self-governance is attainable.[46]

But why think that a planning agent with the capacity for self-governance has a normative reason for her self-governance? Given our approach to normative reasons, and given the plausible assumption that self-governance is a human good, she will have this reason for self-governance if, but only if, she has the end of her self-governance. But what is the status of this end?[47]

---

46. See Michael E. Bratman, "Intention, Practical Rationality, and Self-Governance," *Ethics* **119** (2009), 411–43. I here put aside complexities about this inference. For an insightful overview of related issues, see Benjamin Kiesewetter, "Instrumental Normativity: In Defense of the Transmission Principle," *Ethics* **125** (2015), 921–46 (though Kiesewetter focuses on the transmission of what he calls the deliberative "ought," whereas the issue here is the transmission of normative reasons).

47. I take it that the value of X does not by itself induce even *pro tanto* rational pressure to have the end of X: there are too many goods and, in our finite lives, not enough time.

The key is to proceed in two stages. We note first that, as I have argued,

(1) there is an initial self-governance-based, *prima facie* case for REDSG.

We then note that

(2) if a planning agent who is capable of diachronic self-governance conforms to REDSG by having the end it supports, she will thereby have a normative reason (a reason of self-governance) to conform to this norm.

And my conjecture is that, given (1), (2) constitutes a sufficiently systematic connection to a supporting normative reason for REDSG to satisfy the reason desideratum, appropriately understood.[48] Granted, this does not show that there is normative reason to conform to REDSG whether or not one does conform to REDSG. But it does show that if one does conform to REDSG by having the end it supports then there is normative reason in support of this conformity. And my conjecture is that, given (1), this suffices for REDSG to satisfy the reason desideratum, appropriately understood. So we can conclude that REDSG is indeed a norm of practical rationality for such a planning agent. So the end of diachronic self-governance is in this way rationally self-sustaining.

A planning agent with the capacity for diachronic self-governance who conforms to REDSG by having the end it supports will have a reason for her diachronic self-governance, and so for the synchronic self-governance that is partly constitutive of that diachronic self-governance. We now note that this reason also supports conformity to PRSG-P, PCC, and DPR, since each of these norms tracks a constitutive element of relevant self-governance. So we can conclude that these norms also satisfy the reason desideratum, appropriately understood. So given the initial self-governance-based case for these norms we can conclude that they too are norms of practical rationality for a planning agent.

Return now to a planning agent who has the capacity for self-governance and is reflecting on basic norms involved in her planning agency. She will see that the best rationale for these norms treats self-governance, both synchronic and diachronic, as the basic consideration that supplements a

---

48. This is where my talk, in my formulation of the reason desideratum, of a "systematically present" reason is doing important work.

two-tier pragmatic rationale. She will see that given that she is, as there is reason to be, a planning agent, the application to the particular case of the norms that are central to her planning agency is supported by appeals to the significance of her self-governance. She will thereby be in a position to see the rational dynamics of her planning agency as having a justifying rationale that involves both two-tier-pragmatic and self-governance-based support. In this way her plan dynamics will make sense to her and be reflectively stable. And that is what we needed to show to defend the planning theory from the challenge posed by the myth theorists.[49]

49. Many thanks to audiences at the Royal Institute of Philosophy, the University of Nebraska, and Lund University, and to participants in my winter 2016 seminar on plan rationality at Stanford University. Special thanks to: Ron Aboodi, Facundo Alonso, Gunnar Björnsson, Olle Blomberg, John Broome, David Copp, Jorah Dannenberg, Luca Ferrero, Amanda Greene, Carlos Núñez, Herlinde Pauer-Studer, Sarah Paul, Björn Petersson, David Plunkett, Johanna Thoma, Han van Wietmarschen, Gideon Yaffe, and an anonymous reviewer. [For further developments, see my "Introduction: The Planning Framework," this volume, essay 1, at 14–17.]

CHAPTER 11

A Planning Agent's Self-Governance Over Time

What is it to govern your thought and action not only at a time but also over time? Let's focus the question a bit. We are planning agents. Almost all of our intentional activity is embedded in planned temporally extended activity that is structured by prior partial plans. These plans settle practical issues, pose problems of means and the like, filter solutions to those problems, and guide action. These structures of planning support important forms of cross-temporal and social organization in ways that are compatible with our cognitive and epistemic limits. Given their basic role in cross-temporal organization, we can expect these planning structures to play a central role in diachronic self-governance. So let's ask, more specifically, what is it for a planning agent to govern her thought and action over time?[1]

In the background are two ideas. The first is that self-governance over time involves, in part, responding to certain common threats to important

1. This essay develops ideas about a planning agent's diachronic self-governance that are sketched in "Rational Planning Agency," *Royal Institute of Philosophy Supplement* (2017) 80 [this volume, essay 10]. I offer a brief overview of the ideas in both of these essays in my "Plan Rationality," in Ruth Chang and Kurt Sylvan, eds., *The Routledge Handbook of Practical Reason* (forthcoming). Many of these ideas are drawn from my Pufendorf Lectures, delivered at Lund University in June 2016. I presented earlier versions of the present essay at the August 2016 Workshop on "Time in Action" at Oslo University; as part of my Franz Brentano Lectures on Practical Philosophy at the University of Vienna in April 2017; and at the Copenhagen workshop on Shared and Temporally Extended Agency in April 2017. Many thanks to the audiences on these occasions and to Philip Pettit, Sergio Tenenbaum, Johanna Thoma, and Gideon Yaffe.

forms of cross-temporal organization and stability. Our account of a planning agent's diachronic self-governance needs to say more about those threats and the response characteristic of diachronic self-governance. Second, we do not want to see such self-governance as, at bottom, the workings of a self who is separate from the psychic economy and stands back and pulls the strings. We want a model of a kind of cross-temporal psychic functioning that ensures a planning agent's relevant self-governance over time. So let's see.

1. SELF-GOVERNANCE AT A TIME AND OVER TIME

An initial idea is that for a planning agent to govern her action over time, she needs at the least to be synchronically self-governing at relevant times (or small temporal intervals) along the way. But what is such synchronic self-governance? Here we can draw from Harry Frankfurt's appeal to "where (if anywhere) the person himself stands."[2] Self-governance involves guidance of thought and action by the agent's relevant practical standpoint. The standpoint needs to guide choice that is in accord with that standpoint; and the standpoint itself needs to be sufficiently coherent to constitute a clear place where the agent stands on relevant practical issues. In this way we understand synchronic self-governance without an irreducible appeal to a little person in the head who is pulling the strings.

A planning agent's self-governance over time involves, then, such synchronic self-governance at relevant times or during small temporal intervals along the way.[3] On this model, not all cases of successful self-management

2. Harry Frankfurt, "Identification and Wholeheartedness," as reprinted in Harry Frankfurt, *The Importance of What We Care About* (Cambridge: Cambridge University Press, 1988), 159–76, 166. See also Gary Watson, "Free Agency," *Journal of Philosophy* 72 (1975): 205–20, 216.

3. In saying this I am supposing that synchronic self-governance can involve self-governance during a relevant, small temporal interval. (This is in the spirit of Sergio Tenenbaum's thought that "a 'synchronic' norm is not necessarily a time-slice norm." See Sergio Tenenbaum (2016) "Reconsidering Intentions," *Noûs*. doi:10.1111/nous.12160: 14. Can we say more about such intervals? My tentative proposal is that we look for intervals within which relevant basic concerns and plans are constant, there is not reconsideration of relevant plans, and there are not relevant action plans that specify different stages to be carried out at different times within that interval. Given that we are normally involved in planned temporally extended activities within which our plans specify different stages over time, we can expect these intervals normally to be small. And in any case, once there is reconsideration of a relevant plan we can no longer continue to understand the process as simply one of synchronic self-governance. Nevertheless, it remains possible that one fails to act in accord with one's standpoint during a relevant interval even if we cannot specify a specific moment in that interval at which this failure occurred. (These comments were aided by correspondence with

over time will constitute such diachronic self-governance. Ulysses has a strategy of self-management over time by tying himself to the mast, thereby blocking his self-governance when the sirens call; but his successful diachronic self-management is not diachronic self-governance.[4]

There is a partial parallel here with rational planning agency quite generally. In rationally planning my actions over a stretch of time, I at least implicitly suppose that, given my plan, when the times of action arrive it will be rationally permissible for me to carry out my plan then. Rational planning for a temporally extended stretch of activity needs to accommodate the supposed rational execution of the plan at times along the way. This is a norm of rational planning. In the case of diachronic self-governance, what we have is not a rationality norm but a metaphysical constraint: an individual's self-governance over time needs to accommodate her self-governance at each relevant time (or relevant temporal interval) along the way. In each case we have a principle of over-time/at-a-time coordination.

I think we should retain such over-time/at-a-time coordination of diachronic and synchronic self-governance.[5] But I also take it that diachronic self-governance is not merely a concatenation of self-governance of the same person at various times along the way.[6] It involves, as well, appropriate *interconnections* across time. What interconnections?

2. INTERCONNECTIONS: THE PLAN-THEORETIC MODEL

As I see it, the basic context in which the issue of a planning agent's diachronic self-governance arises is one in which the agent is engaged in plan-shaped temporally extended activity.[7] This suggests that a planning agent's

Sergio Tenenbaum, though they are in the service of an approach to diachronic self-governance that I do not think he would endorse. And see Tenenbaum, "Reconsidering Intentions," at 21–22.)

4. This paragraph responds to a query from Gideon Yaffe.

5. Agnes Callard (in conversation) and Jennifer Morton (in correspondence) have pointed to cases in which a breakdown in synchronic self-governance at t results in downstream changes that then support later, associated diachronic self-governance. As I understand it, such later diachronic self-governance begins at a time later than t. But I agree that we might—as it were, by courtesy—speak of the earlier breakdown in synchronic self-governance at t as the time at which, in an extended sense, the diachronic self-governance begins.

6. See my "Time, Rationality, and Self-Governance," *Philosophical Issues* 22 (2012): 73–88, at 81 [this volume, essay 6, at 143].

7. Granted, even for a planning agent there may be cases of intentional agency that are not embedded within such planned temporally extended activity: spontaneously scratching an itch, perhaps. But in such cases of spontaneous activity the question of whether the agent is diachronically self-governing does not arise in a clear way.

diachronic self-governance involves synchronically self-governed choices at the relevant times along the way of a relevant planned temporally extended activity, where these choices over time are tied together by the interconnections characteristic of planned temporally extended activity.

What interconnections are these? Well, the plans that guide such temporally extended activity will settle relevant practical questions and will normally at least implicitly cross-refer to each other: one's plan for today will typically involve a reference to one's earlier and later plans; and vice versa. These issue-settling, cross-referring plans will frame much of one's practical thought and action over time: they will pose problems of means and preliminary steps in filling in one's so-far partial plans as time goes by and in ways that, taken together, mesh; and they will filter options that are potential solutions to those problems. In playing these roles these plans will induce forms of psychological connectedness and continuity of intention and plan that are in the spirit of broadly Lockean models of personal identity over time.[8]

Given these roles of plans in structuring the agent's temporally extended practical thought and action, we can expect that her standpoints at times along the way will be plan-infused.[9] These standpoints will involve both plans for temporally extended activities and relevant general policies, including policies about weights for deliberation.[10] In planned temporally extended activity these plan-infused standpoints will be interconnected in the cited ways. And this leads to the proposal that the cross-temporal interconnections that are characteristic of a planning agent's self-governance over time, given self-governance at times along the way, involve the interconnections that are characteristic of relevant planned temporally extended activity. This is the *plan-theoretic model* of these interconnections.

A complexity is that, given the hierarchical structure of plans, these cross-temporal interconnections can be at different levels. In particular, there can be such interconnections at the level of an overarching plan

8. For this last idea, see my "Reflection, Planning and Temporally Extended Agency" as reprinted in my *Structures of Agency* (New York: Oxford University Press, 2007), at 28–33. And see Gideon Yaffe, *Liberty Worth the Name: Locke on Free Agency* (Princeton, NJ: Princeton University Press, 2000), chap. 3. This paragraph draws from my "Rational Planning Agency."

9. See my "Three Theories of Self-Governance" as reprinted in my *Structures of Agency* (Oxford: Oxford University Press, 2007), 222–53; and my "Rational Planning Agency."

10. See my "Three Theories of Self-Governance," at 239, where I call these "self-governing policies." For an overview of my approach to a planning agent's self-governance at a time, see my "A Planning Theory of Self-Governance: Reply to Franklin," *Philosophical Explorations* 20 (2017): 15–20.

despite a breakdown in interconnection at a more specific level of sub-plans. Perhaps I continue with my overall plan to earn a law degree but change my sub-plan from one focusing on criminal law to one focusing on tort law. There are relevant cross-temporal continuities of intention at the level of the overall plan; but there is a breakdown in continuity in my sub-plans concerning area of concentration. Such upper-level continuities would help support my diachronic self-governance. And it may well be that I now sensibly believe, perhaps in light of new information, that I have conclusive reason to make the change in my lower-level plans. So sticking with my prior plan in favor of criminal law would be stubbornness, not synchronic self-governance. However, if, in contrast, there were available a way of continuing with my lower-level plans so that there would be self-governance at times along the way and relevant cross-temporal interconnections at *both* lower and higher levels of the hierarchy, then the plan-theoretic model will say that a breakdown in plan continuity at the lower level would to some extent diminish the extent of diachronic self-governance.

This plan-theoretic model has an important implication. Consider Sartre's young man. He must choose between staying with his mother and fighting with the Free French.[11] Suppose at t1 he chooses to stay with his mother. At t2, however, he reconsiders and changes his mind and decides to fight with the Free French. Both at t1 and at t2 he sees the conflict as a conflict of non-comparable values. So it seems that at each time in acting on his choice he is synchronically self-governing, since his choice and action at each time cohere with and are guided by a basic value of his, one that he supposes is not outweighed or overridden in the circumstance. However, in shuffling from his decision at t1 to his decision at t2[12] he is breaking the cross-temporal interconnections characteristic of planned temporally extended activity. If, in contrast, he had stuck with his initial decision to stay with his mother, his intentions over time would have been connected in these ways. In shuffling from one decision to another, though he is self-governing at each time, he does not satisfy the plan-theoretic model of the interconnections involved in self-governance over time. In contrast, he would satisfy that model were he to stick with his prior decision.

11. Jean-Paul Sartre, "Existentialism Is a Humanism," in *Existentialism from Dostoevsky to Sartre*, edited by Walter Kaufmann. rev. and expanded. (New York: Meridian/ Penguin, 1975), 345–69. The problem I note in this paragraph owes to John Broome, "Are Intentions Reasons? And How Should We Cope with Incommensurable Values?" in Christopher W. Morris and Arthur Ripstein, eds., *Practical Rationality and Preference: Essays for David Gauthier* (Cambridge: Cambridge University Press, 2001), 98–120, esp. 114–9.
12. I owe the terminology of "shuffling" to Richard Kraut (in conversation). In my "Time, Rationality, and Self-Governance," I call this brute shuffling.

Granted (and to return to the complexity noted earlier), even if he shuffles in this way he might satisfy the plan-theoretic model, of the interconnections involved in self-governance over time, at the level of some persisting, higher-level plan—for example, a plan to give due regard to duties of loyalty. Nevertheless, there was available to him a way of resisting shuffling and continuing with his lower-level plans so that there would be self-governance at times along the way *and* relevant interconnections at both lower and higher levels of the hierarchy of his plans. So, on the model, his shuffling diminishes the extent to which he is diachronically self-governing.

But why accept this plan-theoretic model of relevant interconnections?

3. THE ARGUMENT FROM SETTLING FUNCTION

I begin by considering an argument that is in the spirit of an earlier essay.[13] This argument is not, however, conclusive. So I will turn to a second argument.

This first argument draws from the settling function of intentions and plans, and can be articulated by way of a pair of premises. The first premise concerns a functional role that is characteristic of intention:

> (i) The functional roles of prior intentions and plans include settling relevant practical matters in a way that supports the cross-temporal intention-interconnections that are characteristic of planned temporally extended activity.

The second premise draws on an insight from Sydney Shoemaker. Shoemaker noted that the psychological continuity that plays a basic role in Lockean theories of personal identity over time "is just the playing out over time of the functional natures of the mental states characteristic of persons."[14] And an analogous idea seems apt here:

> (ii) The cross-temporal interconnections that are characteristic of a planning agent's self-governance over time involve the "playing out over time of the functional natures of the" relevant plan states.

When we put (i) and (ii) together we get

13. "Time, Rationality, and Self-Governance."
14. Sydney Shoemaker, "Personal Identity," in Sydney Shoemaker and Richard Swinburne, *Personal Identity* (Oxford: Basil Blackwell, 1984), at 95.

(iii) The cross-temporal interconnections that are characteristic of a planning agent's self-governance over time involve those interconnections that are characteristic of planned temporally extended activity.

And that is the plan-theoretic model of the relevant interconnections.

On reflection, however, one might challenge premise (i).[15] Why not instead say only that the relevant functional role of plan states is to support the cross-temporal intention-interconnections that are characteristic of planned temporally extended activity so long as the agent continues to judge that considerations on balance strongly favor the plan? And Sartre's young man does not judge that considerations on balance strongly favor his plan to stay with his mother, though he does judge that these considerations weakly favor that plan.

So if we are going to defend the plan-theoretic model we need to see if there is a further argument in its defense. And I think that there is. The argument I think I see[16] appeals to a version of a parallel that has struck many philosophers—a parallel between the cross-temporal organization of an individual's activity and interpersonal, social organization.

4. ACTING "TOGETHER" WITH ONESELF AT DIFFERENT TIMES: THE SHARED AGENCY MODEL OF DIACHRONIC SELF-GOVERNANCE

The idea is that in diachronic self-governance one and the same person's agency at different times is drawn together in ways that to some extent parallel the ways in which different agents are interconnected when they act together. I do not say that in diachronic self-governance there are, literally, multiple agents acting together. I retain the common sense thought that there is one agent who acts at different times; and this contrasts with interpersonal shared agency involving multiple agents. Nevertheless, there is a revealing, if partial, parallel between an individual's diachronic self-governance and interpersonal shared agency. And this parallel helps explain the significance to us of such diachronic self-governance. In diachronic self-governance I am not just governing my relevant actions at each relevant time along the way. In addition, my thought and action at the

15. See Luca Ferrero, "Diachronic Constraints of Practical Rationality," *Philosophical Issues* 22 (2012): 144–64, at 160.

16. An argument that goes beyond my earlier discussion of a planning agent's self-governance over time in my "Time, Rationality, and Self-Governance."

times along the way are, at least implicitly, interwoven and interconnected in ways that support the helpful metaphor that "we"—that is, me at these different times—are thinking and acting "together."

Now, others have explored the idea of a bargain between the agent at t1 and the agent at t2.[17] Edward McClennen, for example, seeks "a theory of what constitutes a fair bargain between one's different, time-defined selves."[18] The agent at t1 strikes a bargain with his later t2-self, a bargain that enjoins his t2-self to stick with the agent's decision at t1. The idea of a bargain, however, seems to involve a kind of reciprocal interrelation that is not possible here. After all, the person-stage at t1 will not be around when the person-stage at t2 acts, and will not be in a position to respond to whether that later person-stage keeps up her end of the bargain.[19]

My proposal that a planning agent's diachronic self-governance involves an intrapersonal analogue of shared agency is not the proposal of a bargain between the person at t1 and the person at t2. Instead, the proposal is that certain structural features of socially shared agency have intrapersonal, cross-temporal analogues,[20] and that this helps support the idea that these intrapersonal analogues are an aspect of a planning agent's diachronic self-governance.

How then should we understand relevant forms of shared agency? In other work[21] I argue that a basic idea here is that of a shared intention: a shared intention of the participants to J is central to a shared intentional activity of J-ing together. And I argue that this shared intention is, in basic cases, constituted by a web of interconnected intentions of each of the participants in favor of their J-ing, together with associated cognitive

17. Edward McClennen, *Rationality and Dynamic Choice: Foundational Explorations* (Cambridge: Cambridge University Press, 1990); Edward McClennen, "Rationality and Rules," in Peter A. Danielson, ed., *Modeling Rationality, Morality, and Evolution* (Oxford: Oxford University Press, 1998), 13–40; George Ainslie, *Picoeconomics: The Strategic Interaction of Successive Motivational States within the Person* (Cambridge: Cambridge University Press, 1992).

18. "Rationality and Rules," 25.

19. I make a related point in response to a similar idea from George Ainslie in my "Planning and Temptation," as reprinted in my *Faces of Intention* (Cambridge: Cambridge University Press, 1999), 48. As I note there, Frank Döring makes a related point in response to McClennen.

20. Carol Rovane explores a related parallel between "long-term activities" and "joint activities" in *The Bounds of Agency: An Essay in Revisionary Metaphysics* (Princeton, NJ: Princeton University Press, 1998), 144 ff.

21. Michael E. Bratman, *Shared Agency: A Planning Theory of Acting Together* (New York: Oxford University Press, 2014).

attitudes of those participants. This web of attitudes of the participants is constituted as follows:

(A) The participants each have intentions in favor of J, intentions that interlock in the sense that each intends that they J in part by way of the intentions of each that they J.[22]

(B) Each intends that they J in part by way of mutual responsiveness of each to each in the execution of these intentions of each, and so by way of relevant sub-plans of each that mesh with each other.

(C) Each believes correctly that there is persistence interdependence between the intentions of each that they J.

(D) Each believes that if these intentions do persist they will indeed J.[23]

(E) All this is out in the open among the participants.

When such a structure of interconnected attitudes leads to the joint J-ing by way of the intended mutual responsiveness and mesh, there is shared intentional action.

And now my proposal is that the cross-temporal, intrapersonal "glue" characteristic of a planning agent's diachronic self-governance involves intrapersonal analogues of the interpersonal connections characteristic of shared intention and shared intentional agency. These intrapersonal analogues of conditions of shared intention and shared intentional agency support the metaphor that in diachronic self-governance the synchronically self-governing agent at each time is acting "together" with the synchronically self-governing agent—namely, herself—at other times, in a sense of "together" that comes from our theory of shared agency.[24] And an idea in the background of this *shared agency model* of the cross-temporal interconnections

22. Since these intentions, as it were, interlock with themselves they involve a kind of reflexivity.

23. As I indicate in *Shared Agency* at pp. 76–7, such a belief condition is, strictly speaking, too strong if what we are seeking are necessary conditions for shared intention. But since what we are seeking is, rather, sufficient conditions for robust forms of shared intention, it is reasonable to appeal here to such a belief condition. (And see below, note 30.) More generally, in *Shared Agency* I do not claim that the conditions highlighted there (and cited here) are strictly necessary for shared intention or shared intentional action. I leave open the possibility of other, perhaps weaker, forms of shared agency. However, my conjecture here is that these strong conditions of shared agency help give us an apt model of a planning agent's diachronic self-governance.

24. In my *Shared Agency* I discuss—and note important complexities concerning—the mirror image of this idea, namely, the idea that shared agency involves "quasi-Lockean" interconnections between relevant participants. See pp. 97–8 and 128.

involved in a planning agent's diachronic self-governance is that it helps explain the significance to us of such diachronic self-governance.[25]

In thinking about a planning agent's self-governance over time it is tempting to appeal to a kind of cross-temporal narrative unity: there is a "story" that ties together the different elements over time. Depending on what counts as such narrative unity, this idea may apply to many cases. But according to the shared agency model, the more basic cross-temporal unity at work in diachronic self-governance is the unity involved when the agent is acting "together" with herself over time, in a sense of "together" that comes from the theory of shared agency.

5. PLANNED TEMPORALLY EXTENDED AGENCY AND SHARED AGENCY

The next step is to argue that planned temporally extended agency does indeed involve intrapersonal, cross-temporal analogues of conditions of socially shared intention. In this way the shared agency model helps support the plan-theoretic model of the cross-temporal connections that are characteristic of a planning agent's diachronic self-governance.

There will, of course, be important differences between my planned temporally extended agency and our acting together. In particular, our acting together will normally involve two-way causal interactions: what I think and do affects what you think and do, which affects what I think and do. In contrast, there will be a causal asymmetry in the case of my planning agency over time: what I think and do now can causally influence what I think and do later, in a way in which what I think and do later cannot causally influence what I think and do now. (Though my present anticipation of what I will think and do later can of course affect what I think and do now.) So the analogies between planned temporally extended agency and shared intentional agency will at most only be partial. But we can still ask whether these partial analogues, if such there are, shed light on diachronic self-governance.

So let's consider conditions (A)–(E) of shared intention and see what their analogues would be in a case of an individual's planned temporally extended activity. To do this, let's work with an example. Suppose that, given expected time pressures at this evening's interview, I decide at t1

25. A further, interesting question that I will not try to pursue here is whether, and to what extent, this shared agency model can help us understand the legal doctrine of *stare decisis*.

on strategy A for responding to certain anticipated questions at t2. At t1 I form an intention to engage in A at t2. I also fill in this plan a bit: I develop at t1 a partial sub-plan for A-ing at t2. Later, t2 arrives, conditions are as I had at t1 anticipated, and I proceed to fill in my sub-plans further and follow through with A then, at t2. Let's see if there are, in this temporally extended activity, analogues of conditions (A)–(E) of shared intention.

To keep track, let's use *italics* to indicate a relevant analogue condition. Begin with (A), the interlocking condition. And consider the relation between my intention at t1 to A at t2 and my intention at t2 to A at t2. An initial point is that in so intending at t1 I do not think my intention will simply reach its ghostly hand over time and shape my action at t2.[26] Instead, I will normally suppose that my intention at t1 will persist between t1 and t2, shape associated thought and action along the way, and thereby issue at t2 in my updated intention to A then.[27] It is this updated intention to A that I expect will issue in my A-ing: I certainly do not expect some unrelated intention at t2 to do this work. And this is, at least implicitly, how I intend this process to work its way through. So, at least implicitly, my intention at t1 to A at t2 *interlocks* with my intention at t2 to A then: at t1 I intend, at least implicitly, that I A at t2 by way of my intention at t2 to A at t2; and at t2, at least implicitly, I intend to A then as a way of following through with my intention at t1 to A at t2.[28] So we have this intrapersonal analogue of condition (A) of shared intention.

Consider now the first part of condition (B), the intended mutual responsiveness condition. In the intrapersonal case, at t1 I intend, at least implicitly, that my intention at t2 to A at t2 works its way through to action in ways compatible with my present intentions (at t1) concerning how to A at t2. Further, at t2 I intend, at least implicitly, to A in a way that fits with my intentions at t1 concerning how to A. So there is a kind of *intended mutual responsiveness* (though not mutual causal interaction) between my

---

26. *Intention, Plans, and Practical Reason*, p. 5.

27. While my intention persists from t1 to t2 it will also normally be filled in with further sub-plans. The persistence of intention that is characteristic of planned temporally extended agency is compatible with filling in the partial, hierarchical structure that is normally involved in prior intention. (I am responding here to an inquiry from Thomas Smith.)

28. The idea that relevant contents of intentions can be tacit or implicit is also an aspect of the background view of shared intention. See *Shared Agency*, 104–5. I also note there the possibility that "certain less demanding social psychological phenomena might in certain cases to some extent functionally substitute for these more demanding attitudes of each" (105). And we can allow for an analogous possibility in the intrapersonal case. So in the shared case and in the intrapersonal case there are analogous possibilities of non-explicit but implicit content and less demanding functional substitutes.

intentions at t1 and at t2. So, there is this intrapersonal analogue of the first part of condition (B) of shared intention.

Consider now the second part of (B), the intended mesh condition. In the intrapersonal case, at t1 I intend, at least implicitly, that the sub-plans I have so far constructed for A-ing at t2 mesh with the sub-plans I will construct and act on at t2, and at t1 I intend, at least implicitly, that I A at t2 by way of those meshing sub-plans at t2. Further, at t2 I intend, at least implicitly, to A by way of sub-plans at t2 that mesh with the partial sub-plans I had formulated at t1. So at t1 and at t2 I intend, at least implicitly, that my A-ing at t2 go by way of sub-plans at t2 that *mesh* with my sub-plans at t1. So, there is this intrapersonal analogue of the second part of condition (B) of shared intention.

Consider now condition (C), the condition of correct belief in interdependence. In the intrapersonal case, my intention at t1 to A at t2 depends on my expectation that, if conditions at t2 are as I at t1 expect them to be, I will continue so to intend at t2. Further, at least in some cases, at t2 I know that if I had not intended at t1 to A at t2 then I would not at t2 be intending to A then.[29] So my intention at t1 is dependent on my expectation of my later intention. And my later intention may be accompanied by the knowledge that it depends on my earlier intention. So, there is at least a partial analogue of condition (C).

Consider now condition (D), an expectation of success condition. In the intrapersonal case, at t1 I believe that, given that my intention does persist, I will A at t2. And at t2 I believe that, given that my intention to A has persisted, I will indeed A at t2.[30] So there is, throughout t1-t2, conditional *expectation of success* in A-ing.

Finally, all of these analogues in the intrapersonal case will normally be *out in the open* for me throughout t1-t2. At each stage along the way I will be in a position to know that I have so far satisfied the cited conditions and justifiably to expect that I will continue to do so. So there is an analogue of condition (E) of shared intention.

So in my planned temporally extended activity there are intrapersonal analogues of interlocking intentions, intended mutual responsiveness and mesh in sub-plans, and expectations of success. There is at least a partial analogy with the condition of true beliefs about interdependence. And

---

29. See my remarks below about the snowball effect.

30. Here I am mirroring the belief conditions cited in the above model of shared intention, where that model aimed at sufficient conditions for robust shared intention. As noted above (note 23), we could weaken those belief conditions somewhat, and then those weaker belief conditions would be reflected in our account of relevant shared agency analogues. But to keep our discussion manageable I put this complexity aside here.

throughout there can be cognitive accessibility to all these elements, and so an analogue to the out-in-the-open condition. Appeal to these shared-agency-analogue conditions supports the metaphor that *I at t1* and *I at t2* are acting and thinking *together* in an intrapersonal *analogue* of shared intentional activity.

Indeed, there are kinds of shared intentional activity that are even closer to such cases of planned individual activity over time. For example, in the multigenerational shared activity of the building of a cathedral, the interrelations among the agents of different generations will involve causal asymmetries similar to those in the intrapersonal temporally extended case.[31] So in this respect there will be an even closer analogy between such social cases and the cited kind of temporally extended individual planned activity.

Of course, the cited cross-temporal structure in the case of my temporally extended planned activity may not be present in cases in which the world develops between t1 and t2 in ways that are counter to my relevant expectations at t1 about conditions at t2. But what matters for present purposes are cases in which these expectations are realized and one does indeed act over time in ways that involve carrying out one's prior plan. And in such cases, planned individual activity over time involves cross-temporal intrapersonal connections that are substantially analogous to the interpersonal connections characteristic of shared intention.

Recall now that according to the shared agency model, the cross-temporal connections that are characteristic of a planning agent's diachronic self-governance involve intrapersonal analogues of conditions of socially shared intention. What we have just seen is that such intrapersonal analogues are provided by the intention interconnections characteristic of planned temporally extended agency. Further, and as noted earlier, the issue of a planning agent's diachronic self-governance normally arises within the background of planned temporally extended agency. Taken together, these points support the conjecture that the interconnections characteristic of planned temporally extended agency are central to a planning agent's diachronic self-governance. And that is the plan-theoretic model of these cross-temporal interconnections. A striking fact at the bottom of the plan-theoretic model of the cross-temporal, intrapersonal glue characteristic of diachronic self-governance is that the cross-temporal structure of planned temporally extended activity involves an intrapersonal analogue of acting together. We have sought a deeper rationale for that plan-theoretic model, and now we have it, one that draws on the shared agency model.

31. The example owes to Seamus Miller. I discuss it in *Shared Agency*, 100.

6. WILLPOWER AND AN END OF ONE'S DIACHRONIC SELF-GOVERNANCE

Let me turn now to a further question about a planning agent's self-governance over time. Suppose that you know you will be tempted to drink heavily tonight at the party.[32] You now think that, in light of what matters to you, this is a bad idea. However, you know that at the party your evaluation will shift in favor of drinking more. You also know that if you did drink heavily, your evaluation would later shift back and you would regret that. So this morning you resolve to drink only one glass tonight. The problem is that, as you know, if you were to stick with your resolve at the party, you would act against what would then be your present evaluation. And we normally suppose that action contrary to one's present evaluation is a breakdown in self-governance.

What if you abandon your prior resolve and drink heavily at the party, given your present evaluation in favor of that? Well, in that case your intentions and plans over time will not conform to the plan-theoretic model of the connections involved in diachronic self-governance. And that will tend to block your diachronic self-governance.

So in neither case will you be, in a clear way, diachronically self-governing. But it also seems an important commonsense idea that willpower can be a central case of diachronic self-governance. What to say?

We sometimes avoid such problems by, prior to the party, changing the world outside our minds in a way that induces new reasons to stick with our prior resolve. One might, say, make a side bet. This is the snowball effect.[33] Again, we sometimes manage to resist reconsideration of our prior resolve, and this can many times be a good strategy, especially given the normal costs and risks of such reconsideration.[34] Both snowball effects and sensible resistance to reconsideration provide important support to the

---

32. See Richard Holton, *Willing, Wanting, Waiting* (Oxford: Clarendon, 2009). And see my "Toxin, Temptation, and the Stability of Intention," as reprinted in my *Faces of Intention* (Cambridge: Cambridge University Press, 1999); my "Temptation and the Agent's Standpoint," *Inquiry* 57 (2014): 293–310 [this volume, essay 7]; and my "Rational Planning Agency." In this paragraph I draw from that last essay.

33. See my *Intention, Plans, and Practical Reason*, 82, and my "Agency, Time, and Sociality." *Proceedings and Addresses of the American Philosophical Association* 84, no. 2 (2010): 7–26, 10 [this volume, essay 5, at 114–15.] In a standard case of a snowball effect, the new reason to stick with one's prior intention is induced by an initial stage in the execution of that intention (e.g., buying a nonrefundable airplane ticket), a stage whose aim is not that of inducing such a reason. Here I extend the idea of a snowball effect to include cases in which the new reason is induced by activity (e.g., making a side bet) whose aim is to induce that reason.

34. This is a general theme in my *Intention, Plans, and Practical Reason*.

stability of our temporally extended agency. But cases of temptation and potential willpower seem sometimes to involve something further.[35] After all, it seems that there will be many cases of temptation in which we do in fact reconsider our prior resolution and we are not protected by some prior side bet or other snowball effect.[36]

A thought here is that we have available a form of theoretical reasoning that can support sticking with our prior resolve. After all, in such a case you will at the time of temptation know that your then-present evaluation diverges from your earlier and expected-later evaluation. This might lead you to adjust your then-present evaluation to be more in line with your different evaluations at these different times. This might be an aspect of a form of theoretical reasoning that aims at smoothing out differences in judgment across time.[37] Could we appeal to such theoretical reasoning to explain how willpower can comport with self-governance?

Well, at the time of temptation you will think that your earlier and later evaluations are mistaken, and so wonder why you should change your present evaluation in order to smooth out these cross-temporal differences in evaluation. And it is not clear why you should have any intrinsic concern with such diachronic theoretical constancy—why such a concern would not simply be an undefended concern with cross-temporal theoretical tidiness.[38] But in any case, what is central for present purposes is that such theoretical thinking is not directly concerned with or responsive to the presence of the prior resolution. Yet what we are trying to explore is the potential role of that prior resolution in diachronic self-governance. A related point is that we seek an account of willpower that also applies to resistance to shuffling in cases like that of Sartre's young man. But in such cases of persisting non-comparability, there is already constancy of evaluation over time: the problem is that this constant evaluation underdetermines what to do. So appeal to cross-temporal theoretical smoothing will not explain what blocks shuffling.

35. Here I am disagreeing with Holton's approach in his *Willing, Wanting, Waiting*.
36. Sarah Paul, "Review of Richard Holton's *Willing, Wanting, Waiting*," *Mind* 120 (2011): 889–92.
37. There is a parallel here with Bas van Fraassen's "Reflection" principle in his "Belief and the Will," *Journal of Philosophy* 81 (1984): 235–56. Related ideas are in Sarah Paul, "Doxastic Self-Control," *American Philosophical Quarterly* 52 (2015): 145–58; and Arthur Lau, "Temptation, Resolution, and Epistemic Self-Trust" (unpublished manuscript, Stanford University 2013). I discuss these ideas further in "Temptation and the Agent's Standpoint," section IV.
38. This parallels concerns that have been raised about certain apparently basic norms of practical rationality. See below note 44.

Perhaps we should instead challenge the assumption that in the conflict, at the time of temptation, between prior resolution and present evaluation it is the present evaluation that speaks for the agent and shapes her then-present standpoint. Perhaps we should instead say that in some cases it is the prior resolution that speaks for the agent. That is why acting in accord with that prior resolution at the time of temptation can cohere with syn-chronic self-governance.[39] Further, given that the evaluation at the time of action is made in light of what matters to the agent, and given that what matters to the agent is shaped by her standpoint, this impact of the prior resolution on the agent's standpoint can then ground a re-shift in the eval-uation so that it favors sticking with one drink.[40]

But given just these two elements—prior resolution and present evaluation—and given the normal status of the agent's evaluation, it is going to be difficult to explain why the prior resolution trumps the evaluation in shaping where the agent stands.[41] A more straightforward strategy would be instead to appeal explicitly to a third element, one that can explain this significance of the prior resolution to present standpoint. And a natural idea here would be to appeal to an end in the agent's standpoint that favors follow-through with the prior resolution and thereby potentially supports both a shift in standpoint and a re-shift in evaluation, both in the direction of will-power. In playing this dual practical role, such an end could help explain how willpower can cohere with both synchronic and diachronic self-governance.

What is it to have an end? Well, to have X as an end is, roughly, to have a noninstrumental concern in favor of X. This is not the same as having an intention in favor of X. First, not all intentions are ends in this sense, since some intentions are solely instrumental. And, second, even for a planning agent not all ends are intentions, since—in contrast with intentions—it is common to have ends one knows are not co-realizable.

The proposal, then, is that a relevant end, in this sense of end, can, to-gether with the cited prior resolution, play a dual role of supporting both a re-shift in evaluation and a re-shift in standpoint. But, how precisely should we conceptualize this proposed dual role of such an end? Should we say that this end, together with the prior resolution, directly supports a re-shift of evaluation in favor of willpower, and that given this re-shifted

39. A related idea is in my "Temptation Revisited," as reprinted in Michael E. Bratman, *Structures of Agency* (New York: Oxford University Press, 2007), 264–74.

40. A related idea is in my "Temptation and the Agent's Standpoint."

41. I made some efforts in this direction in "Temptation Revisited" at 271–4 and 278; but I now think that these efforts will not apply in a sufficiently general way to cases of potential willpower.

evaluation there is a corresponding shift in what the agent's standpoint supports? Or should we say that this end, together with the prior resolution, directly supports a shift in standpoint, and that given this shift in standpoint there can be a corresponding shift in evaluation (since this evaluation is made in light of what matters to the agent, and what matters to the agent is shaped by her standpoint)?

It seems to me that the second proposal—one that prioritizes the impact of the end on the agent's standpoint—fits best with our underlying model of self-governance. The idea is that what is fundamental is what is favored by the agent's standpoint. This shapes what matters to the agent. And the relevant evaluations are evaluations in light of what matters to the agent. What was wrong with the earlier, simple proposal that it is the prior resolution, rather than the present evaluation, which dominantly speaks for the agent was not that it focused primarily on the impact of these different elements on the agent's standpoint. The problem, rather, was that, in the absence of the sort of third element to which we are now appealing, it seemed difficult to defend this priority of the prior resolution in shaping the agent's standpoint. Once we introduce this third element, however, we potentially have a straightforward explanation of the impact of the resolution on the agent's standpoint. And we thereby potentially have a straightforward explanation of its impact on the agent's relevant evaluation.

But what end is this? One idea, due to Jordan Howard Sobel, would simply be that the agent as a matter of fact "puts a premium on steadfastness."[42] In a related proposal, Wlodek Rabinowicz highlights the idea that one's preferences may well be "influenced by [one's] previously chosen plan of action."[43] In each case the idea would be that the agent has an end of "steadfastness," or of fitting with a "previously chosen plan," and this end,

42. Jordon Howard Sobel, "Useful Intentions," in his *Taking Chances: Essays on Rational Choice* (Cambridge: Cambridge University Press, 1994), 237–54, at 249.

43. In exploring the idea of preferences that are "influenced by the previously chosen plan of action" Rabinowicz notes the parallel with Sobel's paper. Such preferences are at the heart of Rabinowicz's model of "wise choice." But, as I go on to note in the text, we can ask whether giving such significance to continuity with the past is an undefended concern with mere cross-temporal mental tidiness. To answer we need to embed such cross-temporal continuity within a larger framework. And that is what the appeal to diachronic self-governance—an appeal to which I turn below—tries to do.

That said, both Sobel and Rabinowicz highlight an idea that is also part of the model I will be discussing, namely: that however we understand this concern for cross-temporal continuity, it is one concern among others and can be overridden in a particular case. Thus Rabinowicz: "The influence of the previously accepted plan on my preferences at node *n* may, but need not, be decisive." See Wlodek Rabinowicz, "To Have One's Cake and Eat It Too: Sequential Choice and Expected-Utility Violations," *Journal of Philosophy* 92 (1995): 586–620, at 606.

together with the prior resolve, explains how her standpoint at the time of temptation gives independent significance to relevant cross-temporal interconnections in a way that potentially shifts her standpoint to favor willpower and thereby supports a corresponding re-shifting of evaluation in favor of willpower. So an end along the lines of Sobel's and Rabinowicz's discussions would potentially play the cited dual role of shaping standpoint and thereby shaping evaluation.

But here the worry is that in appealing to such an end we are appealing simply to a concern in favor of mere cross-temporal psychic tidiness. And we do not want a central element in diachronic self-governance to involve such a brute concern with tidiness.[44]

What we need, then, is an end that, in tandem with the prior resolve, can play these two coordinated roles by favoring something that involves but goes beyond cross-temporal coherence. Here we might consider a proposal by Thomas Kelly, in the context of a discussion of sunk costs, that it can be sensible to have an end of redeeming one's own earlier actions, of preventing them from having been in vain.[45] And this end is not simply a concern with cross-temporal mental tidiness. But even if we agree with Kelly that such a backward-looking end can sometimes be sensible, its application will not be sufficiently general to solve our problem about willpower. Perhaps one's earlier resolve not to drink heavily at the party has already issued in actions that have themselves had significant costs, and so an end of preventing those costly actions from being in vain might support follow-through at the time of the party. But this is a special case. One may simply have decided in the morning not to drink heavily in the evening, and now the time—and the temptation—has arrived. There has been no significant prior, costly action that might be the target of redemption.

44. An analogous worry is at the heart of a challenge that has been posed by Joseph Raz and Niko Kolodny to norms of plan rationality. I agree with these philosophers that if these norms were simply responsive to mere psychic tidiness then it would be unclear why they should have normative significance. But in my "Rational Planning Agency" [this volume, essay 10] and my "Introduction: The Planning Framework" [this volume, essay 1] I argue that these norms are not simply responsive to mere psychic tidiness: they are responsive to conditions of self-governance. In turning later in this discussion to an end of diachronic self-governance, I am pursuing a related strategy with respect to present issues about diachronic self-governance. See Joseph Raz, "The Myth of Instrumental Rationality," *Journal of Ethics and Social Philosophy* 1, no. 1 (2005); and in Nico Kolodny, "The Myth of Practical Consistency," *European Journal of Philosophy* 16 (2008): 366–402. Talk of "psychic tidiness" is from Niko Kolodny, "How Does Coherence Matter?," *Proceedings of the Aristotelian Society* 107 (2007): 229–63, at 241.

45. Thomas Kelly, "Sunk Costs, Rationality, and Acting for the Sake of the Past," *Noûs* 38 (2004): 60–85, esp. 73–5.

What we need is a more generally applicable end, but one that is not simply a concern with cross-temporal mental tidiness. And a natural proposal, based on a kind of inference to the best explanation, would appeal to a (perhaps implicit) end of one's diachronic self-governance itself—where that diachronic self-governance is understood along the lines we are currently developing.[46] This is not merely an end of diachronic coherence, though diachronic self-governance involves cross-temporal coherence. This end of one's diachronic self-governance would sometimes support willpower in the face of temptation, since such willpower would involve the cross-temporal continuity and interconnection of plan structures that is, I have argued, an element in diachronic self-governance. In this way this end of one's diachronic self-governance would be poised to help stabilize the agent's temporally extended, planned activities in the face of anticipated temptation.

Further, such cases of temptation—where these sometimes take the form of temptations to procrastinate—pervade our lives.[47] If the end of diachronic self-governance is part of the structure of a planning agent's response, in diachronic self-governance, to such pervasive sources of instability, we can plausibly see that end as a central element in a planning agent's self-governance, one that stands guard against such instability. A planning agent's self-governance over time involves coordination of two kinds of coherence within planned temporally extended activity: the synchronic coherence involved in self-governance at relevant times along the way, and the coherence involved in relevant cross-temporal continuities and interconnections of intentions over time. The proposal is that this coordination of these two forms of coherence is normally supported by standpoints that include the end of diachronic self-governance, and that

46. One consideration in favor of appeal to this specific end is that this appeal fits well with a plausible theory of plan rationality. I explain this in "Rational Planning Agency" and "Introduction." This connection with issues about plan rationality is also relevant to my assessment of an alternative, intellectualistic strategy developed by J. David Velleman. In his "Centered Self," in his *Self to Self* (Cambridge: Cambridge University Press, 2006), 253–83, at 272, Velleman says: "my intellectual drives . . . favor fulfilling my past intentions." But, as I note in "Rational Planning Agency," this will lead to a cognitivist treatment of basic norms of plan rationality, and there are good reasons to be wary of such a cognitivism.

47. Sarah Paul, "Diachronic Incontinence is a Problem in Moral Philosophy," *Inquiry* 57 (2014): 337–55; Sergio Tenenbaum and Diana Raffman, "Vague Projects and the Puzzle of the Self-Torturer," *Ethics* 123 (2012): 86–112, esp. section III; Chrisoula Andreou, "Temptation, Resolutions, and Regret," *Inquiry* 57 (2014): 275–92; Chrisoula Andreou and Mark D. White, eds., *The Thief of Time: Philosophical Essays on Procrastination* (Oxford: Oxford University Press, 2010).

the presence of this end stands guard to support this coordination in the face of pervasive potential threats to the needed stability over time.

So by modeling a planning agent's diachronic self-governance as involving this end of her diachronic self-governance, we provide for the possibility of diachronically self-governing willpower. We help explain the potential robustness of diachronic self-governance in the face of certain characteristic threats of instability. And we do this by appeal to an end that—in contrast with mere mental tidiness—is, plausibly, worth wanting.

Is there an analogous argument that synchronic self-governance involves an end of synchronic self-governance? Well, what is needed for synchronic self-governance is guidance by the substantive concerns that constitute the agent's then-present standpoint. And it is not clear why these substantive concerns must include a concern specifically with self-governance. In contrast, when we turn to diachronic self-governance we face a distinctive, time-induced issue of coordination between present standpoint and cross-temporal continuity. The end of one's diachronic self-governance is a response to that issue. If this is right, there is an asymmetry here. However, insofar as synchronic self-governance is an element in diachronic self-governance, there will be an indirect argument for the need for an end of synchronic self-governance.

The next step is to see more precisely how the presence of this end of diachronic self-governance would help make possible a form of willpower that coheres with both synchronic and diachronic self-governance.

7. DIACHRONICALIZED STANDPOINTS

The first step is to note that the relevant end will not simply be an end of maximizing the amount of one's diachronic self-governance—an end that would argue against taking a nap. It will, rather, be an end in favor of one's diachronic self-governance given that certain preconditions are met. In particular, this end will come to bear at a given time if the agent is engaged in a relevant planned temporally extended activity and her standpoint at that time—a standpoint that includes this very end—would support a choice that also satisfies the intention-interconnection conditions of diachronic self-governance. Since this conditional end concerns the role of a standpoint that itself includes this end, this is a reflexive (and conditional) end in favor of diachronic self-governance.

We can now distinguish two cases. In a simple case, the support of the standpoint at that time for a choice that coheres with one's diachronic self-governance does not depend on the presence in that standpoint of the end of that diachronic self-governance. This may happen in a case of potential shuffling given ongoing non-comparability in which, even in the absence of the end of diachronic self-governance, the standpoint supports—albeit, weakly—refraining from such shuffling. In a second, more complex case, the support of the standpoint for a choice that coheres with one's diachronic self-governance depends on the way this end in favor of that diachronic self-governance—an end that is itself in that standpoint—favors that choice in part because that choice would satisfy the diachronic interconnection conditions on diachronic self-governance. As we have begun to see, this may happen in a case of potential willpower in the face of temptation. In either case, and this is the central idea, the agent's standpoint at that time—one that includes this conditional, reflexive end in favor of one's diachronic self-governance—would support the joint satisfaction of the conditions of both synchronic and diachronic self-governance.

Let's see in more detail how this works in a temptation case. In such a case the agent's conditional and reflexive end of her diachronic self-governance would support willpower if that end were brought to bear on that willpower; and, given her planned, ongoing temporally extended activity, it will be brought to bear if her standpoint at the time of temptation, *supplemented by the support this end would provide*, would support that willpower. If the agent's conditional and reflexive end of diachronic self-governance is sufficiently important to her to make it true that her standpoint at the time of temptation, supplemented by the support this end would provide, would support that willpower, then the agent satisfies the relevant preconditions, and her conditional end in favor of her diachronic self-governance does indeed support sticking with her prior resolve.

A complication is that this end in favor of her diachronic self-governance may not always be sufficiently important to the agent to re-shift her standpoint in this way in a temptation case. After all, that standpoint involves a complex web of elements, only one of which is this end. Other ends can in a given case trump the potential impact of this conditional end in favor of diachronic self-governance.[48] When other ends do trump they block relevant diachronic self-governance (though they need not block synchronic self-governance), and so they block the satisfaction of the relevant precondition. This is what happens when the agent decisively rejects her earlier plan, despite her end in favor of her diachronic self-governance. But sometimes in a temptation case, this end in favor of diachronic self-governance

48. This is the parallel with views of Sobel and Rabinowicz anticipated in note 43. It is also a feature of Velleman's view cited in note 46.

would have sufficient priority to support sticking with the prior resolve in a way that is sufficient to re-shift the agent's standpoint so that it now favors sticking with her prior resolve. In such a case the agent's sticking with her resolve can cohere with both synchronic and diachronic self-governance. The agent will thereby be in a position to re-shift her evaluation concerning further drinking: she can now favor abstaining since that would comport with her self-governance, both at the time and over time, and so—given her end of her diachronic self-governance—with where she now stands. We thereby explain how willpower can sometimes (though not always) cohere with self-governance.

So a way to ensure that at least some cases of willpower involve synchronic self-governance at the time of resisting temptation is to appeal to the cited conditional end in favor of one's diachronic self-governance. As noted, this end will be reflexive in the sense that it supports a choice insofar as that choice would comport with both diachronic and synchronic self-governance *given this very end* (and its impact on the agent's standpoint, and so on synchronic self-governance, and so on diachronic self-governance).

The next point is that once this conditional, reflexive end is on board it will also favor constancy of decision in the face of non-comparability. Sartre's young man, having chosen to stay with his mother, comes to a time when he reconsiders. At this time he satisfies the relevant precondition: he has a standpoint that (weakly) supports the choice to continue helping his mother, where that choice would thereby comport with synchronic self-governance and, given the history, with diachronic self-governance. So, this choice to continue with his mother—in contrast with a shuffled choice instead to fight with the Free French—would be supported by his conditional, reflexive end in favor of his diachronic self-governance.

Granted, there is no guarantee that this will result in his standpoint *strongly* favoring the option previously chosen. A basic feature of non-comparability is that if A and B are non-comparable, it is possible to add into the mix a further consideration, C, in favor of A, and yet it still be true that A together with C remains non-comparable with B.[49] Nevertheless, we have an explanation of why, even if the non-comparability remains, shuffling in such a case is a breakdown in diachronic self-governance, whereas resistance to shuffling can comport with diachronic self-governance and so be supported by the end of diachronic self-governance.

In supposing that the agent's standpoint includes the cited conditional, reflexive end in favor of her diachronic self-governance, I am supposing

49. Joseph Raz, *The Morality of Freedom* (Oxford: Clarendon, 1986), 325–6.

that this standpoint is, as I will say, *diachronicalized*: it includes an element that can sometimes accord significance to relevant plan-infused cross-temporal interconnections, interconnections that are not merely cross-temporal mental tidiness. And the idea is that a planning agent's diachronic self-governance in the case of willpower involves a standpoint that is diachronicalized in this way, and that such a standpoint will also support a planning agent's diachronic self-governance in resisting brute shuffling.

8. LATER REFLECTION AND PLAN-INDUCED TEMPORAL FOOTPRINT

We need one further idea. Suppose that in Gregory Kavka's toxin case you decide at t1 to drink a disgusting toxin at t3.[50] You make this decision at t1 because you know that given that decision you will get a great reward at t2. You also know throughout that your reward at t2 depends on your decision at t1 but does not depend on your following through with that decision at t3. You decide at t1 to drink at t3, you get the reward at t2, and t3 arrives. At t3 you are faced with a choice of whether to stick with your intention to drink the toxin at t3. If you stick with it, your intentions during t1-t3 will satisfy the shared-agency-analogue conditions with respect to this time interval. But won't you nevertheless be acting contrary to your standpoint at t3? Well, on our way to a model of a planning agent's diachronic self-governance we have supposed that you have the conditional, reflexive end of your diachronic self-governance. So we need to ask whether, given this end, your standpoint at t3 may turn out to support drinking the toxin. If it does then your drinking the toxin at t3 may fully comport with both your synchronic and your diachronic self-governance. But that seems wrong.

In response we might try simply to say that in this toxin case at t3 your end of your diachronic self-governance will not outweigh your end of not getting very sick. But in discussing the temptation case, we supposed that your end of your diachronic self-governance might sometimes in effect outweigh your end of drinking more wine. And it is not clear how we could defend in a principled way this purported, systematic difference between the cases.

I think there is a structural issue here, one distinct from the question of the relative weights an agent assigns to avoiding the discomfort of toxin-drinking in comparison with diachronic self-governance. We can articulate this structural issue by considering your relevant reflections at a later time,

50. Gregory S. Kavka, "The Toxin Puzzle," *Analysis* 43 (1983): 33–6.

t4.[51] In particular, we consider your reflections at t4, on the basis of what you at t4 know were your relevant non-evaluative beliefs at t3, on your decision at t3. In the temptation case, if you did stick with your prior resolve to resist the temptation, such reflections at t4 would, we may assume, *not* issue in regret about your decision at t3. In the toxin case, in contrast, if you did at t3 stick with your prior resolve to drink toxin, such reflections *would*, we may assume, issue in a kind of regret at t4 about your decision at t3. Drinking toxin is, after all, awful. In the toxin case—in contrast with the temptation case—sticking at t3 with your prior intention would be something you would regret at t4 when reflecting in the cited way on that decision.

This suggests that sticking with your intention at t3 to drink the toxin does not fit into the kind of cross-temporal structure of plan-infused attitudes that is an element of diachronic self-governance. And this is a contrast with the kind of temptation case at issue here. The end of one's diachronic self-governance conditionally supports sticking with one's resolve in a temptation case in part because sticking with one's resolve fits together, in shared-agency-analogue ways, not just with one's earlier resolve but also with one's relevant, anticipated later attitude concerning one's exercise of willpower. In sticking with one's resolve one is acting "together" with oneself at both earlier and later times. It is this relevant anticipated later regret at abandoning one's resolve that distinguishes this temptation case from the toxin case in which what is anticipated is, rather, relevant later regret at having followed through with one's intention to drink the toxin. In drinking the toxin one would not be acting "together" with oneself at the later time, t4. This is what allows us to resist the idea that drinking the toxin would be an element in diachronic self-governance and so potentially be supported by the conditional, reflexive end of one's diachronic self-governance.

But why does this yet later time matter? The answer seems to be that appeal to such later times is at least implicitly built into the plans that frame the relevant temporally extended activity. The planned temporal shape of the activity will frequently extend to relevant later times—to, as I once said, plan's end.[52] In the temptation case we are thinking of the planned project of resisting temptation as extending beyond the moment of expected temptation and including one's relevant later reflections on earlier follow-through. And in the toxin case we are thinking of the plan for

51. This is a basic idea in my "Toxin, Temptation, and the Stability of Intention" and my "Temptation and the Agent's Standpoint."
52. "Toxin, Temptation, and the Stability of Intention," section IX.

getting the money as extending beyond the time of drinking the toxin and including one's relevant later reflections on earlier follow-through. In each case, diachronic self-governance with respect to the planned temporally extended activity needs to involve relevant shared-agency-analogue plan-theoretic continuities that extend through to plan's end. And that is why the conditional, reflexive end of one's diachronic self-governance, while it will sometimes support willpower, will not (on current assumptions) support drinking the toxin. It will not support drinking the toxin because following through with the intention to drink will not fit appropriately with one's relevant, anticipated regret, at plan's end, concerning such follow-through.

9. A PLANNING AGENT'S DIACHRONIC SELF-GOVERNANCE

We now have in place the building blocks for a model of a robust form of a planning agent's self-governance over time:

First, the agent is engaged in *planned temporally extended activity*. Given the hierarchical structure of plans, this planned temporally extended activity can be shaped by a higher-level plan that remains in place even as lower level sub-plans are adjusted. And these plans specify a *temporal footprint*, one that will commonly include one's relevant later responses to one's then-earlier efforts.

Second, there is synchronic *self-governance at (during) relevant times (small temporal intervals) along the way* in the execution of the plan that frames the relevant temporally extended activity. This synchronic self-governance involves coherence of standpoint and coherence of choice with coherent standpoint.

Third, there are appropriate *cross-temporal interconnections* between relevant plan-infused attitudes. These interconnections involve cross-temporal interconnections of intention that are characteristic of planned temporally extended activity, all in the context of self-governance at times along the way. These plan-theoretic interconnections induce associated shared-agency-analogue interconnections. And these shared-agency-analogues support the metaphor that in the temporally extended activity involved in diachronic self-governance the agent at different times along the way is "acting together" with herself at the other relevant times along the way.

As noted, a complexity is that there can be these interconnections at a higher level of the hierarchy of plans despite breakdowns in interconnection at a lower level of sub-plans. Such higher-level interconnections can, together with other relevant elements, sometimes suffice for diachronic self-governance. However, if the breakdown at the lower level could have been avoided in a way that cohered with diachronic (and so, synchronic) self-governance at that level, then that lower-level breakdown diminishes the extent of diachronic self-governance even given the higher-level interconnections.

Fourth, the standpoints at times along the way are *diachronicalized*: they include a conditional, reflexive end in favor of one's diachronic self-governance. A precondition of this end is that the agent is engaged in a relevant, planned temporally extended activity, and his diachronicalized standpoint at the time at issue would support the joint satisfaction of conditions of both synchronic and diachronic self-governance. This conditional, reflexive end to some extent helps coordinate the coherent standpoints at each relevant time along the way with the cross-temporal interconnections involved in diachronic self-governance. It does this by sometimes inducing within the standpoint at a given time relevant significance of the cited connections across time. And the time frame that is relevant to this end of diachronic self-governance is specified by the plan that frames the underlying temporally extended activity.

In short, this model of a planning agent's self-governance over time highlights: (1) planned temporally extended activity, and an associated time frame; (2) self-governance at (during) relevant times along the way of that activity; (3) plan-infused cross-temporal interconnections that have a structure that is to some extent analogous with the interpersonal structure of interlocking intentions of individuals in shared agency; and (4) diachronicalized standpoints at (during) relevant times along the way. These diachronicalized standpoints help support the coordination between (2) and (3) in response to characteristic threats to stability.

Such diachronic self-governance on the part of a planning agent is responsive to common threats of instability within her temporally extended agency, namely: threats of potential shuffling and of temptation. These responses to these threats involve diachronicalized standpoints and go beyond snowball effects and sensible non-reconsideration. But these responses need not involve an implausible rigidity. We highlight the twin ideas that a planning agent's diachronic self-governance normally involves the end of her diachronic self-governance and can involve the stability of prior intentions in cases of resisting shuffling and in some cases of willpower. But we also acknowledge the Sartre-inspired thought that in some cases "the prior project collapses into the past in the light of a new project which rises on its ruins."[53]

---

53. *Being and Nothingness* (Hazel Barnes translation) (New York: Washington Square Press, 1984), 612.

BIBLIOGRAPHY

Ainslie, George. *Breakdown of Will*. New York: Cambridge University Press, 2001.

Ainslie, George. *Picoeconomics: The Strategic Interaction of Successive Motivational States within the Person*. Cambridge: Cambridge University Press, 1992.

Ainslie, George. "Precis of *Breakdown of Will*." *Behavioral and Brain Sciences* 28, no. 5 (2005): 635–50.

Alonso, Facundo. "Shared Intention, Reliance, and Interpersonal Obligations." *Ethics* 119, no. 3 (2009): 444–75.

Andreou, Chrisoula. "Incommensurable Alternatives and Rational Choice." *Ratio* 18, no. 3 (2005): 249–61.

Andreou, Chrisoula. "Temptation, Resolutions, and Regret." *Inquiry* 57 (2014): 275–92.

Andreou, Chrisoula, and Mark D. White, eds. *The Thief of Time: Philosophical Essays on Procrastination*. Oxford: Oxford University Press, 2010.

Anscombe, G. E. M. *Intention*. Ithaca, NY: Cornell University Press, 1963.

Arpaly, Nomy. *Unprincipled Virtue*. Oxford: Oxford University Press, 2003.

Arpaly, Nomy, and Timothy Schroeder. "Praise, Blame and the Whole Self." *Philosophical Studies* 93, no. 2 (1999): 161–88.

Bennett, Jonathan. "Morality and Consequences." In *Tanner Lectures on Human Values*, edited by Sterling M. McMurrin, 45–116. Cambridge: Cambridge University Press, 1980.

Binkley, Robert. "A Theory of Practical Reason." *The Philosophical Review* 74 (1965): 423–48.

Blackburn, Simon. *Ruling Passions: A Theory of Practical Reasoning*. Oxford: Oxford University Press, 1998.

Bratman, Michael E. "Agency, Time, and Sociality." *Proceedings and Addresses of the American Philosophical Association* 84, no. 2 (2010): 7–26. [This volume, essay 5.]

Bratman, Michael E. "A Planning Theory of Self-Governance: Reply to Franklin." *Philosophical Explorations* 20, no. 1 (2017): 15–20.

Bratman, Michael E. "A Thoughtful and Reasonable Stability." Comments in *Taking Ourselves Seriously and Getting It Right* by Harry G. Frankfurt, edited by Debra Satz, 77–90. Stanford, CA: Stanford University Press, 2006.

Bratman, Michael E. "Castañeda's Theory of Thought and Action." In *Faces of Intention*, 225–49. New York: Cambridge University Press, 1999.

Bratman, Michael E. "Cognitivism about Practical Reason." In *Faces of Intention*, 250–64. New York: Cambridge University Press, 1999.

Bratman, Michael E. "Constructivism, Agency, and the Problem of Alignment." In *Constructivism in Practical Philosophy*, edited by James Lenman and Yonatan Shemmer, 81–98. Oxford: Oxford University Press, 2012.

Bratman, Michael E. *Faces of Intention*. New York: Cambridge University Press, 1999.

Bratman, Michael E. "Following Through with One's Plans: Reply to David Gauthier." In *Modeling Rationality, Morality, and Evolution*, edited by Peter A. Danielson, 55–66. New York: Oxford University Press, 1998.

Bratman, Michael E. "I Intend that We J." In *Faces of Intention*, 142–61. New York: Cambridge University Press, 1999.

Bratman, Michael E. "Intention and Means–End Reasoning." *The Philosophical Review* 90, no. 2 (1981): 252–65.

Bratman, Michael E. "Intention, Belief and Instrumental Rationality." In *Reasons for Action*, edited by David Sobel and Steven Wall, 13–36. Cambridge: Cambridge University Press, 2009. [This volume, essay 3.]

Bratman, Michael E. "Intention, Belief, Practical, Theoretical." In *Spheres of Reason*, edited by Simon Robertson, 29–61. Oxford: Oxford University Press, 2009. [This volume, essay 2.]

Bratman, Michael E. *Intention, Plans, and Practical Reason*. Cambridge, MA: Harvard University Press, 1987; Reissued CSLI Publications, 1999.

Bratman, Michael E. "Intention, Practical Rationality, and Self-Governance." *Ethics* 119, no. 3 (2009): 411–43. [This volume, essay 4.]

Bratman, Michael E. "Intention Rationality." *Philosophical Explorations* 12, no. 3 (2009): 227–41.

Bratman, Michael E. "Modest Sociality and the Distinctiveness of Intention." *Philosophical Studies* 144, no. 1 (2009): 149–65.

Bratman, Michael E. "Planning Agency, Autonomous Agency." In *Structures of Agency*, 195–221. New York: Oxford University Press, 2007.

Bratman, Michael E. "Planning and the Stability of Intention." *Minds and Machines* 2, no. 1 (1992): 1–16.

Bratman, Michael E. "Planning and Temptation." In *Faces of Intention*, 35–57. New York: Cambridge University Press, 1999.

Bratman, Michael E. "Plan Rationality." In *The Routledge Handbook of Practical Reason*, edited by Ruth Chang and Kurt Sylvan. Routledge, forthcoming.

Bratman, Michael E. "Practical Reasoning and Acceptance in a Context." In *Faces of Intention*, 15–34. New York: Cambridge University Press, 1999.

Bratman, Michael E. "Rational and Social Agency: Reflections and Replies." In *Rational and Social Agency: The Philosophy of Michael Bratman*, edited by Manuel Vargas and Gideon Yaffe, 294–343. New York: Oxford University Press, 2014.

Bratman, Michael E. "Rational Planning Agency." In *Philosophy of Action, Royal Institute of Philosophy Supplement*: 80, edited by Anthony O'Hear, 25–48. Cambridge: Cambridge University Press, 2017. [This volume, essay 10.]

Bratman, Michael E. "Reflection, Planning, and Temporally Extended Agency." In *Structures of Agency*, 21–46. New York: Oxford University Press, 2007.

Bratman, Michael E. "Setiya on Intention, Rationality, and Reasons." *Analysis Reviews* 69, no. 3 (2009): 510–21.

Bratman, Michael E. "Shared Agency." In *Philosophy of the Social Sciences: Philosophical Theory and Scientific Practice*, edited by Chris Mantzavinos, 41–59. Cambridge: Cambridge University Press, 2009.

Bratman, Michael E. *Shared Agency: A Planning Theory of Acting Together*. New York: Oxford University Press, 2014.

Bratman, Michael E. "Shared Cooperative Activity." In *Faces of Intention*, 93–108. New York: Cambridge University Press, 1999.

Bratman, Michael E. "Shared Valuing and Frameworks for Practical Reasoning." In *Structures of Agency*, 283–310. New York: Oxford University Press, 2007.

Bratman, Michael E. *Structures of Agency*. New York: Oxford University Press, 2007.

Bratman, Michael E. "Temptation and the Agent's Standpoint." *Inquiry* 57, no. 3 (2014): 293–310. [This volume, essay 7.]

Bratman, Michael E. "Temptation Revisited." In *Structures of Agency*, 257–82. New York: Oxford University Press, 2007.

Bratman, Michael E. "The Fecundity of Planning Agency." In *Oxford Studies in Agency and Responsibility*, Volume 1, edited by David Shoemaker, 47–69. Oxford: Oxford University Press, 2013.

Bratman, Michael E. "The Interplay of Intention and Reason." *Ethics* 123, no. 4 (2013): 657–72. [This volume, essay 8.]

Bratman, Michael E. "Three Theories of Self-Governance." In *Structures of Agency*, 222–53. New York: Oxford University Press, 2007.

Bratman, Michael E. "Time, Rationality, and Self-Governance." *Philosophical Issues* 22, no. 1 (2012): 73–88. [This volume, essay 6.]

Bratman, Michael E. "Toxin, Temptation, and the Stability of Intention." In *Faces of Intention*, 58–90. New York: Cambridge University Press, 1999.

Bratman, Michael E. "Two Faces of Intention." *The Philosophical Review* 93 (1984): 375–405.

Bratman, Michael E. "Two Problems About Human Agency." In *Structures of Agency*, 89–105. New York: Oxford University Press, 2007.

Bratman, Michael E. "Valuing and the Will." In *Structures of Agency*, 47–67. New York: Oxford University Press, 2007.

Bratman, Michael E., David Israel, and Martha Pollack. "Plans and Resource-Bounded Practical Reasoning." *Computational Intelligence* 4, no. 3 (1988): 349–55.

Broome, John. "Are Intentions Reasons? And How Should We Cope with Incommensurable Values?" In *Practical Rationality and Preference: Essays for David Gauthier*, edited by Christopher W. Morris and Arthur Ripstein, 98–120. Cambridge: Cambridge University Press, 2001.

Broome, John. "Does Rationality Give Us Reasons?" *Philosophical Issues* 15, no. 1 (2005): 321–37.

Broome, John. "Have We Reason to Do as Rationality Requires? A Comment on Raz." *Journal of Ethics and Social Philosophy Symposium* 1 (2005): 1–8.

Broome, John. "Is Rationality Normative?" *Disputatio* 2, no. 23 (2007): 161–78.

Broome, John. "Normative Requirements." *Ratio* 12, no. 4 (1999): 398–419.

Broome, John. *Rationality Through Reasoning*. Hoboken, NJ: Wiley-Blackwell, 2013.

Broome, John. "Reasons." In *Reason and Value: Themes from the Moral Philosophy of Joseph Raz*, edited by R. Jay Wallace, Philip Pettit, Samuel Scheffler, and Michael Smith, 28–55. Oxford: Oxford University Press, 2004.

Broome, John. "The Unity of Reasoning?" In *Spheres of Reason*, edited by Simon Robertson, 62–92. Oxford: Oxford University Press, 2009.

Broome, John. "Wide or Narrow Scope?" *Mind* 116, no. 462 (2007): 359–70.

Brunero, John. "Cognitivism about Practical Rationality." In *Oxford Studies in Metaethics*, Vol. 9, edited by R. Shafer-Landau, 18–44. Oxford: Oxford University Press, 2014.

Brunero, John. "Instrumental Rationality, Symmetry, and Scope." *Philosophical Studies* 157, no. 1 (2012): 125–40.

Brunero, John. "Self-Governance, Means-Ends Coherence, and Unalterable Ends." *Ethics* 120 (2010): 579–91.

Brunero, John. "Two Approaches to Instrumental Rationality and Belief Consistency." *Journal of Ethics and Social Philosophy* 1, no. 1 (2005): http://www.jesp.org.

Calhoun, Cheshire. "What Good Is Commitment?" *Ethics* 119, no. 4 (2009): 613–41.

Castañeda, Héctor-Neri. *Thinking and Doing*. Dordrecht, The Netherlands: Reidel, 1975.

Chang, Ruth. "The Possibility of Parity." *Ethics* 112 (2002): 659–88.

Chang, Ruth. "Voluntarist Reasons and the Sources of Normativity." In *Reasons for Action*, edited by David Sobel and Steven Wall, 243–71. Cambridge: Cambridge University Press, 2009.

Christensen, David. "Clever Bookies and Coherent Beliefs." *The Philosophical Review* 100, no. 2 (1991): 229–47.

Christensen, David. "Diachronic Coherence versus Epistemic Impartiality." *The Philosophical Review* 109, no. 3 (2000): 349–71.

Copp, David. "The Normativity of Self-Grounded Reason." In *Morality in a Natural World*, 309–54. Cambridge: Cambridge University Press, 2007.

Cullity, Garrett. "Decisions, Reasons, and Rationality." *Ethics* 119, no. 1 (2008): 57–95.

Dancy, Jonathan. "Replies." *Philosophy and Phenomenological Research* 67, no. 2 (2003): 468–90.

Davidson, Donald. "Incoherence and Irrationality." In *Problems of Rationality*, 189–98. Oxford: Oxford University Press, 2004.

Davidson, Donald. "Intending." In *Essays on Actions and Events*, 2nd ed., 83–102. Oxford: Oxford University Press, 2001.

Davis, Wayne. "A Causal Theory of Intending." *American Philosophical Quarterly* 21, no. 1 (1984): 43–54.

Evnine, Simon. *Epistemic Dimensions of Personhood*. Oxford: Oxford University Press, 2008.

Feigl, Herbert. "The 'Mental' and the 'Physical'." *Minnesota Studies in the Philosophy of Science* 2 (1958): 370–497.

Ferrero, Luca. "Decisions, Diachronic Autonomy, and the Division of Deliberative Labor." *Philosophers' Imprint* 10, no. 2 (2010): 1–23.

Ferrero, Luca. "Diachronic Constraints of Practical Rationality." *Philosophical Issues* 22, no. 1 (2012): 144–64.

Ferrero, Luca. "Inescapability Revisited." Unpublished manuscript, April 2016.

Ferrero, Luca. "What Good Is a Diachronic Will?" *Philosophical Studies* 144, no. 3 (2009): 403–30.

Fuller, Lon. "Positivism and Fidelity to Law: A Reply to Professor Hart." *Harvard Law Review* 71, no. 4 (1958): 630–72.

Frankfurt, Harry. "Alternate Possibilities and Moral Responsibility." In *The Importance of What We Care About*, 1–10. Cambridge: Cambridge University Press, 1988.

Frankfurt, Harry. "Freedom of the Will and the Concept of a Person." In *The Importance of What We Care About*, 11–25. Cambridge: Cambridge University Press, 1988.

Frankfurt, Harry. "Identification and Wholeheartedness." In *The Importance of What We Care About*, 159–76. Cambridge: Cambridge University Press, 1988.

Frankfurt, Harry. *Necessity, Volition and Love*. Cambridge: Cambridge University Press, 1999.

Frankfurt, Harry. "On the Necessity of Ideals." In *Necessity, Volition and Love*, 108–16. Cambridge: Cambridge University Press, 1999.

Frankfurt, Harry. "The Faintest Passion." In *Necessity, Volition and Love*, 95–107. Cambridge: Cambridge University Press, 1999.

Frankfurt, Harry. *The Importance of What We Care About*. Cambridge: Cambridge University Press, 1988.

Frankfurt, Harry. "The Problem of Action." In *The Importance of What We Care About*, 69–79. Cambridge: Cambridge University Press, 1988.

Frankfurt, Harry. *The Reasons of Love*. Princeton, NJ: Princeton University Press, 2004.

Gauthier, David. "Assure and Threaten." *Ethics* 104, no. 4 (1994): 690–721.

Gauthier, David. "Commitment and Choice: An Essay on the Rationality of Plans." In *Ethics, Rationality, and Economic Behavior*, edited by Francesco Farina, Frank Hahn, and Stefano Vannucci, 217–43. Oxford: Oxford University Press, 1996.

Gauthier, David. "Intention and Deliberation." In *Modeling Rationality, Morality, and Evolution*, edited by Peter A Danielson, 41–54. New York: Oxford University Press, 1998.

Gauthier, David. *Morals by Agreement*. Oxford: Oxford University Press, 1986.

Gauthier, David. "Rationality and the Rational Aim." In *Reading Parfit*, edited by Jonathan Dancy, 24–41. Oxford: Blackwell, 1997.

Gauthier, David. "Resolute Choice and Rational Deliberation: A Critique and a Defense." *Noûs* 31, no. 1 (1997): 1–25.

Gauthier, David. "Rethinking the Toxin Puzzle." In *Rational Commitment and Social Justice: Essays for Gregory Kavka*, edited by Jules L. Coleman and Christopher W. Morris, 47–58. Cambridge: Cambridge University Press, 1998.

Gibbard, Allan. "Morality as Consistency in Living." *Ethics* 110, no. 1 (1999): 140–64.

Gibbard, Allan. "Reply to Critics." *Philosophy and Phenomenological Research* 72, no. 3 (2006): 729–44.

Gibbard, Allan. *Thinking How to Live*. Cambridge, MA: Harvard University Press, 2003.

Gibbard, Allan. *Wise Choices, Apt Feelings*. Cambridge, MA: Harvard University Press, 1990.

Gilbert, Margaret. *A Theory of Political Obligation*. Oxford: Oxford University Press, 2006.

Gilbert, Margaret. "Shared Intention and Personal Intentions." *Philosophical Studies* 144, no. 1 (2009): 167–87.

Gilbert, Margaret. "Walking Together: A Paradigmatic Social Phenomenon." *Midwest Studies* 15, no. 1 (1990): 1–14.

Greenspan, Patricia. "Conditional Oughts and Hypothetical Imperatives." *Journal of Philosophy* 72, no. 10 (1975): 259–76.

Grice, Paul. "Intention and Uncertainty." *Proceedings of the British Academy* 57 (1971): 263–79.

Grice, Paul. "Method in Philosophical Psychology (From the Banal to the Bizarre)." Presidential Address, *Proceedings and Addresses of the American Philosophical Association* 48 (1974–5): 23–53.

Harman, Gilbert. *Change in View: Principles of Reasoning*. Cambridge, MA: MIT Press, 1986.

Harman, Gilbert. "Practical Reasoning." In *Reasoning, Meaning, and Mind*, 46–74. Oxford: Oxford University Press, 1999.

Harman, Gilbert. *Reasoning, Meaning, and Mind*. Oxford: Oxford University Press, 1999.

Harman, Gilbert. "Willing and Intending." In *Philosophical Grounds of Rationality: Intentions, Categories, Ends*, edited by R. Grandy and R. Warner, 363–80. Oxford: Oxford University Press, 1986.

Hieronymi, Pamela. "The Wrong Kind of Reason." *Journal of Philosophy* 102, no. 9 (2005): 437–57.

Hobart, R. E. "Free Will as Involving Determination and Inconceivable Without It." *Mind* 43, no. 169 (1934): 1–27.

Holton, Richard. "Intention as a Model for Belief." In *Rational and Social Agency: The Philosophy of Michael Bratman*, edited by Manuel Vargas and Gideon Yaffe, 12–37. New York: Oxford University Press, 2014.

Holton, Richard. *Willing, Wanting, Waiting*. Oxford: Clarendon Press, 2009.

Hume, David. *A Treatise of Human Nature*, edited by L. A. Selby-Bigge. Oxford: Oxford University Press, 1978.

Hussain, Nadeem J. Z. "The Requirements of Rationality." Unpublished manuscript, Stanford University, ver. 2.4.

Jollimore, Troy. "Why Is Instrumental Rationality Rational?" *Canadian Journal of Philosophy* 35, no. 3 (2005): 289–308.

Kagan, Shelly. *The Limits of Morality*. Oxford: Oxford University Press, 1989.

Kavka, Gregory. "The Toxin Puzzle." *Analysis* 43, no. 1 (1983): 33–6.

Kelly, Thomas. "Sunk Costs, Rationality, and Acting for the Sake of the Past." *Noûs* 38, no. 1 (2004): 60–85.

Kenny, Anthony. *Will, Freedom, and Power*. Oxford: Blackwell, 1975.

Kiesewetter, Benjamin. "Instrumental Normativity: In Defense of the Transmission Principle." *Ethics* 125, no. 4 (2015): 921–46.

Kolodny, Niko. "How Does Coherence Matter?" *Proceedings of the Aristotelian Society* 107, no. 1 (2007): 229–63.

Kolodny, Niko. "Instrumental Reasons." In *The Oxford Handbook of Reasons and Normativity*, edited by Daniel Star. Oxford: Oxford University Press, forthcoming.

Kolodny, Niko. "Reply to Bridges." *Mind* 118, no. 470 (2009): 369–76.

Kolodny, Niko. "State or Process Requirements?" *Mind* 116, no. 462 (2007): 371–85.

Kolodny, Niko. "The Myth of Practical Consistency." *European Journal of Philosophy* 16, no. 3 (2008): 366–402.

Kolodny, Niko. "Why Be Rational?" *Mind* 114, no. 455 (2005): 509–63.

Korsgaard, Christine. "The Normative Constitution of Agency." In *Rational and Social Agency: The Philosophy of Michael Bratman*, edited by Manuel Vargas and Gideon Yaffe, 190–214. New York: Oxford University Press, 2014.

Korsgaard, Christine. "The Normativity of Instrumental Reason." In *The Constitution of Agency*, 27–68. Oxford: Oxford University Press, 2008.

Korsgaard, Christine. *Self-Constitution: Agency, Identity, and Integrity* Oxford: Oxford University Press, 2009.

Korsgaard, Christine. *The Sources of Normativity*. Cambridge: Cambridge University Press, 1996.

Lau, Arthur. "Temptation, Resolution, and Epistemic Self-Trust." Unpublished manuscript, Stanford University, 2013.

Lehrer, Keith. *Self-Trust: A Study of Reason, Knowledge, and Autonomy*. Oxford: Oxford University Press, 1997.

Locke, John. *An Essay Concerning Human Understanding*, edited by Peter H. Nidditch. Oxford: Oxford University Press, 1975.

McCann, Hugh. "Settled Objectives and Rational Constraints." *American Philosophical Quarterly* 28, no. 1 (1991): 25–36.

McClennen, Edward F. "Pragmatic Rationality and Rules." *Philosophy & Public Affairs* 26, no. 3 (1997): 210–58.

McClennen, Edward F. *Rationality and Dynamic Choice: Foundational Exploration.* Cambridge: Cambridge University Press, 1990.

McClennen, Edward F. "Rationality and Rules." In *Modeling Rationality, Morality, and Evolution,* edited by Peter A. Danielson, 13–40. Oxford: Oxford University Press, 1998.

McDowell, John. "Some Remarks on Intention in Action." *Amherst Lecture in Philosophy* 6 (2011). http://www.amherstlecture.org/mcdowell2011/mcdowell2011_ALP.pdf.

Millgram, Elijah. "Segmented Agency." In *Rational and Social Agency: The Philosophy of Michael Bratman,* edited by Manuel Vargas and Gideon Yaffe, 152–89. New York: Oxford University Press, 2014.

Mintoff, Joe. "Rational Cooperation, Intention, and Reconsideration." *Ethics* 107, no. 4 (1997): 612–43.

Morton, Jennifer. *Practical Reasoning and the Varieties of Agency.* PhD diss., Stanford University, 2008.

Morton, Jennifer. "Toward an Ecological Theory of the Norms of Practical Deliberation." *European Journal of Philosophy* 19, no. 4 (2011): 561–84.

Morton, Jennifer, and Sarah K. Paul. "Grit." Unpublished manuscript.

Nagel, Ernest. "Goal-Directed Processes in Biology." *Journal of Philosophy* 74, no. 5 (1977): 261–79.

Núñez, Carlos. "The Independence of Practical Reason." Unpublished manuscript.

Núñez, Carlos. *The Will and Normative Judgment.* PhD diss., Stanford University, 2016.

Parfit, Derek. *Reasons and Persons.* Oxford: Oxford University Press, 1984.

Paul, Sarah K. "Diachronic Incontinence Is a Problem in Moral Philosophy." *Inquiry* 57, no. 3 (2014): 337–55.

Paul, Sarah K. "Doxastic Self-Control." *American Philosophical Quarterly* 52, no. 2 (2015): 145–58.

Paul, Sarah K. "How We Know What We're Doing." *Philosophers' Imprint* 9, no. 11 (2009): 1–24.

Paul, Sarah K. "Review of Richard Holton's *Willing, Wanting, Waiting.*" *Mind* 120, no. 479 (2011): 889–92.

Quinn, Warren. "The Puzzle of the Self-Torturer." In *Morality and Action,* 198–209. Cambridge: Cambridge University Press, 1993.

Rabinowicz, Wlodek. "To Have One's Cake and Eat it Too; Sequential Choice and Expected Utility Violations." *Journal of Philosophy* 92, no. 11 (1995): 586–620.

Rabinowicz, Wlodek. "Wise Choice: On Dynamic Decision-Making without Independence." In *Logic, Action, and Cognition,* edited by Eva Ejerhed and Sten Linstrom, 97–109. Dordrecht, The Netherlands: Kluwer, 1997.

Railton, Peter. "On the Hypothetical and Non-Hypothetical in Reasoning about Belief and Action." In *Ethics and Practical Reason,* edited by Garrett Cullity and Berys Gaut, 53–80. Oxford: Clarendon Press, 1997.

Railton, Peter. "Normative Guidance." In *Oxford Studies in Metaethics,* Volume 1, edited by Russ Shafer-Landau, 3–34. Oxford: Oxford University Press, 2006.

Raz, Joseph. "Instrumental Rationality: A Reprise." *Journal of Ethics and Social Philosophy Symposium* 1 (2005): 1–19.

Raz, Joseph. *The Morality of Freedom.* Oxford: Clarendon Press, 1986.

Raz, Joseph. "The Myth of Instrumental Rationality." *Journal of Ethics and Social Philosophy* 1, no. 1 (2005): 1–28.

Reisner, Andrew. "Unifying the Requirements of Rationality." *Philosophical Explorations* 12, no. 3 (2009): 243–60.

Rosenthal, David. "A Theory of Consciousness." In *The Nature of Consciousness: Philosophical Debates*, edited by Ned Block, Owen Flanagan, and Guven Guzeldere, 729–53. Cambridge, MA: MIT Press, 1997.

Ross, Jacob. "How to Be a Cognitivist about Practical Reason." In *Oxford Studies in Metaethics*, Vol. 4, edited by R. Shafer-Landau, 243–82. Oxford: Oxford University Press, 2009.

Rovane, Carol. *The Bounds of Agency: An Essay in Revisionary Metaphysics*. Princeton, NJ: Princeton University Press, 1998.

Rubenfeld, Jed. *Freedom and Time*. New Haven, CT: Yale University Press, 2001.

Sartre, Jean-Paul. "Existentialism Is a Humanism." In *Existentialism from Dostoevsky to Sartre*, edited by Walter Kaufmann, rev. and expanded, 345–69. New York: Meridian/Penguin, 1975.

Sartre, Jean-Paul. *Being and Nothingness*, translated by Hazel Barnes. New York: Washington Square Press, 1984.

Scanlon, T. M. *What We Owe to Each Other*. Cambridge, MA: Harvard University Press, 1998.

Schroeder, Mark. "Means-End Coherence, Stringency, and Subjective Reasons." *Philosophical Studies* 143, no. 2 (2009): 223–48.

Schroeder, Mark. *Slaves of the Passions*. Oxford: Oxford University Press, 2007.

Schroeder, Timothy. "Donald Davidson's Theory of Mind is Non-Normative." *Philosophers' Imprint* 3, no. 1 (2003): 1–14.

Searle, John. "Collective Intentions and Actions." In *Intentions in Communication*, edited by Philip R. Cohen, Jerry Morgan, and Martha E. Pollack, 401–15. Cambridge, MA: MIT Press, 1990.

Searle, John. *Intentionality: An Essay in the Philosophy of Mind*. Cambridge: Cambridge University Press, 1983.

Searle, John. *The Construction of Social Reality*. New York: The Free Press, 1995.

Sellars, Wilfrid. "Thought and Action." In *Freedom and Determinism*, edited by Keith Lehrer, 105–39. New York: Random House, 1966.

Setiya, Kieran. "Cognitivism about Instrumental Reason: Response to Bratman." Workshop on Practical Rationality, University of Maryland, April 2005.

Setiya, Kieran. "Cognitivism about Instrumental Reason." *Ethics* 117, no. 4 (2007): 649–73.

Setiya, Kieran. "Explaining Action." *The Philosophical Review* 112, no. 3 (2003): 339–94.

Setiya, Kieran. "Intention, Plans, and Ethical Rationalism." In *Rational and Social Agency: The Philosophy of Michael Bratman*, edited by Manuel Vargas and Gideon Yaffe, 56–82. New York: Oxford University Press, 2014.

Shah, Nishi. "How Truth Governs Belief." *The Philosophical Review* 112, no. 4 (2003): 447–82.

Shah, Nishi, and J. David Velleman. "Doxastic Deliberation." *The Philosophical Review* 114, no. 4 (2005): 497–534.

Shapiro, Scott. *Legality*. Cambridge, MA: Harvard University Press, 2011.

Shemmer, Yonatan. "Practical Reason: From Philosophy of Action to Normativity." Unpublished manuscript, University of Sheffield.

Shoemaker, Sydney. "Personal Identity." In *Personal Identity*, edited by Sydney Shoemaker and Richard Swinburne, 67–132. Oxford: Basil Blackwell, 1984.

Shpall, Sam. "The Calendar Paradox." *Philosophical Studies* 173, no. 3 (2016): 801–25.

Simon, Herbert. *Reason in Human Affairs*. Stanford, CA: Stanford University Press, 1983.

Smart, J. J. C. "Extreme and Restricted Utilitarianism." *Philosophical Quarterly* 6 (1956): 344–54.

Smith, Michael. "Internal Reasons." *Philosophy and Phenomenological Research* 55 (1995): 109–31.

Smith, Michael. "The Structure of Orthonomy." In *Agency and Action*, edited by John Hyman and Helen Steward, 165–93. Cambridge: Cambridge University Press, 2004.

Sobel, Jordan Howard. "Useful Intentions." In *Taking Chances: Essays on Rational Choice*, 237–54. Cambridge: Cambridge University Press, 1994.

Stalzer, Kenneth. *On the Normativity of the Instrumental Principle*. PhD diss., Stanford University, 2004.

Strawson, Peter. "Freedom and Resentment." In *Free Will*, 2nd ed., edited by Gary Watson, 72–93. Oxford: Oxford University Press, 2003.

Styron, William. *Sophie's Choice*. New York: Random House, 1979.

Tenenbaum, Sergio. "Reconsidering Intentions." *Noûs* (2016). doi:10.1111/nous.12160.

Tenenbaum, Sergio, and Diana Raffman. "Vague Projects and the Puzzle of the Self-Torturer." *Ethics* 123, no. 1 (2012): 86–112.

Thompson, Michael. *Life and Action*. Cambridge, MA: Harvard University Press, 2008.

Tomasello, Michael. *Why We Cooperate*. Cambridge, MA: MIT Press, 2009.

van Fraassen, Bas. "Belief and the Problem of Ulysses and the Sirens." *Philosophical Studies* 77 (1995): 7–37.

van Fraassen, Bas. "Belief and the Will." *Journal of Philosophy* 81, no. 5 (1984): 235–56.

Vargas, Manuel. "Some Doubts about Inverse Akrasia." Unpublished manuscript, University of San Francisco, 2013.

Velleman, J. David. "Deciding How to Decide." In *The Possibility of Practical Reason*, 221–43. Oxford: Oxford University Press, 2000.

Velleman, J. David. *How We Get Along*. Cambridge: Cambridge University Press, 2009.

Velleman, J. David. "On the Aim of Belief." In *The Possibility of Practical Reason*, 244–81. Oxford: Oxford University Press, 2000.

Velleman, J. David. *Practical Reflection*. Princeton, NJ: Princeton University Press, 1989; Reissued Stanford, CA: CSLI, 2007.

Velleman, J. David. "Replies to Discussion on *The Possibility of Practical Reason*." Philosophical Studies 121, no. 3 (2004): 277–98.

Velleman, J. David. "The Centered Self." In *Self to Self*, 253–83. Cambridge: Cambridge University Press, 2006.

Velleman, J. David. "The Possibility of Practical Reason." In *The Possibility of Practical Reason*, 170–99. Oxford: Oxford University Press, 2000.

Velleman, J. David. *The Possibility of Practical Reason*. Oxford: Oxford University Press, 2000.

Velleman, J. David. "What Good Is a Will?" In *Rational and Social Agency: The Philosophy of Michael Bratman*, edited by Manuel Vargas and Gideon Yaffe, 83–105. New York: Oxford University Press, 2014.

Velleman, J. David. "What Happens When Someone Acts?" In *The Possibility of Practical Reason*, 123–43. Oxford: Oxford University Press, 2000.

Wallace, R. Jay. "Normativity, Commitment, and Instrumental Reason." With postscript in *Normativity and the Will*, 82–120. Oxford: Oxford University Press, 2006.

Walzer, Michael. *Just and Unjust Wars*. New York: Basic Books, 1977.

Watson, Gary. *Agency and Answerability*. Oxford: Oxford University Press, 2004.

Watson, Gary. "Free Action and Free Will." In *Agency and Answerability*, 161–96. Oxford: Oxford University Press, 2004.

Watson, Gary. "Free Agency." In *Agency and Answerability*, 13–32. Oxford: Oxford University Press, 2004.

Williams, Bernard. "Deciding to Believe." In *Problems of the Self*, 136–51. Cambridge: Cambridge University Press, 1973.

Williams, Bernard. "Internal and External Reasons." In *Moral Luck*, 101–13. Cambridge: Cambridge University Press, 1981.

Williams, Bernard. "Internal Reasons and the Obscurity of Blame." In *Making Sense of Humanity*, 35–45. Cambridge: Cambridge University Press, 1995.

Wolf, Susan. "The True, the Good, and the Lovable: Frankfurt's Avoidance of Objectivity." In *Contours of Agency: Essays on Themes from Harry Frankfurt*, edited by Sarah Buss and Lee Overton, 227–44. Cambridge, MA: MIT Press, 2002.

Yaffe, Gideon. *Liberty Worth the Name: Locke on Free Agency*. Princeton, NJ: Princeton University Press, 2000.

Yaffe, Gideon. "Trying, Intending, and Attempted Crimes." *Philosophical Topics* 32 (2004): 505–32.

INDEX

assurance, rational structure of, 170–6, 182. *See also* deliberative procedure

autonomy, 46n64, 48–50, 98n59
  Velleman's account of diachronic, 47n65, 179
  See also diachronic self-governance; self-governance; synchronic self-governance

bad ends, problem of, 81–2, 101–2, 103–4, 107–9

Baier, Annette, 118n14

belief
  vs intention, 114, 141, 185
  truth-aim of, 40–2, 43n57, 62–4n32, n34
  See also belief closure; belief-involvement of intention; cognitivism

belief closure, 53–4, 56, 60, 62, 64, 71, 74
  role in instrumental rationality, 54, 55n7, 60, 62, 64, 66–7, 71, 73–4
  See also belief-involvement of intention; cognitivism

belief-involvement of intention, 19–21
  believing one intends X involves believing X (Broome), 20, 70–1
  intending involves a belief that it is possible one will so act (Wallace), 20, 22–5, 37
  intending involves a belief that one will so act, 20, 26, 37, 59–60
  intention as a reflexive belief (Harman), 20–1, 25, 27, 30–5, 37, 68
  as source of rational pressures on intention, 19–20, 21–7, 37–41, 43
  See also belief closure; cognitivism

Bennett, Jonathan, 32n33

Binkley, Robert, 22n12, 52n1

Blackburn, Simon, 79n13, 135n8

bomber (case), 32–6. *See also* intending means vs expecting side-effects

bootstrapping worries, 75n61, 81–2, 127n43, 129n46

Broome, John, 5n11, 9, 19–20, 27n24, 28n26, 54, 59n18, 70–4, 81–2n20, 87, 90n42, 91n43, 100, 102, 107–8, 123n28, 140n21, 141n24, 147–8n34, 150n4, 151, 156n19, 193, 207n17

Brunero, John, 8n19, 18n2, 23n13, 134n4, 146

Buridan (case), 127–8, 140–1. *See also* non-comparability of options

Calhoun, Cheshire, 141n23

Caligula (case), Gibbard's, 108n73. *See also* Iago (case)

Callard, Agnes, 226n5

Castañeda, Héctor-Neri, 1–2n2

Chang, Ruth, 81–2n20, 125n36

Christensen, David, 130n48, 158n25

clutter avoidance (Harman), 53n3, 60n21

cognitivism, 3–5, 19–20, 59, 122, 194–5, 204
  compromised, 29–31, 36–7
  and the grounding of consistency, 19, 21, 23–4, 37, 39–41, 63–4, 195
  and the grounding of means-end coherence, 19, 21–3, 25–7, 29–32, 37–9, 43, 64, 66, 92–3
  about instrumental rationality, 53–6, 59–60, 64, 66, 70–4, 92–3
  and the problem of agglomeration, 23–4, 37
  and the problem of false beliefs about one's own intentions, 27–32, 37, 62, 66–74, 93, 122, 195
  and the problem of intended means vs expected side-effects, 32–7
  and the problem of intending without believing one will so act, 61–2, 72–3
  and the problem of means-end incoherence that is not incoherence of belief, 31–2, 93
  supplemented, 24, 27–9, 34, 36–7, 39
  Velleman's intellectualism, 45, 62–6, 176–7, 242n46
  See also belief closure; belief-involvement of intention

coherence of intention, 5, 7, 187, 210–11
  of choice with standpoint, 211–12, 217, 248
  condition of self-governance, 5, 7–8, 13n28, 210–12, 216–17, 219
  cross-temporal, 163n36, 179, 214, 216, 241–2
  rational pressure for, 18–19, 66, 217
  social, 119–20

desires, 97
  vs intentions, 1, 42, 78, 97, 114, 136, 145, 185, 193, 197, 203, 213
  higher-order (Frankfurt), 159
  practical reason and satisfaction of intrinsic (Harman), 25–6, 31
  for self-knowledge (Velleman), 25n20
detachment of rationality. *See* factual detachment of a reason (Broome)
diachronalized standpoint, 245–6, 249. *See also* diachronic self-governance: end of
diachronic norm, 8, 11, 127–30, 139–48, 208–9, 217–19. *See also* diachronic plan rationality; diachronic self-governance; planning norms; stability of intention; stability, norm of
diachronic plan rationality, 8–9, 11, 13, 127, 132–3, 139–40, 150, 200–1n42, 214, 217–22
  as an aspect of self-governance, 147–8
  in the face of non-comparability, 127–30, 140–2, 150–1, 218
  in the face of temptation, 151, 154–6
  rational non-reconsideration (RNR) model of, 150–6, 163
  standpoint function supplement to RNR, 163–7
  and the threat of shuffling (*see* shuffling, brute)
  See also deliberative procedures/standards; diachronic norm; diachronic self-governance; judgment shift (Holton); present evaluation, rational priority of; reconsideration; temptation
diachronic self-governance, 8–11, 143–5, 224–6
  end of (*see* end of diachronic self-governance)
  as a form of temporally extended agency, 180
  "glue" of, 129, 146, 232–3
  interconnections of, 144, 214, 226–9, 244
  metaphysics of, 226
  relation to synchronic self-governance, 10–11, 214, 216, 225–6
  as a response to destabilizing threats, 224–5

shared agency model of (*see* shared agency model of diachronic self-governance)
  See also autonomy: Velleman's account of diachronic
Döring, Frank, 231n19

end, to have an, 208, 239
  as a ground of normative reasons, 12
  vs to have an intention, 239
end of diachronic self-governance, 11–13, 15, 216–21, 242–6, 249
  and later reflection on follow-through, 246–8
  rationally self-sustaining, 13–15, 17, 222
  reflective stability of, 16–17
  status of, 218–21
  and willpower, 242–6
end of self-governance, 12–14, 216, 219–21
  as contingent or essential, 12, 14–15
  status of, 221–3
  See also end of diachronic self-governance; synchronic self-governance: end of
endorsement, 79–80, 135. *See also* agential authority (where the agent stands); reflective endorsement
Etchemendy, John, 133n1, 153
Evnine, Simon, 158n25
explanatory coherence (Harman), 21, 26n22, 60n19

factual detachment of a reason (Broome), 87
  invalidity of, 87, 102n65
  and nonmodifiable intentions (Setiya), 88–9, 90–2, 94–5, 100–2, 104
  and volitional necessities, 105–9
  See also nonmodifiable intentions; smoker (case), Setiya's; transmission of reasons
fecundity of planning agency and structures, 2, 131, 191, 194, 199, 201, 206. *See also* two-tier pragmatic approach
Feigl, Herbert, 21n11
Ferrero, Luca, 14n30, 96n57, 111n2, 141n24, 205n12, 230n15

Tenenbaum, Sergio, 151n9, 209n22, 225–6n3
theoretical reason
  as grounds for norms of intention (*see* cognitivism)
Thompson, Michael, 155n18, 176n13, 181–2n36, 192n20
threats, rational structure of, 170n10, 171–6. *See also* deliberative procedure/standard
time
  human agency in relation to, 110–11
  intention stability over (*see* stability of intention)
  rationality at a (*see* synchronic plan rationality)
  rationality over (*see* diachronic plan rationality)
  self-governance at a (*see* synchronic self-governance)
  self-governance over (*see* diachronic self-governance)
  See also cross-temporal organization of thought and action; diachronic norm; temporal footprint, plan-infused; temporally extended activity/agency
Tomasello, Michael, 121n21
toxin puzzle, Kavka's (case), 80n16, 154n15, 181, 246–8
tracking thesis, 5, 7–8, 11
  and diachronic rationality, 8, 11
  reflective significance of, 7
  and synchronic rationality, 7–8
transmission of reasons, 80, 89, 135, 197–8n35
  vs detachment, 91n43
  and non-modifiable intentions, 87–92, 94–5, 100–4
  and the problem of akratic intentions, 81, 102
  and the problem of bad ends, 81–2, 101–5, 107–9
  vs a reason to avoid means-end incoherence, 90
  and volitional necessities, 105–9
  See also factual detachment of a reason (Broome); means-end coherence; transmission of reasons principle
transmission of reasons principle, 89–90, 138, 221n46

  vs means-end coherence, 193
  role in justification of planning norms, 98–9, 103–4, 139, 197
  vs wide-scope, local rationality constraint, 135
  See also transmission of reasons
two-tier pragmatic approach, 2, 16, 152–3, 205–6
  and appeal to self-governance as supplement, 5–8, 180–1, 183, 209–10, 221–2
  To deliberative procedures, 169–70, 174–5
  a need to go beyond, 2–7, 156, 175–6, 206–7
  and the particular case, 3, 6–7, 123, 155
  of the rational non-reconsideration (RNR) model, 153–5, 163–4n37
  and threat of fragmentation, 175–6
  tracking thesis/considerations of self-governance as a supplement for, 5–8, 222–3
  See also planning norms: and application to the particular case; rule worship worry (Smart)

Ulysses (case), 226
underdetermination. *See* non-comparability of options

van Fraassen, Bas, 157, 158n25, 164, 238n37
Vargas, Manuel, 160n32, 163n35
Veek, Reuben, 34
Velleman, J. David, 3, 3–4n7, 4n8, 10, 19, 21, 25n20, 32n24, 38–43, 45–6, 47n65, 54–5, 60–1n22, 62–3, 64n36, 65–6, 92n46, 118n14, 122, 125, 176–7, 179, 180n33, 189n11, 194, 195n30, 204n9, 210n24, 215, 242n46, 244n48
Velleman's intellectualism. *See* cognitivism
video games (case), 23–4n16, 57n12, 200n41, 203n5
volitional necessities (Frankfurt), 105–9, 165n41

walking together (case), Gilbert's, 111, 116, 190